THE HOLLYWOOD HALL OF SHAME

THE
HOLLYWOOD
HALL OF
SHAME

The Most Expensive Flops in Movie History

HARRY AND MICHAEL MEDVED

A PERIGEE BOOK

PERIGEE BOOKS
are published by
The Putnam Publishing Group
200 Madison Avenue
New York, New York 10016

Published simultaneously in Canada by General Publishing Co. Limited, Toronto.

The authors gratefully acknowledge permission from the following to reprint excerpts in this book:
The Curtis Publishing Company for material from "The Greatest Story Ever Told" by William Trombley, in *The Saturday Evening Post*, copyright © 1963 by The Curtis Publishing Company.
William Morrow & Company for material from *Wide-Eyed in Babylon* by Ray Milland, copyright © 1974 by Ray Milland.
W. W. Norton & Company for material from *Marlene: The Life of Marlene Dietrich* by Charles Higham, copyright © 1977 by Charles Higham.

PHOTOGRAPH CREDITS AND ACKNOWLEDGMENTS:
United Artists, Universal Pictures, American International Pictures, Columbia Pictures, Twentieth Century-Fox, RKO Radio Pictures, Paramount Pictures, Warner Brothers, Metro-Goldwyn-Mayer, Tarik International Films, Associated Film Distribution, Museum of Modern Art, Academy of Motion Picture Arts and Sciences.
All photographs from the personal collections of Harry Medved, Kevin Allman, Sol Genuth, and Michael Medved.

LIBRARY OF CONGRESS CATALOGING IN PUBLICATION DATA

Medved, Harry.
The Hollywood hall of shame.

1. Moving-pictures—United States—Plots, themes, etc. I. Medved, Michael. II. Title.
PN1997.8.M42 1984 791.43'75'0973 83-19431
ISBN 0-399-50714-0
0-399-51060-5 (hc)

Book design by Helen Barrow
Line drawings by Claire Nelson
First Perigee printing, 1984
Printed in the United States of America
1 2 3 4 5 6 7 8 9

For our mother, Renate Medved . . .
who *never* ran over budget

Acknowledgments

Those who believe in poetic justice will find comfort in the fact that this book, like the movies it describes, ran disastrously behind schedule and over budget. Life, as they say, imitates art, and writers are sometimes overwhelmed by the subjects they choose to portray. In any event, our painful struggle to bring this project to a successful conclusion gave us new sympathy—and an uncomfortably close personal identification—with some of the filmmakers whose efforts are recounted in these pages. Were it not for the invaluable assistance of a few key individuals, we might still be toiling away at a project that became—to paraphrase Michael Cimino—far "larger, richer, deeper" than its ambitious authors (or their patient publisher) had ever anticipated.

Above all, we are indebted to our close friend Sol Genuth, whose good sense and good humor helped this book find its final form. After working with him on *The Golden Turkey Awards* and a half-dozen other professional and personal projects, we should not have been surprised at the tremendous value of his contributions, but one is never prepared to take genius for granted.

Also joining us on this book for a second time around was Kevin Allman, journalist and boy wonder. He cheerfully accomplished some of the most thankless research tasks, laying the groundwork for all that followed, and left his mark on every stage of the production.

Lori Twersky rounded out our trio of remarkable researchers. She wrote to us as a stranger in response to our last book and concluded work on this one as our friend. We benefited in particular from her extraordinary background in films from the silent era.

Charles Higham and Robert Windeler, good friends and distinguished Hollywood historians, provided generous and sagacious advice at the early stages of this project.

Other colleagues and confidants who offered information, opinions, or moral support included Bruce Akiyama, Judd "Sky Hook" Magilnick, Denise Kurtzman Magilnick, Bennett Yellin, Daniel and Susan Lapin, David Medved, Amy V. Lowe, the assembled Altschulers, Charlie and Sara Kaufman, photo flash Harry Green, Wendy Lapidus, Richard Lamparski, Muki the Wonder Hound, Robin, Joshua and Aaron Genuth, Killer Kalby, and the long-suffering staff at the research library of the Academy of Motion Picture Arts and Sciences. We also owe a special debt to literally scores of individuals—most of whom wish to remain anonymous—who worked on the films in this book and shared their experiences and information with us.

Judy Linden, our brilliant editor at Perigee, provided just the right mix of hand-holding and nagging, while Superagent Richard Pine, and Superlawyer Gregg Gittler, stood behind the project when it needed it most.

Nancy Medved not only provided moral support (as usual) and invaluable computer expertise but also offered constructive contributions during every stage of the writing of this book. To our most consistent (if inconspicuous) co-author, a fond hail and farewell!

One final note, intended especially for those readers (and you know who you are!) who pore with consummate care over every word and every sentence in books such as this one. As you proceed through the Hall of Shame, you will no doubt discover many comments that approach, and sometimes cross, the boundaries of good taste. There are remarks in these pages that may be construed as offensive to Italians, Germans, blacks, women, children, Jews, Arabs, Catholics, Irishmen, Koreans, Japanese, and gay people. If, in our desire to cover every base, we have inadvertently omitted any major group as a target for our sophomoric abuse, then allow us to apologize in advance.

The Curators

HARRY MEDVED, twenty-two, prepared for his work as a curator of *The Hollywood Hall of Shame* by co-authoring the best-selling books *The Fifty Worst Films of All Time* (1978) and *The Golden Turkey Awards* (1980). In frequent television appearances and as host of "Worst Film Festivals" on four different continents, he has emerged as the world's leading authority on Hollywood's most dubious achievements. In 1981, he served as senior researcher and special consultant on Paramount's feature film *It Came From Hollywood*—a movie that is appropriately displayed in the "Basement Collection" of the Hall of Shame. Harry is currently studying film production at U.C.L.A., where he is making slow, steady, majestic progress toward an eight-year B.A.

In addition to collaborating with his younger brother, Harry, on two previous volumes on motion pictures, MICHAEL MEDVED, thirty-four, has also written three "serious" books, including the best-sellers *What Really Happened to the Class of '65?* and *Hospital: The Hidden Lives of a Medical Center Staff*. An honors graduate of Yale, Michael worked as a teacher, a political speechwriter, and an advertising creative director before devoting himself full time to writing books and watching movies. Since 1981, his weekly film reviews have been broadcast nationally on WTBS, "The Super Station," and in 1983 he appeared as on-air host for *The Worst of Hollywood*—a ten-part television series for Great Britain's Channel Four. While evaluating the motion picture work of others, he has also risked participation in Hollywood embarrassments of his own, serving as a screenwriter on three major studio projects and creating a historical mini-series that is currently under production for ABC-TV.

Contents

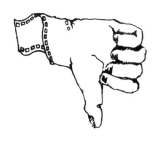

ON THE VANITY OF EARTHLY GREATNESS

The tusks that clashed in mighty brawls
Of mastodons, are billiard balls.

The sword of Charlemagne the Just
Is ferric oxide, known as rust.

The grizzly bear whose potent hug
Was feared by all, is now a rug.

Great Caesar's bust is on the shelf,
And I don't feel so well myself.

—ARTHUR GUITERMAN

BOMBS AWAY

As any two-year-old can tell you, human waste has a fascination all its own. Most of us feel a guilty thrill when we read detailed descriptions of lavish Roman orgies, glittering receptions at the court of Versailles, or millionaire banquets of the Gilded Age. In the twentieth century, however, we must turn to Hollywood for the most inspiring examples of wretched excess; the motion picture business has, over the years, squandered millions upon millions on projects that brought scant financial or artistic return.

The Hollywood Hall of Shame honors these monumental flops, providing immortality, of sorts, to fabulous failures that the film industry would prefer to forget. Most of these movies turned out to be so embarrassingly awful that they deserved their cruel fate at the box office; others, such as D. W. Griffith's classic silent, *Intolerance*, are remembered today as masterpieces. The unifying element of the various exhibits in this Museum of Mistakes is not wretched artistic quality—though many of the entries would easily qualify—but rather public rejection of the finished product.

In our previous books on motion pictures—*The Fifty Worst Films of All Time* (1978) and *The Golden Turkey Awards* (1980)—we celebrated egregious examples of awfulness, regardless of cost. Multimillion-dollar fiascoes, such as the 1973 remake of *Lost Horizon*, found themselves cheek by jowl with unspeakable sci-fi cheapies, such as *Robot Monster*, which appear to have been produced in someone's garage. This time, in contrast, we concentrate exclusively on big budget bomberinos, telling the inside story of how the films were made, what went wrong during production, and why they failed at the box office. We focus on the huge gap between the bright hopes of the participants as they initially conceived these projects and the grim reality of the finished product as finally released. Any idiot can set out to

make a cheap, tawdry, exploitative little film and come up with a cheap, tawdry, exploitative little film, but it takes a certain genius to attempt a grand and glorious masterpiece and to produce instead an overstuffed golden turkey. Touring the crowded exhibit areas of the Hollywood Hall of Shame is an experience akin to viewing colossal ruins from the ancient world—it reminds us of the futility of all mortal efforts at permanence and grandeur.

The films described here are not, in all cases, without their admirers. Some of them have even been nominated for Academy Awards as Best Picture of the Year, including such patently undeserving contenders as *Cleopatra* (1963) and *Doctor Dolittle* (1967). The honors bestowed on such projects should not be taken too seriously, however, since the Academy is well known for its propensity to look with favor on big budget movies that are in trouble at the box office. The hope is that an Oscar nomination will help these wounded dinosaurs make a sudden financial recovery and thereby benefit the industry as a whole. Unfortunately, such miraculous and illogical resurrections, though portrayed persuasively in *E.T.* and the Bible, have seldom occurred in the cold practical world of the entertainment business.

The twenty-three films featured in the main galleries of our Exhibition of Excess represent only a tiny fraction of the literally thousands of financial flops that have afflicted Hollywood over the years. Inevitably, we have used a good deal of personal discretion in making our selection. Some titles—such as *Cleopatra, Darling Lili,* and *Heaven's Gate*—are obvious and inevitable choices, guaranteed a place of honor by the sheer size of the financial loss they entailed. Other films are included on the basis of particularly bizarre or intriguing production histories (*Hotel Imperial*), disastrous personal consequences for the principal participants (*The Conqueror*), or an

16

unusually inane fundamental concept (*Hello Everybody!*). To paraphrase Tolstoy: All successful pictures are alike; every unsuccessful picture is unsuccessful in its own way. We have tried to present a varied and balanced view of these distinctive roads to ruin. In all cases we have considered not only quantitative criteria (measuring the dollars-and-cents totals of major disasters) but also qualitative factors (assessing the flair and panache with which the money disappeared).

What all this means is that a number of otherwise deserving movies, which clearly rank among the biggest money losers of all time, could not, for lack of space, be included among the full-length displays in our principal exhibit area. These spacious corridors, which are intended for the general public, have therefore been supplemented by a special Basement Collection designed for confirmed connoisseurs of filmic fiascoes. Here, we present a "dishonor roll" of more than two hundred films that are duly noted and briefly described, covering the period from 1913 through 1982. If your favorite failure was not properly honored in the main gallery, do not despair; the chances are it is in our basement compendium.

It is neither accidental nor arbitrary that movies of the last few years are clearly over-represented in this list; the rising cost of producing even the most modest sort of motion picture has greatly increased the opportunities for ambitious producers to churn out new candidates for the Hall of Shame. Today, the *average* Hollywood feature costs more than $10 million; by comparison, a classic spectacle such as *Gone With the Wind*, considered the most lavish and expensive epic of its era, cost only $4 million. With the ridiculously inflated budgets of today's motion pictures threatening the future of the entire industry, the time seems particularly ripe for Hollywood to look back to the past and to re-examine its own wasteful ways.

Even without the special contemporary relevance of this museum, we would feel a special affection for the films assembled here. We suspect—and hope—that the exhibits which follow will betray that affection. There is something irresistibly appealing about grand, doomed gestures, and all of the films which appear in these corridors clearly fall under that heading. In 1940, Count Galeazza Ciano offered the memorable phrase: "Victory always finds a hundred fathers, but defeat is an orphan." In these terms, the Hollywood Hall of Shame may be seen as a desperately needed orphanage, in which these lost and battered films have been lovingly adopted and have, after many trials and tribulations, found a home at last.

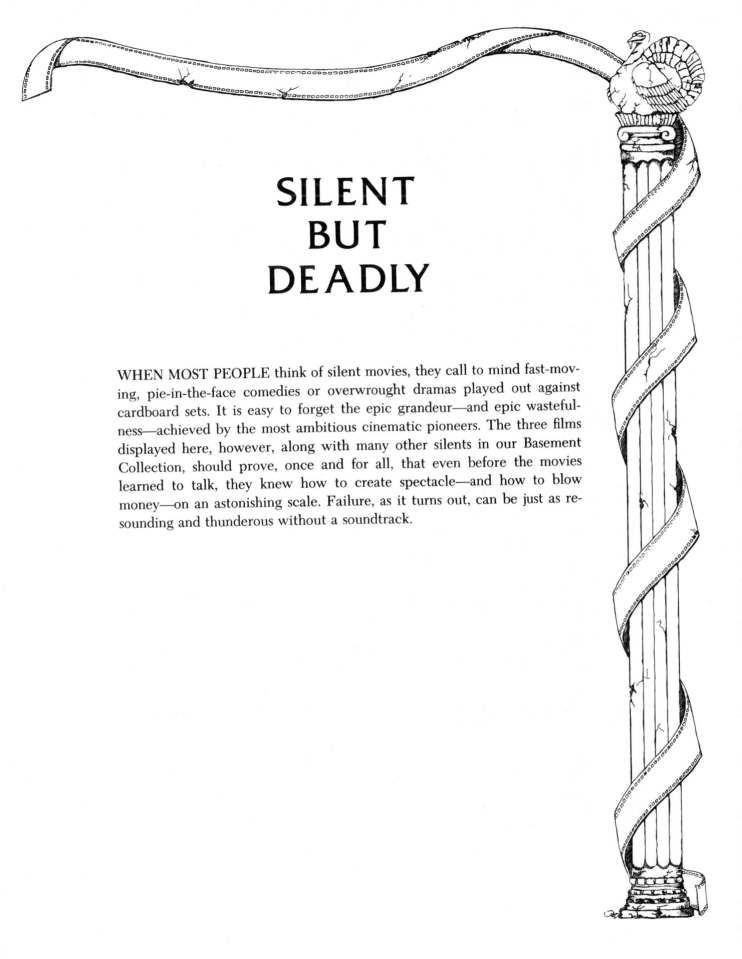

SILENT
BUT
DEADLY

WHEN MOST PEOPLE think of silent movies, they call to mind fast-moving, pie-in-the-face comedies or overwrought dramas played out against cardboard sets. It is easy to forget the epic grandeur—and epic wastefulness—achieved by the most ambitious cinematic pioneers. The three films displayed here, however, along with many other silents in our Basement Collection, should prove, once and for all, that even before the movies learned to talk, they knew how to create spectacle—and how to blow money—on an astonishing scale. Failure, as it turns out, can be just as resounding and thunderous without a soundtrack.

"An Eye for Grandeur": D. W. Griffith not only introduced such crucial cinematic breakthroughs as the close-up and the fade out, but he also produced and directed Hollywood's first multi-million-dollar box office bomb.

INTOLERANCE

(1916)

Wark Producing Company
Conceived, produced, and directed by D. W. Griffith
Cameraman: Billy Bitzer
Author of Titles: Anita Loos

THE MODERN STORY
Starring Mae Marsh ("The Little Dear One"); Robert Harron ("The Boy");
Monte Blue (Strike Leader); Tod Browning (A Crook); Miriam Cooper
(A Prostitute); and Walter Long ("The Musketeer of the Slums").

THE BABYLONIAN STORY
Starring Alfred Paget (Belshazzar); Constance Talmadge ("The Mountain Girl");
Elmer Clifton (The Rhapsode); Seena Owen ("The Princess Beloved");
and Elmo Lincoln ("The Mighty Man of Valor").

THE FRENCH STORY
Starring Eugene Pallette (Prosper Latour); Margery Wilson ("Brown Eyes");
and Josephine Crowell (Catherine de Medici).

THE JUDEAN STORY
Starring Howard Gaye ("The Man of Men—The Nazarene")
and Erich von Stroheim (The Pharisee).

"The Great Innovator"

It is only appropriate that the same man who is credited with the introduction of such crucial cinematic innovations as the close-up, the tracking shot, and the fade out, should also be the one to invent the multimegaton Hollywood bomb. In this aspect of filmmaking, as in so many others, D. W. Griffith blazed a bold trail for all others to follow.

Before Griffith, the motion picture industry avoided costly mistakes for one very good and very simple reason: movies were considered such a trivial and low-grade form of entertainment that they seldom cost more than a few hundred dollars to produce. Then about 1912, a number of Italian films—including the original *Quo Vadis?*—arrived in the United States and showed that expensive screen spectacles could draw huge crowds at much higher

admission prices than had ever been charged before. Inspired by this example, Griffith—a veteran director of cheapie one-reelers—set to work in 1914 on his Civil War epic *Birth of a Nation*. His backers worried when costs rose to $100,000, making it the most expensive American movie made up to that time, but their doubts were quickly erased by the enthusiasm of the public response following the film's release. *Birth* became a national phenomenon, praised as a work of art by nearly everyone who saw it and publicly endorsed by the president of the United States. It also earned an incredible box office gross that has been estimated at $50 million.

In a sense, Griffith became a victim of his own success. He had already begun another project before the release of *Birth of a Nation*, but after the dimensions of triumph became clear, he worried that the new film, *The Mother and the Law*, might be consid-

The Persian invaders make a desperate attempt to storm the walls of Babylon—making good use of the largest set ever constructed for a motion picture. The bearded battlers on both sides had been recruited from L.A.'s skid row district, and frequent injuries on the lot proved that the director had no difficulty whatever in whipping up the proper blood lust among his extras.

ered "measly" and "anti-climactic." The movie offered a melodrama of contemporary urban life in which a poor but honest couple suffers at the hands of callous bosses, supercilious "uplifters," criminal gangs, and the penal system. In view of the success of his previous effort and the millions of dollars pouring into his coffers, Griffith decided to expand the scope of his latest movie to include stories from several periods in history, each one illustrating the disastrous results of man's intolerance to his fellow man. The episodes he selected concerned the massacre of the French Huguenots in 1572, the destruction of Babylon by Cyrus the Great in the sixth century B.C., and the ministry of Jesus in ancient Judea. The resulting film might not be a masterpiece of coherent organization but it would, in any event, be varied and interesting.

Elephants and Extras

Babylon had always been a symbol of doomed grandeur, and Griffith resolved that *his* Babylon would be, if anything, even more grand than the original. On a vast tract of empty land at the intersection of Hollywood and Sunset Boulevards, within view of the neighborhood's modest residential bungalows, arose a set so colossal that even today, some seventy years after its construction, it still holds the record as the largest structure ever created for a motion picture. Griffith's Babylon featured city walls as high as a twelve-story building and an elaborately decorated interior courtyard that extended for more than a mile. Nor would D. W. content himself with false fronts and papier-mâché. His towering walls had to be strong and broad enough to allow King Belshazzar's golden chariot to drive along their rim during a key battle sequence.

Griffith went to great lengths to assure historical accuracy of his sets and costumes, but on one particular detail he refused to allow mere facts to interfere with the purity of his artistic vision. He decided in the midst of the production that this elephantine project required several plaster elephants—what better representation could be found for bizarre size and overwhelming power? Though his researchers tried to dissuade him, insisting that elephants are not native to the Fertile Crescent and that the ancient Babylonians had never even seen them, the great director refused to give in, and to no one's surprise, he ultimately got his way. When the boss gave the word, eight plaster pachyderms soon appeared atop massive pedestals at both sides of the breathtaking courtyard set.

Despite their tremendous size, these elephantine effigies could not, on their own, satisfy Griffith's lust to make use of the beasts in his movie; he also rented a number of real elephants from a local circus and put them to work pushing the huge Persian attack towers, each one more than 120 feet tall, up against the walls of Babylon. Several times shooting had to stop when these touchy animal stars decided that they preferred romancing some of the lady elephants who also happened to be on the lot to the dull and tedious business of pushing around D. W.'s silly towers. Eventually, all female pachyderms were banned from the set because of their distracting influence on the production.

Amorous elephants were not the only participants in Griffith's epic undertaking to experience confusion; no one, except the great man himself, had any clear idea what was going on, or how the various stories were supposed to fit together. Working, as usual, without a written script, Griffith delighted in keeping all aspects of his "great game" strictly in his head. He supervised production from various movable towers, adjustable scaffolds, and even from an anchored balloon floating high above his mammoth set.

The constant presence of some 4,000 extras only added to the bedlam at his studio. Many of these employees were housed in temporary shacks thrown up across the street from the lot, but Griffith made sure they had the best possible sanitary accommodations. As cameraman Karl Brown remembers: "Even the latrines had been dug, not silly little privies, but big, majestic twenty-holers as befit the majesty and dignity of our production."

Unfortunately, the extras who used these facilities

Flying High in 1915: D. W. Griffith directs a crowd scene in Intolerance *from his vantage point in an anchored balloon. Notice the banner in the background bearing the picture's original title,* The Mother and the Law.

were not the sort of people who could fully appreciate such refinements. Most of them had been recruited from skid row in downtown Los Angeles and were described by one member of the regular cast as a group of "booze hounds and down-and-outers." Despite their generous pay of two dollars a day, they caused countless problems. They were supposed to be Persian and Babylonian soldiers, but they ruined many a shot by pushing their false beards up from their chins and onto their foreheads in order to avoid sweating under the hot California sun. They also displayed sadistic abandon when it came to the battle scenes and ignored repeated instructions to "go easy" on one another. Swords, arrows, and spears were all used to devastating effect, and on one memorable day some sixty-seven extras took their bleeding wounds to the first-aid tent.

Though the extras displayed instinctive skill at mayhem, it proved more difficult to inspire them to the erotic heights demanded by the gigantic orgy scene. This particular sequence had been demanded by the film's New York backers, who worried that Griffith had not sufficiently protected their investment by including "enough sex." With his mania for historical detail, D. W. wanted the cast to abandon itself to its libidinous revels with appropriate oriental

In Griffith's Intolerance, *the orgy sequence alone cost $200,000—more than the entire budget of* Birth of a Nation, *the previous record holder as "Most Expensive Film Ever Made."*

music playing on the set. Unfortunately, it proved impossible to locate an authentic Babylonian combo for the occasion, so Griffith turned to Boyle Heights, the Jewish immigrant enclave of Los Angeles. In order to create the properly exotic atmosphere, he hired a gray-bearded Chasidic ensemble to play traditional Jewish wedding dances while the heavily costumed extras staged their bacchanal.

That's the Way the Money Went

The cost of this single extravagant orgy was more than twice as much as the entire budget for *Birth of a Nation,* while the wardrobe for "The Princess Beloved" (Seena Owen), King Belshazzar's main squeeze, proved more expensive than all the costumes used for both Union and Confederate armies in

the previous film. Griffith's own accounting department estimated the overall cost of the new movie at $1,900,000—making it nineteen times more expensive than the world's previous record holder for cinematic extravagance.

As they began adding up these staggering expenditures, the bankers and businessmen behind Griffith's studio convened an emergency meeting to call a halt to the madness. They ordered the embattled director to curb his excesses and to bring the movie to a quick conclusion, or else they would withdraw their money and the production would collapse. Enraged and insulted by their ultimatum, D. W. refused to compromise his principles and proved willing to put his money where his megaphone was. In a gesture of characteristic flamboyance, he offered to buy out all of his nervous partners, giving them legally binding notes that promised to pay interest for the continued use of their funds until he could pay them back in full from the gigantic profits he expected from his film.

Enough Blame to Go Around

Those profits never developed for several reasons. One factor was certainly the film's unconventional structure, with four separate stories stitched together with only the weakest of threads. As Griffith himself explained the basic concept to the press, "The stories begin like four currents looked at from a hilltop. At first the four currents will flow apart, slowly and quietly. But as they flow, they grow nearer and nearer together, and faster and faster, until in the end, in the last act, they mingle in one mighty river of expressed emotion." According to Griffith's original plan, it would take this mighty river more than eight hours on screen to get its currents together: he announced to his shocked subordinates that he would divide *Intolerance* into two segments of four hours each to be shown on successive nights. Hemorrhoid sufferers everywhere no doubt rejoiced when Griffith changed his plans and trimmed the film to a single presentation three hours in length. Nevertheless, for many viewers the constant intercutting from one century and one story to another (creating something

The Pharisees display an appropriately intolerant reaction to "The New Kid in Town"—all part of the thrills and chills in "The Judean Story."

of a "Meanwhile, back in Babylon . . ." effect) made the three hours seem like three weeks. As one critic observed in the press after one of the premiere showings: "The universally heard comment from highbrow or nobrow who tried to get it all in an evening: 'I am so tired!' "

Another factor in the film's failure with the public was beyond Griffith's control, and these historical circumstances may, in fact, have been the straw that broke the elephant's back. *Intolerance*, particularly in its final minutes, was a passionate pacifist statement, with a tableau of modern-day soldiers laying down their guns and turning their eyes to a band of angels overhead. This theme seemed well-attuned to American sensibilities in 1915, with the United States maintaining official neutrality and a great sense of moral superiority to the European powers who were busily butchering each other on the battlefields of World War I. Then in April 1917, before *Intolerance* had even opened in most parts of the country, Woodrow Wilson declared war on the Kaiser. Suddenly a wave of martial fervor swept the country, our boys began marching merrily "Over There," and Griffith's message of tolerance and forbearance seemed as timely as the introduction of pay toilets at the height of a dysentery epidemic.

"Look on My Works, Ye Mighty, and Despair!"

Griffith lost everything in the financial disaster associated with the film. His creditors even took control

Evil co-writers help Catherine de Medici (Josephine Crowell) plan the massacre of Huguenots in order to provide a fitting climax to "The French Story" in Intolerance.

King Belshazzar (Alfred Paget) and "The Princess Beloved" (Seena Owen) receive the bad news that Babylon is doomed. Little did the actors know that a similar fate awaited D. W. Griffith's Intolerance.

of his Hollywood studios and barred the master director from ever setting foot on the premises. It took him more than twenty years to fully repay the personal debts he had incurred for the sake of *Intolerance.* Though he went on to make many more films before his death in 1948, friends reported that Griffith, who sank steadily deeper into alcoholism, never fully recovered from the blow he suffered with the failure of his masterpiece.

Like his creator, the great Babylonian set for *Intolerance* rotted in public for years, long past its days of glory. No one seemed able to raise enough money to have the huge structure torn down, and it remained a bizarre point of interest prominently featured on sight-seeing tours of Hollywood. A number of local residents even launched a drive to preserve "Griffith's Folly" as a Hollywood monument of sorts. By this time, however, Babylon had already reached

an advanced state of decay, with weeds sprouting through the steps and the huge plaster elephants crumbling into dust. The Los Angeles Fire Department finally settled the issue in 1930 by condemning the entire structure as a fire hazard and ordering the rubble cleared as soon as possible to make way for new homes.

In contemplating the fate of Griffith's grand fantasy, and so many other monumental ruins in the Hollywood Hall of Shame, it is hard not to think of Shelley's *Ozymandias:*

> And on the pedestal these words appear:
> "My name is Ozymandias, king of kings:
> Look on my works, ye mighty, and despair!"
> Nothing beside remains. Round the decay
> Of that colossal wreck, boundless and bare,
> The lone and level sands stretch far away.

QUO VADIS?

(1925)

A production of U.C.I. (Unione Cinematografica Italiana)
Produced by Giuseppe Barattolo
Directed by Arturo Ambrosio and Georg Jacoby and Gabriellino D'Annunzio
Director of Photography: Kurt Courant
Based on the novel and play by Henryk Sienkiewicz

Starring Emil Jannings (Nero); Lillian Hall Davis (Lygia); Elena di Sangro (Poppaea); Elga Brink (Domitilla); Rina De Liguoro (Eunice); Alphons Fryland (Vinicius); Bruto Castellani (Ursus); Gino Virotti (Chellon Chellonides); R. Van Riel (Tigellinus); and Andre Habay (Petronius).

"The Grandeur That Was Rome"

The idea of taking an old, previously successful film and bringing it up to date in a thrilling modern version has always held a magical allure for hit-hungry producers. In 1921, however, when executives of the Roman film consortium U.C.I. announced plans for an expensive remake of a vehicle that had already been done *twice* within the past ten years, many observers suspected that the Italian executives had been consuming more than their normal share of Chianti. Actually, the choice of such a moth-eaten and overly familiar property as the 1896 novel *Quo Vadis?* demonstrated the desperate straits into which the national film industry had fallen.

In the years just prior to World War I, Italian filmmakers led the way for the rest of the world, turning out more than 400 movies a year, including the popular Roman spectacles that inspired D. W. Griffith and a host of other imitators. Then came the political and economic turmoil of the war and its aftermath, which did the industry irreparable harm, as did the destructive cut-throat competition between the leading Italian studios. With most of the major companies on the verge of bankruptcy, they finally decided to pool their resources in a concerted, last-ditch effort to restore the glory and glitter of former years.

In this context, it made sense for the Italians to turn to the tried-and-true formula that had worked so well in the past: spending millions upon millions of lire on an exotic pageant featuring dissolute Romans,

pious Christians, and hungry lions. The material of *Quo Vadis?* seemed absolutely foolproof, but then, between the time the latest remake was announced in 1921 and the day production actually began in 1924, something went terribly wrong.

That something was named Benito Mussolini, a dictator of iron whim who ordered invasions and assassinations as casually as another man might order lunch. He came to power in 1922 amid a flood of propaganda that compared him to the ancient Caesars and promised a revival of the old Roman Empire. Suddenly, a film about a mad emperor and his imperial henchmen persecuting a bunch of lovable Christian martyrs became a politically touchy proposition. The producers of *Quo Vadis?* responded to this situation by abandoning the anti-Roman point of view of the original material and generally wimping-out on all fronts. In their version the Christians were okay guys with nothing special against Rome, and they sure weren't rebels against the Emperor or anything like that—they were just these dull, harmless kids who prayed a lot. As for the Romans, they were okay guys too, maybe a little wild sometimes, and sure, they liked to party hearty, but hey, doesn't everybody like to kick back and have a good time once in a while? Even Nero himself came off as well-meaning and inoffensive in this film, with titles appearing regularly on screen to tell the audience that he was "a man," and "just a man," and "just a good man," and to assure all concerned parties that the filmmakers implied not even the slightest criticism of Our Boy Benito in their characterization of the power-mad

The three co-directors (from left to right, Arturo Ambrosio, Georg Jacoby, and Gabriellino D'Annunzio) argue over the best way to stage one of the elaborate crowd scenes in their silent spectacular, Quo Vadis?

Emperor. In fact, *Quo Vadis?* clearly suggests that Nero's only serious fault was that he lacked the personal strength and decisiveness of some of the latter-day Roman leaders the producers all knew and loved.

Too Many Cooks Spoil the Minestrone

As if the ideological balancing act between Catholic and Fascist sensibilities did not cause enough confusion on the set, the U.C.I. executives compounded the situation by hiring three (count 'em, three!) co-directors for their epic.

The first man on the spot was Arturo Ambrosio, a veteran of numerous Italian spectacles. But as plans for *Quo Vadis?* moved forward, the producers discovered that they did not have enough money to realize their ambitious plans without seeking aid from abroad. At this point a group of German investors came riding to the rescue, galloping over the Alps with bags full of fresh gold. Their local film industry, like its Italian counterpart, had fallen onto lean times, so these Teutonic tycoons welcomed the opportunity to put their money into a surefire Roman extravaganza that promised enormous profits. To make sure that the proper atmosphere of efficiency and discipline prevailed on the set, however, the Germans insisted that one of their countrymen act as cameraman and another take over the reins as direc-

tor. The producers already had made a commitment to Arturo Ambrosio, but they desperately needed the German backing, so they finally agreed to hire Georg Jacoby—fair-haired boy of the Berlin bunch—as Ambrosio's co-director.

One might have thought that four hands on the helm were more than enough, but the nervous producers began to worry about the film's box office potential in Italy after a German star (Emil Jannings) was signed to play the lead part of the Emperor Nero. As insurance on the homefront, the U.C.I. executives went searching for a big Italian name and finally came up with the biggest name in the country next to Mussolini himself: they approached Gabriele D'Annunzio and offered him the position of third co-director, along with a handsome fee for his services.

Sometimes called the "John the Baptist of Fascism," D'Annunzio was a degenerate, eccentric, and wildly popular writer who used to boast publicly of drinking wine from the skull of a virgin who had committed suicide for his sake. Despite his involvement in such heartwarming amusements, D'Annunzio still found time to play a role in national politics, to propagandize tirelessly for his hero, Mussolini, and to personally design the official Fascist uniform. Whenever Italian filmmakers used one of his poems, novels, or stories as the basis for a movie, the film became an inevitable smash hit. Producers realized that D'Annunzio's connection with a film was a virtual guarantee of its box office success, so they began paying him 40,000 lire per film simply to use his name in

A newspaper ad for the silent stinker, Quo Vadis? Somehow, the nature of Emil Jannings' grotesque overacting as Nero manages to come across clearly even in this promotional layout prepared by the American distributor.

the credits and advertising. D'Annunzio sneered at these lavish sums as "merely a means of buying meat for my dogs," but when the producers of *Quo Vadis?* suggested that he participate in the project, his hounds must have been hungry. D'Annunzio accepted their offer, without the slightest intention of expending his precious time or energy on the movie. Instead, he dispatched his son, Gabriellino, to represent him on the set, just as he had used the boy in the past to take his place with some of his cast-off mistresses.

Unfortunately for the future of the production, Gabriellino had a far more passionate interest in motion pictures than his father did, and he became immediately embroiled in violent arguments with his two co-directors. Costly delays took place as the various bosses argued over who would get to do what, and with whom, and then to muddy the waters still further, the German investors selected a supplementary "production supervisor" who soon claimed that *he* should be the one in charge. The bitter battles over creative control and on the question of who should receive primary credit for the film's expected triumph raged without interruption until *Quo Vadis?* had been clearly rejected by critics and the public. Then, suddenly, each of the overweening egos associated with the production stepped forward and cheerfully acknowledged that it was actually one of his colleagues who had made all the key decisions.

Beastly Behavior

Along with the laughable human errors, the fates themselves fully co-operated in creating problems for U.C.I.'s Roman extravaganza. Midway through the shooting schedule, actor Bruno Kastner became seriously ill and had to drop out of the project. All sequences in which he appeared had to be reshot at enormous cost. To add to the air of gloom, a slave girl extra was seriously burned during the climactic scene showing the destruction of Rome. But then the most disturbing incident of all involved one of the forty-five lions who took part in the production. To make them behave ferociously in front of the cameras, the beasts were starved for days at a time. So when the largest of the lot was accidentally released, he was in a particularly foul mood. He immediately leaped into the midst of a crowd scene in progress, seized one of the extras, and proceeded to maul him. A few minutes later, with cast and crew watching helplessly, the lion had succeeded in killing his quarry, but the animal trainers were still reluctant to take drastic ac-

German star Emil Jannings as Nero and Rina De Liguoro (who, off-screen, was an honest-to-goodness Italian countess) as Eunice were both part of the multi-national muddle known as Quo Vadis?

tion. After all, lions were harder to come by than extras. They tried to coax the creature into abandoning the corpse, but he indignantly refused and continued to toy with it, convinced that he had killed the extra fair and square. It was only when the lion actually began eating the body that his keeper reluctantly took out a rifle and shot the temperamental animal star.

Unfortunately, the cameras failed to capture any of this action for posterity, but there was still more than enough gory footage in the finished film to satisfy even the most grisly appetites. After lulling the audience into a torpor by sequences so static and stylized they have aptly been described as "the dullest orgies ever filmed," the three directors planned to startle viewers awake with sudden interludes showing the sadistic grand-scale slaughter of Christians. These blood baths, everyone agreed, were enough to bring viewers to the edge of their seats, unless they were already busy being sick under them. To assure realism in the mutilation scenes, the half-starved lions were turned loose on a multitude of dummies that had been stuffed with generous cuts of over-ripe horsemeat. These figures were manipulated, puppet fashion, by members of the crew out of camera range, while the happy carnivores proceeded to rip through clothing to tear the meat into bloody fragments.

No, the Italian "cheesecake" extras are not auditioning for commercial work advertising underarm deodorants. They are merely part of the Good Life as lived to the hilt by the Emperor Nero (Emil Jannings).

The human actors, meanwhile, found it difficult to throw themselves into their roles with similar enthusiasm; reviewer Mordaunt Hall in the *New York Times* observed that "the players appear often to be conscious of their Roman apparel and senatorial wreaths." One star, however, made a noble attempt to upstage the raging beasts and turned in a performance so ludicrous and out of control that it deserves to be hailed as a camp classic. As Nero, Emil Jannings literally drools, rolls his eyes, twitches, gags on his own tongue, and during the orgy scenes, manages a fairly convincing impersonation of the Pillsbury Dough Boy during its mating season. Jannings had shown himself to be an actor of range and skill in other silent films such as *The Last Laugh* (1924) and *Variety* (1925), but apparently the strain of attempting to portray an ambivalently characterized Nero under three quarreling directors proved too much for him. Later in his career, he won the very first Academy Award as Best Actor for his roles in *The Way of All Flesh* and *The Last Command.* He went on to become the greatest star of German cinema under the Third Reich and preferred, quite naturally, to forget all about his controversial outing in *Quo Vadis?*

A Cunning Strategy

The producers also would have liked to forget about the film—especially after they saw the ghastly finished product—but the size of the investment they had sunk into the project made such a course of action unthinkable. In the midst of their despair, a group of clever Yanks stepped forward with a promising scheme to provide *Quo Vadis?* with a free ride to glory. The executives at First National Pictures, which owned American rights to distribute the movie, pointed out that MGM was in the middle of preparations for release of its epic production of *Ben-Hur*, starring Francis X. Bushman. If the Italians and First National rushed *Quo Vadis?* into the theatres ahead of the vastly superior Metro product, they could capitalize on the interest in Romans and early Christians generated by MGM's vaunted publicity machine. According to this theory, gullible filmgoers would hardly notice the difference between *Quo Vadis?* and *Ben-Hur*, and even if they did, they would prefer rampaging lions to racing chariots any old time.

The history of the film's run in New York City shows how poorly their plans worked out. It opened at a movie house charging the then exorbitant ticket price of $2.00. A mere two weeks later, that price had gone down to $1.65. At the end of three months, the film had shifted to lesser theatres that first attempted to charge 65¢, then dropped it within a week to 40¢ per ticket. Perhaps if First National had been willing to go all the way and offered cash payments to patrons who were willing to come in and actually see the film, they might have attracted decent crowds; as it was, the much-heralded Italian import, which had been expected to run at the prestige houses for more than a year, disappeared from sight long before *Ben-Hur* was even released and had no effect whatever on the success of the latter film.

Today, when movie buffs hear the title *Quo Vadis?*, they think either of the influential 1912 smash hit or of the profitable remake in 1951 starring Peter Ustinov and Robert Taylor. Here, in the Hollywood Hall of Shame, however, the all-but-forgotten 1925 version has pride of place; after all, it made a major contribution to driving the entire national film industry into the ground. After the worldwide failures of *Quo Vadis?* and its sister production *The Last Days of Pompeii*, the struggling Italian studios lost their desperate gamble. They closed up shop for more than ten years, until revived by Mussolini himself for yet another Roman costume drama, *Scipio Africanus.* But that, as they say, is another story, and another wing (Fascist Follies) in our Exhibition of Excess.

Meanwhile, back in Tinseltown, a hopelessly hokey and expensive production describing the great deluge and the destruction of the world by water was about to provoke the wrath of the unforgiving Movie God. . . .

NOAH'S ARK

(1929)

A Warner Brothers Production
Produced by Darryl F. Zanuck
Directed by Michael Curtiz
Story by Darryl F. Zanuck; adapted by Anthony Coldeway

Starring Dolores Costello (Miriam, a Handmaiden, and "Marlene of Vienna");
George O'Brien (Japheth, son of Noah, and Travis, an American Soldier);
Noah Beery (King Nephilim and Nickoloff, an Atheist Russian);
Guinn "Big Boy" Williams (Ham and Al); Paul McAllistar (Noah and The Minister);
Myrna Loy (Slave Girl and Dancer); Malcolm Waite (Shem and Bulkah);
Lions, Tigers, Bears, Okapis, Dik-diks, Crocodiles, Raccoons, etc, as Themselves.

The Biggest and the Best

No Hollywood mogul ever demonstrated greater te-
nacity or endurance than the late Darryl F. Zanuck
during the fifty years of his incredible career. Who
else could have perpetrated an unmitigated disaster
such as *Noah's Ark* at age twenty-seven and yet have
emerged from the wreckage with his power and his
"boy wonder" reputation virtually intact? Zanuck
recalled the experience fondly at a testimonial dinner
of the Screen Producers Guild in 1953: "I decided to
become a genius.... I knocked everything, even
Warner pictures. One day Jack Warner said he bet I
thought I could run the studio better than he did. I
told him I was *sure* I could. The following Monday
morning he made me executive producer. Now that I
had the job of genius, I was going to make the greatest picture of all time. I picked a man who is now one
of the finest directors in the business, Mike Curtiz. I
got top stars and I made *Noah's Ark*, one of the biggest flops ever turned out. Now Jack Warner and his
brothers were certain I was a genius." That certainty,
of course, was fully shared by Zanuck himself, who
never wavered in self-confidence or drive from the
time he began his career as a teenaged screenwriter
during World War I until he was finally ousted from
his post as head of Twentieth Century-Fox in 1971.

Whatever his contributions to the world of motion
pictures, Zanuck's off-screen personality made an
even more vivid impression on his contemporaries.
He smoked an endless series of huge black cigars that
seemed totally out of proportion to his diminutive
frame. His other trademark was a sawed-off polo
mallet, which he swung at his side as he paced his office and dictated an inexhaustible stream of memos,
letters, and ruminations. Wherever he went, he was
followed so closely by an elite corps of handpicked
yes-men that comedian Fred Allen suggested, "He
should put out his hand every time he makes a right
turn." One of the more charming aspects of this re-

*The Boy Wonder at His Desk in 1929: Darryl F. Zanuck
became head of production at Warner Brothers at age
twenty-seven, after several years scripting dozens of the
studio's films under various aliases. He no doubt wished
that he could have attached an alias to his involvement
with* Noah's Ark.

Noah's son Japheth (George O'Brien) meets with a group of irate neighbors, who express their displeasure with his family's shipbuilding program.

fined and mild-mannered individual was his reported habit of approaching aspiring actresses and backing them against the wall, with the modest declaration: "You've had nothing until you've had me! I am the biggest and the best! I can go all night and all day."

One can only hope for the sake of the young ladies involved that he delivered on these promises more effectively than on his 1928 pledge to Warner Brothers to make the "biggest and the best" movie of all time. Reviewers can at least vouch for the length of the resulting film, which did indeed seem to "go all night and all day" when it was finally screened for the public.

"The Little Wounded Bird": By 1929, Dolores Costello had replaced the versatile Rin Tin Tin as Warner Brothers' top box office star.

The Formula for Success

Zanuck's original plan for *Noah's Ark* was to emulate the spectacular success of Cecil B. De Mille's 1923 version of *The Ten Commandments*. De Mille's approach, inspired at least in part by Griffith's stylistic experiments with *Intolerance*, had been to parallel scenes of Moses and the Exodus to sequences from modern life that illustrated the same "Eternal Moral Dilemmas." In writing the script for *Noah's Ark*, Zanuck unabashedly borrowed this technique, juxtaposing the story of Noah and his sons, Shem, Ham, Bacon, Sausage, and Japheth, with a bizarre melodrama of faith versus depravity during World War I ("The Deluge of Blood") and its aftermath. Each of the actors was asked to play a double role, representing the same "type" of character in both the Biblical and contemporary stories.

This scheme proved to be a major challenge to the film's star, Dolores Costello, who had recently replaced the redoubtable Rin Tin Tin as Warner Brothers' top box office attraction. Miss Costello boasted the same sort of acting range as the celebrated canine, though instead of striking heroic poses, she specialized in rendering the type of heroine known as "The Little Wounded Bird." Over the years, she had perfected the astonishing feat of batting her eyelashes and gaping at the camera at the same moment; if given enough time to prepare, she could also pout. The secret of her mass appeal seemed to be the deep protective feelings she aroused in men when they saw her in the throes of some horrendously difficult situation, such as trying to remember her lines. At the time of *Noah's Ark*, she happened to be married to another Warner Brothers star: the great John Barrymore. (One of the most notable products of their seven-year union was a granddaughter, Drew Barrymore, who won rave reviews for her role as Elliot's little sister in Steven Spielberg's *E.T.*) Unlike her husband, Miss Costello proved unable to make a smooth transition from silent stardom to a career in talkies, though her fans insisted that her chirpy, cutesie-pie voice blended perfectly with her image of defenseless and ethereal blond loveliness. If a Hostess Twinkie could talk, it would undoubtedly sound very much like Dolores Costello.

Meanwhile, the director for the project suffered language problems of his own—he was a "Mad Hungarian" who had been imported to Hollywood for the specific purpose of guiding *Noah's Ark* to completion. Zanuck had screened some of Michael Curtiz's Budapest productions and had been particularly impressed by a film called *Moon of Israel*, which used the crossing of the Red Sea as dramatic background for an outrageously schmaltzy love story between a Hebrew slave girl and a son of the Pharaoh. In later years, Curtiz directed some of Hollywood's finest films, including classics such as *Captain Blood* (1935), *Casablanca* (1943), and *Mildred Pierce* (1945), but on the set of *Noah's Ark* he seemed troubled and confused. He fell ill several times during the course of the filming, and Darryl Zanuck had to somehow overcome his well-known shyness to rush forward and take over the directing chores himself. The presence of the beloved producer only added to a level of hysteria on the set that had already reached epic proportions.

A Floating Menagerie

One of the reasons for that hysteria was the constant presence of numerous exotic—and contentious— wild animals. Zanuck boasted to the press of the fantastic zoo he had assembled for the film, including "sacred oxen of India, rare okapi of the Congo, yaks, single-striped zebras, and the dik-dik, smallest of the deer." All of these esoteric creatures, along with more prosaic species such as elephants, tigers, hawks, and bears, were herded together on an actual floating ark that used thousands of feet of lumber and could carry hundreds of people and beasts.

The human actors were even more numerous than the animal participants in the film. In seeking to "out–De Mille De Mille," Warner Brothers succeeded in out-Griffithing Griffith, by hiring the ridiculous total of 7,500 extras and equipping them with some 6,000 specially made wigs and 3,000 false beards. (Presumably, the female extras were allowed to perform without false beards.) Zanuck also devised a new technological marvel to provide appropriate makeup for the extras in their big scenes. As the *New York Times* reported, "A number of spraying machines were built and installed for the purpose of spraying exposed portions of the bodies of principals and extras with a prepared copper-colored dye." According to the studio, this tint represented "the shade of human skin in Noah's era," though the basis for this important historical discovery remains undisclosed. In any event, the waterproof coloring was compounded of various fruit juices, and as the *Times* reported, "the stars passed in front of one of the spraying machines and their arms, chests, legs and hands were quickly turned the desired shade before they passed on to their assigned position in the day's scene."

Being sprayed with prune juice, however, represented only one of the many indignities to which the poor extras were subjected. For them, the most difficult scene involved the flood's destruction of the gi-

To ensure the proper skin tone for his extras in some of the experimental color sequences in Noah's Ark, *Zanuck ordered that they be sprayed each day with a body dye specially concocted from various fruit juices.*

And the Rains Came . . . : Water from specially constructed reservoirs in the Hollywood Hills runs down spillways onto the Temple of Moloch set in a fateful (and fatal) sequence in Noah's Ark.

gantic "Temple of Moloch." This sprawling set had been constructed within a "studio tank," essentially a huge concrete lake. For months, engineers worked on accumulating 15,000 tons of water in a series of reservoirs in the Hollywood Hills, then designing a complex system of chutes and spillways to carry it with maximum impact onto the set. When the flood waters came whooshing down these channels cunningly concealed atop the temple columns, the entire set was supposed to collapse, and the studio tank would be flooded within minutes. At the height of the devastation, the extras were supposed to scurry around the tumbling masonry and to splash about for a while in the rising waters.

The day before shooting this awesome scene, director Curtiz explained the procedures to chief cameraman Hal Mohr. As he visualized the resulting chaos, Mohr asked, "Jesus, what are you going to do about the extras?" and the director calmly replied, "Oh, they're going to have to take their chances." As cinematographer Mohr later recalled the episode, "When they started talking about how to do it, I ob-

jected, not as a cameraman, but as a human being, for Christ sake, because it seemed to me they were going to kill a few people with these tons of water and huge sets falling on them. . . . We had stuntmen who knew what they were doing, but we also had several hundred other people who didn't know what it was all about. . . . They would do anything you'd tell them, just to get a day's work, but they had no idea what the hell was going to happen. I wouldn't have any part of it, but they insisted they were going to do it, so I told them to shove the picture, and walked off the set."

During the filming, Hal Mohr's worst fears were fully realized. As the torrents slammed down on the unsuspecting hordes the expressions of terror were absolutely genuine. Three extras died on the set, another lost his leg, and a half-dozen more were crippled by broken limbs. Surveying this devastation, Zanuck and his henchmen merely shrugged their shoulders with the implied comment, "That's show business," and did their best to keep the scandalous story out of the newspapers.

That's the Way the Money Went

As one of the trade papers proudly announced after viewing the finished film: "They show everything conceivable under the sun—mobs, mobs and mobs, Niagaras of water, a train wreck, war aplenty, crashes, deluges and everything that goes to give the picture fan a thrill." These thrills, Janis Joplin notwithstanding, did not come cheap. The film cost somewhere between $1.5 and $2.5 million, depending on whose estimates are to be believed. Unfortunately, the expenditure of such huge sums did not prevent audiences from feeling cheated when they left the theatres. Ads for *Noah's Ark* had capitalized on the thrilling novelty of the newly developed "talkies" by billing it as a "Vitaphone Talking Picture," despite the fact that it included only a few brief sound sequences, added as an afterthought to protect the studio's hefty investment. Despite these precautions, as MGM's Dore Schary later observed concerning *Noah's Ark*: "That one never even made it to Mount Ararat."

The Finished Product

When the film premiered in New York, Zanuck attempted to conceal the puniness of his achievement behind a gigantic fig leaf of wild and wooly hype. Full-page ads promised "THE MOST COLORFUL AND SPECTACULAR OPENING IN THE HISTORY OF SHOW BUSINESS—A RIOT OF COLOR ON LAND AND IN THE SKY—ALL THIS WILL ATTEST TO THE GENIUS OF THE WARNER BROTHERS—AND WILL EARN DUE PRAISE." The first-night festivities included a blimp in the shape of an ark floating high above the theatre, a bank of colored spotlights to create a rainbow effect, a huge neon sign showing the ark with electric raindrops pouring over it, and elaborate simulations of clouds and lightning to entertain the patrons inside the theatre while they waited for the film to begin.

Meanwhile, the promotional material designed for theatre owners used Biblical cadences to extoll the virtues of this "Colussus of All Pictures":

The DELUGE is here! Wherever THE SPECTACLE OF THE AGES opens, a torrent of GOLD sweeps down upon the box office! A tidal wave of POPULARITY rolling up MIRACULOUS grosses! Records swept away in the GOLDEN FLOOD! Get ready to ride the flood tide of PROSPERITY with *NOAH'S ARK*!

Exhibitors would have been better advised to get ready to drown in the muddy waters of public and critical rejection.

The Critics Rave

"An idiotic super-spectacle with parallel Old Testament and Jazz Age sequences—Moses against Scott Fitzgerald. . . . Widely conceded to be the worst picture ever made."

—ALVA JOHNSON, *The New Yorker*

"A solid bore, with a very second rate war story in which everything from *The Big Parade* to date has been shabbily copied."

—*New York Post*

"You never saw so much rain in your life. . . . A wet blanket—just plain awful."

—*Los Angeles Times*

"Frequently borders on the ridiculous. . . . After sitting through this cumbersome production, one feels that it is a great test of patience."

—MORDAUNT HALL, *New York Times*

After the Flood

In the wake of the *Noah* disaster, there was some talk that Darryl Zanuck and the Warner Brothers might actually go down with the ark, but huge profits from the studio's all-talkies—in particular its Al Jolson musicals—helped to keep the enterprise afloat. Zanuck never wasted time brooding over his monumental failure but went on immediately to better, if not bigger, things. With *Little Caesar* (1930) he helped to initiate the series of hard-edged gangster movies that

"After the Deluge": The officially approved studio still depicts some of the human cost of the Lord's work but neglects to show the three extras who actually drowned on the set during the course of the production.

A Horde of Extras Scramble for High Ground: Their idol-worshiping antics caused the destruction of the world by a deluge of water, while an inane and incoherent script caused the failure of the film through a deluge of audience indifference.

eventually defined a distinctive Warner Brothers style. In 1933, at age thirty-one, Zanuck left the studio and organized the Twentieth Century Company, which rapidly merged with an older operation to become Twentieth Century-Fox.

Regardless of these triumphs of his maturity, Zanuck's youthful indiscretion with *Noah's Ark* still caused him occasional embarrassments. A few years after the film's release he was vacationing in Mexico and came into a bar with assorted friends and followers. There, he was recognized by screenwriter Arthur Caesar. Caesar had never been introduced to Zan-

uck, but he immediately came up behind him and gave him a swift kick in the seat of the pants.

"Say!" Zanuck exclaimed in horror. "What was that for?"

Quoth Caesar: "That was for *Noah's Ark*. From now on, watch it!"

The same sort of unceremonious warning would have been appropriate for the careless Captains of Industry who created the rambling wrecks that we will view as we move on to a new gallery of our museum, but it is unlikely that it would have enabled them to avoid their disastrous indulgence. . . .

THE TITANS
AND
THEIR TOYS

THOSE TWO PLAYFUL plutocrats, William Randolph Hearst and Howard Hughes, had much in common. They inherited great wealth, then increased it many times over, had an uncanny knack for making headlines and enemies, and developed a nearly obsessive fascination with the world of Hollywood and motion pictures.

Part of that fascination involved romantic adventures with glamorous film stars, though the twin titans differed markedly in their treatment of these human toys. Hearst remained deeply devoted to his companion Marion Davies for the last thirty-three years of his life; Hughes, on the other hand, enjoyed a succession of Hollywood love interests. Hearst labored mightily to make Miss Davies a star, but he insisted that she be accepted as a very special kind of star. He wanted people to look at her and see nothing but purity and goodness; Hughes wanted people to look at his protégée Jane Russell and see nothing but . . . well, breasts. As he himself so eloquently put it: "There are two good reasons why men go to see her. Those are enough."

Despite their contrasting approaches toward star-making, Hearst and Hughes shared the same profligate philosophy when it came to spending money on motion pictures. Neither man, after all, needed films as a means of getting rich; they viewed their Hollywood experiments as a source of personal entertainment, not additional income.

In view of this general approach, it is hardly surprising that these merry millionaires made lasting contributions to the history of irrational cinematic waste. Three particularly spectacular examples of their idiotic overspending are on display in the elegant, ornate, and heavily gilded corridor of the Hollywood Hall of Shame you are now about to enter.

CAIN AND MABEL

(1936)

A Cosmopolitan Production
A Warner Brothers Picture
Executive Producers: Hal Wallis and Jack L. Warner
Directed by Lloyd Bacon
Screenplay by Laird Doyle and Earl Baldwin; Story by H. C. Witwer
Music and Lyrics by Harry Warren and Al Dubin

Starring Marion Davies (Mabel O'Dare); Clark Gable (Larry Cain);
Roscoe Karns (Aloysius K. Reilly); David Carlyle (Ronny Cauldwell);
Walter Catlett (Jake Sherman); Allen Jenkins (Dodo); and William Collier, Sr. (Pop Walters).

The Mogul and His Mistress

When considering the relationship between William Randolph Hearst and Marion Davies, a recitation of the bare facts will lead inevitably to the worst possible conclusions. He was fifty-four when they met; she was nineteen. He was the fabulously wealthy "Lord of the Press," heir to an important mining fortune and owner of twenty-nine newspapers across the country; she was an ambitious chorus girl with a charming smile and a good pair of legs. He spent millions in an often frustrating effort to make her Hollywood's number-one star, while she remained, in the eyes of her most outspoken critics, nothing more than a talentless floozy.

This caustic view of the Hearst-Davies partnership—immortalized by Orson Welles in his thinly veiled treatment of their relationship in *Citizen Kane*—ignored the generous and genuine nature of the love between them. Hearst wanted to marry Miss Davies and certainly would have done so except for the fact that his socialite wife—and mother of his five sons—absolutely refused to grant him a divorce. For her part, Miss Davies remained unmistakably devoted to her man, even after he suffered severe financial setbacks during the last decade of his long life. She impressed all who met her as bright, charming, and incurably warm-hearted, while her film work showed that she had a natural flair for light comedy. It is ironic that Hearst, despite his fervent commitment to her success, may have actually harmed her career by his insistence that she play sweet, long-suffering heroines in stuffy costume dramas, roles for which she was singularly ill-suited. Nearly all of these films—and there were dozens of them, starting with *Cecelia of the Pink Roses* in 1918—lost money in a big way, but the normal rules of Hollywood logic never applied to Miss Davies. She dropped one major bomb after another, but the studios continued to compete with one another for the privilege of holding an exclusive contract for her services. Whatever her failing as a box office draw, Maid Marion brought with her certain fringe benefits, most notably the wealth and connections of her faithful friend, W. R. For one thing, Davies' involvement with a given studio meant favorable reviews for all of that studio's products from the Hearst newspapers. W. R. felt no shame whatever when it came to using his power of the press to promote the future of his favorite star or to attack those who dared to stand in her way.

Needless to say, Hollywood's studio heads appreciated this sort of ruthlessness, and over the years Hearst and Marion wandered from Paramount to MGM to Warner Brothers, making a series of deals between these established studios and their own production company, Cosmopolitan Pictures. Although this lavishly funded enterprise occasionally produced movies without its principal star, everyone understood that these ventures were merely light-hearted diversions from the serious and noble work of Making the World Safe for Marion Davies. Hearst's selfless and single-minded dedication to this crusade caused him to lavish fortunes on even the most trivial details of her pictures and inflated their cost to astronomical and nonsensical levels. Fortunately, the mighty

Hearst and Davies at a party shortly after her retirement from Hollywood in 1937. To the rest of the world the former star may have begun to resemble a faded flower, but in the eyes of her number-one fan she remained an incomparable American Beauty rose.

mogul maintained a sense of humor about the entire situation. When a friend once said to him, "You know, there's money in the movies," Hearst readily agreed. "Yes," he smiled, "mine."

Shooting the Works

In 1934, Miss Davies faced a crossroads in her career when she failed to win two parts at MGM (Elizabeth Barrett Browning in *The Barretts of Wimpole Street* and the title role in *Marie Antoinette*) that W. R. particularly wanted her to play. After bitter struggles with Metro's production chief, Irving Thalberg (who eventually cast his own wife, Norma Shearer, in both coveted roles), Hearst stormed off the MGM lot, taking Marion and her bungalow along with him.

This was not quite as easy as it sounds since the bungalow in question was a fourteen-room Spanish-style mansion, specially constructed to provide for Miss Davies' every comfort during filming. She wept for days on end until W. R. promised to move the building across town to Burbank, where Marion was supposed to begin a new contract with Warner Brothers. The gigantic structure was divided into three sections, placed onto tractor trailers, and dragged through the streets of Los Angeles, where it attracted curious crowds. When the building finally arrived at its new resting place, an entire wall surrounding the sound stage had to be removed in order to admit it onto the Warners' lot.

It was an appropriately portentous moment, because Hearst had great plans for Marion's comeback. He would show the world—and particularly those doubting executives at MGM—that despite her age

(38) and despite the unflattering pounds that had recently added new dimensions to her figure, Miss Davies' greatest days of stardom still lay ahead of her. To prove this point, her first film with Warner Brothers was *Page Miss Glory* (1935), in which she played a *teenager* who wins a national contest as "The Most Beautiful Girl in America." This was a plot premise that would have been believable only if the script had specified that it was a *Hearst* newspaper sponsoring the competition. Her next effort, *Hearts Divided* (1936), was a love story from the Napoleonic Era intended as W. R.'s "stick it in your ear!" response to MGM's *Marie Antoinette*.

Marion's lackluster acting helped to sink both films, but Hearst resolved to press on and on, in the best Captain Ahab tradition, with the forlorn hope that the moviegoing public might yet validate his taste in mistresses. In the language of a studio press release concerning Marion's next project, W. R., along with the Warner Brothers, decided to "SHOOT THE WORKS in a happy, hilarious Jamboree of Joy!!!" Even those who condemned Miss Davies as a serious actress conceded her gifts as a comedienne. So be it, then; Hearst would temporarily set aside his personal preference for soggy melodrama and make her latest—and greatest—film a musical comedy in which she would sing, act, wisecrack, and otherwise dazzle the world. The chosen vehicle for this stunning display of the lady's abilities was a tired magazine short story nearly ten years old entitled "Cain and Mabel." It described the magical transformation of initial hostility into undying love in the relationship between a championship boxer named Larry *Cain* and a Broadway musical star named *Mabel* O'Dare (get it?). To make sure that the actor cast as the fighter-hero packed the right sort of box office punch, Hearst dug deep into his seemingly bottomless pockets to secure the services of The King of Hollywood himself, "borrowing" Clark Gable from MGM to lend lustre to Marion's do-or-die picture. At first, Gable hesitated (having participated in a previous Hearst-Davies fiasco called *Polly of the Circus*), but in the end he decided—no doubt along with his accountant—that he could not possibly resist playing the role in W. R.'s "happy, hilarious Jamboree of Joy."

The Ideal Woman

The first cloud to appear on this otherwise sunny horizon concerned the casting of the second male lead. Initially, Dick Powell seemed perfect for the part of Ronny Cauldwell, the sophisticated Broadway crooner who competes (unsuccessfully) with the

rough-hewn Larry Cain for the favors of the beauteous Mabel. Powell had appeared in both of Marion's
films for Warner Brothers, and she obviously enjoyed
working with him. Hearst worried, however, that
their relationship might have become too friendly. As
he approached his seventy-fourth birthday, W. R.
was not about to relax his grip on a lady who had cost
him so much good money over the years. In the good
old days, when he was still young and full of fun, he
wouldn't have bothered with social niceties but
would have come straight to the point and shot
Powell through the heart. During one celebrated
sailing expedition in 1924, he had reportedly murdered producer Thomas Ince in a complex case of
mistaken identity, after flying into a rage at Charlie
Chaplin's flirtation with Miss Davies. In any event, as
an old man, Hearst proved willing to settle for a less
definitive form of revenge: he simply nixed Dick
Powell at the last moment for his assigned part in
Cain and Mabel. This left Warner Brothers in an
awkward situation and the studio turned, in desperation, to a newcomer named David Carlyle. To make
the young man look sufficiently debonair for his role,
the makeup department fitted him with a false
moustache—at the same time that it removed Clark
Gable's own very genuine facial hair. Director Lloyd
Bacon (*42nd Street, Knute Rockne—All American*)
insisted that "a prizefighter didn't look right with a
moustache," and despite Gable's forcefully stated
displeasure with that verdict, he finally agreed to

shave. His main interest in the project was drawing
the paycheck and completing the film without making waves, and this pliable, professional approach led
to notable restraint in his love scenes with Marion
Davies. Hoping to profit from Dick Powell's example, he scrupulously avoided kissing his co-star on the
lips. Even at moments of soaring passion, he went no
further than nuzzling Marion's cheek with his nose,
then glancing shamefacedly over his shoulder as if to
ask, "Is that all right, Mr. Hearst?"

What was not all right, as far as W. R. was concerned, was Marion's heavy drinking on the set. She
had already begun to slide into the chronic alcoholism that marred her middle years, and Hearst tried,
without notable success, to keep her under control.
He instructed his spies at the studio to confiscate any
liquor they found on the set, but Marion devised various means of outsmarting them. She hid bottles in
bushes or flowerpots and enjoyed quick gulps of liq-
uid encouragement whenever the informers were
looking the other way. Her favorite hiding place was
the toilet tank of the bathroom, where she kept an
emergency supply of high-quality hooch. She would
frequently excuse herself during filming to "powder
her nose," returning to the sound stage in much better spirits than when she had left. She also employed
spies of her own at the studio's main gate to warn her
when W. R. was on his way so she could be properly
prepared by the time he arrived.

Hearst's daily appearance on the set was usually
the signal for a break from filming. As the old man
walked up, with two well-groomed dachshunds on a
leash, he would take a few moments to chat privately
with Marion or else order a lunch recess that would
last several hours. These meals were often elaborate,
elegant affairs in Miss Davies' private bungalow to
which members of the cast and crew might be invited. Marion's favorite dachshund, Gandhi, was always a particularly honored guest, occupying his
own place at the table and eating sliced London broil
from a silver tray.

However lavish the behind-the-scenes arrangements, they paled beside the excesses that took place
in front of the cameras. The action of *Cain and
Mabel*, such as it is, grinds to a halt at several points
to accommodate gigantic production numbers that
are supposed to be part of Mabel's regular Broadway
routine. The scale of these extravaganzas suggests
halftime at the Superbowl, and they make so little
sense in the context in which they appear that they
lead inevitably to the conclusion that the projection-
ist has confused his reels and is accidentally showing
excerpts from the wrong movie. In the midst of all

*The Sweetheart of San Simeon Meets the King of Holly-
wood: Clark Gable hated the fact that he had to sacrifice his famous moustache for his role in* Cain and
Mabel, *but director Lloyd Bacon insisted that professional prize fighters were invariably clean shaven, so off
it went.*

"The Ideal Woman": Marion Davies as Queen Guinevere in one of the absurdly elaborate musical sequences from Cain and Mabel. *She remained static and stationary, sweetly fluttering her eyelids while dancing chorines and gigantic sets on moving platforms churned furiously around her.*

this sudden and frantic activity, the Sweetheart of San Simeon scarcely moves a muscle. Draped in outrageously elaborate gowns, surrounded by 160 energetic chorus girls and gaudy, rapidly shifting sets, she is thrust forward and backward on tricky moving platforms, while striking a stationary pose with her hands clasped and her eyes turned toward the heavens. The main purpose of these incongruous interludes was to show Hearst his light of love in the guise of various "Ideal Women" through history, including a Renaissance *contessa* gliding along in a Venetian gondola, Madame du Barry at Versailles, or Lady Guinevere on the eve of her wedding to King Arthur. In this nuptial sequence, the extent of Hearst's excitement is represented on screen when a gigantic organ suddenly appears from nowhere. In order to prevent the film losing its wholesome family appeal, this enormous instrument is used to play music through its various pipes (whew!) rather than simply sitting there and inspiring awe. In case anyone missed the underlying point, however, each of its milk white, smoothly polished organ pipes is crowned by a scantily clad chorine, perched with difficulty far above the ground and wearing a smile of satiated bliss.

No doubt inspired by all this symbolism, one of the studio's workmen became so excited that he could not stop himself from wandering across the back of the sound stage in his cap and overalls during a key moment in the Apotheosis of Marion Davies. When prints of the film are screened today, this poor bumbling oaf is still visible, shuffling from one side of the screen to the other, making his own unhurried way into cinema immortality. The cameraman failed to notice his bravura performance, but the film editor caught it when he sat down to cut the movie. By that time it was already too late; shooting the sequence a second time, with all its sets, costumes, and chorus girls, would have been far too costly, so the film went out to the public with its distinctive beauty mark left intact.

The Knock-Out Punch

Premiere audiences found themselves so thoroughly overwhelmed by the generally wretched quality of the movie that they scarcely noticed such trivial details as the wandering workman. Ads for *Cain and Mabel*, meanwhile, warned wary patrons, "It's Unlike Any Musical You've Ever Seen Before—Timed

Frustrated dance director Bobby Connolly is surrounded by some of the 160 chorus girls who participated in the "Night in Venice" musical fantasy sequence in the William Randolph Hearst–Marion Davies "do or die" picture, Cain and Mabel.

to the Tantalizing Tempo of Today!!!" Not even such upbeat and emphatic alliteration could lure patrons into the theatres: during its first seven days *Boxoffice* magazine described business as "average," but it dropped off to "below average" in its second week and continued to fade after that. In desperation, the Warners' publicity department decided to forget about Marion Davies altogether and to concentrate on the Clark Gable angle. The ads screamed, "THRILL TO THE FAMOUS GABLE KNOCK-OUT PUNCH! He's got what it takes to make a champion—and he's always in there swinging—whether it's a glove affair or a love affair!" Another studio campaign attempted to hype the movie based on sheer size: "BIGGER STAR VALUES! BIGGER STORY! BIGGER PRODUCTION! BIGGER PROMOTION!" This ambitious two-page spread, however, forgot to add the key designation "BIGGER BOMB!" *Cain and Mabel* ran in most places less than a

month and earned back so little of its tremendous cost that the press reported that Hearst's personal losses on the project amounted to nearly three million dollars.

"As Much As We All Loved Her . . ."

Cain and Mabel bombed with such enormous destructive force that even some relatively innocent bystanders were injured in the blast.

One such victim was David Carlyle, Dick Powell's replacement and the hapless second lead. When he saw the finished film and watched the dismal public response, Carlyle thought seriously about giving up his career as an actor. "I was absolutely crushed," he recalls. "I was so convinced, so completely convinced, of the poor job I did on this film, because of lack of experience, that I said then and there, 'This is the last time anybody's going to hear the name, "David Carlyle!" ' I figured the only way to get away from that picture and from the disaster was to change my name." After *Cain and Mabel*, Carlyle became known as Robert Paige and went on to a career of more than thirty years in feature films and television.

Marion Davies, however, was too well known to change her name, no matter how sorely she might have been tempted to do so. After the humiliating fiasco of *Cain and Mabel*, she made only one more film: *Ever Since Eve* (1937), an inane comedy about a woman who is so irresistible to men that she must buy a pair of Plain Jane glasses to keep them from pursuing her. No such special measures were required to keep fans away from the theatres: though its relatively modest budget made *Eve* a far less costly disaster than *Cain*, it was, nonetheless, an unmitigated flop. As Warner Brothers executive Hal Wallis recalled in his memoirs, "We realized we were in real trouble . . . Marion was showing the effects of drinking, overeating and late hours. She was forty-one, and it showed. *Ever Since Eve* was her last picture with us, and the end of her career. As much as we all loved her, we were relieved."

Hearst's declining financial fortunes prevented Marion from staging a comeback; moreover, the two lovers began to feel increasingly estranged from the Hollywood community after the savage portrayal of their association in *Citizen Kane* in 1941. In case nostalgia for the old days struck either of them in the security of Hearst's mountaintop castle at San Simeon, they had, ready at hand, a bulky souvenir from *Cain and Mabel*. One of the absurdly expensive musical sequences in the picture had featured a specially constructed carousel, and W. R. ordered it dismantled piece by piece and shipped to the grounds of his estate.

Hearst confounded his enemies by surviving to the ripe age of eighty-eight. Marion was with him to the end, but ten weeks after his death in 1951 she married an old family friend who happened to be eight years younger than she was. It was, of course, her first *marriage*, but she had only ten years to enjoy it before she died of cancer at age sixty-four.

In her obituary, *Time* magazine described her as "The Hearstwhile Empress of Hollywood" and looked back in astonishment at the string of financial disasters among her forty-six films. A more generous assessment came from her friend, writer Anita Loos, best known for her novel *Gentlemen Prefer Blondes.* "More money was squandered on Marion than on all of the gold-diggers of the fabulous Twenties," Miss Loos recalled. "But she never had to dig."

UNDERWATER!

(1955)

A Howard Hughes Presentation
An RKO Radio Picture
Produced by Harry Tatelman
Directed by John Sturges
Screenplay by Walter Newman, based on a story by Hugh King and Robert B. Bailey

Starring Jane Russell (Theresa); Gilbert Roland (Dominic);
Richàrd Egan (Johnny); Lori Nelson (Gloria);
Robert Keith (Father Cannon); and Joseph Calleia (Rico).

A Multi-Talented Pair

Whenever Howard Hughes grew bored with running his billion-dollar business enterprises (Hughes Aircraft, TWA, Summa Corporation), dating beautiful women (Katharine Hepburn, Mitzi Gaynor, Ida Lupino, Ava Gardner), or winning headlines with his feats as a pilot (setting a new record for around-the-world flying in 1938), he took a break from his exertions by dabbling in motion pictures. Over the course of thirty years, beginning in 1925, he moved in and out of Hollywood, producing a dozen films, some of which he directed himself. All of his movies were, of course, reckless and expensive, but some of them, including *Hell's Angels* (1930), *Scarface* (1932), and *The Outlaw* (1943), justified their inflated budgets with conspicuous box office success. Finally, at the end of his movieland adventures, the beginner's luck of the bashful billionaire appeared to run out altogether. In 1955, Hughes racked up an incredible double score with two disastrous turkeys (*Underwater!* and *The Conqueror*), both of which merit full displays in the Hollywood Hall of Shame.

The failure of *Underwater!* was intimately connected with the fading lustre of its star, Miss Jane Russell. Since discovering her ample talents in 1940, Hughes had poured millions into a campaign to force America to sit up and take notice. From the beginning, the mighty mogul himself set the tenor for these efforts. When he saw his first photographs of Miss Russell, a former chiropodist's assistant from Bemidji, Minnesota, Hughes confided to his aide Noah Dietrich: "Today I saw the most beautiful pair of knockers I've ever seen in my life!" This poetic statement not only summed up Miss Russell's mass appeal but pointed the way for all the publicity that followed. During the shooting of her first film, *The Outlaw*, Hughes complained to his staff, "We're not getting enough production value out of Jane's breasts!" Using his aviator's knowledge of aerodynamics, lift, thrust, and drag, the producer took matters into his own hands and personally designed a revolutionary new bra to guarantee maximum mileage from his star's twin-engine fuselage. To advertise the film's release, Hughes hired a skywriter who decorated the skies above Hollywood with a mysterious logo: THE OUTLAW ⊙ ⊙. Playwright George S. Kaufman responded to such antics by describing the film, in neo-Dickensian terms, as "The Sale of Two Titties." Ad campaigns for future Russell films followed the same contours, with lines such as "THEY DON'T COME ANY BIGGER!" (*The Tall Men*, '55); "SEE JANE RUSSELL SHAKE HER TAMBOURINES ... AND DRIVE CORNEL WILDE!" (*Hot Blood*, '56); and "JANE RUSSELL IN 3-D. ... IT'LL KNOCK *BOTH* YOUR EYES OUT!" (*The French Line*, '54).

By the mid-fifties, however, the Russell boom had begun to deflate, as passionate fans of glandular grandeur started turning their attention from Jiggling Jane to a promising newcomer named Marilyn Monroe. Seeking novel means to bolster the sagging fortunes of his number-one star, Hughes became intrigued with the newly developed diving technology known as S.C.U.B.A. (Self-Contained Underwater Breathing Apparatus). As one of his longtime associates recalled, "He just fell in love with all the underwater gear ... He was a real gadgets buff and these things just grabbed his attention." Before the invention of the new equipment, exploration of the ocean floor required a rubber suit, helmet, metal shoes, and

Richard Egan and Gilbert Roland (with towel) film a key scene in the 300,000 gallon unnatural lake specially constructed for Howard Hughes' **Underwater!**

an air supply on the surface. Suddenly, divers could swim about on their own, free of such encumbrances, and most important for Hughes' purposes, Miss Russell could wear a series of revealing bathing suits that prominently displayed her own built-in aqualungs. With this uplifting purpose in mind, he bought an unpublished story called "The Big Rainbow" about diving for pirate gold in the Caribbean and hired a number of veteran writers to adapt it for the screen.

Sunken Treasure

Jane is cast as Theresa—a Cuban hot tamale with plenty of *salsa* in her veins. Her accent in the picture brings back fond memories of episodes of *I Love Lucy* in which the heroine comically impersonates her husband, Ricky Ricardo. The only problem is that La Russell is not trying for comedy in *Underwater!*, and if you've forgotten for a moment about her essential seriousness, then, BA-BA-LOO!, just wait till she starts strutting her stuff in those bathing suits. Her husband in the movie is one Richard Egan, an appropriately hunky co-star, who, according to an *L.A. Times* prediction before the film's release, "is the young man who will inherit the Clark Gable roles." As it turned out, he was lucky to inherit the John Agar roles and is best remembered today as

Elvis Presley's competition for the love of Debra Paget in *Love Me Tender* (1956). In *Underwater!*, Russell and Egan play a pair of daring but honest adventurers who dive indomitably for sunken treasure, despite interference from several roving sharks and one opportunistic human shark (Joseph Calleia). In the end, despite their tireless—and decidedly tiresome—efforts, they come up with absolutely nothing—a fate that presaged the future of the producers' hopes for substantial profits from this movie.

Even allowing for Howard Hughes' expenditure of tens of thousands of dollars for all the latest aqualung equipment for his own entertainment and edification, *Underwater!* never should have been a particularly expensive picture. The traditional way of handling this sort of adventure yarn was to stage the underwater sequences in a studio tank while filming the action through a glass wall. Then the cast and crew might take a few extra days to pick up location footage on a brief sailing expedition off the California coast. In 1955, the entire project should have been brought in with a total cost of no more than $300,000. This optimistic and sensible assessment, however, failed to reckon with Howard Hughes' unparalleled genius for devising novel ways to waste his money. Since the action of the film was supposed to take place in the Caribbean, he logically decided that most of the picture must be shot in Hawaii.

Jane Russell checks Richard Egan's hair for sea lice, while he thoughtfully monitors her heartbeat, in a tender interlude from **Underwater!**

Transporting the players and technical personnel to the islands was a minor matter; moving the sets proved a far more formidable challenge. On direct instructions from The Boss, more than forty tons of simulated "sunken galleon" was constructed at the RKO studios in Hollywood, then placed on giant floats, hauled by tugboat across the Pacific, and ceremoniously deposited on the ocean floor.

Despite these heroic and costly efforts, the executives back home were less than delighted with the footage from Hawaii and decided that filming some Caribbean scenes in the actual Caribbean might not be such a bad idea after all. Unfortunately, their timing in reaching this decision left a good deal to be desired: when the weary filmmakers finally reached their new location they found the entire sea beset by storms and hurricanes. At the outset, a bargeful of expensive camera equipment went down to the briny deep. After the weather cleared and the seas calmed, the problems continued. As one member of the crew recalled, "Storms had so kicked up the ocean bottom that the sand was in suspension—and so the water was not clear. It was muddy, and the sky was full of clouds. It was totally unfilmable."

In the final analysis, Hughes and his colleagues might just as well have tried to shoot the entire project in the Bermuda Triangle. After months of struggle and thousands of feet of film, every bit of location footage was scrapped—more than a million dollars gone to Davy Jones locker. RKO was careful not to let the precise figures become public, but it was estimated that well over half the movie's astonishing budget of $3.5 million went to unused footage.

Back at the studio, and back at their drawing boards, the RKO executives resolved to start over and do what should have been done in the first place: to shoot the bulk of the picture in a back-lot tank. Hughes, however, stubbornly refused to accept an ordinary tank as the setting for his masterpiece: instead, he commanded studio employees to set to work building a huge unnatural lake that held 300,000 gallons of water. As one RKO veteran remembered, "There was an unsettled, nutty flavor about the whole production. They dug this hole on one of the sound stages, filled it with water, and came up with the biggest damn swimming pool you ever saw. It was more than thirty feet deep, with portholes on the sides so you could shoot through it. They brought in two big sharks, and a couple of yachts from Newport Beach, and floated them around in there. Everybody was very proud of that big hole; they brought all kinds of visitors to gape at it."

More Fun Than a Barrel of Sea Turtles

The real problem facing the studio, however, was how to lure *paying* visitors to gape at the finished film. Recognizing the mediocre quality of his prod-

Stand-ins did most of the actual swimming and diving for the leading players in Underwater! *As this still makes clear, Jane Russell's "double" conspicuously lacked the distinctive water wings that had always kept the great star's career afloat.*

uct, Hughes determined that the only way to rescue his investment and save public humiliation was to launch a national publicity campaign of unprecedented flamboyance and intensity. The centerpiece of this historic effort was one of the most unusual premieres in the history of motion pictures. For a film of such "magnificence" and "lasting importance" as *Underwater!*, RKO explained, the normal mink-pearls-and-limousines premiere simply would not do. Instead, the inaugural showing of this spectacular new film took place entirely underwater. One hundred and fifty invited guests were equipped with their own aqualung equipment and dropped into a deep, quiet Florida lake, where a special screen and projector had been set up to roll the picture. They sat on theatre benches anchored to the lake bottom and tried to watch the soporific action on screen, when not distracted by passing sea turtles, assorted fishies, and lovely "usherwets," who slithered by periodically in skimpy bathing suits and swim fins.

The lucky mortals selected to participate in this momentous experiment in entertainment were film critics and Hollywood reporters from the nation's leading magazines and newspapers. They arrived at Jacksonville airport on board two deluxe specially chartered Super-Constellations borrowed from TWA (another Hughes Corporation). From there, a colorful police-escorted motorcade took them 100 miles to the site of the two-day gala at Silver Springs. Considering their harsh treatments of his previous efforts, Hughes must have been tempted to drop all the critics into the drink and to leave them there, but he realized that his only hope for publicizing the new film was to keep the journalists alive and to show them a good time. Understanding that the way to a reporter's heart is through his liver, RKO provided an open bar for the duration of the affair, so that even before they jumped into the soup for the fateful screening, most members of the press had already been marinating for some time.

While searchlights circled the critic-infested waters of Silver Springs, Jane Russell remained in her hotel room and sulked. She told frustrated RKO publicists that she didn't feel like "putting on a show" (which meant putting on her bathing suit), but in the end she gave in to their pleas and made a brief appearance, splashing around the lake with her co-star, Richard Egan. By that time, however, technical problems had already begun to dim the festive atmosphere of the premiere, as spectators discovered when they attempted to view the film underwater. Its soundtrack came across as a series of unintelligible glumps and gurgles. Considering the quality of

From left to right, Gilbert Roland, Richard Egan, Lori Nelson, and Joseph Calleia all feel understandably seasick in the midst of Underwater!

the dialogue in the movie, this may actually have been an improvement, but the first-night audience failed to appreciate that fact as the reporters swam to the surface en masse and made their way back to the bar. When the welcome words "The End" finally shimmered across the underwater screen, only the patient usherwets remained in their places.

The embarrassing fact that the entire crowd walked out on—or rather, paddled away from—the film's premiere showing did not prevent Hughes from achieving his main purpose with this soggy debut. Newspapers across the country provided reams of free publicity in discussing the novel extravaganza, with witty headlines such as "MOVIES ARE WETTER THAN EVER" or "NEW HUGHES PICTURE MAKES BIG SPLASH." Weekly *Variety* even ran a page-one story about the great event under the inane—and inscrutable—heading: "JANIE, MAKE WITH THE LUNGS: SEXSATIONAL RKO CHEESECAKE DUNK." Unfortunately for Hughes and Russell, none of this public enthusiasm for the Florida gala managed to rub off on the picture itself; as one reporter observed, it was only a shame that they couldn't release the party to the public instead of the film. Despite the fact that the *Hollywood Reporter* happily predicted that *Underwater!* would "get back ten times its cost," the film was resoundingly rejected by the public and proved to be the biggest flop of all the seven Hughes-Russell collaborations. It was also the last picture they made together, and for Miss Russell it was something of an Underwaterloo. She continued to work in motion pictures till the 1960s, but her days as a major star—and a recognized box office draw—were clearly be-

The premiere of Howard Hughes' new film took place, appropriately enough, entirely underwater, with 150 invited guests equipped with their own aqualungs, who watched a special screen set up at the bottom of a Florida lake. Here, some of the enthusiastic journalists show greater interest in one of the "usherwets" provided for the occasion than in the thrill-packed adventure film that unspools before their eyes.

hind her. In the last fifteen years she has made assorted cameo appearances in movies and on TV, appeared on Broadway in *Company*, and personally designed a luxury adobe-style apartment complex in the San Fernando Valley called, believe it or not, Taco West. She has also received a good deal of national exposure as the official representative for the Playtex "18 Hour Living Bra." Jane's good-natured TV pitch to "all you full-figured gals" shows that she has developed an admirable sense of humor concerning the basis of her own former notoriety. It was undoubtedly more difficult to manage that same sort of detachment back in 1955 during a particularly embarrassing and memorable occurrence associated with the debut of her immortal undersea adventure.

An Historic Unveiling

To film historians, the world premiere of *Underwater!* is significant not only for its own tacky sake, but because it marked the coming-out party for another buxom Jane who immediately succeeded Miss Russell in the hearts of mammary fans everywhere: Jayne Mansfield.

Miss Mansfield's Hollywood "career" was virtually nonexistent until she managed to wangle an invitation to the fiesta in Silver Springs. On the char-

tered flight from California to Florida, she contrived to sit next to the editor of *Variety*, while her generously proportioned chest drew approving comments from other gentlemen of the press on board the plane. Before she arrived in the Sunshine State, she had already devised a bold plan to win national media attention.

The morning of the gala premiere was officially set aside for cheesecake shots of Jane Russell splashing around the pool of her hotel. Journalists waited in deck chairs, pads at the ready, and photographers had their cameras loaded for bare, awaiting the arrival of the world-famous star.

Russell, as usual, took her own sweet time, and Jayne Mansfield took advantage of her tardiness by walking out into the pool area, clad in the smallest bikini anyone had ever seen. As she wiggled her way toward the water, photographers immediately took note of her charismatic corpus and began snapping a few shots. She smiled at them and proceeded to the diving board, pretending to be totally unaware of the near panic she had incited among the nation's entertainment reporters. As she jumped gracefully into the pool she took the fateful step that changed the course of her entire life. As she herself remembered it, "I dived in, undid my bikini top, and came up bouncing."

This carefully planned accident had a profound impact on the gentlemen who stood at poolside, watching the free show. As Miss Mansfield, in feigned horror, grasped herself firmly, clambered out of the pool, and ran for cover, flashbulbs began popping in earnest as the newshounds recognized a major story when they saw it. By the time Jane Russell finally made it down for her planned session with the press, more than one photographer was already out of film.

The shots, widely reprinted, made an overnight sensation of Miss Mansfield; one article about the incident was appropriate—if rather tastelessly—headed: "JAYNE OUTPOINTS JANE!" On the strength of the public response to this episode, Warner Brothers immediately signed the new celebrity to a seven-year contract starting at $250 a week.

Miss Mansfield would have preferred to have been discovered by Howard Hughes himself and to have replaced the aging Russell as the billionaire's favorite bundle, but by the time of the *Underwater!* premiere, The Great Man had turned his attention to still bigger things. He was already hard at work on a project of even more dubious sanity—and far greater cost—than *Underwater!*, and the result is on display in our next exhibition case in the Hollywood Hall of Shame.

THE CONQUEROR

(1956)

A Howard Hughes Presentation
An RKO Radio(active) Picture
Produced and Directed by Dick Powell
Written by Oscar Millard

Starring John Wayne (Temujin—later known as "Genghis Khan"); Susan Hayward (Bortai);
Pedro Armendariz (Jamuga); Agnes Moorehead (Hunlun); Thomas Gomez (Wang Khan);
John Hoyt (The Shaman); William Conrad (Kasar); Ted De Corsia (Kumlek); Lee Van Cleef (Chepei);
and Billy Curtis (Midget Tumbler).

Selling Out

Once upon a time, RKO studios enjoyed a reputation in Hollywood as a "class act joint." It produced high-quality black-and-white films featuring such distinguished stars as Katharine Hepburn, Fred Astaire, Ginger Rogers, Cary Grant, Orson Welles, and King Kong. But then, in 1948, disaster struck: Howard Hughes purchased the studio outright for $23,489,478. Hughes had already established a personal style as an independent producer during the previous twenty years; he liked gaudy, tacky "big stories," full of buxom broads, macho males, and plenty of furious action. Soon, RKO studios began showing the personal stamp of its eccentric new owner and turned out pictures with all the grace and finesse of the billionaire's legendary (and useless) wooden airplane the Spruce Goose. Even before sinking $3.5 million on *Underwater!*, Hughes wasted comparable fortunes on similarly inane projects such as *Jet Pilot* (1951) and *Vendetta* (1950), causing the price of RKO stock to plummet by more than fifty percent. The climax to his low-flying regime—and the most expensive film in the studio's history—began production in 1955, when Hughes set out to make "The Genghis Khan Story," otherwise known as *The Conqueror*.

There was something in the heartwarming saga of the twelfth-century Mongol chieftain who cut a bloody swath through all of Asia that touched a deeply responsive chord in Hughes' own megalomania. Sensing, perhaps, that this new picture would be his last, he resolved to leave Hollywood with a big noise. Agent Ingo Preminger (Otto's brother) wanted

to take part in this expensive explosion and mentioned to Hughes that one of his clients, screenwriter Oscar Millard, was a well-known expert on the subject of Genghis Khan. As Millard recalled years later, "I was, in fact, such an authority on Genghis Kahn that when I prudently looked him up in the Britannica in the half hour before the meeting, I had trouble finding him because I couldn't spell his name." Suitably impressed by the depth of the writer's knowledge and research, Hughes hired him to craft a screenplay, in which Millard deliberately set the dialogue in "stylized, archaic English. Mindful of the fact that my story was nothing more than a tarted up Western, I thought this would give it a certain cachet and I left no lily unpainted . . . Nevertheless, the screenplay was hailed as sensational and Hughes announced the then unheard-of budget of $6 million—in today's money a little short of the cost of *Heaven's Gate*." Musical star Dick Powell (who had recovered from his unhappy experience with another idiosyncratic millionaire concerning the casting of *Cain and Mabel*) won the chance to produce and direct this thud-and-blunder spectacle—a big break for a former crooner with only one previous directorial credit. RKO, meanwhile, hoped to sign Marlon Brando for the prize role of "The Mightiest of Warriors." The Method Man would have been an interesting choice as Genghis Khan, lending a touch of high-camp intensity to Oscar Millard's mock-Shakespearean lines, but fate had other plans and intervened.

In the mid-fifties, John Wayne stood at the peak of his phenomenal popularity, having been voted America's Number-One Box-Office Attraction in

Howard Hughes called a Hollywood press conference in 1948 to announce his acquisition of RKO Studios for the bargain price of $23,489,478. Within eight years he had succeeded in running the once flourishing production company into the ground with a series of tacky, expensive, and indulgent motion pictures.

1954. His contract with RKO called for one more picture, and Wayne planned to work with his friend Dick Powell as soon as the fledgling director completed work on his much-heralded Mongolian epic. As luck would have it, Wayne arrived early for a meeting one afternoon in Powell's office and killed time by flipping idly through a pile of papers on the desk. There, he came across the script of *The Conqueror* and began reading it with interest. It was this chance encounter that led ultimately to what Jack Smith of the *L.A. Times* aptly described as history's "most improbable piece of casting unless Mickey Rooney were to play Jesus in *The King of Kings.*" Wayne asked Powell if he could borrow the script overnight, and then, next morning, the Duke called in to say, "Let's do this one—it's great!" As Powell remembered later, "I asked him if he was serious and he said he was. . . . I was unprepared for the situation, but John was insistent. . . . Besides, who was I to turn down Wayne?"

The director then called screenwriter Millard, expecting him to be delighted with the news. "Are you sitting down?" Powell said. "We've got John Wayne!" Millard somehow managed to keep his enthusiasm under control. "When he starts mangling those lines," he moaned, "he's going to be a big joke . . ." Powell, however, reassured him. "He's promised to work with a dialogue coach and a tape recorder. He's very enthusiastic. Swears he'll work his fanny off." As if to prove the point, the Duke immediately began dieting and taking fencing lessons to prepare for this "role of a lifetime."

Expectations for the film continued to rise as RKO signed Susan Hayward for the role of Bortai, a Tartar princess who is kidnapped and raped by good ol' Genghis and later, in the finest Hollywood tradition, becomes his adoring wife. Miss Hayward maintained a sense of humor about her role. "Me, a red-haired Tartar princess!" she recalled years later. "It looked like some wild Irishman had stopped off on the road to old Cathay."

Fun in the Sun

With John Wayne as Genghis Khan and Susan Hayward as his hot-blooded Asian bride, it would have been consistent for RKO to have used the Amazonian rain forest to represent Mongolia's Gobi desert. Instead, they decided to shoot the picture in Utah, using the scenic canyon lands surrounding the village of St. George. According to the studio press book, this town was a "clean, green Mormon community of 4,300 in the midst of 500 miles of desert," and since Mormon was Howard Hughes' favorite brand of human (he usually picked them as his aides because he trusted their moral values), it seemed, in all respects, the perfect location.

The more serious (and tragic) consequences of shooting the film in this particular stretch of desert did not become apparent until years later, but almost immediately, as the production began, cast and crew started suffering from the heat. Temperatures at times rose to 120 degrees, causing particular distress for the leading actors, who sweated beneath inches of yellow makeup and black lacquer eyebrows, intended to make them look suitably Mongolian. As the star, Duke Wayne carried an extra burden: an artificial Fu Manchu moustache that wound its sinister way down both sides of his mouth. Some of the lucky extras, at least, managed to avoid such encumbrances: RKO hired 300 Indians from the nearby Shivwit Reservation to play Tartar horsemen and, as the studio cleverly pointed out, these Native Americans needed no touch of movie magic to make them look Oriental and exotic.

The Indian extras were natural horsemen, and Dick Powell took full advantage of their prowess by including more than a half-dozen different scenes of various heavily costumed riders galloping down the same steep desert incline. Whenever the action of the film begins to lag, the director throws in a sequence showing a horse turning somersaults in the sand and throwing its rider; in the key battle sequence so many mounts collapse before your eyes that you begin to think you are watching the equestrian equivalent of a car crash movie. Second lead Pedro Armendariz ("The Clark Gable of Mexico" and Wayne's close friend off screen) participated in

*Leo Gordon, as one of the Mongol minions, stands guard over the recently captured Princess Bortai (Susan Hayward),
the latest acquisition of Genghis Khan,* **The Conqueror.**

one unscheduled six-horse pileup and required eight
days in the hospital and twenty-six stitches to re-
attach his jaw to his face.

Meanwhile, Susan Hayward became involved in a
series of nasty spats with one of the many exotic animals Hughes shipped to Utah to join his human menagerie. During one memorable scene, she is
supposed to express her contempt for her personal
conqueror, Wayne, by kicking his pet black panther
in the rear. The beast, as it turned out, did not take
kindly to such treatment and offered to shorten Miss
Hayward's shapely leg if she tried it again. In desperation, the filmmakers rented a particularly docile
mountain lion and painted it black so it could stand
in for the panther, assuming that no one would object
to one more interracial masquerader on the set. Unfortunately, the animal developed a taste for its own
makeup and licked most of it from its body, causing
further delays. All this helped to place Miss Hayward
in such a foul humor that she threw a major tantrum
when cameraman Joseph LaShelle took several shots
of her pixieish nose from what she considered to be a
decidedly unflattering angle. The indignant star ultimately persuaded Hughes to fire the man in the middle of the production.

When Oscar Millard arrived in Utah on board a
Hughes-chartered plane to attempt some last-minute
script changes, he found the atmosphere on location
to be unmistakably troubled and chaotic. "The company had just missed being wiped out by a flash
flood," he remembered, "and Duke Wayne had been
drunk for three days. Not that it made much difference; except when a bender bloated him, it was hard
to tell. His performance drunk or sober was the way
other actors tend to perform if drunk."

These comments, coming as they did shortly after
the Duke's death, were not only uncharitable, but
smacked of scapegoatism. Certainly, Mr. Millard had
an interest in blaming Wayne for the fiasco of *The
Conqueror*, but if the truth be know, it was the script,
more than any other single factor, that raised the film
from the realm of ordinary mediocrity into the rare-
fied air of the unforgettably awful.

Lines of Sheer Poetry

The action of the film commences with John Wayne
on horseback (what else?) high on a hill alongside his
"blood brother" Jamuga (Pedro Armendariz). They
are looking down on Susan Hayward making her way
across the desert with her feckless husband and a
brace of faithful water buffalo (since the Borax

Genghis Khan (John Wayne) woos the Tartar spitfire Bortai (Susan Hayward) with his simple eloquence: "Yer beautiful in yer wrath! . . . I shall keep you, and, in responding to my passions, yer hatred will kindle into love!"

Twenty Mule Team would never do for the Gobi desert). Wayne begins drooling (he is undoubtedly aroused by either the girl or the buffalo) and suggests, much to his sidekick's chagrin, that they attack the caravan.

TEMUJIN: Tempting . . .

JAMUGA: Tempting, but unwise, my brother. Listen to me . . .

TEMUJIN: There are moments fer wisdom, Juh-mooga, then I listen to you—and there are moments fer action—then I listen to my blood. I feel this Tartar wuh-man is fer me, and my blood says, "TAKE HER!"

The fair prize is duly seized, after much shouting and a few horses inexplicably falling down, but back at the Mongol camp Jamuga is still worried about his pal's passion for the new babe on the block:

JAMUGA: There is no limit to her perfidy!

TEMUJIN: She is a wuh-man—*much* wuh-man! Should her perfidy be less than that of other wimmen?"

She soon manages to demonstrate this perfidy by attempting to decapitate Temujin with his own sword. He successfully dodges the blow and embraces the lusty lassie with a bemused leer.

TEMUJIN: Yer beautiful in yer wrath! I shall keep you, Bortai! I shall keep you, *and*, in responding to my passions, yer hatred will kindle into love!

This feminist notion is nicely illustrated in the climactic rape scene, in which Bortai's protesting fists beat for several moments against the Macho Mongol's broad back, then slowly unclench as she hugs him to her with sudden fervor. By the standards of 1955, this ridiculous sequence was considered so racy that a representative of the Breen Office (Hollywood's "moral watchdog" agency) demanded changes when he reviewed the original script. As a result, before the Duke is allowed to wrestle his Tartar woman to the sand, he is required to look toward the camera and declaim: "Know this, wuh-man—I take you fer WIFE!" This turns out to be a good decision in any event, since according to Temujin, after Bortai "all other women are like the second pressing of the grape."

This facility for poetic expression helps Temujin maintain popularity with his friends, and Bortai is ultimately forced to recognize that he is, after all, Mr. Right.

BORTAI: Tell of Temujin, Jamuga. I know of him only that, of a sudden, my hatred for him could not withstand my love.

JAMUGA (*With eyes fixed on the horizon*): He has a quality of spirit that *commands* love, and makes men greater than themselves. Lacking this spirit, I found fulfillment in our brotherhood, and strove to inspire him to the greatness he knew not yet was in him. That was the purpose of my life.

BORTAI: *Was*, Jamuga?

JAMUGA: He now has greater inspiration, Bortai!

As the entire inspired mess stumbles toward its conclusion, Temujin wins a major battle against his Tartar archenemies and is crowned with a new title: Genghis Khan, or "Perfect Warrior." At this moment of blazing triumph, he rides off into the sunset with Bortai, while Jamuga's voice comes onto the soundtrack as narrator, with all the earnest solemnity of a suburban rabbi publicly congratulating a Bar Mitzvah boy on his big day. "And the Great Khan made such conquests as were undreamed of by mortal men," he informs us. "The tribes of the Gobi flocked to his standard and the farthest reaches of the desert trembled under the hooves of his hordes. At the feet of his Tartar woman he laid all the riches of Cathay, and from forth their loins sprang a race of conquerors."

. . . and from forth our stomach springs yesterday's breakfast.

Long-Range Consequences

As might be expected, critics howled at *The Conqueror* while many audiences found it hilarious as a work of unintentional comedy. Howard Hughes, however, considered the film "a masterpiece" and invested the unprecedented sum of $1.4 million in a publicity campaign to "help" the public appreciate the movie's finer points. This massive advertising blitz, along with the box office magic of John Wayne's name, managed to generate $4.5 million in business (making it the eleventh top-grossing film of 1956), but these receipts still fell far short of earning back the tremendous cost of the production and the publicity.

The box office failure of *The Conqueror* left RKO in the middle of the Gobi desert without a water buffalo. The studio had been losing money for years while serving as a tax write-off for Howard Hughes, but the dismal reception accorded "The Mightiest of All Motion Pictures" served to destroy the billionaire's enthusiasm for his multi-million-dollar toy. Having run a once proud studio into the ground, he now sold it to a tire and rubber company—on terms surprisingly advantageous to himself—and abandoned all further dreams of Hollywood glory.

If the story ended there, *The Conqueror* would never have qualified for its coveted position in the Hollywood Hall of Shame. Most other relics on display here performed far worse at the box office than John Wayne's horse opera of the wild, wild east; its grosses, after all, were disappointing but not disastrous. It is the ultimate cost in terms of death and suffering—rather than simple calculations of dollars and cents—that earns *The Conqueror* a special niche in the history of cinematic disasters.

As they toiled away under the blistering sun of the Utah desert, all members of the company knew it was hot, but no one realized just how hot it was. In 1953, the U.S. government had exploded eleven atomic devices at its testing ground in Yucca Flat, Nevada—just 137 miles away from the town of St. George. The largest of these explosions measured fifty-one kilotons—nearly four times as powerful as the bomb that leveled Hiroshima—and the cumulative effect of the blasts spread substantial fallout throughout the region. Snow Canyon, Utah, where much of the action of *The Conqueror* was shot, acted as a natural reservoir for windblown atomic material, and the presence of radioactive isotopes remained dangerously high through the thirteen weeks of the production. Members of the cast and crew, blissfully unaware of the situation, frolicked in the midst of atomically charged dust storms and consumed with relish tons of

The Princess Bortai (Susan Hayward) performs the seductive (and symbolic?) "sword dance" before making an attempt to separate Duke Wayne's head from his brawny shoulders. As Good Ol' Genghis (Wayne) aptly commented earlier in the picture: "She is a wuh-man—much wuh-man!"

contaminated food and water. To make matters worse, Hughes shipped sixty tons of radioactive dirt back to Hollywood to recreate the desert location on a sound stage for retakes, and in so doing provided his employees with further exposure.

In the three decades that have passed since the major atomic tests at Yucca Flat, nearly half the population of the tiny town of St. George has developed cancer of one form or another. These grim statistics are comparable to the records compiled for the unwitting members of *The Conqueror* cast and crew. Of 220 Hollywood professionals who worked in Utah on the production, ninety-one have contracted cancer and forty-six of them have died from it. A director of radiological health at the University of Utah told reporters that "with these numbers, this case could qualify as an epidemic. . . . In a group this size, you'd expect only thirty some cancers to develop. But with ninety-one, I think the tie-in to their exposure on the set of *The Conqueror* would hold up even in a court of law."

John Wayne, Susan Hayward, and Dick Powell all fought lengthy and losing battles against cancer. Pedro Armendariz developed cancer of the kidney four years after his role in *The Conqueror* and man-

During a break from filming The Conqueror, John Wayne *listened to a Geiger counter test and posed for this publicity photo with his sons Michael and Patrick (with bare chests). Back in 1955, rumors of radioactivity on the Utah location were treated as a joke; twenty years later, after ninety-one members of* The Conqueror *cast and crew developed cancer, no one was laughing.*

aged to survive until 1963, when his doctors informed him he had terminal cancer of the lymphatic system. The Mexican star, who was fifty-one, shot himself through the heart the same day he heard the news. By the time Agnes Moorehead (who played John Wayne's mother in the film) was diagnosed with uterine cancer in 1974, rumors had begun to spread through Hollywood of some sort of "radioactive germs" associated with the Utah location. "I should have never taken that part," Miss Moorehead confided to Debbie Reynolds. Near the end of her life she told her friend Jeanne Gerson (who played Susan Hayward's nurse in *The Conqueror* and herself developed breast cancer): "Everybody in that picture has gotten cancer and died."

The memory of mayhem runs like a dark undercurrent beneath the glittery surface of many of the films in the Hollywood Hall of Shame. A lion dined on a extra in *Quo Vadis?*; three extras drowned on the set of *Noah's Ark*. The cruel impact of *The Conqueror*, however, brought down nearly half the cast and crew, including all the major stars. Never before in Hollywood history had so many innocent people made the ultimate sacrifice in so worthless—and tasteless—a cause.

According to one of Hughes' closest associates, "Howard felt guilty as hell" as he gradually became aware of the deadly impact of the radioactive desert sands. Perhaps this sense of guilt helps to explain his continued obsession with this silly celluloid paean to Genghis Khan. One year after selling RKO, Hughes startled the film community by paying the staggering sum of $12 million to buy back just two of the 700 films in the studio's library: *Jet Pilot* and *The Conqueror*. He quickly withdrew these twin "classics" from circulation, protecting them from the slings and arrows of an outraged public. Since theatregoers failed to respect such high art, the increasingly erratic billionaire locked away all existing prints of *The Conqueror* and decreed that he alone would enjoy the privilege of seeing it; and see it he did, in splendid isolation, night after night. His aides estimated that Hughes must have screened *The Conqueror* hundreds, if not thousands, of times. As Jack Smith observed, "I assume that a projectionist would have had to be on duty, since the producer would hardly have done that menial job himself, but perhaps Hughes had him blindfolded while the film was running. That certainly would have been the merciful thing to do."

Despite public curiosity about this unusual picture, for some twenty years it remained Hughes' closely guarded private treasure, since he would never allow it to be "butchered" on late-night TV. After the billionaire's death, it was finally auctioned off and sold to Universal, which in turn rented it to cable television. There, discerning viewers can now enjoy two hours of sheer insanity—if they manage to forget about costs and cancer—and thrill as in days of yore to conquests undreamed of by mortal men, as the tribes of the TV wasteland flock to the Duke's standard, and the farthest reaches of the desert tremble once again under the hooves of his hordes.

And so the Great Khan rides again, but his earth-shaking ambitions—and even those of Howard Hughes himself—must pale before the wild attempts at cinematic grandeur by the two power-mad politicos featured in the next gallery of our Exhibition of Excess. . . .

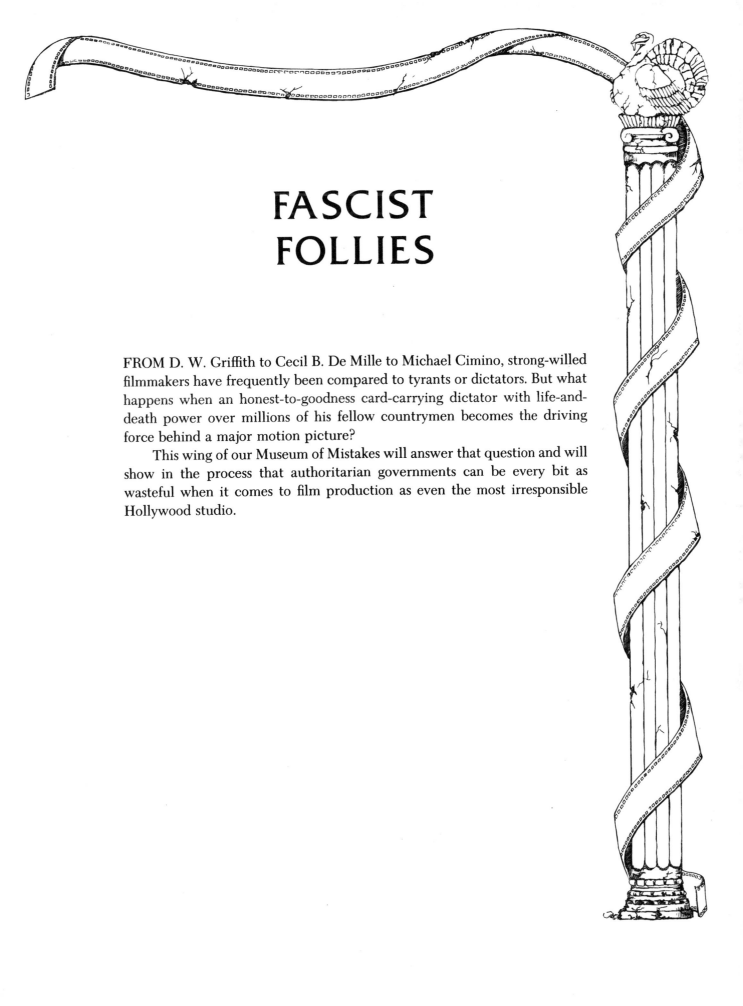

FASCIST FOLLIES

FROM D. W. Griffith to Cecil B. De Mille to Michael Cimino, strong-willed filmmakers have frequently been compared to tyrants or dictators. But what happens when an honest-to-goodness card-carrying dictator with life-and-death power over millions of his fellow countrymen becomes the driving force behind a major motion picture?

This wing of our Museum of Mistakes will answer that question and will show in the process that authoritarian governments can be every bit as wasteful when it comes to film production as even the most irresponsible Hollywood studio.

SCIPIO AFRICANUS (SCIPIONE L'AFRICANO)

(1937)

A production of E.N.I.C.
(Ente Nazionale Industrie Cinematografiche)
Production Chief: Vittorio Mussolini
Produced by Federic Curiosi
Directed by Carmine Gallone
Screenplay by Camillo Mariani dell'Anguillara, S. A. Luciani,
and Carmine Gallone, in collaboration with Silvio Maurano

Starring Annibale Ninchi (Scipio); Camillo Pilotto (Hannibal); Isa Miranda (Velia); Memo Benassi (Cato); Fosco Giachetti (Massinissa); Francesca Braggiotti (Sofonisba); Marcello Giorda (Siface); and Lamberto Picasso (Hasdrubal).

Our Boy Benito

Despite the bad press he has received in history books, Benito Mussolini was an unusually artistic sort of dictator. He played the violin with considerable skill, wrote novels and plays full of action and romance, and, most important for our purposes, established himself as Italy's *numero uno* movie fan. His widow, Rachele Mussolini, recalled that his special favorites were Laurel and Hardy, and whenever his heroes appeared on the screen, "Benito would then be almost childlike, showing unsuppressed pleasure and applauding every custard pie that hit its target." He proved equally enthusiastic in expressing his disapproval of entertainments that bored or disturbed him. Mrs. Mussolini vividly remembered one particular evening at the theatre when, to express his annoyance, "Benito had taken off his shoe and thrown it at the actors." Had he lived until the 1970s, one can readily imagine Il Duce as a happy audience participant at midnight screenings of *The Rocky Horror Picture Show.*

It was only to be expected that a man with such strong feelings about the dramatic arts should nurse major creative ambitions of his own. Despite his busy schedule as a tyrant, he somehow found time to write a play about Napoleon, which later served as the basis for a better-than-average German film called *The Hundred Days* (1935). Though Benito received proper screen credit for his contribution to this

project, his movie aspirations were far from satisfied. His chief goal in this regard was the restoration of the Italian film industry to the international pre-eminence it had enjoyed during the first two decades of the twentieth century. Mussolini witnessed—and to some extent encouraged—the disastrous productions of *Quo Vadis?* and *The Last Days of Pompeii,* which helped to ruin the industry in the 1920s, and his dreams for a revival of the national cinema became one of his most cherished goals.

In pursuit of this noble purpose, Mussolini's first step was a new emphasis on government-sponsored newsreels. He felt an undoubted fascination with his own image on the screen and decreed that ordinary Italians should share this enthusiasm. While his fellow citizens continued to flock to the theatres to expose themselves to the "corrupting influence" of the American films that dominated the market, they would at the same time enjoy the officially mandated treat of watching movie reports on the latest activities of their beloved leader. As Vernon Jarratt observed in his book *The Italian Cinema:* "It was a very lucky cinema patron indeed who, at some time or other in the programme, did not find the Duce's voice blaring out from the loudspeaker behind the screen as he cut his first sod on a housing project, reviewed his mighty troops, helped to get in the harvest or just orated from some balcony."

These newsreels thoroughly pleased Mussolini, but like all true film fanatics, and most of the unfortunate dreamers included in our Display of Disasters, he continued to fantasize about someday creating "The Greatest Movie Ever Made." To bring that vision closer to reality he pumped millions from the public coffers into construction of a brand-new super studio: Cinecittà, or "Cinema City," which soon boasted the largest and finest filming facilities in Europe. All that remained was the choice of a suitable vehicle to harness the new equipment and to then show the world the glories of Fascist film.

Mussolini felt certain that he had found such a property when he came up with the original concept for *Scipio Africanus.*

A Chip Off the Old Block

Scipio Africanus?

To the uninitiated it sounds like the name for a new brand of peanut butter specifically designed to appeal to residents of America's big-city ghettos.

Roman history buffs, however, will instantly recognize the subject of Mussolini's film fantasy as one of the great heroes of antiquity: Publius Cornelius Scipio, who won the honorary title Africanus to commemorate his stunning victory over the Carthaginians in North Africa in 202 B.C.

Il Duce had more than a passing interest in this figure from the distant past. Scipio, who assumed dictatorial powers from the confused and cautious Senate, was the one who first established Roman control of North Africa and added immeasurably to the wealth and power of the Republic. Mussolini, meanwhile, had been condemned by most nations of the world in 1935 for his bloody invasion of defenseless Ethiopia in a bid to win additional African territory for his much heralded "New Empire of the Caesars." Shortly after securing this glorious victory, the official Fascist propagandists described their fave-rave, Benito, as "Defender of the Prestige of Rome, Protector of Islam, and Mother of All Mediterranean Peoples." (His hapless subjects in Libya, Somalia, and Ethiopia would certainly have agreed he was a *Mother,* but the other titles might have been more controversial.) Even before Italy's superfilm on Scipio went into production, Il Duce's admirers had begun referring to him as Mussolini Africanus. When you add to this coincidence the fact that historians describe Scipio as handsome, noble, selfless, kind, virile, thrifty, brave, clean, and reverent, then the parallel with Mussolini is obvious and complete.

Plans for a new film on Scipio's magnificent exploits began taking shape while the Ethiopian war continued to rage, and spokesmen for the Italian film

That fun-loving dictator, Benito Mussolini, works closely with an imported German camera crew, bringing his special cinematic expertise to bear on the set of **Scipio Africanus.**

industry made no bones about the fact that one of the purposes of the project was to show their nation's "historic claim" to an African empire. To make sure that this message came across with the proper artistry, Mussolini selected a twenty-one-year-old boy wonder of unparalleled skill and genius to take overall charge of the production. How had this Roman whiz kid qualified for the job, despite a lack of any prior experience making movies? Atsa right, he'sa da *bambino* of Il Duce himself: Vittorio Mussolini.

The year before assuming his rightful place as leader of his nation's film industry, Vittorio was busy winning headlines for his fearless role in the Ethiopian war. He had requested—and received—the privilege of flying the very first bombing mission against terrified and helpless Abyssinian tribesmen. Later, he wrote of this inspiring experience in his book, *Wings Over Ambe*, and described war as "the most beautiful and complete of all sports." But it was not only his experience with bombs that prepared him for his work on *Scipio;* as much as he enjoyed killing, Vittorio loved movies even more. As a teenager he had, in fact, served as film critic for one of his father's newspapers. With this invaluable apprenticeship behind him, the young man proceeded to occupy the largest office at the Cinecittà complex and began supervising construction of a life-size replica of the Roman Forum.

Heroic Efforts

Though the plot of the new film described the struggle of Scipio against Hannibal in the Second Punic War, the scale of the production was anything but puny. Vittorio refused to use miniatures of any kind and instead employed 500 workmen to build a set that rose to a height of 175 feet. Cost was no object,

Atsa My Boy!: After an exhaustive nationwide talent search, Il Duce wisely selected his twenty-one-year-old son, Vittorio Mussolini (right), to supervise production of Scipio Africanus.

since whenever the project ran out of money, Vittorio went to one of the government-controlled banks and made its director the proverbial "offer he couldn't refuse." The funds thus "loaned" to the production company went to pay for such indulgences as 100 seaworthy Roman galleys, launched with much fanfare at the port of Ostia, and some 500 camels for use in one three-minute segment of film.

For the climactic scene of the Battle of Zama, Vittorio borrowed 12,000 regular troops from the War Ministry and also arranged for 1,000 Libyan horsemen in flowing robes to portray the Numidian cavalry of Hannibal. The Libyans were less than delighted with this assignment, especially when twenty-five of their number suffered serious injury during the filming. Mussolini's soldiers apparently had the time of their lives in taking out their aggressions on these unfortunate Arabs during the course of their make-believe battle.

No truly mammoth production could be complete without elephants, and the fabulous flying Mussolinis, father and son, combed every circus in Italy, gathering together all the pachyderms they could find. Research showed that Hannibal had some eighty of the fearsome beasts at his disposal for the Battle of Zama, and yet, try as they may, the filmmakers could come up with only nineteen elephant loaners for their production. Ever resourceful, Vittorio devised an ingenious means of handling the discrepancy: in addition to the flesh-and-blood elephants, they created sixty papier-mâché stand-ins and ordered extras to push them along in the background as if they were alive.

The director of this exotic charade, along with the rest of the gigantic film, was none other than Carmine Gallone—the same auteur whose profligate ways on *The Last Days of Pompeii* helped to ruin the Italian film industry some eleven years before. A balanced consideration of Gallone's work shows that he had both strengths and weaknesses as a director. His chief strength was an uncanny ability to waste money; his primary weakness was a lack of attention to detail. This chronic sloppiness eventually placed the entire *Scipio* project in jeopardy. During one of the early screenings of the finished film for middle-rank Fascist officials, members of the audience noted in horror that despite the millions of lire spent on costumes and props, in several scenes a number of extras could be seen wearing wristwatches beneath their Roman togas. Even worse, during much of the heroic footage showing the Battle of Zama, telephone wires were unmistakably visible in the distance. In response to heated demands that he remove the offending material, Gallone pleaded that it was impossible since he could not cut those sequences without destroying the continuity of his masterpiece. At last it was decided to leave the film as it stood, hoping that critics and viewers would already be sound asleep from an hour of soporific exposition before they reached the segment where they could spot wristwatches and telephone poles.

The Costliest Roman of Them All

Scipio Africanus in its final form lurches forward at such a solemn, ponderous pace that the elephants within the film appear by comparison to move like gazelles. The dramatic highlight of the entire production is a brief sequence in which a papier-mâché pachyderm receives a spear directly in its eye and

the soundtrack goes wild with the noise of bellowing beasts. There is also abundant noise from bellowing humans, with particular emphasis on Scipio himself (Annibale Ninchi), who uses Mussolini's characteristic gestures and intonation to deliver several lengthy tirades on such favorite Fascist themes as the sanctity of the state, the necessity of discipline, and Rome's "inevitable destiny" as an African power. Just to make sure we can tell the good guys from the bad guys, Hannibal (Camillo Pilotto) is depicted as an overweight bully with a scruffy beard and an eye patch, who resembles no one so much as Bluto in the old Popeye cartoons. Not only is the Carthaginian commander shown to be barbarous and cruel, but he is also portrayed as a dirty old man, slobbering with lust at the mere thought of corrupting the virtue of a beauteous Roman virgin (Isa Miranda).

Hail, Scipio: Annibale Ninchi, as Scipio Africanus (a sort of second-century Il Duce), salutes his loyal fans from an imposing podium, thoughtfully provided as part of his Roman flagship.

Il Duce reviews some of the Libyan troops who have been recruited to portray Hannibal's Numidian cavalry in Scipio Africanus. The facial expressions and posture of these slave-labor extras bear eloquent testimony to their enthusiasm for their participation in the production.

The lavish trappings for these melodramatics helped elevate the cost of the film to what our old friend Jamuga the Mongol might describe as "levels undreamed of by mortal men." *Life* magazine reported that the Italians squandered the equivalent of $2 million on the picture, at a time when the average European film cost less than $100,000.

Vittorio and his papa considered this expenditure a worthwhile investment in national prestige and expected that their colossal undertaking would win new friends for the Fascist regime wherever the film was shown. *Scipio* did, in fact, attract considerable attention at its debut showing in New York (where one critic suggested that it "probably cost more than the War in Ethiopia"), but universally scornful reviews prevented the Italians from gaining a national distribution deal. *Variety* described the picture as "undramatic and wooden," while Bosley Crowther in the *New York Times* observed that "there are moments in the film when one feels that it is not so much the noble days of Republican Rome that one is witnessing as the last act of *Aïda*." A few "art houses" eventually agreed to run *Scipio* very briefly, but the great majority of Americans never even heard of it.

This failure in the New World was deeply disappointing to Mussolini, but not entirely unexpected, since, as he had made clear many times, most citizens of the decadent U.S.A. could not possibly understand "the Roman virtues." The utter rejection of his film by the public in Italy, however, was far more painful and proved difficult to explain. Though it opened with all the hoopla normally associated with a coronation, *Scipio*'s engagement at Rome's first-run houses lasted only one week. The terrified theatre

owners would have loved to please the government by featuring the film indefinitely, but it was simply impossible to go on screening it to theatres that were absolutely empty. Much to Il Duce's chagrin, his fellow countrymen continued to prefer even the schlockiest movies from Hollywood studios to the hometown heroics of Scipio Africanus. Though Benito could require movie houses to show newsreels of his exploits by government decree, he had not yet devised a means of forcing the ordinary citizen to go out to a theatre and pay his hard-earned money to see a film he didn't like.

The Last Refuge

Dr. Johnson once observed that "Patriotism is the last refuge of a scoundrel," and by the final months of 1937, Vittorio Mussolini clearly had been driven to desperate measures. He prepared an article for a leading periodical in which he stressed the importance of the national film industry and went on to chide his fellow countrymen for their total indifference to *Scipio Africanus*. "The public must not stay away when an Italian film is projected," he wrote, "because it is necessary to love it even as we love the most rebellious of our sons. The people must come to love their own films, even if this causes them great displeasure." In other words, "My Daddy said you're supposed to go see my movie, even if you end up hating the damn thing." Unfortunately, these exhortations failed to produce the desired response, and *Scipio* was consigned to free showings on various public occasions and at yearly assemblies in grade schools throughout Italy.

Attempting to draw a lesson from his colossal failure, Il Duce concluded that he could not make the sort of triumphal films he wanted to make without the participation of big name American stars. With this in mind, he sent Vittorio to Hollywood to scout the situation and see who was available. The result was a bizarre plan for a lavish production of Verdi's *Rigoletto* starring those two noted operatic stars, Stan Laurel and Oliver Hardy. The entire concept may have seemed like someone's idea of a joke, but Vittorio had actually won approval from his father's two favorite stars, and from producer Hal Roach, before the political situation between America and Italy began to deteriorate and forced cancellation of this ambitious international project. Back in Italy, Vittorio and his proud papa continued to dream of future flings at Fascist filmmaking, until they both had to abandon these activities due to a pressing engagement with World War II.

During the war, Italian schoolboys continued to be subjected to *Scipio* on a regular basis. Government officials hoped that the movie would inspire the right sort of fighting spirit in the nation's youth, but instead it became a standing joke. Class clowns learned to mimic the actors, and they particularly enjoyed rendering obscene versions of Scipio's stirring speeches. For an entire generation of students, *Scipio* *Africanus* served as a fitting symbol of the Mussolini regime, highlighting both its grand pretensions and its utter fraudulence. If you find an Italian of the right age and with the right sort of memory and ask what he or she recalls of the film, chances are you will get a knowing chuckle along with a specific mention of the movie's single most memorable feature: "Oh yes, who could forget it! That's the one where they are all wearing wristwatches along with their togas!"

The nineteen elephants featured in the recreation of the Battle of Zama (202 B.C.) in Scipio Africanus *were unfortunately upstaged by telephone poles that appeared on the horizon. These inadvertent details of set decoration are barely visible in this still, but highly noticeable on screen.*

KOLBERG

(1945)

A production of U.F.A. (Universum Film Aktien Gesellschaft)
Directed by Veit Harlan
Screenplay by Veit Harlan and Alfred Braun, in collaboration with Thea von Harbou,
and with officially uncredited contributions by Dr. Joseph Goebbels

Starring Kristina Söderbaum (Maria); Heinrich George (Nettelbeck);
Horst Caspar (Gneisenau); Paul Wegener (Colonel von Loucadou);
and Gustav Diessl (Major Schill).

One Happy Nazi

By 1939, Dr. Joseph Goebbels should have been one happy Nazi. He had achieved virtually everything that an ambitious Aryan boy could possibly desire: fame, wealth, three palatial homes, scores of gorgeous mistresses, a devoted *Hausfrau* for a wife, six blond-haired children, and a position—as Minister for Public Enlightenment and Propaganda—that made him the second most powerful man in the entire Reich. Why, then, did he continue to lose sleep over his one burning, unfulfilled ambition? How had he become so totally obsessed with an unseemly vision of himself as a German answer to David O. Selznick who would give the world an unforgettable battlefield epic comparable in scope to *Gone With the Wind*?

To answer that question, one must understand that Goebbels, as his biographer Helmut Heiber observed, "remained a frustrated 'artist' all his life." Like his buddy and mentor Adolf Hitler, Dr. G. began putsching and shoving only after he had failed to win recognition as a creative genius. While Hitler's chosen field was painting, Goebbels dreamed of himself as a great writer. At age twenty-four he won a Doctor of Philosophy degree from Heidelberg for a lengthy dissertation on a minor dramatist named Wilhelm von Schutz. With his academic credentials well in hand, Goebbels unleashed his own creative furies and turned out a romantic novel called *Michael*, which was promptly rejected by all leading publishers. After another few months of trying without success to write articles for liberal periodicals, Goebbels decided at last to put such flighty concerns behind him and to settle down to good, steady, respectable work: writing propaganda for the newly organized Nazi party.

He definitely had a flair for public relations; a number of historians have described Goebbels as "The Man Who Invented Adolf Hitler." But building the public image of a megalomaniac dictator, while doubtless a pleasant and stimulating endeavor, could not satisfy all of Dr. Goebbels' inner needs. He continued to nurse artistic aspirations and eventually focused them on a consuming interest in motion pictures.

After the Nazi rise to power in 1933, he indulged that interest by assuming personal control of every aspect of the German film industry. He not only determined which scripts would be produced but also kept close tabs on all the more important projects, following their progress from the first rushes to the final editing process. As he himself put it, he was "an impassioned devotee of cinematic art." Under his leadership, the Germans produced some 1,363 feature films, each of which Goebbels viewed personally before it was released to the public. In all three of his homes, he maintained private screening facilities in which he showed the native German products that were part of his work, along with foreign films for pure pleasure. Movies from Hollywood held a special fascination for him, and he became increasingly impatient with the fact that German artists could not compete more successfully on the international market with the "Jews and Communists" in California.

Goebbels' jealousy reached a peak in 1939 when, shortly after its release in the United States, he managed to obtain a print of *Gone With the Wind*. As it turned out, he not only respected this movie, but fell in love with it. He told his associates that he considered Selznick's movie "a painting, while our own German films are merely photographs." If such sentiments seemed unpatriotic, then frankly, Gretchen, he didn't give a damn. But he did resolve shortly thereafter that his chief legacy to the Master Race would be a Master Movie that would go beyond its American prototype in cinematic grandeur and romantic sweep. He personally selected what he considered to be the ideal subject for this epic film: the story of the town of Kolberg and its last-ditch heroic stand against the French during the Napoleonic wars.

A Gathering of Heroes

Goebbels began outlining his project in 1941, but he had no desire to rush into production. For one thing, he worried over the timing of the film and wondered what response it would provoke from the German people. During the early years of the war the Nazi armies advanced on all fronts, winning one smashing victory after another, and the public might have had a difficult time accepting a movie about a desperate defensive struggle to protect the sacred soil of the Fatherland. By 1943, however, the bloom was off the blitzkrieg. German troops had begun to retreat under the onslaught of Russians and Americans, so the fight-to-the-death story of the brave town of Kolberg took on new urgency and relevance. On June 1, Dr. G. issued a written order to veteran director Veit Harlan that read:

I commission you to make a film epic, *Kolberg*. The film is to show, through example of the Prussian city which gives the film its title, how a common resolution at home and at the front can overcome all enemies . . . I authorize you to request whatever help and support you deem necessary from all Army, Government and Party agencies, and you may refer to this film which I have hereby commissioned as being made in the service of our intellectual war effort.

Harlan had been chosen for the singular honor of creating this important picture because, over the years, he had earned the title of "Dr. Goebbels' Favorite Director." In 1940, he had thrilled all Nazi officials, including the Führer himself, with his direction of the infamous anti-Semitic diatribe *Jud Süss* (*The Jew Suess*), which went on to become a huge hit throughout occupied Europe. As filming began on *Kolberg*, Harlan called a press conference to explain his high-minded artistic intentions for the new project. "I want to show the heroism of our Prussian ancestors," he nobly declared. "I want to say to today's public: this is the core of which you were born, and it is with this strength that you will today rise to victory!"

As his personal contribution to this heroic effort, Harlan selflessly cast his wife, Kristina Söderbaum, in the starring role. Though Swedish-born, Miss Söderbaum had won millions of German fans with her frequent screen appearances as the Reich's favorite "child bride," portraying sweet, vivacious virgins in the style of a Nordic Mary Pickford. In *Kolberg*, she plays "Maria, a farmer's daughter," who urges her brothers and boyfriend to die for the glory of Prussia and considers it an honor when they follow her advice.

The film's other leading character is Nettelbeck, the mayor of the town, who defies the military authorities in order to organize civilian resistance to the French. For this pivotal role, Goebbels and Harlan selected Heinrich George, a distinguished actor whose real-life theatrics exceeded even his florid performances on screen. Before 1933, he identified himself as a radical Communist; then, as soon as he discovered that he could seduce more women as a follower of Adolf Hitler, he was transformed, literally overnight, into a fanatically dedicated Nazi. In the midst of orgiastic revels, he used to demand a moment of silence, then force his drinking companions to fall to their knees with him to offer a prayer of thanks to the Führer. After the war, Herr George received scathing reviews from the Red Army and died in a Soviet prison camp in 1946.

Would-be movie mogul Joseph ("Doc") Goebbels with some of his eager-beaver aides. Could they be reviewing production plans for **Kolberg**?

Colonel Loucadou (Paul Wegener) and General Gneisenau (Horst Caspar) prepare to die for the Prussian Fatherland.

The Law of Madness

The last months of 1943 hardly seemed an auspicious moment for the German film industry to start production on a sumptuous and ridiculously expensive cinematic spectacle. Italy had already surrendered to the Allies, the Russians had begun their inexorable march to the west, while American and British bombing raids caused increasing shortages and hardships for the civilian population. Such trivial distractions, however, could not be allowed to interfere with Doc Goebbels "important plan" for cinematic greatness. As director Veit Harlan later recalled, a "law of madness" applied at all times on the *Kolberg* set. "Hitler as well as Goebbels must have been obsessed," he concluded. "They had the idea that the film could be more useful to them than even a military miracle, because they no longer believed in victory in any rational way. In the cinema's dream factory, miracles happened more quickly than they do at the front."

While major buildings remained bombed-out hulks in some of Germany's most important cities, hundreds of workmen labored to construct an enormous set at Neustettin designed to resemble Kolberg of the Napoleonic era. Were Nazi troops needed to

hold off the Russians on the eastern front? Too bad. Dr. Goebbels needed them as extras for *Kolberg*, and he diverted entire units for months at a time. Were German citizens going hungry because the railroads had a difficult time shipping enough food to the cities? Too bad. The good doctor needed 100 boxcars full of salt to create "snow" for *Kolberg*'s touching Christmas scene. Were German boys dying in battle because the industrial plants couldn't turn out enough ammunition to keep them supplied? Too bad. Goebbels ordered the factories to turn out hundreds of thousands of blank bullets for *Kolberg*.

This same bizarre sense of priorities led German chemists to take time off from their military duties to prepare millions of feet of expensive and exotic color negative stock especially for the film. It would, of course, have been far easier to have shot *Kolberg* in black and white, but Selznick had used color for *Gone With the Wind*, so Goebbels refused to consider anything else. The rehearsals and filming went on and on, over the course of a full year, producing more than ninety hours of developed film for the beleaguered editors to consider. This footage featured some of the most elaborate and confusing battle scenes in cinema history, for which Dr. Goebbels and

A small sample of the 187,000 Wehrmacht extras who were reassigned from the front to lend authenticity to Kolberg—*intended as a Nazi answer to* Gone With the Wind.

his henchmen employed a remarkable total of 187,000 *Wehrmacht* troops. To place this mighty army in context, we should remember that director Harlan had at his disposal more than *three times* the combined number of French and Prussian soldiers who participated in the actual battle that the movie was trying to recreate. There is no way to explain this idiotic discrepancy other than to suggest that due to inflation an army of, say, 40,000 just didn't go as far as it once did. In any event, the hordes of extras never complained; no matter how temperamental the director or how uncomfortable the costumes they were forced to wear, facing German cameras presented fewer inconveniences than facing Russian guns.

The Cost of Greatness

If Goebbels had been required to pay for all the free military manpower used in the film, the cost of his production would have been twice or three times what it was. Even as matters stood, the budget of 8,500,000 marks (the equivalent of $2,125,000) made it by far the most expensive motion picture ever made in Germany. A full one-fourth of this grotesque cost went to pay for sequences that Goebbels decided to cut from the film at the last moment. The offending scenes showed the horrors of warfare in particularly bloody and realistic terms; Dr. Goebbels reasoned that the German public would not go to the theatres to watch the same sort of devastation that they could look out their windows and see in even more realistic terms for free.

This same concern for the sensibilities of the Master Race led Dr. G. to treat all information concerning the production of *Kolberg* as a closely guarded state secret. Despite his confidence in the courage of his countrymen, Goebbels worried that they might resent the lavish arrangements surrounding the production, and throughout 1944 the world knew nothing at all of the bizarre activities at Neustettin. When the film was finally released to the public, everyone would of course be aware of the incredible dimension of the project, but by that time, Goebbels felt sure, the German people would be so inspired and uplifted by what they saw on the screen that they would forgive and endorse all sacrifices made for the sake of cinematic glory.

Uplift and Inspiration

Perhaps the most striking, and easily the most obnoxious, feature of the finished film is the musical score,

Nettelbeck (Heinrich George) tells Maria (Kristina Söderbaum): "You're a really fine person, Maria. You weren't afraid to die. You stayed in your place, and you did your duty."

full of bombastic marches, banal love themes, and angelic choral hymns designed to encourage the fighting Prussians on the screen. The composer was Norbert Schultze, best known for his nostalgic ballad of wartime love, "Lili Marlene." In the score for *Kolberg*, the insinuating charm of this celebrated song is totally absent, and instead the audience is assaulted relentlessly and mercilessly by brass bands, a full orchestra, and a gigantic chorus. The main choral theme of the film, "EIN VOLK STEHT AUF!" ("A People Arise!"), is repeated so many times and with so deadening an effect that under any sort of normal circumstances it would serve as a cue for An Audience to Arise and walk out of the theatre.

Along with Schultze's ponderous score came still more music to the ears of any true-blue Nazi: inspiring and interminable patriotic speeches. Through an astonishing coincidence, the text of these declamations bore a haunting resemblance to various radio talks and public exhortations delivered by Dr. Goebbels to the citizens of the Reich. The propaganda minister had determined that he would spare nothing—not even his own creative genius—in the do-or-die effort to make *Kolberg* an artistic triumph. To achieve this purpose he became an uncredited screenwriter on the project and personally scripted key lines for the hero, Nettelbeck. Goebbels, for example, lovingly created a stirring scene in which Mayor Nettelbeck attempts to persuade General

Gneisenau to help the citizens in defending the town. "Commander, we haven't yet fired our last bullet!" he cheerfully declares. "Even if we have to hang on to the soil of our town with our fingernails, we won't let go. No, they will have to hack our hands off one by one, kill us one after the other . . . Better to be buried under the ruins than to capitulate. I have never gone on my knees to anyone before. Now I'm doing it. Gneisenau, Kolberg must *not* be surrendered!" The general (Horst Caspar) is so moved by the simple eloquence of the mayor that he commands him to get up (A Mayor Arises!), embraces him smiling broadly, and delivers the movie's single most upbeat line: "That is what I wanted to hear from you, Nettelbeck! Now—we can die together!"

This declaration proved singularly prophetic concerning the fate of the finally completed film and its principal creator.

The Gala Premiere

It is common enough for producers of feature films to encounter difficulties in trying to orchestrate glittering premieres, but it is safe to say that the problems faced by Joseph Goebbels in his plans for the long-awaited debut of *Kolberg* were more or less unprecedented. He had decided to release the film for the first time as part of the morale-building *Atlantikfestung* (Atlantic Festival) scheduled for January 30, 1945, in the occupied French city of La Rochelle. By the time the great day arrived, however, Goebbels had to abandon whatever visions he may have entertained of sleek limousines, searchlights, and footprints in cement, due to the unfortunate fact that La Rochelle had been totally surrounded by the Allies. Nevertheless, a premiere is a premiere, and the propaganda minister ordered the Luftwaffe to fly a daring mission behind enemy lines to drop the newly completed film by parachute so it could be shown as scheduled to the first-night crowd.

The notices that followed the first night's festivities within the besieged garrison were universally enthusiastic, since the only response that has been preserved was a hearty telegram to Goebbels from the German Commandant at La Rochelle:

Opening performance of color film *Kolberg* took place today in La Rochelle Theatre for soldiers of all units of defence zone. Deeply moved by the courageous action of the Kolberg fortress and incomparable artistic presentation, we add, to our gratitude for the dispatch of the film, our renewed vow to emulate the heroic struggle at home and not to fall short of them in our perseverance and initiative. Long live Germany, long live our Führer!

Less than two weeks later, the movie's otherwise triumphant first run was cut short when La Rochelle surrendered to the Americans. But, not to worry, Goebbels had already provided for his movie's Berlin premiere. Unfortunately, the UFA-Palast Theatre, where the festive showing was supposed to take place, had recently been bombed into popcorn by the Allies, and most of the capital's other movie houses were, in fact, already *kaput*. Goebbels' staff at last located a small theatre that was still in working order and opened the film there with as much fanfare as they could muster. Few Berliners could be persuaded to attend the screenings, however; most people chose to remain in their bomb shelters day and night, and the only ones who actually saw the film were a handful of government employees who were ordered to show up and sit through it.

Through it all, Goebbels refused to give up on the future of his masterpiece and kept expecting courageous Germans to risk death, if necessary, in order to view the great spectacle on the screen. In his diary of May 18, 1945, he made the melancholy observation that despite the heroic struggle depicted on film, the real-life town of Kolberg had just surrendered to the Russians. "We have now had to evacuate Kolberg. I will ensure that the evacuation is not mentioned in the official press report. In view of severe psychological repercussions on the *Kolberg* film, we could do without that for a moment."

Twilight of the Gods

Goebbels managed to attend one final screening of his favorite film, on April 17, 1945. He ordered all the members of his staff to sit with him through the showing, even though they had already watched the movie countless times. After the show, the good doctor made a rousing speech to his associates. "Gentlemen," he began, "in a hundred years' time they will be showing another fine color film describing the terrible days we are living through. Wouldn't you like to play a part in the film? . . . I can assure you it will be a fine and devastating picture, and for the sake of this prospect it is worth standing fast. Hold out now, so that a hundred years hence the audience does not hoot and whistle when you appear on the screen."

In response, his colleagues looked at Goebbels as if he were ready for the giggle-works, and one staff member mumbled to another, "Merely to be a bit player in a picture a hundred years hence seems hardly worth dying for now." When the Russians encircled Berlin five days later most of Goebbels' assistants decided to take a rain check on playing heroic roles in his imaginary film of the future and flew the coop for Obersalzburg, where they could surrender to the notably less ferocious Americans. Meanwhile, Goebbels himself retreated to the *Führerbunker* in the company of his family and his Main Man, Mr. H. Hitler reportedly killed himself on April 30, leaving Goebbels in charge of what remained of the "Thousand Year Reich." The good doctor lasted less than a day in this position, before administering fatal injections of prussic acid to each of his six children, poisoning his wife, and shooting himself in the head. His chauffeur had been left with instructions to douse the bodies in gasoline and to set them aflame, so Goebbels could bid the world *auf Wiedersehen* in properly cinematic style.

After the war, all prints of *Kolberg* were seized by Soviet and American forces, and screenings of the film were strictly forbidden. Despite these precautions, copies of the movie turned up mysteriously in Argentina, where it played under the title *Burning Hearts* and no doubt delighted a substantial number of escaped Nazis during the 1950s.

Veit Harlan, meanwhile, spent nearly twenty years trying to live down his reputation as the most notorious Nazi film director. He stood trial in 1948 for war crimes but won acquittal by persuading the court that he had exercised very little artistic control on the propagandistic and anti-Semitic projects that bore his name. Harlan testified that Goebbels had once threatened to "smash him like a bug on the wall" if he showed too much independence, and made a point of holding one of the Harlan children in Germany as a hostage whenever the director and his wife were allowed to travel abroad. After his acquittal, Harlan suffered several heart attacks, while his wife, the former star Kristina Söderbaum, suffered a long series of nervous breakdowns. When West Germany's Second Television Network began making plans for a broadcast of *Kolberg* in 1963, Harlan volunteered to spearhead an effort to bring the old

warhorse "up to date." "With a few cuts and new synchronization," he said, "I can turn *Kolberg* into a democratic film." The television executives never took advantage of his offer, since public protests forced cancellation of the scheduled broadcast. Harlan died of cancer later that same year.

In 1966, *Kolberg* finally made its long-awaited return, released as a theatrical feature by Atlas Films. Presented as an historical document of the Nazi period, bracketed with twenty minutes of newsreel footage showing speeches by Goebbels that paralleled Nettelbeck's speeches in the film, it opened in West Germany to "good but not great business" (*Variety*). Left-wing groups offered noisy protests wherever the film was shown and tried in several cases to shut down the theatres that dared to play it. In Munich, pacifist pickets carried signs that read "Goebbels Triumphs!" Critics refused to take the movie seriously or to consider it on its own terms, writing instead about the historical significance of its re-release. The British film magazine *Sight and Sound* reported that "young people, trained in the school of American action cinema," found Goebbels' spectacle "badly made" and "ludicrous," while the *New York Times* wrote that "there have been waves of giggles accompanying some particularly sentimental scene or obvious piece of propaganda."

Whatever its shortcomings and stupidities, *Kolberg*, on one level at least, commands our respect. With its breathtaking waste of German manpower and matériel at a crucial juncture in the European conflict, it made a major contribution to the Allied war effort. Considered from this perspective, few productions in history have had so practical and beneficial an effect.

Certainly, the execrable and idiotic entertainments included in the next corridor of our museum lacked any such positive impact. They advanced the interests of absolutely no one—least of all the curiously beloved stars whose questionable talents they were intended to showcase.

DISASTROUS DEBUTS

HOLLYWOOD, as the old saying goes, is always in the market for new talent and will often turn to other arenas of the entertainment business in order to find it. Over the years, various singers, dancers, swimmers, football players, ice skaters, and TV personalities have made a smooth transition to big screen stardom, transferring their popularity from one medium to another. Enterprising producers are invariably attracted to the commercial possibilities of such "crossover" stars, but their success is by no means assured. For every John Travolta, who leaps effortlessly from a popular TV series to a string of movie triumphs, there is a Henry Winkler, whose feature film ventures have been consistent disappointments; for every Elvis Presley, who used his musical gifts to become a major box office draw, there is a Bob Dylan, who has twice embarrassed himself with feeble attempts to project his charisma on the silver screen.

In the Hollywood Hall of Shame, however, we cannot be satisfied with ordinary failure; we are looking for disasters that are grandiose in scope and bizarre in content. Fortunately for our purposes, the two beloved entertainers featured in this next gallery began (and ended) their careers as movie stars with rickety, overpriced vehicles that are eminently worthy of consideration. This corridor in our museum commemorates the blighted hopes of major studios that blew millions on these "sure thing" sucker bets, trying to cash in on the national notoriety of this unlikely pair, but ending up with two inane and unsalable experiments. We must leave unanswered the larger, fundamental question raised by these experiences: how did two such dubious musical talents as Kate Smith and Liberace ever attract their legions of fans in the first place? This phenomenon is one of those deep mysteries of nature, along with water divining, the migration secrets of birds, and the indomitable will of salmon to spawn upstream, which will, no doubt, remain forever unexplained.

HELLO EVERYBODY!

(1933)
Paramount
Directed by William A. Seiter
Screenplay by Dorothy Yost and Lawrence Hazard, based on a story
by Fannie Hurst
Music and lyrics by Arthur Johnson and Sam Coslow

Starring Kate Smith ("Kate Smith"); Randolph Scott (Hunt Blake);
Sally Blane (Lily Smith); George Barbier (Mr. Blair); Charley Grapewin (Jed);
and Ted Collins ("Ted Collins").

Sitting on Top of the World

By the mid-1930s, Kate Smith had already established herself as an American Institution—like the Statue of Liberty, Smokey the Bear, or Ebbetts Field. When England's King George VI and Queen Elizabeth visited their former colonies, she was introduced to the royal couple by no less a fan than Franklin D. Roosevelt. "This is Kate Smith," the President said. "This is America."

Needless to say, it took a small town to produce so enormous a talent—in this case, Greenville, Virginia, where Kate was born in 1910. Her papa was a wholesale distributor of magazines who was unable to provide any formal music lessons for his plump and promising child, but Kate nonetheless developed her golden voice by singing in church choirs beginning at age four. While still a teenager, this gifted prodigy journeyed to New York City in quest of fame and fortune.

The good news is that she found a part in a stage show almost immediately; the bad news is that her role in *Honeymoon Lane* called for her to portray Tiny Little, a comic relief fat girl who is constantly ridiculed by the other characters. Miss Kate handled this opportunity with such natural aplomb that she went on to an even more substantial role in another show. As co-star of the George White musical *Flying High,* our versatile songstress portrayed Pansy Sparks, who is repeatedly insulted by Bert Lahr and the other comics in the cast. Their sparkling repartee included witty lines such as, "That girl is sitting on top of the world—nothing else would bear her weight," and "When she sits down it's like a dirigible coming in for a landing!" On stage, Kate withstood these barbs with a stoic smile, but after each performance she would run to her dressing room in tears.

By the time she was nineteen, Kate had begun to think about abandoning her show business career, but destiny had other plans and soon anointed her through the agency of one Ted Collins. An artists and repertoire representative for Columbia Records, Collins missed his commuter train home one fateful night in 1930 and decided to take in a performance of *Flying High.* The raw country girl who portrayed Pansy Sparks immediately captured his imagination, and so began one of the greatest manager-talent relationships in the history of the entertainment industry. The partnership lasted until Collins' death in 1964, and many of Kate's friends suggested that the reason she never married was that the connection with Ted was so much deeper than conventional matrimony.

Under the guidance of her homespun Svengali, Kate became a vaudeville star virtually overnight, then made the big jump to radio. From the moment of her first broadcast on CBS on May 1, 1931, her three trademarks were already in place: the cheerful greeting "Helllooo, Everybody!"; the romantic theme song, "When the Moon Comes Over the Mountain"; and the folksy close, "Thanks for listenin'!" Her good-hearted simplicity and her rich contralto voice made her, within months, the number-one radio attraction in the United States, displacing crooner Rudy Vallee. Using the production company she formed with Collins (The Kated Corporation), Miss Smith went on to a succession of hit records, ultimately recording over 2,000 songs. As Ted noted with glee, despite the fact that there was plenty of Kate to go around, the adoring public simply could not get enough of her. In 1938 she launched a second daily radio show, *Kate Smith*

A studio publicity still shows off the new camera that Paramount designed in order to capture the awesome scope of its most promising new star.

Speaks, in which, instead of music and entertainment, she would offer her thoughts on the Great Issues of the Day, such as "what we oughta do about this Hitler fella" and "the best recipe for chocolate fudge I ever heard." That same year, Kate won the exclusive right to sing Irving Berlin's "God Bless America" on the radio, and many Americans were soon suggesting that it be made the new national anthem. Fervent patriotism was always a part of the Great Lady's appeal, and during World War II she traveled over 500,000 miles to entertain the troops while managing to sell $600 million in war bonds—an all-time record. In the 1950s, Kate triumphantly entered the new medium of television, where the daily *Kate Smith Hour* on NBC remained a popular show for most of the decade. Kate Smith fans might be somewhat more restrained in their enthusiasm than, say, the devotees of the Rolling Stones, but they remained committed enough over the course of thirty years to make her a huge star of TV, the concert hall, and the recording studio. The only arena she never managed to conquer was the realm of motion pictures and that, as we shall see, was not for lack of trying.

"A Great Big Bucketful of Money"

In the early 1930s, as the Kate Smith phenomenon first afflicted the American public, each of the major Hollywood studios wanted the opportunity to con-

struct a feature film that would use the beloved star as its sturdy foundation. Kate and Ted, anxious to prove that they were more than a pair of bumpkins who had just fallen off the turnip truck, demonstrated their skill as cagey and tenacious negotiators. They forced the studios to bid against one another and wound up with what one old Hollywood hand remembers as "a great big bucketful of money" before they finally agreed to sign with Paramount.

Part of Paramount's grand strategy called for devising a suitably saccharine vehicle for the Divine Miss S.; her fans, after all, were not exactly ready for *King Lear*. With this situation in mind, the studio hired Fannie Hurst, who had enjoyed huge success with her sob-story best-sellers, *Imitation of Life* and *Symphony of Six Million*. Miss Hurst wrote the story of a poor farm girl with a God-sent voice who makes it big (even though she is unusually big to begin with) as a radio star. The on-screen name of this highly original "fictional" character is, believe it or not, "Kate Smith." Meanwhile, Kate's contract with Paramount also required a substantial movie role for her alter ego, Ted Collins. In the final script for Miss Smith's starring vehicle, Ted is required to stretch his dramatic abilities to their limits by his consummate portrayal of an agent and manager cunningly known as "Ted Collins." By using these real names, the studio bosses hoped to pull a fast one on all those pumpkin heads in the provinces; hopefully, they would come galumphing into their local theatres convinced that they were seeing the honest-to-goodness true life story of their number-one heroine, while the antics they watched on the screen bore little resemblance to the actual details of Kate's past.

The main problem for Paramount was creating a suitable love interest for its overweight star, but scenarist Hurst managed to solve that dilemma in best soap-opera style. At the beginning of the picture, Kate falls hard for a city slicker played by Randolph Scott. He flirts harmlessly with her but saves his serious attentions for the lady's younger and substantially slimmer sister, who is played by Sally Blane—real-life sister of Loretta Young. The noble Kate stoically accepts the situation as she stands at her balcony and moans at the moon while watching the two slender love birds making hootchie-kootchie on the patio below. In public, she hides her true feelings, encourages her sister to marry the boy of her dreams, and then leaves the family homestead for the big city because she can't stand living so close to the man who, as she sings, "Shoulda Been for Me!" Once she arrives in New York, she becomes, naturally, an instant radio sensation and in the process manages to defeat the greedy designs of the power and water

Sally Blane gets the guy (Randolph Scott), but Big Sister Kate Smith wins radio stardom in the course of the gut-wrenching tearjerker, Hello Everybody! *Paramount tried to sell this white elephant to the public with ads proclaiming: "While her golden voice brings happiness to millions, it hides a sob and a tear in her own great heart!"*

company against the poor folks back home, thereby winning the gratitude of every extra on the sound stage.

Charging at the Camera

Unfortunately, Kate's attitude toward her real-life co-workers failed to inspire similar gratitude. From the moment she arrived in California, she seemed to be uncomfortable. As she tersely observed in her autobiography: "I didn't much like the movie capital, as I'm not fond of parties and staying up late, but I did appreciate the opportunity to see the West Coast." We spoke with Sally Blane, Kate's co-star in *Hello Everybody!*, who distinctly recalled the atmosphere on the set. "You see, she was very different from picture people," Miss Blane recalled. "I'd been here since I was five or six years old, and it just felt like Kate Smith didn't belong, as far as I could see. You got the feeling that she didn't approve of Hollywood; she just wanted to take their money. It felt to us like an intrusion. She came with her whole entourage. California was supposed to be for actors, everyone was supposed to be good-looking and pretty, and here we had this big stout woman who just had nothing to do with us."

From the day shooting began, director William Seiter (*Sons of the Desert* [1933], *Room Service* [1938]) discovered that "The Queen of the Air" might be many things to many people, but she was certainly no actress. Even the most trivial scenes had to be shot and reshot so many times that the cost of the film, already high because of the big fee for Kate and Ted, began mounting to appalling levels. In frustration and embarrassment, Kate the Great ordered a "locked set"—prohibiting anyone except the director and the technical crew from watching her at work.

This ban even extended to the studio's other stars, notably including Mae West. The blonde bombshell was then engaged in her first starring role for Paramount, a small-scale production called *She Done Him Wrong*, while the studio heads devoted most of their attention to their sure winner, *Hello Everybody!* Mae wanted to spend an afternoon watching the filming on this major undertaking while checking out her competition, but Kate absolutely refused to allow her near the production. "I don't want that immoral woman about!" said America's First Lady of Song, and when Kate put her foot down, it usually registered on the Richter scale.

The most difficult moments in the production came when the filmmakers attempted to extend Kate's horizons even beyond singing and acting.

Kate Smith (see if you can spot her) leads the poor-but-honest "common folk" in protesting the greed of the water and power company, as represented by white-haired villain George Barbier—all part of the soppy social commentary in Hello Everybody!

Paramount had promised exhibitors that their sensational new film would not only show Kate *singing* (no problem) but also *acting* (big problem) and *dancing* (forget it!). Ultimately, director Seiter (described by Sally Blane as "a darling man but the world's most unimaginative director") lavished nearly as much time and effort on a two-minute sequence of Kate Smith dancing as Darryl Zanuck spent on the destruction of the entire human race in *Noah's Ark*. The final results on screen can only suggest the untold joys of the rehearsals and the countless outtakes. As she begins singing "Dinah . . . Nothing Ever Could be Finah . . ." Kate comes charging at the camera like the front four of the Pittsburgh Steelers, claps her hands, and begins wiggling her feet and furiously waving her arms while wearing a torrid "hot-cha!" smile on her face. As *Variety* reported, "Her dance, to 'Dinah,' got a howl out of the preview audience." Nevertheless, it clearly served as an inspiration for the fascinating Sea Mammal show that is featured today at the popular San Diego attraction, Sea World.

Something for Everybody

According to Arthur Mayer, at the time a leading Paramount executive and, years later, one of the "witnesses" in Warren Beatty's *Reds*, the studio spent more than $2 million on *Hello Everybody!*, making it the most expensive movie musical in history up to that time.

In a desperate attempt to ensure a return on its investment, the studio attempted to throw in something for everybody, including an extremely touching number designed to thrill all the "colored folk" in the audience. After Kate becomes a radio star in the movie, she receives a special request from a black orphanage to dedicate a song specially to them. She responds on the air by saying, "And now, folks, I'd like to sing this next song for a lot of little colored children who are listenin' in an orphanage in New York City. Here you are, kids!" Then as Kate's soothing words waft their way over the airwaves, the film cuts to a series of close-ups of the delighted darkies who are listening to her song—in this case an absolutely astonishing production number called (honest to God) "Pickaninnies' Heaven":

> Little pickaninnies
>   Listen to the tale
> Of a place that I know
> It's twice as high as the moon
> You get there in a balloon
>   Haven't you been told
>   Of the place where all the good little
>   pickaninnies go?
>
> I've just been there
>   So I oughta know!
> Great big watermelons
> Go round and get in your way . . .
> Luscious pork chop bushes
> Bloom right outside your door
>   In a pickaninnies' heaven!
>
> I've heard them say
> Go down a Swanee River
> Made of real lemonade . . .
> And though the Good Lord
> Took your Mammy
> She'll be waiting for you there
>   In the pickaninnies' heaven!

More Than Conventional

With the shooting of the film finally completed, Paramount faced a difficult problem in marketing its Great White Hoke. As the studio pressbook pointedly observed, "More than 75,000,000 members of this country's radio population has [sic] listened to 'The Queen of the Air,' but only a handful of people have seen her." In addressing the question of how the public might cope with their first movie glimpse of

this American institution, the Paramount executives decided to take the water buffalo by the horns and to deal with the inevitable questions about Kate's weight with candor and good humor. Publicity for the film described Miss Smith as "212 pounds of vital young womanhood" and fearlessly described "the entire avoirdupois situation."

No one has ever looked upon the radio star as anemic. Even at her birth, Kate was plump and the ensuing years gave further poundage. Furthermore, the young woman has no desire to diet. She is healthy as she is, and that, Kate believes, is one of the most important things in life.

Not long ago, after her successful personal appearance at the Ambassador, Atlantic City, she ordered a chocolate parfait. The waiter unfortunately spilled it over her dress. She cheerfully accepted the deluge. 'But,' she added, 'I will have my sweet revenge!' So she ordered four more parfaits—on the house.

The fact that Paramount flooded the newspapers with this sort of publicity clearly indicates that the studio understood that its hot new star was something more than a conventional romantic heroine. As ads for the film proclaimed: "THE VOICE THAT BROUGHT ROMANCE INTO THE HOMES OF AMERICA NOW BRINGS A *NEW* KIND OF ROMANCE TO THE TALKING SCREEN!" And what kind of romance was it? A love affair between a girl and her chocolate parfait? No, Paramount explained, what Kate represented was "A LADY BOUNTIFUL WITH A READY SONG ON HER LIPS TO HIDE THE ACHE OF EMPTINESS IN HER OWN GREAT HEART! SHE HELPED EVERYBODY BUT HERSELF!" In other words, the promotional campaign employed a most unconventional marketing strategy: it tried to win movie popularity for Miss Smith by making her an object of pity. It would have been far more appropriate if the studio had asked the public to pity the poor executives who poured millions into this entire lamebrained enterprise, with thoroughly disastrous results.

Box Office Records

Following its debut in January 1933, *Hello Everybody!* set box office records almost immediately: reports from several cities across the country indicated that no film in history had ever done such wretched business during the first week of its release. In many theatres, the movie didn't even last a week—it closed after five days and crawled out of town with its trailer between its legs. Not even the anticipated core audience—the Happy Hayseeds of Hillbilly Hollow—turned out to see Miss Kate. Instead, they flocked to another, far more wholesome 4-H

Kate Smith horrifies her on-screen brother and sister, Jerry Tucker and Marguerite Campbell, by threatening to eat them in a tender domestic scene from Hello Everybody!

Club–approved entertainment: the original *State Fair*, starring Will Rogers, Janet Gaynor, and Blue Boy the Hog. In the last analysis, even die-hard fans of great girth and heroic proportions turned their backs on Kate Smith and found more satisfaction in another newcomer named King Kong—who ended up as one of the top of box office draws 1933.

After the spectacular failure of her film, Kate Smith packed up her bags, said "Goodbye Everybody!" and left Hollywood for good. She returned to New York to resume her position as "Queen of the Air," suffering the ignominious fate of earning another $30 million for herself and Ted Collins during the balance of her career. She never again attempted a starring movie role, though she did make a brief appearance in a 1943 film called *This Is the Army*. It

was a thick slice of wartime promotional puffery, and this time Miss Kate made no attempt to act or (thank heavens!) to dance. She simply walked onto a sound stage and sang "God Bless America" at the request of the star of the picture, Ronald Reagan, who played "The Stage Manager."

In 1982, this same Mr. Reagan, now cast as Stage Manager of the United States, was reunited with Miss Smith to present her with a well-deserved Presidential Medal of Freedom. It is hardly surprising that the proclamation drawn up to honor her on this occasion neglected to mention her brief film career. We have done our best, as selfless patriots, to correct this unconscionable omission, all the while keeping in mind Kipling's words: Judge of the Nations, spare us yet, Lest we forget—lest we forget!

SINCERELY YOURS

(1955)

Warner Brothers
Produced by Henry Blanke
Directed by Gordon Douglas
Screenplay by Irving Wallace
Musical Adviser: George Liberace

Starring Liberace (Anthony Warrin); Joanne Dru (Marion Moore);
Dorothy Malone (Linda Curtis); William Demarest (Sam);
Lurene Tuttle (Mrs. McGinley); and Richard Eyer (Alvie Hunt).

The Miracle Worker

In recent times, we have become so accustomed to viewing Liberace as a figure of parody and derision that it is easy to forget the intense adulation that he inspired some thirty years ago. At the height of his popularity, his weekly television show went out to some 30 million viewers on more that 200 stations, reaching even more people than the *I Love Lucy* series. "Mr. Entertainment" won two Emmy awards and drew nearly 10,000 fan letters every week, most of them from the middle-aged matrons who made up his core audience. "I love your smile, dimple and mischievous wink—like a little boy's!" wrote one of them, while another pleaded that she would "just love a piece of your shirt or an old sock, but I know that is too much to ask." Some of Liberace's more fanatic followers even came to believe that their hero possessed magical healing powers. On more than one occasion cripples traveled hundreds of miles to his concert appearances and begged for a single touch that might change their lives. In the same spirit, Warner Brothers humbly approached The Great Man, hoping that he would help to heal their mid-fifties box office anemia and magically transform warmed-over manure into cash-box gold.

He had, after all, performed much the same feat with his TV show. The critics always despised Liberace and considered him, in the words of William Connor of the *London Daily Mail*, "The biggest sentimental vomit of all time!" Such harsh words, however, did nothing to slow the triumphal progress of the pianistic prodigy who was born Wladziu Valen-

tino Liberace in the romantic city of Milwaukee, Wisconsin. Despite a singing voice that had been aptly described as that of a "dormouse with adenoids," despite an irritating habit of mixing, say, Chopin's Nocturne in E Flat with sprightly renditions of "Three Little Fishies" and "Tico Tico," despite a set of florid costumes that made Maria Montez look like a wallflower, the perpetually smiling glamor boy with the candelabrum on his piano captured the hearts of middle America. If there was one quality more than any other that characterized his public image, it was sweetness, though it took the public many years to fully appreciate just how sweet Liberace was. At the beginning of his career, he still went to great lengths to present himself as "America's most eligible bachelor," made none the less desirable by the fact that at the age of thirty-two he still lived at home with his mother, Frances, and his bandleader brother, George.

Working in close harmony with one another, this trio of Liberaces moved in short order from a successful nightclub act to a local Los Angeles TV series to a national show that became an overnight sensation. The executives at Warner Brothers never claimed to understand the Liberace craze—that would have required a spiritualist, or at least an expert in deviant psychology—but they did recognize a phenomenon when they saw one. The movie men eagerly paid a huge (but undisclosed) sum for the privilege of signing "The People's Pianist" to his first starring role. If they provided him with plenty of changes of costume (twenty-nine in all) and the opportunity for numerous piano solos (including works by Liszt, Tchaikovsky, Mozart, Chopin, along with "Tea for Two," "The Beer Barrel Polka," "The Notre Dame Fight Song," "Chopsticks," and other favorites), then how could they possibly miss?

The studio and its new star both worked hard to provide an answer to that question.

The Man Who Played Odd

To script a musical melodrama that would suitably display the charm and talent of its wavy-haired golden boy, Warner Brothers selected a promising young screenwriter named Irving Wallace. It was not, to put it mildly, Mr. Wallace's finest hour as a writer, though it would be unfair to give the future novelist exclusive credit for the mush-minded disaster that emerged from his typewriter. The studio executives had ordered him to update a silly 1932 "weepie" called *The Man Who Played God,* in which George Arliss plays a brilliant concert pianist who tragically loses his hearing. The remake also describes the adventures of a classical pianist, but this time around our hero is something more than your run-of-the-mill Artur Rubinstein–Vladimir Horowitz type artist. Liberace plays the brilliant and lovable Anthony Warrin, a fearless crusader on behalf of "Music for the Masses." What this means is that after concluding a Carnegie Hall performance of the Tchaikovsky Piano Concerto Number One, he delights his audience by offering as encore a tinkly sing-along version of "When Irish Eyes Are Smiling." As one of his admirers pithily observes in the course of the film, "He respects the classics, but from a sitting position, not from his knees." Despite this admirable moderation in the choice of a preferred position, our hero contracts a mysterious disease that renders him suddenly deaf. This dramatic development is portrayed on screen by the use of a unique dramatic device described as "point of hearing," in which, through the magic of motion pictures, we directly experience Liberace's frustrating condition as sounds fade in and out and large chunks of dialogue are rendered unintelligible. This is actually an improvement over the rest of the film, since some of the hero's dramatic soliloquies will cause the viewer to wish that he had been struck dumb as well as deaf. At the point of suicide, for instance, he looks down from the railing of his skyscraper penthouse and declaims: "Maybe I am a coward! Maybe I don't have the courage and heroics you like to see in people. But I know how I feel inside. And I know how the people down there feel! And it makes me wonder. Wonder . . . about God. A God that hasn't time. Hasn't time to help anyone who needs Him!"

"Mr. Entertainment": Liberace flashes his famous grin during a break from filming his debut vehicle as a star of feature films. Warner Brothers felt certain that he, if anyone, was the man who could put the tinsel back into Tinseltown.

To help our pathetic princeling endure this dark night of the soul, the screenwriter has thoughtfully equipped him with a group of friends and followers who can help pass the time until the end of the movie and the inevitable operation ("It's like a miracle!") that magically restores his hearing. Joanne Dru plays his secretary, who hides a deep unselfish love for her boyish boss beneath a mask of brisk efficiency. Dorothy Malone is his glamorous fiancée, the sort to make the oldsters in the audience whisper, "She's just not his type—can't he see that it's the secretary who really loves him?" William Demarest, meanwhile, presents a standard-issue version of that familiar figure from all such films: the gruff, tough-talking manager with the heart of gold. None of these devoted groupies, however, had the heart to raise an obvious point from the past: that one Ludwig van Beethoven (a fair musician in his own right, though perhaps not quite as talented as Liberace) managed to continue

The Toast of the Town: With 30 million Americans watching his television show every week, Liberace seemed all but certain of stardom on the silver screen. To ensure his success, Warner Brothers hired a young screenwriter named Irving Wallace to craft a preposterous script that would match the sentimental appeal of "The People's Pianist." Dorothy Malone plays his spoiled and fickle fiancée, who in the end loses the gorgeous Mr. Glitter to his loyal and humble secretary, Joanne Dru.

his career despite a handicap similar to that of the hero of this film.

Anthony Warrin, on the other hand, abandons his musical pursuits and takes up an exciting new career as his neighborhood's most prominent Peeping Tom. After obtaining a set of powerful binoculars, he sits on his balcony all day and surveys the passing scene with passionate interest. While jaded moviegoers might suspect that this proclivity suggests that Liberace has discovered a YMCA in the immediate vicinity, his penthouse actually overlooks Central Park. Through his recent mastery of lipreading, he snoops on unsuspecting visitors to the park and discovers "much unhappiness in the world below." Since the holiday season is approaching (and Warner Brothers planned to release this film as Christmas fare for the whole family), Mr. Entertainment now decides to become Mr. Santa Claus and to help these unfortunates in any way he can.

First, there is a little crippled boy (Richard Eyer) who comes to the park with his grandfather. Alvie wants to play football "more'n anything," but without an expensive operation he doesn't stand a chance. Liberace steps in immediately and pays for the wondrous cure, throwing in a piano rendition of the "Notre Dame Fight Song" at no extra charge.

Next, we go from the Fighting Irish to the Frightened Irish, in the person of a sweet, elderly dearie

from The Old Sod whose married daughter is ashamed of mama's unsophisticated immigrant ways. As our hero perceptively comments: "A small American tragedy: Mrs. McGinley gets everything from her daughter except recognition, respect and love!" To remedy the situation, America's Smiling Sweetheart stages his own version of *Queen for a Day*, taking Mrs. McGinley (Lurene Tuttle) on a shopping spree around town and turning her into an elegant matron ready for the highest of high society.

This latest triumph is no sooner in hand when—horrors!—the roving binoculars find his fiancée in the park confessing her love to another man. In his response to this provocation, Liberace demonstrates that he has transcended the traditional role of the macho male (as if anyone ever had any doubt) by graciously acknowledging the situation and "giving her the freedom" to marry the other guy. Meanwhile, he settles down with his faithful secretary, who returns the favor by persuading him to undergo the risky operation that eventually restores his hearing. In the grand finale, he makes a triumphal return to Carnegie Hall, where, in addition to the nauseous mix of classics and kitsch that is, after all, his stock-in-trade, he offers a brief soft-shoe dance routine that brings the stuffed shirt crowd to its feet in grateful applause. There is actually good reason for this gratitude: the movie, at long last, is over.

"The Box Office Staff of Life"

In view of the wretched quality of *Sincerely Yours*, Warner Brothers kept the cost of the production a closely guarded secret. When confronted with rumors that the picture had gone way over budget and that Liberace had received an unprecedented fee for his performance, studio spokesmen offered only a terse "no comment." The great expectations for the film's commercial prospects could not prevent veteran executives from feeling a sense of embarrassment at having wasted millions on such a simple, saccharine story centered around an untested newcomer to the silver screen.

As Hollywood braced itself for the picture's November release, blockbuster success seemed all but assured. Liberace's concert appearances continued to attract crowds of extraordinary size and enthusiasm, outselling even the tumultuous public performances of teen idol Eddie Fisher. In one stadium show, The People's Pianist sold out a house of 120,000—a figure that most current rock stars could only envy. If such huge hordes eagerly paid premium prices to catch a distant glimpse of their favorite on one of his tours,

Liberace has always been known for his kindly interest in children. Here, in one heart-warming scene from Sincerely Yours, *he shows his tender concern for a crippled boy (Richard Eyer) while his hard-boiled manager (William Demarest, left) knowingly looks on.*

then surely even larger crowds would plunk down the modest cost of a movie ticket to snuggle up to him in the intimacy of their local theatres.

With this calculation well in mind, Warner Brothers staged a huge premiere at the Pantages Theatre on Hollywood Boulevard. In the street, fans filled bleachers for several blocks, cheering each arriving celebrity and greeting Liberace himself with delirious joy. After a few words of thanks, blown kisses, and waves of his bejeweled hands, the man of the hour entered the theatre with his mother on his arm, setting off new cheers from the adoring crowd.

Inside, the critics were notably less affectionate. The *L.A. Times* described *Sincerely Yours* as "unintentionally hilarious," while *Films and Filming* found it "drenched in coy bathos to the point of embarrassment." *The Saturday Review* suggested that "given sufficient intoxication, you could find this movie amusing." Knowledgeable industry observers, however, recalled H. L. Mencken's time-honored maxim

that "nobody ever went broke underestimating the intelligence of the American public." As the *Hollywood Reporter* duly noted after opening night, "This picture will probably make a grand piano full of money for Warner Brothers. It's filled with the corn that is the box office staff of life."

Opening-day grosses from across the country seemed to confirm this optimistic prediction, as matrons by the thousands turned out to see their Chosen One, to enjoy an evening of "culture," and to have a good cry. But within two days of these encouraging returns, ticket sales everywhere suffered a disastrous decline—in some instances falling to an all-time low. In New York, the picture struggled through thirteen days before being pulled totally from the city's screens. In Los Angeles the turnout was even worse, resulting in a premature termination of the picture's scheduled run after one limp week at the box office.

For months thereafter, the leading entertainment reporters in the United States speculated at length on

The Great Profile, Wladziu Valentino Liberace, closes his eyes in order to strike a sensual pose with co-star Dorothy Malone.

the reasons for the Great Liberace Disaster. One Hollywood astrologer suggested that the film had been shot at a time when Liberace's stars had arranged themselves in a particularly inauspicious alignment. This explanation was no less definitive than the conclusion by the *Hollywood Reporter* that "what the public can see for nothing on their TV sets, they won't pay for as a picture attraction." In all the public debate over the film's cruel fate, no one came up with the most obvious analysis: that *Sincerely Yours* failed for the simple reason that it was so incredibly awful that even those who enjoyed the excesses of Liberace's television show couldn't bring themselves to endure it.

A Climax, of Sorts

Needless to say, Warner Brothers failed to exercise their option to produce another film with the Miracle Man from Milwaukee, and he made no further appearances on the big screen until 1965, when he played a parody of himself as an unctuous casket salesman in Tony Richardson's brilliant satire *The Loved One.* This paucity of motion picture work did not leave Liberace inactive: he continued his work as a TV entertainer and a concert artist, drawing fees of $50,000 a week for his appearances in Las Vegas. The

bitter experience of his one starring venture in the movies never dimmed his lustrous smile, but it did contribute to the breakup of his long-standing partnership with his brother George. The older Liberace, who served as "Musical Adviser" on *Sincerely Yours,* formed his own band shortly after the film's failure but enjoyed his greatest success as the architect of a frozen pizza empire.

In the last two decades, Mr. Entertainment has spent an increasing percentage of his time in Las Vegas, where his flamboyant personal style and unique taste in clothing seemed to blend almost perfectly with the surrounding community. In 1979, his career reached a climax, of sorts, when he opened the "Liberace Museum" as a major tourist attraction in his adopted home town. Located in the Liberace Shopping Plaza, this important cultural resource houses the world's leading collection of Liberace memorabilia, including hundreds of gaudy costumes, pianos studded with rhinestones or painted all colors of the rainbow, candelabra without number, and other artifacts of unquestioned historic importance. Visitors to this museum, however, will be sorely disappointed to discover that it contains no reminders of the most recent headline-grabbing episode in the colorful life of the man once described by *TV Guide* as "The Eighth Wonder of the Show Business World."

In this latest adventure, Liberace became the defendant in a record-breaking $113,178,000 "palimony" suit filed against him by a twenty-three-year-old dancer and part-time animal trainer named Scott Thorson. The young man claimed that he began dating Liberace when he was seventeen and that the celebrated entertainer persuaded him to give up his education for full-time work as a "chauffeur, bodyguard, confidant, secretary and lover, cohabiting with Liberace at all Liberace's residences." In view of the forty-year age difference that separated the two men and Liberace's lack of an heir apparent to carry on his important work, the veteran pianist with a heart of gold reportedly promised to take legal action to adopt Thorson as his son. Unfortunately, the romance turned sour soon thereafter, and other bodyguards in the star's entourage, allegedly acting on orders from the top, chased Thorson from Liberace's penthouse and physically abused him in the process.

It will be some time before this case reaches a final settlement in the courts, but the sad history of this once-flourishing relationship suggests in eloquent terms the spirit of acrimony that characterized the ill-fated love stories featured in the next corridor of our museum, though, to our deep regret, they must be displayed without rhinestone pianos. . . .

STAR-CROSSED LOVERS

"THE COURSE of true love never did run smooth," notes Shakespeare's Lysander, and the same might be said of the production history of some of Hollywood's biggest budget romances. The two films in this gallery of the Hall of Shame are both bittersweet love stories played out against the background of World War I, and in each case the behind-the-scenes struggles left a trail of casualties to rival any battlefield. Some of the problems of *Hotel Imperial* and *Darling Lili* stemmed from the ineptitude or indulgence of the filmmakers, but primary blame for these colossal failures must be placed upon a strange, malevolent fate that managed to intrude itself at every opportunity. Despite all good intentions, some love affairs are doomed from the beginning.

HOTEL IMPERIAL
(a.k.a. INVITATION TO HAPPINESS; a.k.a. I LOVED A SOLDIER)

(1936-1939)

Paramount

ORIGINAL CREDITS AND CAST

Produced by Ernst Lubitsch
Directed by Henry Hathaway
Screenplay by John van Druten,
with additional dialogue by Grover Jones; based on a play by Lajos Biro

Starring Marlene Dietrich (Anna); Charles Boyer (Lieutenant Nemassy);
Akim Tamiroff (General Videnko); Walter Catlett (Elias);
Paul Lukas (Kuprin); and Stuart Erwin (Anton).

INTERMEDIATE CAST CHANGE

Margaret Sullavan (Anna)

FINAL CREDITS AND CAST

Directed by Robert Florey
Screenplay by Gilbert Gabriel and Robert Thoeren; based on a play by Lajos Biro

Starring Isa Miranda (Anna); Ray Milland (Lieutenant Nemassy);
Reginald Owen (General Videnko); Gene Lockhart (Elias); J. Carrol Naish (Kuprin);
Curt Bois (Anton); and The Don Cossack Russian Male Chorus ("The Cossack Singers").

The Haunted Hotel

Show people are a superstitious lot who will, on the slightest pretext, decide that a given vehicle is a jinx that must be avoided at all costs.

Such was the common view of *Hotel Imperial*, a stage play from Hungary that became the basis for a silent film in 1927. The movie thrilled both the public and the critics, but personal setbacks suffered by its leading participants cast a long shadow over the entire enterprise. During filming, director Mauritz Stiller was suddenly and rudely dumped by his lover and protégée, Greta Garbo. Feeling depressed and humiliated, Stiller returned to his native Sweden, where he died the following year from what many obituaries described as "a broken heart." Similarly stricken was Pola Negri, star of the film and off-screen companion of Rudolph Valentino. During the final days of the difficult shooting schedule for *Hotel Imperial*, Rudy suffered a perforated ulcer and entered the hospital, but Pola could not come to him because of her commitment to the film. A week later Valentino died at age thirty-one, and Negri draped herself dramatically over his coffin during a funeral viewed by hundreds of thousands.

After Valentino's death, Hollywood's mystics decided that *Hotel Imperial* brought with it a mysterious curse; producers, on the other hand, are less sensitive souls who are more concerned with a product's box office potential than with its spiritual vibrations. In the early thirties, Paramount executives viewed the old *Hotel* as a conspicuously commercial property that had achieved great success as a silent and fairly cried out to be remade as a talkie. What's more, it seemed the ideal vehicle for restoring the waning popularity of the studio's biggest star, Marlene Dietrich.

Unrequited Love

Despite the fact that she still received a fee of $200,000 per picture—making her, along with Mae West, the highest paid actress in Hollywood—box office returns showed that the public had become somewhat bored with Miss Dietrich's on-screen image as a glamorous and amoral temptress. In *Hotel*, she could attempt an entirely different sort of role, playing a Polish chambermaid who falls in love with an Austrian cavalry officer during World War I, then heroically risks her life in order to save him. Dietrich hesitated before accepting the part, particularly in view of the bad luck supposedly associated with the picture. In an effort to appease her, Paramount agreed to change the title, coming up with the ingenious designation *Invitation to Happiness*. This insipid title, with its air of hollow and exaggerated optimism, was an obvious attempt to break an ancient jinx, like whistling "Oh, What a Beautiful Morning" during a midnight stroll through a cemetery.

In any event, Paramount's unsolicited *Invitation* came at a time of personal turmoil and professional confusion for Miss Dietrich. For years, the studio had been trying to terminate her association with Josef von Sternberg, the eccentric, extravagant director who had discovered her in Berlin and first made her a star. From the time of their original collaboration on *The Blue Angel* (1930), through a long succession of classic films such as *Blonde Venus* (1932) and *The Devil Is a Woman* (1935), Sternberg's Dietrich remained, as several critics came to observe, more a piece of set decoration than an actress. She appeared in totally outrageous gowns and hairstyles, with lighting and makeup as perfect as possible in films in which visual appeal counted far more than characterization. Dietrich felt comfortable with this formula and maintained complete confidence in Sternberg and his vision, despite the disappointing public response to their latest films and growing strains in their personal relationship. By the mid-1930s, it had become painfully evident that Marlene either could not—or would not—love the great Sternberg in the same way that he loved her. This awkward situation ultimately led the great director to surrender to studio pressure and to abandon their partnership, leaving Marlene to adjust to a new col-

Anna I: During her four weeks on the set, Marlene Dietrich cost Paramount some $900,000, battling continually with director Henry Hathaway, who wanted to make her "ugly" and "a slob" for her role as a Polish chambermaid who is ultimately transformed by love. This photograph indicates clearly who won those arguments.

laborator whose style took after Sternberg's to about the same extent that the work of Sam Peckinpah resembles that of Walt Disney.

Invitation to Oblivion

The man chosen by Paramount production chief Ernst Lubitsch to shape Marlene's new image was none other than Henry Hathaway, a no-nonsense craftsman noted for his stirring adventure yarns. In films such as *Come On Marines!* (1934), *The Lives of a Bengal Lancer* (1935), *North to Alaska* (1960), and

True Grit (1969), Hathaway gave his male stars plenty of chance to display their toughness and courage, but he wasted little time on glamorous females. If Dietrich wanted this particular director to present her in a loving and flattering light, she might have considered asking the Paramount makeup department to transform her into a dead ringer for Duke Wayne. In Charles Higham's invaluable book *Marlene*, Hathaway spoke candidly of his plans to deglamorize the studio's troublesome star:

My idea for *Hotel Imperial* was to start with a shot of a long, wide hallway, and a woman scrubbing and mopping the floor. She has dirty hair and dirty clothes; she is wearing old carpet slippers. She's a slob. As she gets the guy and hides him and as she falls in love with him, she gets progressively prettier. She becomes completely transformed. The first time she wore a clean apron, it would have astonished and excited the audience. It would have driven them wild!

Much to everyone's surprise, Dietrich at first went along with Hathaway's approach to the film. The director had managed to convince her that her astonishing screen transformation, with her body magically secreting false eyelashes and face powder as a natural side effect of falling in love, would prove once and for all that Marlene Dietrich was an *actress* and not a mere clotheshorse. She felt genuine enthusiasm for the project, and all preparations marched forward without a hitch until, a few days before shooting began, disaster struck: Marlene sat down and read through the script in its entirety.

After this grim encounter, Dietrich became convinced that if the screenplay remained unchanged, *Invitation to Happiness* would be for her an Invitation to Oblivion. While her co-star Charles Boyer and the other actors reported for duty, Dietrich refused to work unless she had her way. Hathaway had directed many battle scenes during the early stages of his career, but nothing had prepared him for the bloody warfare that he now witnessed on the set. Four days after shooting had officially begun, producer Benjamin Glazer walked out on the project, telling the press he "would not supervise a story over which the star was given so much authority." Lubitsch stepped into the producer's role himself, which pleased Dietrich, but she still refused to budge on the script. For the time being, they shot around her. Meanwhile, Hathaway and writer Grover Jones burned the midnight oil to rewrite the original screenplay by John van Druten.

Finally, they returned with an acceptable draft and a new title for the film, calling it *I Loved a Sol-dier* in hopes that Dietrich could be coaxed into making love, not war, with her fellow workers on the sound stage. Unfortunately, the skirmishes continued without interruption even after Marlene agreed to step before the cameras. Inevitably, she showed up for her early scenes in far more elegant shape than Hathaway wanted. "Not yet, for Christ's sake!" he shouted. "You can be beautiful later!" Dietrich simply refused to obey, and Hathaway had to run to Lubitsch, who came to the set to "reason with her." As a director in Germany and the United States, Lubitsch had won an international reputation for his sophisticated and stylish films, and Dietrich respected his talent. He was, above all, her compatriot and a sort of substitute Sternberg in these difficult circumstances. Chomping on his cigar while caressing her ego, he proved generally successful in persuading her to "be good" and to cooperate with Hathaway.

On this strained basis, the production staggered forward at the pace of a drugged hippopotamus until the ill-fated project suffered its second major calamity: the Paramount stockholders, increasingly concerned over the high cost and low return of the films Lubitsch created as head of production, suddenly "accepted his resignation" and shipped him back to Europe.

Hathaway recalled the unfortunate effect on Dietrich of this new development:

With Lubitsch gone, she misbehaved. She came on for a scene of scrubbing floors with lipstick on, her hair perfectly groomed, and I was horrified. I said, "Jesus Christ! You can't do this!" She told me, "I have the say now that Lubitsch is gone . . ." We had a hell of an argument. She had become a monster of her own making . . . She said, "If Lubitsch is not coming back, I quit." So I said to them, "Look, forget her. *Just forget her!*"

At that point the studio no doubt wished it could follow Hathaway's advice. Before walking off the picture, Dietrich had completed twenty-eight days of filming. The movie was barely half completed and the cost was already more than $900,000 at a time when the average *completed* film cost less than $200,000. The useless Dietrich footage from *I Loved a Soldier* turned out to be at least as expensive as her most costly collaboration with Sternberg, *The Scarlet Empress*, which, in 1934, had been considered a wildly extravagant flop.

Many of those associated with the new production would have preferred to allow the film to die quietly, but Paramount decided that it had invested far too much already to allow that to happen. Soon after Marlene's departure, the studio's chief executives bravely announced that shooting would continue, while they looked around for an appropriate new star.

The Second Team

They quickly decided on Margaret Sullavan, who, at age twenty-five, seemed on the verge of a brilliant career. Her half-dozen previous films had all been "weepies"—sentimental dramas in which the sweet young heroine suffers oh-so-prettily through various difficult situations—but she had acquitted herself honorably despite the thin material. She obviously lacked Dietrich's star power and sexual magnetism, but the studio felt there had already been more than enough excitement on the set for one picture, thank you very much. Hathaway, who knew precisely what he wanted from his lead actress, seemed delighted by the choice of Sullavan. "She was marvelous," he recalled. "She didn't care how ugly she looked."

The studio cared, however, since it still planned to use the long shots of Dietrich rather than retaking them, and there had to be a least a superficial resemblance between the two stars or else the match-up would never work. Moreover, if Hathaway went too far with his mania for making his leading lady unattractive, who would pay good money to see the picture?

None of these problems seemed insurmountable, nor did they detract from the upbeat mood that now prevailed on the set. The picture had, incidentally, changed names for the third time, reverting to its original title, *Hotel Imperial*. With the superstitious Dietrich having departed from the scene, what reason could there possibly be to worry about the silly idea that this project was cursed?

Then came the fifth day of shooting with Maggie Sullavan, and a long break between takes. The young actress amused herself by flirting with one of her co-stars, Stuart Erwin. He had begun teasing her about her sloppy hair and drab costume, and she responded by squirting him in the face with a concealed water pistol. Giggling like schoolchildren, they chased one another in and out of the scenery as Erwin attempted to grab her and to take the pistol out of her hand. Finally he caught her, they struggled and tripped together over a pile of lighting cables. If this had been a scene for a film they would certainly have fallen into one another's arms, but in the bizarre off-screen world of the Haunted Hotel, matters seldom resolved themselves so neatly. As Sullavan came crashing to the floor, she tried to break the fall with her left hand, then began screaming in pain. A doctor arrived

Anna II: Margaret Sullavan seemed a perfect replacement for Dietrich—until she suffered a serious accident during a break from filming and managed to uphold the tradition of "Paramount's Jinx Picture."

on the scene and ordered an ambulance. The actors and crew gathered on the sound stage, then received the gloomy news from the hospital: the picture's leading lady had broken both bones in her left forearm, and it would be several months, at least, before her cast could be removed. Henry Hathaway remembers that on the next day, "The studio bosses called me and said, 'Do we have to get Dietrich back? Can't Maggie Sullavan wear a sling?' I said, 'God's told me twice not to finish this picture. A heroine with an arm in a sling scrubbing a floor and going to her wedding in a sling? It's ridiculous!'" When Paramount brass refused to listen, Hathaway himself "pulled a Dietrich"—he stormed off the set and quit the picture.

Limbo

With Hathaway and Sullavan gone, the producers approached Bette Davis, Elissa Landi, and Claudette Colbert, asking each of them in turn to take over the lead role. By this time, however, *Hotel Imperial* had become widely known in the press and elsewhere as "Paramount's Jinx Picture," and the various stars sought by the studio all liked their lives and limbs just as they were without having them unexpectedly rearranged.

Without a star, without a director, the *Hotel Imperial* had very little choice but to close its doors and to go out of business. Charles Boyer, Paul Lukas, and the additional members of the cast all had commitments to other projects, and they could not wait around indefinitely for an effective exorcism of the various ghosts and demons that had plagued *Hotel* from the beginning.

Dietrich, meanwhile, went on to make a series of intriguing flops: David O. Selznick's *The Garden of Allah* (with Charles Boyer), Alexander Korda's *Knight Without Armor* (with Robert Donat), and Ernst Lubitsch's *Angel* (with Melvyn Douglas and Herbert Marshall). By the time 1938 arrived, she had failed so consistently that she was labeled "box office poison" and rated 126th in the public popularity according to a major Hollywood poll. With Marlene in these reduced circumstances, the powers at Paramount thought she might consider coming back and completing the picture that she had abandoned nearly two years before. Producer Walter Wanger contacted Dietrich and showed her three reels of the material that was already in the can; she seemed impressed by its quality and expressed strong interest in returning to the project. Next, Wanger contacted Henry Hathaway and told him of Dietrich's interest in bringing the film back to life. The veteran director was sick to death of *Hotel Imperial*, but Wanger assured him that Dietrich had "learned her lesson" and was even ready to apologize for the way she had behaved before. Reluctantly, Hathaway agreed, and the movie seemed ready to rise from the dead until one Monday morning Dietrich unexpectedly showed up at the Paramount executive offices, with Josef von Sternberg in tow. She told the producers "she liked the property, she marveled at it, it was a good chance for her, and she would make it, but only on the condition that von Sternberg directed it." The studio heads sent her home, but Hathaway's response was more succinct. "Tell her to fuck off!" he said.

The Third Team

With the original Dietrich definitively unavailable, Paramount began thinking of manufacturing or importing a Dietrich clone. The long shots from the old footage could still be used under those circumstances, and the expensive sets for the film remained standing—and waiting—on the studio lot. Moreover, with war clouds now gathering in Europe, the time seemed particularly ripe for this drama of daring lovers and clashing armies.

The woman chosen by Paramount to put the entire enterprise back on its feet was Isa (pronounced "E-sa") Miranda, Italy's best-known actress of the 1930s and, just two years before, co-star of Mussolini's notoriously expensive bomb, *Scipio Africanus* (q.v.). With her blonde hair, slinky movements, and husky voice, Miranda was obviously intended to remind filmgoers of a new, improved version of Dietrich, and the use of Sternbergian lighting, makeup, and costumes would help to heighten the resemblance. It hardly mattered that she spoke in an Italian, rather than a German accent—one Fascist country was very much like another, wasn't it, and besides, the character both Miranda and Dietrich had been hired to play was supposed to be Polish. As it turned out, Miranda's English was even worse than expected, and she had to learn most of her lines phonetically, which did little to help her performance. Her purpose on screen was visual, not verbal, and with this in mind, Paramount attempted to make the most of every opportunity to showcase her elegant appearance.

Of course, the script had to be changed to suit this new approach; the Miranda character is no longer an ordinary chambermaid but is now a famous actress who is disguised as a chambermaid. This presumably explains the heavy makeup and elaborate hairstyles

Anna III: Italian import Isa Miranda managed to finish **Hotel Imperial** *without storming off the set or breaking her bones, but critics—and audiences—remained unimpressed by her fluttering eyelids and melodramatic acting style. Co-star Ray Milland obviously wished he were somewhere else.*

The Austrian Cavalry to the Rescue!: Moments after a studio photographer captured this thrilling production still, Ray Milland suffered a bloody equestrian accident that left him unconscious and sent him to the hospital for a two-week convalescence.

that she arranges every morning before she goes out to change the linen in the hotel. The purpose of this cunning disguise is so Miranda can avenge her sister, who died in this same ill-fated hotel a few months ago. Meanwhile, she discovers an Austrian officer (formerly the Charles Boyer part, now played by Ray Milland) who is hiding in one of the rooms. He was trapped behind enemy lines when the Russians took over the town, and he is now looking for an Austrian traitor who is staying at the same hotel and passing secrets to the dreaded foe. It turns out that this rat fink (J. Carrol Naish) is the same cad who did the dirty to Miranda's sister. Since the two pretty young people have so much in common—both wanting to kill J. Carrol Naish—they naturally fall in love. Milland has never before had his hotel room cleaned by such a fascinating woman who is, please remember, Isa Miranda disguised as Marlene Dietrich disguised as an actress disguised as a maid.

The studio attempted one additional disguise—after filming resumed on the long-stalled project, Paramount released a veritable flood of publicity at-

tempting to portray its new star as the greatest *femme fatale* of the twentieth century. Press releases proclaimed her "The Most Dangerous Beauty in All of Europe!" which made Miranda a fitting successor to Dietrich, who, as studio accountants could attest, was the Most Dangerous—or at least the most expensive—Beauty in All of Hollywood. Concerning the new Italian lollapalooza, Paramount further informed the world that she "uses a perfume she mixes herself according to a secret formula prepared for her by a famous French perfume manufacturer . . . Isa cares for her famous beauty with a daily bath of rainwater and goat's milk." But even better than these exotic ablutions, from the studio's point of view, was the fact that Miranda proved to be a pusillanimous pussycat on the set; she was too awed by Hollywood, too grateful for her generous salary, to make trouble during production.

The new director on the project was Robert Florey (*Murders in the Rue Morgue* [1932]; *The Beast With Five Fingers* [1946]), a Frenchman with a reputation for getting films done on time and within budget. He had been selected as the perfect man to beat the jinx that had already delayed the movie for nearly three years, and for the most part filming proceeded without mishap. It's true, there were a few unfortunate accidents involving extras—several were hit with debris during scenes of Austrian bombardment, and one of them suffered a broken leg when his horse was shot out from under him. But extras, it was understood, were only extras, and no one seemed particularly concerned as long as the stars remained unscathed.

As is often the practice, director Florey saved his most exciting and difficult scene for the last day of shooting. This was a furious, headlong cavalry charge through the main street of the ruined town, as Ray Milland leads his Austrian comrades in driving out the Russian heavies once and for all. Milland had shown himself to be an above-average horseman, and he looked forward to leading his "trusty troops of San Fernando cowboys" in their big scene. The charge would begin well out of camera range so the cavalry could work up a good head of steam before turning a corner, bursting through an archway, and careening at full gallop down the rubble-strewn street. In his autobiography *Wide-Eyed in Babylon*, Milland vividly recalls this heroic charge.

We got the signal and away we went with me in the lead. As we turned the corner I was horrified to see they had set another camera on a very low tripod smack in the middle of the street. By this time we were at full stretch with no place to go but straight ahead. There was only one thing to do—clear the camera. My mount was a pretty good quarter horse who could jump, so at the proper moment I hung my hooks into him and he took off. But as he bunched for the take-off the girth broke. I was airborne with just a saddle between my legs heading for what I hoped was a pile of horse manure, only it wasn't. It was a pile of broken masonry with a couple of shovelfuls of the stuff sprinkled over it.

The unfortunate Milland awoke several hours later in Cedars of Lebanon Hospital. He had suffered a concussion, a gash in his skull that took nine stitches to close, and numerous fractures and lacerations on his left hand. During his two-week period of convalescence, director Florey came to visit and assured him that "no real harm had been done." The entire picture could be spliced together "very nicely" even without the conclusion to Milland's reckless gallop as originally planned. Meanwhile, the wounded star felt glad to be alive, realizing, as he wrote years later, that injuries he sustained could have been serious enough to "write finis to my film career."

"Is This the Kiss of Death?"

Billboards for *Hotel Imperial* showed Isa Miranda closing her eyes and kissing Ray Milland, while huge headlines asked the public, "IS THIS THE KISS OF DEATH?" The American people obviously felt that it was and refused to pay money to see the film. The dismal reviews hardly helped, and from the moment of its release, the movie found itself relegated to a singularly ignominious position: it served as the bottom half of Paramount double features, which was about the same prestige as an actor serving as the bottom half of an on-stage horse. *Hotel Imperial*, in other words, ended up as what was probably the most expensive "B" picture ever made. As previously noted, the discarded Dietrich footage cost $900,000, and the brief interlude with Maggie Sullavan ran another $100,000. The embarrassed studio carefully concealed the additional expenses of the final film, but best estimates of those costs—including some 400 cavalrymen, The Don Cossack Russian Male Chorus, and a huge publicity blitz for Miss Miranda—would run to considerably more than $500,000. Another one of the posters for the doomed film showed Miranda in a seductive pose and bore the legend: "HER BEAUTY SENT MEN MARCHING TO DEATH WITH A SMILE!" More than one studio wag suggested that the line might well have been changed to "HER BEAUTY SENT PRODUCERS MARCHING TO BANKRUPTCY WITH A SMILE." Her next two pictures for Paramount did indeed turn out to be flops, though not nearly on so grand a scale as *Hotel Imperial*. In 1940, only one year after her much-heralded arrival in the United States, Isa returned to Italy and abandoned her dreams of Hollywood stardom.

Despite the weak performance of *Hotel Imperial*, 1939 turned out to be a very good year for Paramount. The studio released a number of huge money-makers, including the very popular *Beau Geste* with Gary Cooper and Ray Milland. That particular year also proved to be a lucky one for (surprise! surprise!) Marlene Dietrich. Taking Sternberg's advice, she had reduced her salary demands to $50,000 and won a part in a James Stewart Western called *Destry Rides Again*. It was a tremendous success, showing the fans that she had a sense of humor and even an ability at self-parody, and is well-remembered as her comeback picture. While filming *Destry*, she completed the necessary paperwork to become a U.S. citizen and reaffirmed her refusal to accept Hitler's invitation to return to Germany as his mistress and "The Queen of the Reich Cinema." But that, as they say, is another story.

Through all the different incarnations of *Hotel Imperial*, Paramount had consistently shown its unwillingness to waste anything of value if it could possibly be salvaged, and this policy also applied to usable titles. For reasons that remain unknown, the studio considered *I Loved a Soldier*—one of the interim names for this film—to be a good title, and they recycled it for a World War II romance starring Paulette Goddard and the immortal Sonny Tufts. Ads for the film announced, "She was a welder by day, but wilder by night, and the *answer* to any soldier's 3-day pass." All very well, but the *question* is, was she really only a famous *actress* disguised as a welder?

When sorting through the rubble of the Haunted Hotel, one is left with an inescapable feeling of anti-climax. The final film version is pallid and mediocre—after all that struggle, heartache, bad luck, broken arms, cracked noggins, and blighted careers, the studio came up with a film that, unlike *Noah's Ark* or *The Conqueror*, isn't even bad enough to be interesting. An anonymous screenwriter declared at the time: "For the public, the only reason to actually check into the *Hotel Imperial* is if you want to get a good night's sleep," but in view of the strange story behind the film, even this welcome slumber must be disturbed by nightmares.

Intrigue abounds in the Hotel Imperial *with, from left to right, Robert Middlemass, Russell Hicks, J. Carrol Naish, Henry Victor, Isa Miranda, and Reginald Owen. The strategic problems faced by the Russian officers in the film were not nearly so formidable as the various ambushes and explosions that Paramount confronted in trying to bring the deeply troubled project to completion.*

Director Robert Florey (squatting, center) tries to make some sense of the utter chaos that prevails during the off-again on-again filming of Hotel Imperial. *Pictured with him, on the staircase, are Reginald Owen, Isa Miranda, Ray Milland, and various exotic types recruited from central casting.*

DARLING LILI

(1970)

Paramount
Produced by Owen Crump
Directed by Blake Edwards
Screenplay by Blake Edwards and William Peter Blatty
Music by Henry Mancini

Starring Julie Andrews (Lili Smith); Rock Hudson (Major William Larrabee);
Jeremy Kemp (Von Ruger); Lance Percival (T. C.);
Michael Witney (Youngblood Carson); and Jacques Marin (Duvalle).

Beyond Nuns and Nannies

When Blake Edwards and Julie Andrews fell passionately in love in 1967, it seemed to be a match made in producers' heaven. Andrews had been named America's number-one box office star for two consecutive years, after her triumphant performances on Broadway (*My Fair Lady* and *Camelot*) and her starring roles in two of the most successful movie musicals of all time (*Mary Poppins* [1964] and *The Sound of Music* [1965]). Edwards, meanwhile, had established himself as one of the film community's top directors, having created such major hits as *Operation Petticoat* (1959), *Breakfast at Tiffany's* (1961), *Days of Wine and Roses* (1962), and *The Pink Panther* (1963). With these credits behind them, Andrews and Edwards appeared to be not so much a couple as a multi-million-dollar Hollywood talent merger, with the success of their future joint ventures all but assured. The executives at Paramount can hardly be blamed for having encouraged this happy pair to do whatever they wanted to do as their first project together. At the time, what Edwards and Andrews wanted more than anything else was to change the public's perception of Julie as a virginal and perpetually cheerful songbird and to show the world that she was a serious actress capable of handling a wide range of characterizations. In private, Edwards found his lady friend to be devastatingly sexy, with a provocative streak of daring and wickedness, and he wanted to give Miss Andrews the chance to communicate these qualities on screen. To achieve this purpose, he created the story of a British music hall singer during World War I, who, like the infamous Mata Hari, uses her feminine wiles to seduce vulnerable fighting men into betraying military secrets to

the Germans. To prevent this new Julie from appearing totally despicable, the script calls for her to fall hopelessly in love with one of her intended pigeons, an American aerial ace. To no one's surprise, this grand passion leads to the redemption of our heretofore unscrupulous heroine, as she sacrifices everything for love and betrays her former associates in espionage. As if all this double-dealing weren't shocking enough for the actress known best as Mary Poppins and Maria von Trapp, plans for the film also called for Miss Andrews to perform an alluring striptease, to engage in a wrestling match under the covers with her lover, and to perform a shower scene in which her bare back and shoulders are tellingly revealed. Edwards' co-author on the script was William Peter Blatty, who later won fame for his novel *The Exorcist*, and may, after the failure of this film, have been tempted to explain the sudden and disastrous change of Julie Andrews' on-screen persona as an unfortunate case of demonic possession.

Paramount budgeted $6 million for *Darling Lili* and insisted on insuring its investment by turning the project into a musical extravaganza. After all, the studio had agreed to pay Miss Andrews $1,100,000 plus ten percent of the profits for her participation—an all-time Hollywood record. At those prices, the Paramount executives felt they had the right to demand that Andrews sing for her supper. Blake Edwards objected, but since the studio had already given him his way on the shower scene and other steamy moments, they managed to win this particular point—tit for tat, so to speak. The seven new songs commissioned for the project were composed by Henry Mancini and Johnny Mercer, the same celebrated team that had produced Academy Award–winning ballads for Edwards' previous efforts

Hollywood's Surprise Sex Pot: Julie Andrews leaves nuns and nannies far behind in her Darling Lili *role as a music-hall Mata Hari who flaunts her incomparable feminine charms in order to seduce Allied pilots into betraying key military secrets.*

Breakfast at Tiffany's ("Moon River") and *Days of Wine and Roses.* Sensing that these musical numbers (with unforgettable titles such as "A Girl in No Man's Land" and "Smile Away Each Rainy Day") might not represent Mancini and Mercer's best work, Edwards also included numerous nostalgic songs of the period, including "It's a Long Way to Tipperary" and "Keep the Home Fires Burning." At the same time, the veteran director kept his own home fires burning by employing his uncle as executive producer of the movie, while his father served as studio production manager.

Less Than Congenial Company

Other personnel provided less congenial company during the course of the production. Perhaps the first major mistake concerning the well-laid plans for *Darling Lili* involved the choice of a leading man. Rock Hudson might offer a handsome face and passable

acting skills, but his screen presence proved far too bland for his part as the dashing and charismatic Major Larrabee. In a film in which everything depended upon the sexual fireworks between the two leads, Hudson and Andrews managed to generate about as many sparks as a potential pairing of Jim Nabors and Florence Henderson. Their interaction off-camera turned out to be far more exciting than anything on the screen, as rumors made the rounds describing merciless teasing by Andrews and Edwards concerning Hudson's somewhat ambiguous masculinity. Gossip columnist Joyce Haber reported that Miss Andrews repeatedly told her co-star, "Remember, *I'm* the leading lady," and that Hudson, according to Haber, eventually became so frustrated by this treatment that he took a weekend break from the European location and flew to California for a visit to one of his favorite leather bars in San Francisco.

Julie Andrews, meanwhile, received a more subtle and presumably less satisfying sort of punishment. Her recently completed film, *Star!*, was released

Director Blake Edwards consults the script and coaches his consort, Julie Andrews, on how to handle one of her difficult love scenes with co-star Rock Hudson.

shortly after shooting began on *Darling Lili*, and the critics had a field day attacking it. Producers at Twentieth Century-Fox soon began referring to *Star!* as "their Edsel," and this overproduced musical biography of Broadway immortal Gertrude Lawrence managed to earn back only a fraction of its $12 million cost. Paramount's leading executives became understandably nervous as they watched the debacle unfold, proving that Julie Andrews, despite her popularity, was no guarantee of box office success. They might actually have been tempted to reconsider their extravagant plans for *Darling Lili*, except for the fact that Blake Edwards had already spent millions on the project and it was obviously too late to turn back. Miss Andrews was so deeply enmeshed in the shooting schedule for her new film, in fact, that she refused to make time to attend the gala premiere of *Star!*—a decision that produced outrage from the studio bosses along with intense criticism in the press. The tone of newspaper and magazine stories concerning her activities eventually became so hostile that Edwards barred all reporters from the *Darling Lili* set, and this ban in turn only served to intensify the negative attitudes. He and Andrews soon discovered that critical reports could be just as devastating when filed from a distance as when originating from the location itself.

Certainly, the director, his lady, and their collabo-

rators at Paramount gave the press plenty of material for juicy stories on the painfully slow progress of their troubled film. One hot topic concerned the conflict between the director and his studio over the location for the extensive aerial sequences that provided a dramatic climax for the film. Edwards wanted to shoot these dogfights in South Carolina, but Paramount demanded that he take the cast and crew to Ireland, where the studio had parked some antique airplanes left over from its 1966 hit *The Blue Max*. The chief problem with this scheme was that it failed to take into account the notorious vagaries of weather conditions on the Emerald Isle. It cost the studio $70,000 a day for equipment and personnel while Edwards, Andrews, and company waited helplessly for weeks, hoping for the gloomy, overcast sky to adopt a more appropriately cheerful aspect. In desperation, the company finally decided to begin shooting in spite of the clouds, but a few days after they had done so, the sun came out and stayed out for weeks. Edwards felt that he had no choice but to shut down production once again and pray for the clouds to return—otherwise he could never match the new footage with what was already in the can.

In the midst of this frustrating interlude, Charles Bluhdorn, chairman of Gulf + Western, Paramount's parent company, arrived in Ireland to investigate firsthand why *Darling Lili* was running so far over budget. As his limousine drove up to the location site he was startled to see the entire company, including hundreds of technicians, extras, and stars, in the midst of what seemed to be a carefree picnic, relaxing on the green Irish sod and enjoying a day of sparkling sunshine. Edwards tried to explain to the enraged Bluhdorn that the leprechauns had been playing tricks with the weather, and they were only waiting for the "goddamned sun" to go away, but the corporate money man remained angry and unimpressed.

This indignation only increased after a tour of the local countryside that was initially intended to calm his nerves. Looking out the window of his car, Bluhdorn asked the driver about a huge ancient castle on a scenic hillside. "That's the home of Julie Andrews and Blake Edwards," the chauffeur responded. The visitor soon learned that Paramount paid for these extravagant accommodations and flew into a full-scale fury when Edwards failed to invite him over to the castle for dinner or a drink.

After Bluhdorn's return to the states, the relations between the director and the studio had been permanently poisoned. Paramount ordered the company to move on from the site of their Irish fiasco to the other European locations, but government red tape in Belgium caused further delays. Edwards cheerfully pointed out that he had trimmed the number of extras and crew members so that problems in Brussels cost only $50,000 a day as opposed to the $70,000 they had been wasting in Ireland, but the executives back home took small comfort from this news. By now, the whole world had begun to sense a disaster in the making and those most responsible for the film began pointing fingers of blame at one another. Former Paramount production chief Robert Evans describes the entire situation as "the most flagrant misappropriation and waste of funds I've seen in my career. The primary reason the film went over budget was Edwards' drive to protect 'his lady'; Queen Elizabeth was never treated half as well! The extravagance was unbelievable. He was writing a love letter to his lady and Paramount paid for it."

At last, the *Darling Lili* road show returned to Hollywood to shoot some key sequences on a studio sound stage. Edwards fussed and fidgeted endlessly over these scenes but remained dissatisfied, begging Paramount to allow him to return to Europe for reshooting. The studio brass indignantly refused, ordering him to assemble a finished film from the existing footage. They then crossed their fingers and waited for the completed rough cut. After viewing this version of the movie, one Paramount executive summed up the generally dismal reaction: "It was fifteen million dollars' worth of unusable film—and no picture."

With the studio's ranking officers wandering the lot in a daze and contemplating either suicide or murder, Edwards went back to the cutting room for a last desperate attempt to salvage his bruised masterpiece. To accommodate these heroic efforts, the long-anticipated release date had to be postponed from Fall 1969 till March 1970, while Paramount continued to pay interest on the massive capital invested in the film. These fees, along with the hefty promotional expenses for the movie, brought the total cost to nearly $25 million—more than four times the original budget. Though the picture won some favorable notices from major critics such as Vincent Canby and Roger Greenspun, most reviewers echoed the sentiments of *Time* magazine, which described *Darling Lili* as "aseptic, smooth and foursquare as an ice cube." The response of the public was certainly chilly: according to even the most optimistic accounting, the picture earned only $5 million in box office receipts, making it the single most expensive musical ever produced by Paramount Pictures and one of the most costly flops in Hollywood history.

Sweet Revenge

With admirable pluck, Blake and Julie tried to walk away from the disaster, moving across town to MGM for their next project together. This new movie concerned the heart-rending adventures of an emotionally unstable star who suffers a nervous breakdown after the death of her husband. After *Lili*'s death at the box office, however, the executives at Metro began suffering nervous breakdowns of their own at the prospect of following Paramount's example and blowing tens of millions on Hollywood's most costly couple; they gladly paid Andrews and Edwards one million dollars (another record) in order to escape their commitment to the film and to cut their losses.

At this point, the embattled director and his beloved star may not have had work, but they certainly had one another, having been married in the garden of Andrews' Beverly Hills home on the auspicious day that *Darling Lili* received its first public screening. It was by all accounts a touching ceremony (the wedding, not the screening), though Rock Hudson passed up his opportunity to serve as one of the bridesmaids. Secure within the blissful context of her marriage, which contrasted so strikingly with the mounting hostility of the fickle public, Miss Andrews

Lili Smith (Julie Andrews) reacts with unrestrained laughter when Major Larrabee (Rock Hudson) declares his burning passion for her in the celebrated shower scene in Darling Lili.

The elaborate aerial sequences in Darling Lili *ran millions of dollars above budget because of the unpredictable weather at the movie's Irish location.*

limousine. The result, of course, was *10*, a smash hit that not only served to introduce the formidable Bo Derek to the American public, but returned Blake Edwards to the good graces of the film community. Taking note of the fact that his three most recent Panther features and *10* had together earned more than $300 million on a cumulative budget of less than retired from movies altogether for the next four years. Edwards, meanwhile, crafted two relatively minor Hollywood flops (*Wild Rovers* and *The Carey Treatment*) before packing up his wife and moving to Switzerland. In Europe he directed three more pictures in the highly profitable Pink Panther series, while talking endlessly to anyone who would listen about the way Paramount had "ruined his life" with its callous interference on *Darling Lili*. In 1979, Edwards and Andrews returned to Hollywood to make a comedy that the director had been planning for years—a film inspired by an incident in Brussels in which he had caught a fleeting glimpse of a bride in a

$30 million, the studios were ready to forgive and forget. Edwards, on the other hand, could not let sleeping duds lie and insisted on purging himself of the *Darling Lili* experience once and for all by presenting a thinly disguised treatment of the entire mess in his next film, *S.O.B.* This bitter 1981 comedy described the tribulations of a talented but controversial director (Richard Mulligan) and a musical star (Julie Andrews) struggling to maintain her fading popularity. In order to guarantee box office success for her film-within-the-film, the character portrayed by Miss Andrews agrees to expose her bare breasts in a scene meant permanently to destroy her prospects as a nanny in all the better sort of homes. Despite the positive reviews the real-life Julie Andrews received for the well-preserved state of her private parts, no one suggested that this sort of display could have actually saved as turgid a vehicle as *Darling Lili* any more than it saved *S.O.B.* itself from disappointing returns at the box office. In their next joint effort,

Edwards moved his wife even further away from her halcyon days as Mary Poppins and Maria von Trapp, completing a journey begun some fifteen years before. In *Victor/Victoria* (1982), Julie plays a frustrated opera diva who masquerades as an effeminate young man in order to win jobs as a transvestite cabaret artist imitating heavily costumed glamor girls. (This is almost as confusing as Isa Miranda imitating Marlene Dietrich portraying a famous stage actress disguised as a chambermaid in the *Hotel Imperial*, but not quite.) In any event, this unconventional film became a surprise hit, winning new respect for the commercial and artistic potential of the durable Edwards and Andrews team.

Whatever their ups and downs in the film world, the off-camera romance of Blake and Julie turned out to be a far more satisfying and solid proposition than their ill-fated sob story, *Darling Lili*. In all their years together, they always avoided the sort of world-shaking histrionics that so endearingly characterized the celebrated couple who helped to create the next spectacular ruin on display in a particularly monumental corridor of the Hollywood Hall of Shame . . .

Rock Hudson (as Major Larrabee) explains to his shocked co-pilot why they call it a Bi-Plane.

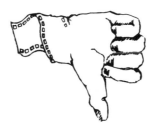

THE
ELIZABETH
TAYLOR
WING

FILMMAKING is a collaborative art form and the creation of a truly memorable movie fiasco requires close teamwork from many individuals. In most cases, the producer, director, writer, and stars must all pitch in with inept and extravagant efforts in order to qualify a movie for one of the coveted positions in the Hollywood Hall of Shame. It is a rare genius indeed whose personal influence on the production process is so powerful and devastating that the participation of this one individual, in and of itself, will give a film a good chance of losing millions of dollars. Elizabeth Taylor is one such individual, and her ability to sink the motion pictures in which she stars has never been excelled.

This remarkable gift did not manifest itself until after her thirtieth birthday and the release of that fabled flop, *Cleopatra* (1963). Before that time, the young Liz had scored considerable box office success with hits such as *National Velvet* (1944), *A Place in the Sun* (1951), *Giant* (1956), *Cat on a Hot Tin Roof* (1958), and *Butterfield 8* (1960). In the light of this honorable past, producers felt justified in treating her well-publicized tour of duty as Queen of the Nile as little more than a disastrous fluke, and Miss Taylor continued to command top dollar for her film roles throughout the sixties. Eventually, however, she compiled a list of discredits so formidable that she made believers out of even her most spirited defenders. This unprecedented string of solid gold turkeys included *Reflections in a Golden Eye* (1967), *Boom!* (1968), *Secret Ceremony* (1968), *The Only Game in Town* (1970), *X, Y and Zee* (1971), *Hammersmith Is Out* (1972), *Night Watch* (1973), *Ash Wednesday* (1973), *The Driver's Seat* (1975), *The Blue Bird* (1976), and *A Little Night Musical* (1977). Her few artistic and commercial successes in this period—*Who's Afraid of Virginia Woolf?* (1966), *The Taming of the Shrew* (1967)—only served as sad reminders of the fact that the lady, for all her faults, had considerable talent. It was not lack of acting skill but rather personal and artistic self-indulgence that kept budgets high and quality low on most of the pictures in which she participated.

The three films on display in this gallery of our museum illustrate Miss Taylor's special style of wastefulness and, though they represent only a fraction of her total achievement in this area, they make a formidable case for her credentials as a project-wrecker. In view of those credentials, it is entirely fitting that she should be the only star in movie history to be honored with her own private wing in the Hollywood Hall of Shame.

CLEOPATRA

(1963)

Twentieth Century-Fox
Produced by Walter Wanger
Directed by Joseph L. Mankiewicz
Screenplay by Joseph L. Mankiewicz, Ranald MacDougall, and Sidney Buchman

Starring Elizabeth Taylor (Cleopatra); Richard Burton (Marc Antony);
Rex Harrison (Julius Caesar); Pamela Brown (High Priestess);
Hume Cronyn (Sosigines); Cesare Danova (Apollodorus);
Martin Landau (Rufio); Roddy McDowall (Octavian);
Carroll O'Connor (Casca); and John Hoyt (Cassius).

The First Twelve Minutes

What began as a cute little political assassination in Sarajevo ended up as the gigantic mess known as World War I, and what began, some thirty-four years later, as a cute little $2 million quickie about the Queen of the Nile ended up as the gigantic mess known as *Cleopatra*—widely acknowledged to be the most expensive film ever made. When asked how the project expanded from a standard Hollywood "tits-and-togas" epic into a disaster of truly monumental proportions, executives at Twentieth Century-Fox simply shrug their shoulders and sigh. "It just grew—like Topsy," said one of them, though it would have been more accurate to observe, "It just grew—like cancer." From the beginning, *Cleopatra* brought suffering and disgrace to nearly all its major participants.

The fiasco began in 1958, when independent producer Walter Wanger bought the rights to an Italian novel by Carlo Mario Franzero called *The Life and Times of Cleopatra*. Twentieth Century-Fox immediately liked the idea of a film based on the book and agreed to put up the money for a mini-spectacle starring Joan Collins in the title role. At this point a series of minor delays held up the beginning of production. Miss Collins became unavailable, and Wanger began talking about Audrey Hepburn as her replacement. Audrey Hepburn as history's most celebrated seductress, the Love Queen of the ancient world? She might have been able to borrow Marni Nixon's voice in order to handle her role in *My Fair Lady*, but it would have been far more difficult for her to borrow a pair of breasts. Recognizing Miss Hepburn's obvious limitations, the producers soon turned their attention to other candidates, focusing at last on Elizabeth Taylor, who had just won an Oscar nomination for her steamy role as Maggie the Cat in *Cat on a Hot Tin Roof*. Intrigued with the idea of those celebrated violet eyes luring Caesar and Antony into unwilling romantic entanglements, Walter Wanger decided to call the actress on the set of her new film, *Suddenly Last Summer*. Her crooner-hubby, Eddie Fisher, answered the phone in the dressing room and related to Liz that Wanger wanted her as his Cleopatra. "Sure," she replied facetiously, "tell him I'll do it for a million dollars." This unheard-of sum, though mentioned in jest, received serious consideration from the producer, and Taylor made history in October 1959, when she signed a contract with Twentieth as the first Hollywood star ever to receive $1 million for a single picture. This generous deal forced a major increase in the entire budget for the project, with projected costs rising from $2 to $6 million, but everyone seemed delighted with the new arrangement.

The studio promptly assembled a distinguished cast and crew to match the stature of their new, world-class Cleo. The gifted Rouben Mamoulian, director of *Golden Boy, Silk Stockings,* and *Blood and*

That Was the Liz That Was: Elizabeth Taylor, recently recovered from her emergency tracheotomy, in her most famous role as Queen of the Nile.

Sand, agreed to helm the project, Peter Finch would portray Julius Caesar, while Stephen Boyd ("hot" from *Ben-Hur* and later to win bad movie immortality with *The Oscar*) was nabbed for Marc Antony. With an official starting date of September 1960, studio executives began traveling through Europe in search of the ideal location to represent the exotic tropical grandeur of ancient Egypt. Their final choice—England—may have seemed a trifle bizarre to most industry observers, but this ill-fated project developed a curious logic all its own. Wanger and Mamoulian eagerly rented all the space at London's Pinewood Studios, while reserving additional facilities at Shepperton and the British MGM lot. They constructed more than eight acres of outdoor sets, featuring imported palm trees flown in for the occasion from Hollywood and the Middle East. A portion of the Thames was even diverted from its normal course to flow through this sprawling Little Egypt and to serve as a stand-in for the River Nile.

Unfortunately, not even the most expensive movie magic could cover the difference in climatic conditions between ancient Alexandria and current-day London. No sooner had shooting begun than the entire set was covered by an impenetrable pea-soup fog. "It was sheer lunacy," recalled director Mamoulian. "The insurance people were nervous ... They said, 'Shoot some film, shoot anything—as long as you can keep the picture going.' Well, we tried it. Rain, mud, slush, fog. . . . On a good day, whenever a word was spoken, you could see the vapor coming from the actors' mouths. It was like a tobacco commercial. We didn't have one piece of usable film with Liz in it." More problems soon arose: a strike of the hairdressers assigned to the production held up shooting for several days, and then one of the lions (obviously inspired by his rampaging predecessor in *Quo Vadis?*, q.v.) broke loose on the set and refused to be recaptured for more than an hour. This big cat-astrophe was nothing, however, compared to the setback Fox suffered six days later when Elizabeth Taylor took ill.

Though her critics in the press at first suspected that she might be malingering, her temperature registered an impressive 103°, and her doctors diagnosed a case of meningitis. For several days, Mamoulian and his associates hoped against hope for a speedy recovery and tried to "shoot around" their star, filming those sequences in which Miss Taylor did not appear. Unfortunately, the script specified her presence in almost every scene, so the company was left to fidget and wait. As Peter Finch recalled, "We just sat around the studio twiddling our thumbs and around four o'clock we'd all end up at the bar. It was a very sad business." Eventually, Miss Taylor's continued incapacity forced the studio to halt production altogether, though the overhead costs continued to add up at the rate of more than $45,000 a day. During this protracted period of gilded limbo, Mamoulian read several new drafts of the screenplay (including one by the distinguished novelist Lawrence Durrell) and rejected them all. From her hospital bed, Liz Taylor wanted to get in on the fun and demanded several script changes of her own, including elimination of the traditional "milk bath" scene and the removal of a torrid sequence with Stephen Boyd in which Antony and Cleopatra are supposed to engage in the Roman equivalent of a game of strip poker. The complex and bitter feuds over the content of the screenplay helped to persuade the weary Mamoulian that not even the Queen of the Nile herself, with or without her famous milk bath, was worth the continued suffering this picture entailed, so he resigned from the project on January 3, 1961.

At that point, producer Wanger welcomed the idea of hiring a new director who might give the wounded production a much-needed transfusion of fresh blood. The donor selected for this purpose was Joseph L. Mankiewicz, who had directed Miss Taylor's previous triumph *Suddenly Last Summer* and had in the past created such outstanding films as *A Letter to Three Wives* (1949), *All About Eve* (1950), and *Julius Caesar* (1953). Mankiewicz hesitated before accepting the assignment, but his agent, impressed by the huge fee offered by Fox, urged his client to "hold your nose for fifteen weeks and get it over with." With thumb and forefinger no doubt firmly pressed against his nostrils, the veteran director began rewriting the script and refurbishing the sets while Walter Wanger, who watched this progress with satisfaction, prophetically observed, "I feel he is going to deliver an unusual picture."

Before Mankiewicz could show his stuff, however, the fates provided another nasty surprise. Liz Taylor, having slowly recuperated from meningitis, came down with a bad case of the flu, which quickly developed into lobar pneumonia. This condition brought her to the point of death; the doctors placed her in an iron lung, but she nonetheless stopped breathing five times. An emergency tracheotomy ultimately saved her life but left a scar on her neck that is visible throughout *Cleopatra* and in all of her subsequent films. Needless to say, the glamorous star's dramatic battle for survival captured the attention of the world. Gossip columnists who had previously vilified Miss Taylor for "stealing" Eddie Fisher from poor Debbie Reynolds, calling her "selfish and cruel to the point of depravity," now praised the one-time "home wrecker" for her courage in the face of adversity and became press cheerleaders in her fight for life. The wave of public sympathy became so overwhelming, in fact, that the Academy voted Liz her first Oscar in 1961 for her mediocre performance as a call girl in *Butterfield 8*.

This honor dramatically increased the prestige and box office appeal that she brought to *Cleopatra*, but the production could hardly benefit from her new clout because the star's delicate health prevented her from returning to work on the damp London set for at least six months. With Peter Finch and Stephen Boyd committed to move on to other projects, Fox had no choice but to close down the London production once and for all, tear down the walls of British Egypt, pay everyone involved, sit back, and decide what the next move should be.

It was now mid-1961, three years after the rights to the Franzero novel had been purchased. The cast and crew had spent some twelve months in London and consumed more than $6 million of the studio's money, but producer Walter Wanger had only twelve minutes of usable footage to show for his efforts.

If at First You Don't Succeed . . .

With the advantage of hindsight, it seems clear that the right decision for Twentieth Century-Fox would have been to bite the bullet, cut its losses, and abandon the ill-fated project for more worthy and promising undertakings. Studio president Spyros Skouras, on the other hand, followed Macbeth's line of reasoning and, had he spoken English with sufficient aplomb, might well have declared, "I am in blood/ Stepp'd in so far that, should I wade no more,/Returning were as tedious as go o'er." In other words, the Fox executives decided that they had already spent so damn much money on *Cleopatra* that they weren't about to pull out now and walk around Hollywood with omelette on their foreheads. Besides, Skouras reasoned, who in his right mind would give up a project that already had received so much priceless free publicity and included a commitment from this year's Oscar winner? On the contrary, the determined studio head (once described by Billy Wilder as "the only Greek tragedy I know") resolved that the

Marc Antony (Richard Burton) takes time to cool off from the sizzling on- and off-screen romance associated with Cleopatra. *Ministering to his needs are three unidentified handmaidens, who no doubt participated in the much-publicized "strike of the slave girls," which added to the picture's already interminable delays.*

Pyramids and Sphinx would rise again to serve as the backdrop for the new, improved *Cleopatra*.

This time around, the studio brass wisely resolved to avoid the London fog and selected Rome's Cinecittà Studios—Benito Mussolini's old stomping grounds—as the location for the born-again production. While designers and craftsmen spent three months building monumental new sets, Wanger and Skouras searched for a fresh group of actors to complement Liz Taylor's long-awaited Cleopatra. Initially, they approached Laurence Olivier for the part of Julius Caesar, but the celebrated thespian read the script and decided to pass, apparently saving himself for more substantive roles in future quality pictures such as *Shoes of the Fisherman, The Jazz Singer,* and *Inchon* (q.v.). In Olivier's place, the producers eventually selected Rex Harrison, gladly accepting a veteran Shavian as a substitute for the century's leading Shakespearian. For the role of Marc Antony, Skouras wanted Richard Burton, who had already proven that he looked great in a toga with his leading roles in films such as *Alexander the Great* and *The Robe*. Burton's legal commitment to the continuing Broadway run of *Camelot* proved to be a minor obstacle, as the studio bought out the remainder of his theatrical contract for $50,000. The star himself had mixed feelings about his return to the screen. As he confided to a friend before leaving for Rome, "I've got to don my breastplate once more to go play opposite Miss Tits."

As all the world knows, his contemptuous attitude toward his co-star changed dramatically as soon as they began working together on *Cleopatra*. Their first fateful off-camera exchange took place within full view of dozens of extras and crew members and began with a rhetorical question from Mr. Burton: "Has anybody ever told you that you are a very pretty girl?" From that point forward, rumors of a romance between the two stars began appearing in the European and American press, despite the concern of Fox executives that this sort of publicity would do further damage to their already wounded production. As press agent Jack Brodsky put it, "Nobody wants this to get out because they feel that the public will crucify her and picket the theatres if she breaks up another family." The official denials from various publicists only served to increase the world's eager speculation over the future of this hot new romance. Director Mankiewicz, meanwhile, pressed for his comment on the juicy rumors, told the press, "As far as I'm concerned, Miss Taylor may fall in love with Mao Tse-tung as long as she finishes her work on the film."

A Public Affair

In late March 1962, Liz and Dick decided, much to the chagrin of the beleaguered studio bigwigs, to make their newfound love a public affair. They provided a feast for scandalmongers and *paparazzi* by appearing together at Rome's leading night spots, where they demonstrated profound dedication to the film by rehearsing their love scenes in the eyes of the world. Their colleagues on the set, duly impressed by the seriousness with which the two stars approached their roles, reported that the dynamic duo took full advantage of their daily lunch breaks to retreat to Miss Taylor's lavish dressing room for a session of "afternoon delight," while every evening they disappeared to an apartment hideaway that had been rented specifically for their trysts. As publicist Jack Brodsky ruefully observed, "Burton-Taylor on set are so close you'd have to pour hot water on them to get them unstuck." Director Mankiewicz found it next to impossible to persuade them to cut short their on-camera lovemaking. As he tried to terminate one particularly protracted kiss, he finally yelled, "Cut! *Cut*! I feel as if I'm intruding!"

The world's press thrived on these stories and continually looked for new angles in describing the endlessly intriguing antics of Miss Taylor. After the Taylor-Burton romance had become old hat, one enterprising Italian newspaper scooped the world with the shocking news that this celebrated love affair was only a fiendishly clever cover-up designed to disguise the awful truth. According to "impeccable sources" quoted in this story, it was Joe Mankiewicz who was actually Liz Taylor's lover, while Burton was merely a "shuffle-footed idiot," ordered by his director to take his co-star out on the town in order to mislead the cuckolded Eddie Fisher and the rest of the world. The morning after this convoluted version of the facts made headlines around the world, Burton showed up for work and amused the entire crew by approaching Mankiewicz with downcast gaze and a long-suffering expression. "Please, Mr. Mankiewicz, sir," he stammered, "do I *have* to sleep with her again tonight?" Even after this little performance, wire service reporters continued to hound the director over the persistent rumors of his involvement with Miss Taylor. In exasperation, "Mank" finally made the startling confession that he was secretly in love with Richard Burton, and it was Liz who was only the cover-up. To prove his point, he went over and kissed Burton on the lips before going back to work and ordering the reporters off the set. To his absolute astonishment, a number of Italian papers ran

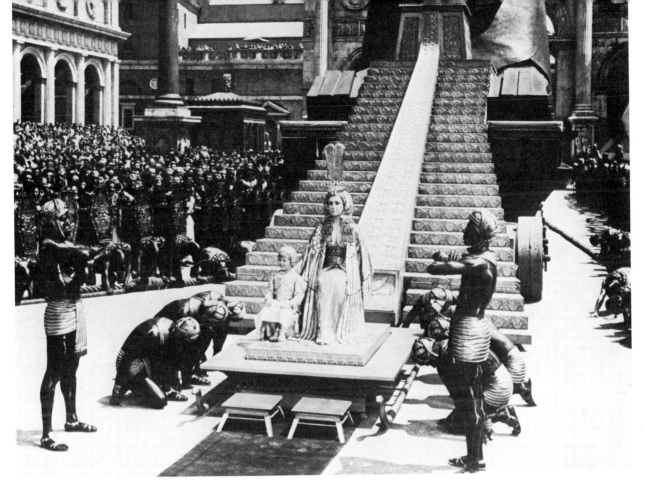

Neither Cleopatra—nor Liz Taylor—had ever been noted for a shy, self-effacing style of personal presentation. Here, the Egyptian queen makes her grand entry into Rome—adding several million dollars to the budget of what many experts still consider the most expensive movie ever made.

the story as a genuine news item of earth-shattering importance.

Unfortunately, Mankiewicz had more serious problems than these putative passions for his two stars. When he had accepted the job of directing *Cleopatra,* he had insisted on scrapping all the Mamoulian material and writing a new script himself. He had asked for several weeks to prepare the screenplay, but with the film already hopelessly over budget and behind schedule, the studio insisted that he begin filming immediately. The Fox executives argued that Mankiewicz could direct during the day and write at night, hoping only that his work on the script would stay a few steps ahead of the shooting schedule. In attempting to follow orders, the director shot everything he wrote without taking time to cut or rewrite and inadvertently cost the studio millions of dollars on wasted footage. As he described the situation once the ordeal was over, "*Cleopatra* was conceived in emergency, shot in hysteria, and wound up in a blind panic." Mankiewicz responded to this sort of pressure with migraine headaches and a nervous

skin disorder, but his doctors provided various pills and regular amphetamine shots to allow him to keep working.

Liz Taylor, of course, also suffered from delicate health but she approached her various infirmities with far less fortitude than Mankiewicz. When she felt ill or upset or simply "not in the mood" for filming, she stayed away from the set and on many occasions kept the cast and crew waiting for hours. She also refused to work during the first three days of her menstrual cycle, so the company enjoyed lengthy and costly breaks on a regular basis. Her eating habits caused further trouble, since her notoriously hefty appetite resulted in visible gains that in turn required tedious refittings of the fifty-eight costumes that Irene Sharaff had designed to emphasize her ample figure. (To paraphrase Mr. Shakespeare's comment on the original Cleopatra: "Neither time can wither, nor custom stale, nor costume designers cope with, her infinite variety.") Some of her co-stars eventually became impatient with the regal treatment demanded by the Queen of Hollywood in her role as Queen of the Nile. Cesare Danova, who played the part of Apollodorus, Cleopatra's jilted lover, pointedly recalled, "Somebody was always running over to ask her, 'How are you, darling? Are you all right, darling? Can I get you anything, darling?' It was a bit sickening." In the face of such criticism, Joe Mankiewicz consistently defended his embattled star. "Any effort to saddle blame on Miss Taylor for the cost of *Cleopatra* is wrong," he declared. "Miss Taylor may have had problems of illness and emotional problems, but she didn't cost Twentieth any $35 million!" No, a mere $20 million would have been a more accurate estimate.

Meanwhile, as the production staggered forward in Italy, even minor participants seemed caught up in the prevailing Alice-in-Wonderland atmosphere. A group of lissome lovelies, for instance, who played Cleopatra's various handmaidens and servants, went on strike to demand protection from the pinching fingers of the aggressive Italians who worked as extras on the film. The producers eventually agreed to pay a special guard to protect the tender rear ends of these sensitive starlets, but not before the "strike of the slave girls" had captured the attention of the world's press. As it turned out, the local extras who worked by the thousands on the film were pinching more than female flesh: according to studio records, these carefree Italians stole incredible quantities of props and supplies, with total losses to theft and graft running into the millions. As director Mankiewicz sympathetically observed, "Not since Marco Polo came back from China had there been the advent of such riches in Italy. . . . I was down in the hold of the ship shoveling coal like an s.o.b., but there was no one on top steering." This lack of overall coordination encouraged an indulgent attitude on the part of all the major stars. One night, Richard Burton disappeared without warning, and not even Miss Taylor knew where he had gone. The next morning, after arriving for shooting more than an hour late, he cheerfully explained that he had been busy observing the "traditional bender" on the occasion of the Welsh holiday in honor of Saint David. He then proceeded to fall asleep on the set, where his snoring helped to ruin an entire day's filming. Not even so consummate a professional as Rex Harrison proved immune to the infectious air of mad abandon and gratuitous sloppiness. "Sexy Rexy" was supposed to deliver the key speech during Cleopatra's spectacular entry into Rome, a huge scene using 5,000 extras, plus hundreds of exotic dancers, chariots, horses, and elephants. The shot had already been delayed half a day by a sudden downpour, but when the weather

cleared and shooting finally began, Harrison kept blowing his lines and forcing numerous retakes of the entire sequence. Each time, the animals had to be regrouped while lucky stage hands had the opportunity to remove the excremental souvenirs that they had deposited on the set during their long, impatient wait for Mr. Harrison to pull himself together.

In addition to these uninhibited expressions of contempt from some of the film's animal stars, the production had to endure further delays caused by the presence of a number of unwelcome beasts. A colony of stray cats had successfully crashed the Cinecittà gates and established vacation homes on some of the *Cleopatra* sets. They no doubt understood that household felines had been considered sacred by the ancient Egyptians and in any event preferred the enclosed comfort of the sound stages to the summer storms and blistering heat of the Roman streets. Members of the crew spent many hours trying to rid the premises of these uninvited guests, but the canny creatures found innumerable hiding places among the various props and palaces. One of these cats cost the production a forty-five-minute delay when it became entrapped under a bed during a love scene and sent out a series of screams that could be heard on the soundtrack. The exasperated director at last called a halt as stage hands dismantled the set and discovered that the animal in question had just delivered a litter of kittens. This blessed event proved far more costly than most human births, since the cost of taking apart and reassembling the set amounted to $17,000.

Rolling Heads

This sort of expenditure caused the Fox executives back home in Hollywood to yowl even more plaintively than the mother cat in labor. *Cleopatra* had obviously begun spinning out of control, and the only hope for retrieving its unprecedented cost was creating a hit of monstrous proportions. As bits and pieces of finished film arrived from Italy, even this forlorn hope began to disappear. On one memorable occasion, studio president Spyros Skouras sat down with Walter Wanger to view several hours of representative footage. As the lights came up and Wanger awaited a reaction from his boss, Skouras remained silent for several minutes. He then turned to the producer and bitterly declaimed, "I wish to hell I'd never seen you in my life!" With no end in sight to the *Cleopatra* debacle and the entire studio tottering on the edge of bankruptcy, Skouras understood the precariousness of his own position. The board of directors of Twentieth Century-Fox had begun clam-

Since Twentieth Century-Fox was burning money anyway on Cleopatra, *why not add a few expensive Roman galleys to the blaze?*

oring for blood, and not even a voluntary pay cut on the part of the top studio executives could appease the wrath of the desperate stockholders. Skouras announced his retirement on June 26, 1962, clearing the way for the company's largest single stockholder and former production chief to come to the rescue as the new president. This would-be corporate savior was none other than our old friend Darryl F. Zanuck, who had gained invaluable experience supervising costly and disastrous productions with his services thirty-three years before as writer and producer of *Noah's Ark* (q.v.). Almost immediately, the veteran mogul brought to bear his refined and distinctive aesthetic sensibility on the troubled *Cleopatra* project. After reviewing rushes of the still-uncompleted film, he perceptively observed, "If any woman behaved to me like Cleopatra treated Marc Antony, I would cut her balls off." Fortunately, Mr. Zanuck never had the chance to attempt this unconventional surgery on Elizabeth Taylor, though he did proceed to cut major and meaty chunks from her film. In his supervision of the editing process, Zanuck placed the emphasis on spectacular crowd scenes while deleting much of the character development and exposition, helping to create a disjointed and superficial melodrama from the unwieldy mass of footage that arrived from Italy. Joe Mankiewicz, of course, resisted this crude ap-

proach to his film and urged Fox to release the movie as a five-hour superfeature with an admission price of $10, or as two separate sequential pictures of two and a half hours each. Zanuck considered these two options and eventually decided on a course that Mankiewicz had not even considered: he gave the director the axe and tossed his bloody head to the still-howling mob of stockholders as a sort of ritual sacrifice. In announcing his latest shake-up, the studio released a terse statement to the press that made no attempt to disguise the bitterness surrounding the Mankiewicz dismissal:

In exchange for top compensation and a considerable expense account, Mr. Joseph Mankiewicz has for two years spent his time, talent, and $35,000,000 of Twentieth Century-Fox's shareholders' money to direct and complete the first cut of the film *Cleopatra*. He has earned a well-deserved rest.

No Rest for the Weary

Even after the filming had at long last been completed and the writer-director rudely sacked, *Cleopatra* continued to cause problems on a major scale. The weekly cost in interest charges alone amounted to $50,000, so that Zanuck fondly and aptly described the project as "this monster hanging on my shoul-

Julius Caesar (Rex Harrison) encounters an unfortunate mishap on the way to a Roman pep rally at the Forum. For Harrison, the "most unkindest cut of all" came when Twentieth Century-Fox excluded his image from the original billboards for Cleopatra—*despite contractual agreements that he would receive equal billing with Burton and Taylor.*

der." Final editing, meanwhile, could not begin until the Mankiewicz version of the finished film arrived from Italy. As luck would have it, these precious reels—representing an investment of nearly $40 million—had been impounded by a Roman court pending settlement of a complex legal dispute between Twentieth Century-Fox and a group of laid-off Italian technicians. No sooner had this sticky and aggravating situation been resolved than Zanuck determined that the movie in its current form contained unusable footage that would have to be reshot, and dispatched a crew to Europe to "pick up" these new sequences for last-minute inclusion in the final cut.

By this time, the publicity barrage for Fox's bloated bonanza had already begun. The world's press had spent so much space describing the project and its problems over the years, and public awareness ran so high that conventional advertising hardly seemed necessary. Instead, Fox launched an understated campaign that simply informed film fans that the legendary epic had at long last arrived. Billboards for *Cleopatra* made no mention of the stars, the credits, or even the title of the film. When people saw the gigantic image of Liz Taylor in her Egyptian hairdo

reclining in her boudoir, they needed no further explanation. Meanwhile, the troubled face of Richard Burton peering lecherously over the lady's voluptuous shoulder reminded the world of the celebrated off-screen romance of the two stars. This cozy sort of advertising pleased everyone except Rex Harrison, who proceeded to sue Twentieth Century-Fox over the fact that his likeness had been excluded from the party in Cleopatra's bedroom, despite contractual promises that he would receive equal billing with Burton and Taylor. Eventually, Harrison won his claim, and billboard artists hastily added his picture, in full battle dress, looming over the queen's other shoulder. For a lesser figure than Cleopatra it may have been somewhat intimidating to have two (count 'em—two!) Roman hunks standing behind her bed while she stretched out and displayed her ample charms to the world, but she was, after all, as John Wayne so eloquently described Susan Hayward in *The Conqueror* (q.v.), "a wuh-man . . . *much* wuh-man!"

The Legion of Decency, meanwhile, found Miss Taylor to be a bit too much wuh-man for the sake of public morals. Before the film's release, they condemned *Cleopatra* as "seriously offensive to decency" (instead of its proper designation, "comically offensive to decency"). This moral outrage seemed more directly inspired by some of the overheated promotional material for the picture than by any sequence in the film itself. One particularly misleading item in the press promised the panting patrons that "More acres of bare flesh will be on view in *Cleopatra* than in any film since *A Day in a Nudist Camp* was exhibited at the 1939 World's Fair in San Francisco." Despite such claims, the only scene of nudity in the entire picture involved a brief view of Miss Taylor's generously upholstered backside as she lay upon a marble slab receiving a massage from one of her slave girls. In view of the star's recently expanded proportions, the studio no doubt reasoned that this one glimpse in itself provided "acres of bare flesh."

With this monumental attraction taking its place in a gigantic spectacle that even in its reduced, tightly edited form ran more than four hours, theatres around the country felt justified in charging the extraordinary price of $5.50 per ticket—nearly three times the cost of a normal first-run feature in 1963. Nevertheless, curiosity about *Cleopatra* had reached such a fevered pitch that advance rentals alone brought in $15 million—making it the top-grossing film of the year before it even opened to the public. For the premiere screening in New York, more than 10,000 people jammed the streets and had to be restrained by a hundred mounted policemen. Eager first-nighters paid a minimum of $100 per person for admission to this gala event and compared the excitement surrounding the debut to the opening festivities for *Gone With the Wind.* Joe Mankiewicz, however, knew better. As he rode to the theatre in his limousine he felt as if he were "being carted to the guillotine in a tumbrel." The reviews—mixed to negative, for the most part—confirmed his fears and sent the executives at Fox into a panic. Curious crowds continued to flock to the theatres, but the film failed to do the sort of phenomenal business the studio needed to stand even the slightest chance of ever earning back its colossal investment. In an effort to save his sinking barge, Zanuck ordered an additional twenty-one minutes cut from the film, and the Academy of Motion Picture Arts and Sciences then did its bit by providing *Cleopatra* with a controversial nomination for Best Picture, but none of it seemed to help. In the end, the film grossed an estimated $26 million in rental income—an amount which *Time* magazine calculates as equivalent to $64.4 million in 1980 dollars. Meanwhile, its $44 million overall cost came to $110.6 million in the same 1980 terms. This means that *Cleopatra* remains well ahead of *Heaven's Gate, Inchon,* and all other rivals as the most expensive picture ever made, while the $46.2 million net loss in current dollars makes it a prime contender for the royal crown as the biggest money loser of all time. Of course, Twentieth Century-Fox has used creative accounting over the years to bolster its feeble claim that the studio's big gamble miraculously paid off and that the Bad Girl of the Nile eventually showed a modest profit. On this matter, the report in *Time* cited above, along with similar estimates in all other impartial periodicals, seems a good deal more reliable than the soothing, self-serving pap from the studio publicity department. The only ones who got rich in the aftermath of *Cleopatra* were the Hollywood lawyers who handled the numerous lawsuits that arose in the wake of the debacle. Walter Wanger sued Twentieth Century-Fox for having fired him from the project at the last moment; Spyros Skouras in turn sued Wanger. Elizabeth Taylor sued Fox, while the studio sued Liz and Richard for $50 million, claiming that their amorous off-screen behavior had helped to destroy the film's prospects.

No matter how many tens of millions were ultimately lost on the project, Taylor and Burton emerged from the wreckage virtually unscathed. They went on to do *The V.I.P.s,* with Liz once again receiving $1 million for her services. Burton, meanwhile, freely admitted to the press that "I find money

The Four Horse-persons of Hollywood's Greatest Financial Apocalypse: Liz Taylor, Rex Harrison, Richard Burton, and a worried Joe Mankiewicz.

very interesting," and explained that his decision to do *Cleopatra* had been based solely on "laziness and cupidity." Despite the fact that the film allowed him to meet the love of his life, he recalled that he "definitely disenjoyed" the whole experience.

Elizabeth's attitude toward her most famous role proved, if anything, even more unfavorable. After screening the finished product for the first time in England, she called it "vulgar" and "something of a disease." She went on to tell the press that this project, for which she had sacrificed so much time, energy, health, and emotion, "surely must be the most bizarre piece of entertainment ever to be perpetrated." She recalled her attendance at the London premiere as one of the low points of her career. "Afterwards, I raced back to the Dorchester and just made it to the downstairs lavatory and vomited."

Unfortunately for Miss Taylor, the worst was yet to come. If *Cleopatra* moved the sensitive star to nausea, then the other films featured in her gallery of the Hollywood Hall of Shame should have ruined her digestion altogether. Her robust on-screen appearance in these next two stinkers, however, suggests that the Great Lady has somehow learned to keep her food down, despite the most embarrassing motion picture roles. . . .

BOOM!

(1968)

Universal
Produced by John Heyman and Norman Priggen
Directed by Joseph Losey
Screenplay by Tennessee Williams, based on his play
The Milk Train Doesn't Stop Here Anymore
and his short story "Man Bring This Up Road"

Starring Elizabeth Taylor (Flora Goforth); Richard Burton (Chris Flanders);
Noel Coward (The Witch of Capri); Joanna Shimkus (Blackie);
Michael Dunn (Rudy); Romolo Valli (Dr. Lullo); and Fernando Piazza (Etti).

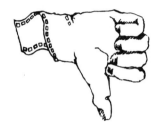

A Sad Decline

Between 1961, when America's motion picture exhibitors voted her the country's number-one box office attraction, and 1967, when she appeared in such dismal vehicles as *Reflections in a Golden Eye* and *The Comedians*, Elizabeth Taylor's popularity suffered a slow, sad decline. Despite the Oscar she won in 1966 for her role as a middle-aged shrew in *Who's Afraid of Virginia Woolf?*, and despite the fact that her status as an international celebrity still allowed her to win top roles, her increasingly matronly appearance and declining commercial drawing power caused Miss Taylor and her agents to worry about the future. In this delicate situation, it seemed only natural to turn back to the proven formula with which she had achieved her greatest critical and financial success. For Liz Taylor, this meant another screen adaptation of a Tennessee Williams play; in *Cat on a Hot Tin Roof* (1958) and *Suddenly Last Summer* (1959), the master dramatist's atmosphere of portentous decadence served as a perfect setting for the young star's smoldering screen presence.

Unfortunately, Williams had already entered a slump all his own, and his mid-sixties productions fell far below the standards of his best work. *The Milk Train Doesn't Stop Here Anymore*, a "religious allegory" based on his own short story "Man Bring This Up Road," served as a case in point. In its original 1963 version, the *Milk Train* came to a screeching halt after only sixty-nine Broadway performances. Williams then reworked the play, and it opened again the next year in a promising new production staged by director Tony Richardson (*Tom Jones, The Loved One*), starring Tallulah Bankhead and Tab Hunter. This latest incarnation proved even less successful than the first version and folded quietly after playing five nights to empty houses.

This troubled play, shunned by the public and savaged by critics, hardly seemed a promising basis for a motion picture, but Universal, as it turned out, had already purchased the rights and managed against all odds to interest the Burtons in making the movie. Elizabeth, abandoning all pretense of youthful glamor, would play Flora Goforth, an aged millionairess who had outlived six husbands but now faced her own death in terrified isolation. Richard Burton would take the part of Chris Flanders, young poet, mystic guru, and gigolo, who moves into the lady's Mediterranean villa and gives her a last fling at love before her pathetic demise. The fact that Burton, who had once been considered the logical heir to Olivier, Gielgud, and the other giants of the British stage, would now gladly accept a role that had been acted on Broadway by Tab Hunter speaks eloquently of the general direction of his career. Nevertheless, Dick and Liz hoped that *Milk Train* would become a bitter, bitchy hit à la *Virginia Woolf*. As columnist Sheilah Graham noted after interviewing the principals, "With all of this enthusiasm, and all the human ingredients, if this picture is not a smash I'll eat my baroque hat." One can only hope for her sake that the chapeau in question was small and tasty.

One Big Happy Family

Before shooting began on the much-touted project, Universal had to confront the obvious problem of the title. *The Milk Train Doesn't Stop Here Anymore* promised the same sort of public appeal on theatre

Considering the performances of the two stars (Elizabeth Taylor and Richard Burton) in the big-screen adaptation of Tennessee Williams' The Milk Train Doesn't Stop Here Anymore, *the producers might well have retitled it* The Ham Truck Has Stalled Here Permanently. *Instead, they called it* Boom!

marquees as the memorable title of Ray Dennis Steckler's recent film, *The Incredibly Strange Creatures Who Stopped Living and Became Mixed-Up Zombies* (1964). Hoping to prove to the world that there were no mixed-up zombies working at the Universal front office, the studio announced that the latest Burton-Taylor epic had been renamed *Boom*. After production began they changed their minds and came up with the new title *Sunburst*. After that they tried *Boom* once again for a short period, then moved on to *Goforth*, before finally settling on *Boom!* (with the all-important exclamation point) shortly before the film's release. As it turned out, that exclamation point proved to be the most exciting part of the picture. When questioned by the press, Tennessee Williams explained the strange title as "the sound of shock felt by people each moment of still being alive." To make sure we get the point, Mr. Burton mumbles that profound monosyllable, "Boom!," several times in the course of the picture, perhaps ex-

The Boom! *Bunch in Full Bloom: from left to right, a visiting sitar player; a frustrated and frigid private secretary (Joanna Shimkus); Flora Goforth, "the richest woman in the world" (guess who?); a mendacious man of medicine (Romolo Valli); a jive-talking gigolo (Richard Burton) with a bag of artsy-nutsy tricks; and a dwarf majordomo (Michael Dunn) with flamboyantly Fascist proclivities.*

pressing his own shock at finding himself in the midst of this dreary mess.

In transferring Tennessee Williams' symbolic drama to the big screen, producer John Heyman and director Joseph Losey decided to "open up" the action in order to emphasize grand sets and spectacular locations. They shot the picture for the most part on a rocky, barren cliff on the island of Sardinia. There, two hundred feet above the crashing waves of the Mediterranean, they built a sprawling pink-and-white mansion out of marble and plasterboard at a cost of more than $500,000. This elaborately decorated set represented the home of "the richest woman in the world," Flora Goforth, and her eccentric domestic ménage, including a nervous, sexually repressed private secretary (Joanna Shimkus), a smarmy attending physician (Romolo Valli), assorted servants, a black giant, a pair of sitar-strumming Hindus, a midget majordomo in boots and riding breeches (Michael Dunn), his team of man-eating schnauzers, a talking myna bird, and a chained ape. Into the midst of this big happy family strolls Richard Burton as a hippy-dippy, long-haired Christ figure known as *Chris* (get it?), armed with a book of poems and a few abstract mobiles. In a previous adventure, this wandering minstrel studied with a holy man in Baja California, and earned the adorable nickname "The Angel of Death" by helping his mentor to commit suicide. As Ms. Goforth's house guest, he engages in endless conversations over the meaning of life, while enjoying her eclectic collection of paintings and sculpture, including an impressive battalion of scowling primitive monoliths that would have been more at home on Easter Island than Sardinia. We eventually learn that these grim totems are supposed to represent her dead husbands (or perhaps more appropriately, the frowning critics). The lady of the house adjusts to this environment by cursing ("Shit on your mother!"), chugging whiskey, popping codeine, throwing temper tantrums, and coughing blood into wads of Kleenex. One of the few bright spots in her grim existence is a visit from an aged homosexual fortune teller known as "The Witch of Capri," who arrives by boat from his own island retreat. This thankless part is played by the distinguished British playwright and actor Noel Coward. In the low point of his long and brilliant career, Coward mincingly delivers witty lines such as, "I have always found girls fragrant in any phase of the moon." Burton also has the opportunity to present scintillating dialogue, as he does when he gazes deep into the heroine's eyes and declares, "My heart beats blood that is not my blood, but the blood of anonymous blood donors." The best and most poetic lines, however, remain for Miss Taylor, including such gems as "Life is all memory," and her moving contemplation of the heavens, "Ah, the insincere sympathy of the faraway stars!" None of this makes much sense, of course, but back in 1968 it all seemed very trendy, timely, and profound, so the company set to work with a great sense of artistic mission.

"Tiresome and Disgusting"

No Elizabeth Taylor movie would be complete without production delays caused by one of the star's celebrated bouts with ill health. In the case of *Boom!* it was bronchitis that struck Her Majesty; she fell ill the same day shooting was supposed to begin, and so, from the outset, the project operated behind schedule.

For the duration of their eleven weeks in the Mediterranean, the Burtons established themselves on board their 110-foot yacht, the *Kalizma*, anchored offshore from the scenic island location. In addition to the crew, the two stars provided floating hospitality for their makeup men, hairdressers, dressers, photograph retouchers, personal secretaries, secretarial assistants, and Elizabeth's two obnoxious, constantly yapping Pekinese dogs. Despite this bulging boatload of fun, Miss Taylor began to feel lonely during her free moments and turned longing eyes on the trained ape who played several scenes with her in the film. This princely primate soon became her pet and received his own comfortable bunk on the *Kalizma*. All went smoothly until one day when the monkey, apparently resentful over the fact that his mistress had a part in the movie that was so much larger than his, decided to take a powder. While Liz and Dick were on the set, the ape disappeared, taking with him a $1,600 jewel case belonging to Miss Taylor. For several days, the star was inconsolable over the loss of this creature, causing further delays in the schedule. The simian scoundrel turned up a year later—long after the Burtons had departed—but he had apparently unloaded the jewel case on the black market and refused to provide any leads as to its whereabouts.

In order to lift Miss Taylor's spirits, producer John Heyman (who also happened, through strange coincidence, to serve as the Burtons' agent) presented his favorite actress with "a small token of his appreciation": a lovely new $60,000 brooch. Such presentations of expensive baubles at a time of stress for the leading lady had become something of a tradition on Liz Taylor films. As her ex-husband Eddie Fisher fondly recalled, "Just a little $50,000 diamond would make everything wonderful for up to four days." Fortunately, Liz had plenty of precious gems to occupy her attention during the filming of *Boom!*; Bulgari of Rome loaned over $2 million worth of stones to decorate the great star, so that she would not have to use her own personal—and even more formidable—collection.

Given their deep commitment to the success of this project, Taylor and Burton had to take special pains not to overwork themselves. They spent many afternoons on the deck of their yacht, playing dominos or hosting drinking parties for their friends. As Mark Shivas reported in the *New York Times*, "If the Burtons don't wish to work early, or late on weekends, they don't. Quite ordinary requests often have to be asked as favors, sometimes through intermediaries. The 'Royal Family' of motion pictures only arrives on the set when everyone is ready, and they don't always wish to rehearse." Director Joe Losey (*The Servant, The Go-Between*) had never worked with Liz and Dick before and so felt totally incapable of lowering the boom. As co-star Joanna Shimkus observed, "Losey was so *nervous* about directing the Burtons that I didn't know when he was shooting, except when he'd yell 'cut!' " After the ordeal had ended, Losey himself recalled, "I enjoyed working with the Burtons, though there is no doubt that their star behavior is sometimes tiresome and disgusting."

In addition to the human difficulties he encountered, Losey also faced the hostility of nature itself in bringing his artistic little picture to completion. Midway through the shooting schedule, an unseasonal storm struck Sardinia, causing flooding on the set and destroying part of Flora Goforth's villa. For several days, Taylor and Burton went back to playing dominos while stagehands worked furiously to repair the damage. This sprawling set had become particularly precious to all concerned since Tennessee Williams had given it his personal blessing. "Oh, how beautiful! How baroque!" he purred when he visited the location for the first time. "Just what I had in mind!" Amazingly enough, Williams maintained his enthusiasm for the production even after he saw the finished film. "It's a beautiful picture," the playwright told the *Los Angeles Times*, "the best ever made of one of my plays. I think Elizabeth has never been that good before. I don't know whether the public is going to buy it, for Lord's sake. I hope they do for Elizabeth's sake, as well as my own. Because I love Elizabeth. . . .

Noel Coward wonders how he ever got involved in this pretentious stupidity, while Liz Taylor shows off some of her characteristically understated wardrobe for Boom!

I can always make out, but inwardly she's a very fragile being. . . . Do you think young people—and they're the moviegoers of today—will understand? I think so. I'd hate to lose them."

"The Sound of a Bomb Exploding"

In the end, it was not only young people Williams lost, but also middle-aged critics, elderly pederasts, wandering poets, and nearly everyone else in the country. Seldom has a major film been greeted with more vigorous or universal contempt. The reviewers, of course, had a field day:

"A pointless, pompous nightmare."
—PAUL D. ZIMMERMAN, *Newsweek*

"An ordeal in tedium."
—RAY LOYND, *Hollywood Reporter*

"A mess."—BRUCE WILLIAMSON, *Playboy*

"Pretentious . . . Ludicrous . . . Why was *Boom!* ever filmed in the first place?"
—LAWRENCE DEVINE, *Los Angeles Herald-Examiner*

"Outright junk."—*Saturday Review*

"Let them [Taylor and Burton] by all means, do their thing, but why film it and charge admission?"

—WILFRED SHEED, *Esquire*

"They display the self-indulgent fecklessness of a couple of rich amateurs hamming it up at the country club frolic, and with approximately the same results.   —*Time*

"A sleek, aberrational and posturing piece of nonsense . . . It is impossible to give a bloody damn about anyone involved in the enterprise."

—CHARLES CHAMPLIN, *Los Angeles Times*

"It stars Elizabeth Taylor and Richard Burton, now well on their way to becoming a comedy team on the order of Laurel and Hardy. The problem is that *Boom!* isn't meant to be funny. . . . The young poet is played by Richard Burton, who now looks exactly like Timothy Leary. Together, they attempt to project an aura of grim mysticism, as if by speaking very slowly and moving as little as possible they might somehow convince the audience that this is serious stuff."   —MICHAEL KORDA, *Glamour*

"Their movie vaudeville team has become one of the great camps of our time . . . Noel Coward seems determined to end his career by making a public fool of himself."   —STANLEY KAUFFMANN, *New Republic*

"The title is explained somewhere, but I'm afraid my attention wandered as the picture flapped along and I'm not sure I got it straight . . . No matter—it is something ambitiously ambiguous and poetic, some sort of metaphysical popcorn to munch while Liz and Richard go about the really serious business of the movie—which is making a million apiece by, respectively, waddling and shambling through poor old Tennessee Williams' self-satire . . . That title could not be more apt; it is precisely the sound of a bomb exploding."   —RICHARD SCHICKEL, *Life*

Bust!

Despite these reviews, the notoriety of the two stars helped *Boom!* to get off to a promising start at the box office. *Variety* described its business in New York City as "wham initial weekend" and predicted that the film's gross "looks socko." But as word-of-mouth caught on, the adjectives describing ticket sales in the daily editions of the trade papers changed from "nice" to "fair" to "wan" to "feeble" until, after the second week, the film's fate wasn't even reported. As a Universal executive pointed out just fifteen days after the picture's release, "*Boom!* isn't doing little

"The Witch of Capri" (Noel Coward) and "The Angel of Death" (Richard Burton) exchange highly charged, richly symbolic dialogue in another action-packed scene from Joseph Losey's Boom!—*hailed by* Newsweek *as "a pointless, pompous nightmare."*

business; it's doing no business at all." At the end of the year, this much-heralded all-star extravaganza had garnered even less business than such cheapie duds as *The Mini-Skirt Mob* and *King Kong Escapes*. To cover its embarrassment, Universal claimed that the movie cost less than $6 million—only a fraction of what Twentieth Century-Fox had wasted on *Cleopatra*—but the actual budget, especially including the extensive advertising and publicity, must surely have been much higher. In any event, this latest flop proved costly enough so that *Variety* pronounced it "one of the biggest box-office losers of the year." When Universal's total earnings for 1968 showed a significant decline from the '67 figures, studio president Lew Wasserman pointed to *Boom!* as the major culprit. Unfortunately, none of the studio's junior executives came up with the bright idea of attempting to re-release the film with an appropriate new title: *Bust!*

Having perpetrated insanity on a glorious, epic scale in *Cleopatra*, and then having given the world a shabby, artsy, and tawdry little fiasco such as *Boom!*, it seemed hard to imagine what Miss Taylor could possibly do in order to top herself. In terms of sheer stupidity on both conception and execution, however, *The Only Game in Town*—the next movie in this exhibit hall—exceeded all her previous work. As Flora Goforth prophetically declaimed in one of the dramatic highlights of *Boom!*: "I spend my life going from one goddamn pointless distraction to another!"

THE ONLY GAME IN TOWN

(1970)

Twentieth Century-Fox
Produced by Fred Kohlmar
Directed by George Stevens
Screenplay by Frank D. Gilroy, based on his play

Starring Elizabeth Taylor (Fran Walker); Warren Beatty (Joe Grady);
Charles Braswell (Lockwood); and Hank Henry (Tony).

Snowbound in Tahiti

In 1970, when producer Fred Kohlmar (*The Last Angry Man, Bye Bye Birdie*) announced specific plans for Elizabeth Taylor's latest cinematic extravaganza, many of his colleagues questioned his sanity. Not only had he agreed to pay the faded star $1,125,000 for her services, but he went along with her bizarre demand to shoot *The Only Game in Town*—with its Las Vegas theme and setting—on a sound stage in Paris, France. True to form, Miss Taylor refused to allow so trivial a matter as making a motion picture to interfere in any way with her domestic arrangements. Since her husband Richard would be in Europe for several months shooting a comedy called *Staircase* (in which he played an aging homosexual alongside their old friend from *Cleopatra* days, Rex Harrison) she naturally insisted that Kohlmar and his cohorts could create a substitute Las Vegas in France that would be even better than the original. One of the production assistants on the film eventually tried to justify this controversial decision to the press. "When you finally get Taylor to commit to a picture, you do whatever she wants," he explained. "If it is a snowbound picture set in the Canadian wilderness and she wants to work in Tahiti because Richard is there doing a pirate picture, you ship snowmaking machines to Papeete." Fortunately, *The Only Game in Town* contained no scenes involving icebergs or glaciers, but it did require the detailed reproduction of the interior of a Nevada casino and an elaborate replica of the Las Vegas skyline. To ensure realism, the producers imported even the smallest props and set decorations from the United States to the production facilities of the Studios de Boulogne. In a triumph of their craft, the set designers succeeded in recreating all the neon and plastic of the desert resort at only four or five times what it would have cost to shoot the entire picture on location. Since *The Only Game in Town* was supposed to be a bittersweet love story, it seemed only fitting that its budget should be inflated by many millions of dollars for the sake of the celebrated romance between Richard and Elizabeth.

Next to the real-life passion of the Burtons, the story of the two fictional lovers in Miss Taylor's new film seemed pallid indeed. She plays Fran, a lonely chorus girl approaching middle age, who falls for Joe, a frustrated musician and compulsive gambler who dreams of escaping Las Vegas for fame and fortune in New York City. These lovable losers made their first appearance in a Broadway stage version of this material that, like *Boom!* before it, showed its true potential as a motion picture property by drawing harsh reviews and sparse audiences. The original play of *The Only Game in Town* starred Tammy Grimes and Barry Nelson and played only thirteen performances before ending its disastrous run in June 1968. By that time, however, Twentieth Century-Fox had already committed $700,000 to playwright Frank D. Gilroy for the rights to turn his latest drama into a feature film. It appeared to be a reasonable decision at the time, since Gilroy's previous play, *The Subject Was Roses*, had not only won the Pulitzer Prize but had also served as the basis for a highly successful movie starring Patricia Neal and Jack Albertson. *The Only Game* may have flopped on Broadway, but in view of its author's winning track record—and the unprecedented sum they had already sunk in the project— the warm-hearted studio execs decided to give the show another chance. Miss Taylor's enthusiasm for the material bolstered their confidence that they had both an artistic and commercial winner on their hands. When Liz heard the script read to her for the

Cleopatra Comes to Vegas, and Everyone Loses: Liz Taylor promised that her role as a show girl in George Stevens' The Only Game in Town *would mark her grand farewell to the silver screen, but the hostile reaction to the film forced her to change her mind.*

first time, she could scarcely contain her enthusiasm. "Stop it," she said. "You're making me cry." This reaction eloquently foreshadowed the response of the studio's accountants as they examined the balance sheets on the finished film.

Deeply Committed

With Elizabeth Taylor deeply committed to the film's success, the producers still faced the problem of signing a co-star of suitable magnitude. Richard Burton would have been obviously absurd in the role of Joe Grady—the sweet-talking, self-destructive Middle American drifter—so it was considered a lucky break for the production that he was busy with other projects of his own. Eventually, the studio announced what seemed to be a stroke of ideal casting: Frank Sinatra himself agreed to take the male lead, and the producers confidently assumed that he would bring the perfect blend of toughness and vulnerability, sleaze and charm, to a very difficult role. In addition to his acting talents, Sinatra had the additional advantage of a long-standing friendship with Miss Taylor; in fact, Hollywood rumors alleged that they had enjoyed a torrid affair during her days as a rising young star on the MGM lot. Whatever the true history of their relationship, the idea that The Voice

himself would be present at Las Vegas-by-the-Seine served to please and reassure Miss Taylor. She was further delighted by the choice of a director for the project; George Stevens had guided her through two of her best performances, in *A Place in the Sun* (1951) and *Giant* (1956), so the entire production had the comfortable, chummy atmosphere of a class reunion.

Liz felt so much at home, in fact, that she soon did what came most naturally to her while working on a movie: she got sick and wound up in the hospital. This time it was an emergency hysterectomy that put her out of commission for several months and set back the shooting schedule before production had even started. At this point Old Blue Eyes, who had a history of developing cold feet after committing himself to film projects, decided that since the movie didn't seem to be going *his* way, he and Elizabeth would remain strangers in the night. Citing the late start for *The Only Game in Town,* he abandoned his contract in order to honor his prior commitment to perform at Caesars Palace, making clear his preference for Las Vegas, Nevada, over Las Vegas, France.

As a replacement for Sinatra, the producers turned at the last moment to Warren Beatty. The young actor had recently earned more than $6 million as producer and star of *Bonnie and Clyde,* and he wanted to follow this huge hit with another film of similar stature. He had been offered plum parts in dozens of movies, including *Butch Cassidy and the Sundance Kid* and *Bob and Carol and Ted and Alice,* but he turned down these shaky, speculative projects so he could concentrate instead on a sure thing like *The Only Game in Town.* Producer Fred Kohlmar happily paid Beatty $750,000 to take over the role of Joe Grady.

Everyone expressed delight at this choice except Richard Burton, who came to resent the growing friendship between Warren and Liz. Burton even managed to rearrange his schedule so that he could be present when his wife and Beatty filmed their most intimate love scenes. On one such occasion, he became so enraged by what he saw that he stormed onto the set, ignoring director Stevens and the whirring cameras, grabbed Miss Taylor firmly by the wrist, and yanked her away from the startled Beatty. Elizabeth immediately burst into tears and claimed that Burton's rough treatment had wrenched her spine out of kilter, aggravating a former back injury. According to several reports in French newspapers, an ambulance then arrived at the studio to take the star back to her hotel, and the entire production lost fifteen more days as they waited for Miss Taylor to recover from this painful experience.

After all the delays and an exhausting eighty-six-day shooting schedule in Paris, Stevens and Kohlmar still lacked enough usable footage to put together a satisfactory motion picture. In spite of the painstakingly accurate reproductions of American streets, supermarkets, casinos, and apartments, they still had to fly the entire company to Nevada for ten intensive days of additional filming in order to finish the film. During this period of panic and pressure, work was interrupted by a new fiasco involving Miss Taylor's pets and pearls, reminiscent of the problem with the larcenous ape from *Boom!* (q.v.) who made off with her beloved jewel case. In this latest episode, work on *The Only Game in Town* ground to a halt for several hours while assorted servants and production assistants helped Elizabeth search for her missing Peregrina Pearl, a bauble worth $37,000. Ultimately, they located this vanished treasure in the mouth of one of the star's dogs, a playful Pekinese who had apparently mistaken it for an especially tempting and expensive brand of chew toy.

After recovering from this disaster, the production moved on to the sound stages at Twentieth Century-Fox for a final week of shooting, and then, after several months in the editing room, the film was ready for release. The studio nonetheless held it back for several months, waiting for precisely the right moment to unleash this masterpiece on the world. Liz Taylor, meanwhile, gave a series of interviews to the press in which she indicated that *The Only Game in Town* would mark her farewell to the silver screen, that she had no greater wish than to retire gracefully after completing such a beautiful film. As it turned out, the picture was not the swan song she had planned, nor even a smoothly executed swan dive, but rather a resounding belly flop as it hit the water.

"When They Drop the Bomb . . ."

The film premiered in January 1970 in Las Vegas (where else?), but the audience for the gala first night surely would have been better off if they had gone over to catch Sinatra's show at Caesars. The critics blasted the film from the beginning and placed particular emphasis on Miss Taylor's portly appearance. While recovering from her recent hysterectomy she had gained considerable weight, and the public had never before seen . . . well, so much of her. As Vincent Canby wrote in the *New York Times*, she resembled "an apple balanced atop a pair of toothpicks"; her overripe figure made no sense whatsoever on a character who was supposed to be earning her living as a Las Vegas dancer. Her costumes only made the situation worse in their all-too-obvious attempt to conceal the fact that her waistline had totally disappeared. These ill-assorted rags included a lopsided miniskirt, a maternity dress, a floppy pantsuit, a cou-

ple of tents, several funny hats, and a flowing blue evening gown, all of which made her appear consistently larger than life—like a colorful Macy's float in the Thanksgiving Day Parade. As for her characterization, she managed to project all the delicacy and refinement of the late John Belushi in drag. Warren Beatty did his best against these impossible odds, but it is small wonder that he went through much of the movie with a hat pulled down over his eyes. As he forces himself to gaze longingly at his co-star, he bears more than a passing resemblance to Charles Grodin trying to cast seductive glances at the divine Miss Piggy in *The Great Muppet Caper;* poor Richard Burton had nothing to worry about.

In addition to these dramatic excesses, Frank Gilroy's script contributed to the general air of unintentional hilarity with some of the most elevating and enlightening dialogue since *Boom!*:

Warren Beatty plays a compulsive gambler in The Only Game in Town, *but it was producer Fred Kohlmar who lost heavily on this sucker bet.*

After meeting in a supermarket and comparing their taste in hats, Fran (Elizabeth Taylor) and Joe (Warren Beatty) decide they are made for each other in **The Only Game in Town.**

WARREN BEATTY (*philosophizing on the nature of love*): Which is worse—the heart abused or the heart unused?

BEATTY: Look, you're just as lonely and hard-up as I am. . . .

ELIZABETH TAYLOR: I don't like that kind of talk!

BEATTY: Look, I don't wrestle, I don't coax. If you want to go to bed, we go. If you don't, we don't.

TAYLOR (*after a long pause*): Carry me?

BEATTY: What?

TAYLOR: Carry me into the bedroom. I like to be carried. Please.

(*After an intense close-up of Miss Taylor's pleading violet eyes, there is a slow dissolve to a scene of the two lovers lighting cigarettes in bed.*)

TAYLOR (*during a lovers' quarrel*): Never darken my door again—unless it's for keeps!

BEATTY (*in his lady's arms*): When they drop the bomb, I hope this is where they find me.

BEATTY (*at the end of the movie*): Marriage is not a pleasing institution, but right now, it's the only game in town, and we're gonna play it!

For theatre owners, however, this particular film was *not* the only game in town, and no one in the world could make them play it after they saw what miserable returns it brought at the box office. In most places the picture played for only one week; nowhere in the United States did it run for more than a month. According to the trade papers it earned a total of less than $1.5 million from around the country while its production budget was estimated at more than $11 million. One can only marvel at the heroic ingenuity that enabled the studio to throw away this sort of money on an intimate little film with only two important characters and nearly all the action taking place in a single apartment. Despite these limited horizons, the nearly $10 million lost on *The Only Game* made it the second most costly disaster in the studio's history—second only to *Cleopatra.* Without the intervening huge success of *The Sound of Music* in 1965, it is entirely possible that the one-two punch of this pair of Liz Taylor fiascoes could have put Twentieth Century-Fox out of business once and for all.

For director George Stevens, *The Only Game in Town* marked the end of a long and distinguished career. In the past, he had created such memorable films as *Swing Time* (1936), *Gunga Din* (1939), *Woman of the Year* (1942), and *The Diary of Anne Frank* (1959), but his most recent project before going down for the count with Taylor and Beatty had been the embarrassing bomb, *The Greatest Story Ever Told* (q.v.). Stevens had originally wanted Liz Taylor as his Mary Magdalene in this Tinseltown version of the life of Jesus, but even without her he managed to lose millions and to ruin his personal reputation. Following this humiliating defeat, Stevens wandered in the wilderness for four years, nursing his wounds, before venturing forth to go to work on *The Only Game in Town*—his last movie effort before permanent retirement.

The film's hostile reception had exactly the opposite effect on Elizabeth Taylor. When it became clear that the picture had been bitterly rejected by the critics and the public, she immediately abandoned all talk of retiring from the big screen and immediately looked for new projects in which to redeem herself. Nevertheless, her magic spell over Hollywood's moguls had finally been broken: never again did she receive million-dollar offers for her screen appearances or the sort of sky's-the-limit budgets that had characterized her previous work.

Writer Frank D. Gilroy managed to recover handily from what he himself described as "the last of the great debacles." He even offered unsolicited advice to Hollywood's producers as to an alternative approach to his material. "Now that everybody has

Here, Liz demonstrates the attitude toward production budgets that earned her a special wing all her own in the Holly-wood Hall of Shame.

taken a bath on it," he told the press, "I've seriously proposed doing it again for half a million dollars and a cast of unknowns. It would make a nice little picture." As if to prove his point, he created precisely that sort of "nice little picture" in 1978, serving as producer and director as well as writer for an intriguing romantic tale called *Once in Paris.* Through the 1980s, he has remained one of the film industry's most respected and unpredictable figures.

It was Gilroy himself who created the most appropriate—if inadvertent—metaphor for the profligate and utterly senseless waste of studio funds on *The Only Game in Town.* A climactic sequence in the film features a bitter argument between Beatty and

Taylor, after which the enraged hero runs off to the casinos. At first, he appears to be on a roll and succeeds at everything, but then his luck changes and he loses heavily. Finally, he walks away from the tables and sits down at one of the fountains in front of the pleasure palace. Taking a last $100 bill from his pocket, he folds it into a little paper boat, sets it afloat, and watches the water carry it down to the gutter.

It is a symbolic if somewhat childish gesture, but considerably less wasteful and foolish than the idiotic entertainments designed especially for children that appear in our next corridor of the Hollywood Hall of Shame....

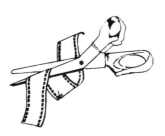

CHILD
ABUSE

ACCORDING TO the conventional Hollywood wisdom, it's hard to lose big money making movies for kids. There are millions of little monsters out there who are capable of forcing their parents to take them to see even the most inane cinematic drivel. This wonderfully unsophisticated audience couldn't care less about big budgets and can be happily entertained without major stars, scenic locations, lavish battle scenes, or dazzling special effects. There are literally scores of producers who have proven by example that all you have to do is throw in a singing clown, a few dwarves, and some lovable animals, and you can, if you're lucky, strike it rich with the kiddies. *Santa Claus Conquers the Martians* (1964) is a prime example of the sort of juvenile junk that, despite an asinine story line and the lowest imaginable production values, has done solid business, year after year. In light of the long history of successful kiddie cheapies, those pioneering producers who managed to blow millions on overblown spectaculars for boys and girls deserve special recognition in our museum. *Doctor Dolittle* and *The Blue Bird* succeed in proving, against all odds, that it is indeed possible for a major motion picture to insult the intelligence of the average four-year-old. These pictures were not only expensive but also embarrassing to all concerned, and they represent the sort of unnourishing pabulum laced with gold dust that will produce upset stomachs in adults as well as children.

DOCTOR DOLITTLE

(1967)

Twentieth Century-Fox
Produced by Arthur P. Jacobs
Directed by Richard Fleischer
Screenplay by Leslie Bricusse, based on the stories by Hugh Lofting
Music and Lyrics by Leslie Bricusse
Dances Staged by Herbert Ross

Starring Rex Harrison (Dr. John Dolittle); Samantha Eggar (Emma Fairfax);
Anthony Newley (Matthew Mugg); Richard Attenborough (Albert Blossom);
William Dix (Tommy Stubbins); Geoffrey Holder (William Shakespeare X);
and Peter Bull (General Bellows).

"Scratching Around"

Between 1912 and 1947, Hugh Lofting, an American writer born in Britain, produced more than a dozen books for children concerning the adventures of Doctor Dolittle—an eccentric English country physician who discovers a way to talk with animals. These volumes, with quaint illustrations by the author, became best-sellers around the world and won recognition as classics of children's literature. For years, various Hollywood producers talked of adapting these beloved tales for the silver screen, but it remained for Arthur P. Jacobs, a former public relations man full of indefatigable energy and bravado, to bring these vague prospects to the point of reality.

In 1963, Jacobs won a commitment of $6 million from Twentieth Century-Fox to produce a movie musical based on the Lofting stories, the highest original budget ever provided for one of the studio's films. (*Cleopatra*, by comparison, initially had been budgeted at only $2 million.) One of the reasons for this unprecedented financial commitment was the classy talent that Jacobs brought to the project: since playwright and lyricist Alan Jay Lerner had combined so successfully with Rex Harrison in educating Eliza Doolittle in *My Fair Lady*, the studio naturally assumed that the same team would achieve comparable results with Dr. John Dolittle in the new musical spectacular. Lerner set to work writing book and lyrics for the film, while Harrison, fresh from his exertions as Julius Caesar in *Cleopatra*, promised to play the lead.

At this early stage in its development, the *Dolittle* project suffered the first of its many serious setbacks. Despite his fervent enthusiasm for the production, Alan Jay Lerner found it difficult to do his job. As producer Jacobs recalled, "He worked on the picture fifteen months on and off, mostly off. We painted an office for him, painted his name on a parking space, and then we waited. And waited some more. I get him on the phone, he tells me he knows what he wants, it's all in his head. More phone calls. He tells me he wants to see me here, I go see him, he tells me he's leaving for New York, I go to New York, they tell me he's in Rome. Well, that's it."

The main problem with Lerner's early departure from the picture was its effect on Rex Harrison. If the truth be known, the former Professor Henry Higgins had no burning desire to play the lead in a musical for kiddies in which he spent his time chatting with sheep and seals; it was only the prestigious presence of Mr. Lerner that had persuaded him to agree to the project in the first place. As Jacobs described what happened next, "Rex had a contract, he was getting more money than God, but when Lerner left, he says, 'Goodbye, sue me, I'm not going to do it.' So we have a picture called *Doctor Dolittle*, six million going in, but no one to play Doctor Dolittle."

After "scratching around" for a while, the studio came up with Christopher Plummer, who had co-starred in the wildly successful *Sound of Music*, as the man to take over the title role. Arthur Jacobs, meanwhile, refused to give up on Rex Harrison and temporarily put aside the issue of a star, concentrating instead on finding a writer to replace Alan Jay

On location at the picturesque English village of Castle Combe, problems multiplied like rabbits for Doctor Dolittle and friends.

Lerner. He finally settled on Leslie Bricusse, the gifted young composer who had collaborated with Anthony Newley on the smash musicals *Stop the World, I Want to Get Off* and *The Roar of the Greasepaint, the Smell of the Crowd*. Bricusse set to work immediately on doctoring *Dolittle*, providing screenplay, music, and lyrics based on the sketchy notes Lerner had left behind. He soon created enough material for Jacobs to show Rex Harrison, who immediately liked what he saw and agreed, in light of the quality of the Bricusse material, to return to the project. This delighted producer Jacobs, but the studio had already made an expensive commitment to Christopher Plummer, so the entire venture suffered from an embarrassment of Dolittles. Though a two-headed llama named the Pushmi-Pullyu figures promi-

nently in the story, no one had anticipated that the movie would feature a two-headed star. The studio therefore disposed of Plummer, but not before paying him his entire agreed-upon fee of $300,000 in return for his agreement to sit out the production. Considering the ultimate fate of the film, there is no question that Plummer enjoyed the best of both worlds. The question that did remain concerned who would direct this gradually congealing epic. Vincente Minnelli and William Wyler were the early front runners. Studio president Darryl Zanuck wanted John Huston, but Jacobs vetoed the idea. "I figured there was already enough temperament with Rex, without getting Huston involved. Minnelli was old-fashioned and Wyler would take fifty takes of every shot and the picture would end up costing $35

120

million. Who else was there?" The answer turned out to be one Richard Fleischer, cartoonist Max Fleischer's amiable son, who, over the years, has managed to direct an astonishing string of cinematic stinkers, including *The Vikings, The Boston Strangler, The Don Is Dead, Tora! Tora! Tora!, Mandingo, Che!*, and the Neil Diamond version of *The Jazz Singer*. With this record in mind, it is only fitting that Mr. Fleischer's name in German translates as "butcher." Before completing *Doctor Dolittle*, he no doubt dreamed of reverting to ancestral type and slaughtering—or sacrificing—some of the animal actors who made his job so difficult.

Riding Roughshod

As usual, Arthur Jacobs summed up the situation with eloquent brevity. "How do you tell an elephant what to do," he moaned, "even if he's the best trained in the world?" This fundamental problem was seriously compounded by the sheer size of the *Dolittle* menagerie: some 1,500 creatures took part in the production. Many of these were understudies, doubles, or stunt beasts. For the key roles of Chi-Chi the Chimp and Jip the Dog, the producers had arranged to have three standbys on hand in addition to the lead players, in case these temperamental profes-

In a prophetic scene from a movie that was destined to emerge as one of the top turkeys of the sixties, a disgusted Doctor Dolittle (Rex Harrison) encounters a flock of the fragrant fowl as Polynesia, the production's temperamental and tongue-tied parrot, offers moral support to her master.

sionals proved, on any given day, to be moody or uncooperative. Gub-Gub the Pig, meanwhile, had to be replaced every month, since porkers grow so quickly that each of these actors soon exceeded the polite and cuddly dimensions intended for the character. Though not formally represented by the Screen Actors Guild, the featured fauna still received regal treatment on the set; it cost the studio an average of $750 per beast per week to look after their needs and keep them healthy and happy.

Despite this care and consideration, mishaps aplenty occurred during the course of the production. The rhinoceros, who was one of the few stars not doubled with a fellow creature, came down with a bug of some sort and had to receive an injection from an elephant gun loaded with penicillin. Also in the infirmary was a small fawn who had snacked on a quart of paint while waiting for her scene and had to have her stomach pumped. A squirrel also became bored between shots and decided to amuse himself by chewing on a banister that was part of the set used to represent the Dolittle home. When the damage finally came to light, the company had to wait for nearly two hours while the nibbled woodwork was replaced. The most serious injury of all, however, involved a giraffe who suffered a nasty case of whiplash while walking from one sound stage to another. According to reporters on the scene, the unfortunate and absentminded beast stepped into a pothole and twisted his neck. It is not known whether the giraffe ultimately secured the services of a lawyer and sued the studio for its negligence.

An ailing rhino on the set taxed the medical knowledge of even the fabled Doctor Dolittle. Eventually, the sensitive star received an injection from an elephant gun loaded with penicillin.

Even when they avoided doing damage to themselves, the pesky varmints in the cast proved difficult to handle. Chi-Chi the Chimp had been trained to slap on cue for one of his big scenes, but while waiting for the technicians to set up the shot he decided to rehearse with a goat who also happened to be on hand. Startled by the unexpected blow to his face, the goat went wild with panic, careened around the set for several minutes scattering props in every direction, and eventually picked up Richard Fleischer's script and ate it. Polynesia, Dolittle's talking parrot, proved similarly temperamental. She had been specially trained to speak a few words, but whenever cameras rolled she maintained stony silence. Eventually, the producers used a human voice to dub Polynesia's lines, but the bird became suddenly loquacious at inopportune moments. One afternoon, during the filming of the huge "Talk to the Animals" production number, Fleischer had been forced to yell "Cut!" time after time while trying to get the scene down perfectly. Finally, during the one take in which every detail seemed to work out properly, Polynesia suddenly squawked "Cut!," causing all activity to stop while the entire crew turned to the director with puzzled expressions.

Rex Harrison, meanwhile, had his own problems. Although he was continually required to perform dangerous and ignominious feats for the sake of Art,

such as riding a rhinoceros or kissing a seal, his most unfortunate moment came when he had to sing his heart out while standing in a field completely surrounded by sheep. As Mr. Harrison remembers it, "First, they had to spray me down for flies. Then the sheep were constantly peeing all over me. The ground was so wet. Oh—agony!!" Our proper Henry Higgins, our noble Julius Caesar, reduced to singing in a kiddie musical while serving as a human fire hydrant for a flock of urinating sheep?! He tried hard to remain philosophical about the whole experience, and his major complaint was the unwillingness of the four-footed stars to rehearse their scenes. "We would just come on set—and roll," he recalls. "I think we wasted many thousands of feet of film."

Problems with location shooting also helped put the production behind schedule. Much of the film could be shot on Hollywood sound stages, but the company also planned to travel to Santa Lucia in the Caribbean and to a quaint village in the English countryside. The name of the town was Castle Combe, and it had recently been selected by the national travel board as "England's prettiest village." It was supposed to represent the site of Dolittle's fictional nineteenth-century residence "Puddleby-on-the-Marsh," so a swift corps of American workmen quickly moved in and removed all signs of contemporary life, including television antennas, automobiles,

The Pushmi-Pullyu, the world's only dancing two-headed llama, engages Doctor Dolittle in appropriately erudite conversation, while the future director of Gandhi, Sir Richard Attenborough (with cane, left), plays a circus owner and sings "I've Never Seen Anything Like It."

and streetlights. They also worked hard to "improve" the general look of the place by adding strategic shrubbery and erecting a temporary sandbag dam to block the town's river.

The citizens of Castle Combe had mixed reactions to this sudden invasion of their sleepy hamlet; most of them resented the inconvenience and the disruption of their daily routine. Their displeasure generally expressed itself in polite grumbling, though one disgruntled resident developed such an intense resentment of the Yankee visitors that he quite literally tried to blow them out of the area. As if the actors and crew had not had enough fun with an uncooperative chimpanzee, a sick rhinoceros, and a giraffe with whiplash, they now had the pleasure of watching a homemade bomb go off under the sandbag dam in an attempt to flood the set and destroy their equipment. The police soon discovered that the mad bomber was a young nobleman and a member of the Queen's guard with the unlikely but highly impressive title of Baronet Sir Ranulph Twistleton-Wykeham-Fiennies, whose ineptitude at pyrotechnics was exceeded only by the length of his name. Sir Ranulph announced to the press that he had taken matters into his own hands to protest the "spoiling" of Castle Combe, which was a prime example of "mass entertainment riding roughshod over the feelings of individuals." The feelings of Fleischer, Harrison, and company were, however, greatly relieved when Twistleton-Wykeham-Fiennies had been turned over to the proper authorities, and they assumed that filming could continue. Little did they know that Sir Ranulph apparently had divine contacts, since Castle Combe was immediately subjected to a most unusual downpour, which continued, without interruption, for several weeks. Under these circumstances, the doctor and his friends could do little; they waited patiently for the weather to clear, but it never did. During fifty-eight days that the company remained in the village, rain fell in fifty-three of them. In desperation, Fleischer decreed that they must pack up their bags and beasts and move on, hoping their luck would change.

The island of Santa Lucia had been chosen as the site of Dolittle's South Seas retreat. According to the script, the good doctor repairs to this remote location as part of his obsessive search for the "Giant Pink Sea Snail"—a sort of benign, molluscan Moby Dick. When the crew arrived in the Caribbean, they failed to discover any such exotic beasts, but they did find precisely what they least wanted to encounter: more rain. The bad weather seemed to follow the production and held them up for several additional weeks.

As director Fleischer commented, "This is really a runaway production; we've run away from every location we've been on." At times, their wretched luck seemed to defy logic, and absolutely everything managed to go wrong. Fleischer in particular remembered an afternoon in England "when I had to do a scene with ducks on a pond. I ask you, what could be easier?" It should have been, you will pardon the expression, like shooting ducks in a barrel, but as soon as they turned the birds loose on the water the pathetic creatures apparently had forgotten how to swim. "There they were, sinking like rocks. It was terrible. Everybody jumped in to save them—it seems it was the molting season and they'd lost their water-repellent feathers."

Producer Arthur Jacobs lost more than feathers in the mad scramble to finish the film. He responded to every setback in a personal and emotional way, causing his colleagues to worry over his health. As one of them observed at the time, "He has no life beyond his work. Arthur has no time for a wife or family or close cronies. You know what he does for relaxation? He works." Midway through 1966, shortly before *Doctor Dolittle* went to the editing room, these exertions resulted in the producer's first heart attack. Another man might have withdrawn from active involvement at this point, but not Jacobs. As soon as he had been released from the hospital he courageously returned to work on the film, confident that this gigantic musical, like its creator, would triumph over every adversity.

Groundless Optimism

At the time of the film's release, Jacobs boasted to *Variety* that it was "the most expensive picture ever made *in Hollywood.*" In his enthusiasm to claim that title, he had obviously forgotten about all the location work that had taken place in England and the Caribbean, or else he considered the resulting footage too worthless to even consider. In any event, the total cost of *Doctor Dolittle* amounted to a staggering $18 million—or three times its original budget. Clearly embarrassed at having spent so much on a whimsical children's musical, the studio issued numerous public explanations of where all the money went. The world soon learned, for instance, that the Great Pink Sea Snail, which Dolittle finally encounters at the end of the film, was actually a forty-foot-long machine that weighed eight tons and cost more than $65,000 to create. Additional funds were lavished on wardrobes for both human and animal stars. Sophie the Seal proved a particularly expensive

Rex Harrison and Anthony Newley try to remember a recipe for escargot as they encounter the "Giant Pink Sea Snail"—a machine that cost the producers of Doctor Dolittle *more than $65,000.*

proposition who required numerous fittings and six different frilly costumes. This seems an especially irresponsible expense when one thinks of all the impoverished and naked seals swimming around in Canadian waters who would be eternally grateful for just one decent cocktail dress.

Samantha Eggar, who plays Dolittle's love interest in the film (but who, unlike various seals, parrots, and llamas, never has the chance to kiss or even to nuzzle the good doctor), used classic British understatement in describing what went wrong with the project. "The original idea was lovely," she said, "but somehow the film got blown all out of proportion." As the costs rose, the pressure to create a monster hit became almost unbearable, and in the end the studio executives had been blinded by groundless optimism. The original soundtrack album received the biggest initial pressing in history—even larger than *The Sound of Music.* Five hundred thousand records found their way into the stores some four months before the picture had been released, which explains why, to this day, so many *Doctor Dolittle* albums can be found in the $1.98 "cut-out" bins. All in all, six different versions of the full musical score with the original English lyrics were recorded and released in conjunction with the movie. In addition, five versions were prepared in Italian, four in French, three in German, and one each in Portuguese, Danish,

Swedish, Dutch, Flemish, and Japanese; but none in Pig, Dog, or Goat, despite Mr. Harrison's formidable linguistic accomplishments on screen. Such diverse artists as Sammy Davis, Jr., Tony Bennett, Jack Jones, Bobby Darin, Andy Williams, Dizzy Gillespie, and André Kostelanetz eventually tried their hands at versions of "Talk to the Animals" and other songs from the movie.

As if this musical assault weren't enough to make the galaxy Dolittle-conscious, the studio arranged a host of merchandising gimmicks that still hold the all-time record for intensity and tackiness. As Arthur Jacobs proudly declared, "Everyone, all the big companies, they want to do some kind of tie-in promotion. You won't be able to go into a store without seeing Doctor Dolittle advertising something." Among the products promoted by this immodest man of medicine were toys, greeting cards, kiddie apparel, cereal, furniture, school supplies, clocks and watches, yo-yos, ceramic ware, Pushmi-Pullyu cuff links and tie clasps, a Dolittle medicine kit, animal crackers, Doctor Dolittle chocolate soda, free toy animals inside each package of Shake-A-Pudding, and, of course, several varieties of Doctor Dolittle pet food. Then there was the "Talking Rex Harrison Doll," which said, "How do you do, I'm Doctor Dolittle" (By George, he's got it!) every time you pulled a string in its back. And for those children who could pull a string or two with their parents, a large, plush two-headed llama could be brought home for a mere $300.

This overpriced effigy of the Pushmi-Pullyu should be remembered as the stuffed animal equivalent of the Edsel, since none of the merry merchandising— nor even the nine Academy Award nominations it ultimately received—could rescue the film at the box office. Mixed-to-negative reviews, along with deadly word-of-mouth reports, helped kill the movie's business after its promising opening. As Arthur Jacobs reported, trying a bit of understatement himself, "It didn't work out the way we'd hoped it would work. I suppose it wasn't sophisticated enough for the older group." After two years in America's movie houses, *Doctor Dolittle* managed to generate only $9 million in revenue—or less than half its original cost.

The *Dolittle* disaster proved little more than a temporary setback to the peripatetic Arthur Jacobs, who continued to devote full energy to his self-appointed mission of creating "quality films for the whole family." In 1969 he produced another expensive musical flop—the $9 million version of *Goodbye, Mr. Chips* starring Peter O'Toole and Petula Clark. Before his sudden death at age fifty-one in 1973, how-

Geoffrey Holder (left, in shells and diaper) gives William Dix, Samantha Eggar, Rex Harrison, and Anthony Newley a foretaste of the critical response to Doctor Dolittle.

ever, Jacobs had succeeded in developing the highly profitable *Planet of the Apes* series, the achievement for which he is probably best remembered today. In these films, he could indulge his interest in communication between human beings and other creatures by presenting highly literate primates from the future and concentrating on gorilla suits and special makeup effects rather than on sinking ducks, mechanical sea snails, or giraffes with whiplash. If he ever felt nostalgia for the good old days, he could have enjoyed a meal of animal crackers on his full set of Doctor Dolittle ceramic ware, or else pulled the string on his talking Rex Harrison doll. Quoth the doctor: "Nevermore!"

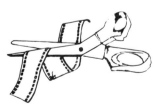

THE BLUE BIRD

(1976)

Twentieth Century-Fox
Produced by Paul Maslansky
Directed by George Cukor
Screenplay by Alexis Kapler, based on the play by Maurice Maeterlinck

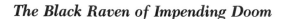

Starring Elizabeth Taylor ("Mother," "Light," "The Witch," "Maternal Love");
Jane Fonda ("Night"); Cicely Tyson ("Cat"); Ava Gardner ("Luxury");
George Cole ("Dog"); Oleg Popov ("Laughter"); Todd Lookinland (Tyltyl); Patsy Kensit (Mytyl);
Robert Morley ("Father Time"); Will Geer ("Grandfather");
Mona Washbourne ("Grandmother"); Richard Pearson ("Bread");
Nadezhda Pavlova ("The Blue Bird"); and Jerry Mathers as "The Beaver."

The Black Raven of Impending Doom

In 1910 the children's play *The Blue Bird*, by Belgian mystic Maurice Maeterlinck, became a major international hit. Its sentimental symbolism charmed adult audiences while the kiddies delighted in watching actors dressed as cats, dogs, and loaves of bread walking around the stage and making fools of themselves. The year after the play's premiere, its author received the Nobel Prize for literature, making *The Blue Bird*—which was easily his most popular and accessible work—well-nigh irresistible to filmmakers. In 1918, Paramount hired the talented Maurice Tourneur to direct the first movie version of Maeterlinck's celebrated drama, and the result was a resounding box office failure. The naive and simplistic conceits that seemed endearing on the stage looked utterly ridiculous on the big screen, but this did not prevent Hollywood from trying again with the same material. This next attempt came in 1940, with Shirley Temple as the little girl on a fantasy quest for true happiness, in a lavish production intended as Darryl Zanuck's answer to *The Wizard of Oz*. As production head at Twentieth Century-Fox, Zanuck had refused to "loan" Miss Temple to MGM for the role of Dorothy, and he wanted to justify that decision by starring her in a "class" children's fantasy that would soon make the children of America forget all about that foolish nonsense with scarecrows, tin woodsmen, and cowardly lions. The resulting *Blue Bird* never got off the ground; critics described it as "hideous kitsch" or a "sad embarrassment to all concerned," and despite the studio's great expectations it proved to be little Shirley's first-ever flop.

In view of this melancholy history, it should have been obvious to everyone that Maeterlinck's Blue Bird of Happiness was, for the movie business, a black raven of impending doom. Nevertheless, in the late 1960s this problem property turned up once again, this time as the basis for an historic development in the history of motion pictures: the first Russian-American co-production. "Expensive movies are sometimes made for strange reasons," *Time* magazine observed. "Quality often has little to do with it. Great amounts of time and huge sums of money are lavished on what Hollywood likes to call 'a project' just because a star was 'available.' *The Blue Bird* belongs to this category, although tangentially. It is probably the first movie in history made because a country was available."

A Division of Responsibility

Needless to say, Russia's availability did not come without a struggle. Negotiations dragged on for three years before the Soviets at last agreed to go along with the plans of producer Edward Lewis (*Spartacus, Seven Days in May*) for a joint venture with Twentieth Century-Fox. Lewis had recently shot *The Fixer* on location in Hungary, and after this intriguing experience behind the Iron Curtain, he was convinced that producing a film in Russia (with, presumably, the enthusiastic approval of the authorities) would not only be good business but would also make a significant contribution to international understanding. This, after all, was the era of détente, with Henry Kissinger and other U.S. officials encouraging link-ups in space and other co-operative projects with the

Elizabeth Taylor played a quadruple role in **The Blue Bird,** *displaying her abundant acting abilities as "Mother," "Light," "Maternal Love," and "The Witch." Here, director George Cukor anoints his versatile star to show his approval of the way in which the makeup department has transformed her for her impersonation of a nasty witch.*

Soviet Union. From their side, the Russians showed more interest in Marlon Brando than in Henry Kissinger, and when Lewis promised them that the great American star would be part of the production package, he finally managed to clinch the deal. With all of the high-level diplomacy involved in these bilateral maneuvers, the choice of Maeterlinck's play as the basis for the new film came almost as an afterthought. Both the American and Russian producers wanted something light and nonpolitical—which meant that they must avoid all descriptions of real life in either of the two countries. So it was they chose a story that takes place entirely in "The Great Forest," "The Garden of Happiness," "The Palace of Night," "The Land of Memory," and other noncontroversial localities. *The Blue Bird* also had the advantage of well-established popularity in the Soviet Union, where it had been treasured as a classic by several generations of children, and the producers felt certain that after the film's release, Maeterlinck's story would become equally well known in the United States.

The plans called for a division of responsibility between the Russian and American production teams. The Soviets would provide crews, sets, locations, costumes, extras, supporting players, and logistical assistance. In return, the Yanks were supposed to come through with top-quality western film stock, the most technologically advanced U.S. equipment, and Marlon Brando. Though it may seem unpatriotic to report it here, the fact is that the Americans were the first ones to drop the ball. When the much-heralded equipment arrived in Leningrad, the disappointed locals discovered only two battered Mitchell cameras, vintage 1955. Even more devastating was the news that the great Brando, in what surely must stand as one of the wisest moves of his career, had decided that he would pass up the chance for a few months in Leningrad working on a kiddie musical. At this point, the Russian filmmakers wanted to nominate producer Edward Lewis for the singular honor of a KGB-sponsored vacation in Siberia, but the wily American eventually appeased them by delivering the sort of big-name Hollywood talent that the starstruck Communists so desperately wanted. In fact, the leading player in *The Blue Bird* was the one international star even more extravagant, overweight, and temperamental than Brando himself—Miss Elizabeth Taylor.

Our old friend, the reigning queen of cinematic excess, agreed to participate in the project because it gave her the chance to display her abundant talents in four different roles: as the mother of the two children at the center of the action, as an evil witch, and as the embodiments of "Maternal Love" and "Light." Before shooting began, Miss Taylor told the press that she planned to adopt a novel approach to this last-named role. "Light can't be saccharine or a Girl Scout leader," she declared. "In the play, she's a goddamn bore, but she will not be a goddamn bore the way I play her. I think I'll put in a few swear words. Everybody's got the wrong image of the film. Give 'em a little cleavage. We can spritz it up."

Miss Taylor's distinctive approach to the screenplay only added to the general confusion that already prevailed. In dividing tasks between the Russian and American production teams, the moguls behind the mess had forgotten about the small matter of a script, so each side proceeded to employ its own writer. The predictable result was two sharply contrasting screenplays that had to be reconciled as the project progressed. The Russian writer Alexis Kapler, a sensitive artist who had spent ten years in Stalin's labor camps, ultimately drew sole credit for the screenplay, but repudiated the producers' changes in his work as an act of "butchery."

These alterations stemmed in part from a desire to accommodate the American celebrities who had committed themselves to the picture. In addition to Miss Taylor, Jane Fonda was on hand to play "Night" (a sexy version of Margaret Hamilton's "Wicked Witch of the West" in *The Wizard of Oz*); Ava Gardner portrayed the lusty hedonist "Luxury"; Cicely Tyson enacted "Cat" (though she insisted that her script designation and costume switch the character from a bad-luck black feline to a homey brown Burmese); and James Coco, adorned in a costume that appeared to have been borrowed from the Milk-Bone dog biscuit commercials, co-starred as "Dog." Popular Russian dancers and actors, meanwhile, handled the challenging roles of "Water," "Fire," "Milk," and "Sugar," though judging from their performances they all would have been better cast as "Ham." Will Geer (of *The Waltons* fame) traveled to the Soviet Union for one big scene (as "Grandfather") in which he sings a song about how boring it is to be dead. To play Tyltyl and Mytyl, the Russian answer to the ever-popular Hansel and Gretel, the production engaged American Todd Lookinland and the British child star Patsy Kensit. The script, however, made no attempt to explain why these two children, who supposedly grew up as brother and sister in the same hut in Mother Russia, spoke in such sharply contrasting accents: one, a mushy California mumble, and the other a precise and high-toned English squeal. Promotional materials for the production described a "stellar international cast," but the highly varied group gathered in Leningrad actually amounted to an ill-assorted menagerie in the style of *Doctor Dolittle*.

Inevitable Chaos

To preside over the inevitable chaos, the producers chose the aging director George Cukor, whose previous credits included such classic films as *Dinner at Eight* (1933), *Camille* (1936), *The Philadelphia Story* (1940), *Born Yesterday* (1950), *A Star Is Born* (1954), and *My Fair Lady* (1964). Cukor had overcome difficult production challenges in the past, but no one had prepared him for the disastrous situation that he discovered after he arrived in Russia. The all-Soviet crews that were supposed to carry out the director's instructions did not understand a word of English, and the interpreters who had been assigned to the set had a difficult time translating the terms used in technical work. Moreover, it soon became apparent that in movie technology, at least, the Russians were

Elizabeth Taylor (left) and Ava Gardner play an elegant game of pattycake while comparing notes on Hollywood dentistry during a break in filming of The Blue Bird.

years, if not decades, behind prevailing Hollywood standards. As Cukor recalls, "The first word I learned in Russian was *problema*." One major *problema* centered around head cinematographer Jonas Gricius, the award-winning cameraman from the famous Russian film of *Hamlet*. Everyone agreed on his artistic talent, but it turned out that he had never before used color film in his life. The strange red flush emanating from Liz Taylor and other leading characters reflected the inexperience of Gricius even more than the embarrassment of the actors, and eventually the producers demoted the Russian to the second unit crew and sent for Englishman Freddie Young (*Lawrence of Arabia, Dr. Zhivago*) to take over primary camera responsibility. In retaliation, the Soviets fired the British publicist from the film and replaced him with one of their own.

Other changes caused more serious problems. James Coco found the Russian food all but inedible, confined himself to a diet of bread and butter, and then gained so much weight that he could barely squeeze into his doggie costume. Eventually he suffered a gall bladder attack and had to abandon the picture, leaving his completed scenes to be reshot by his replacement, George Cole. Not to be upstaged by someone else's illness, Queen Elizabeth decided to make *Blue Bird* an official Liz Taylor blockbuster by developing a major illness all her own. Steven Spielberg's E.T. may have become sick from looking at his

"Cat" (Cicely Tyson, in ruffles and pointed ears) naturally formed a close relationship with "Night" (Jane Fonda). Ms. Fonda seemed to adjust more comfortably to the Russian location than other cast members of **The Blue Bird.** *As one Soviet cameraman recalled their conversations, "I never thought I'd hear Lenin quoted to me from an American."*

phone bill, but the original E.T. (Elizabeth Taylor) came down with a nice case of amoebic dysentery, flew to London for treatment, and held up shooting for two weeks.

Of all the picture's stars, Jane Fonda felt the greatest enthusiasm about working in Russia. She made the trip with her husband, Tom Hayden, and their son, Troy, in tow and enjoyed sharing profound political insights with Russian journalists, including the declaration at one of her press conferences that "It is not the Soviet Union where civil liberties are most infringed, but South Vietnam." Some of the Russian crew members found themselves not merely surprised but astonished at Miss Fonda's clear understanding of the humane and enlightened aspects of the Soviet system. "I never thought I'd hear Lenin quoted to me from an American," said cameraman Gricius.

Ava Gardner also managed a relatively smooth transition to life behind the Iron Curtain. One night

she disappeared without warning, causing a panic among all other participants in a production that was already several months behind schedule. She was found in the small hours of the morning in a local nightclub, dancing with the cabdriver who had brought her there. She explained that she had a sudden urge to cut a rug and couldn't find anyone from the film community willing to go dancing with her. Cooler heads from the production finally persuaded her to dance on back to her hotel room, and she dutifully appeared for work the next day, presumably refreshed from her night on the town.

Cicely Tyson, meanwhile, had serious problems of her own. "There was no one in Russia who could do my hair," she recalled, and when she returned to the States, it was in such sorry shape that she decided to shave her head. The population of Leningrad included less than a *minyan* of blacks, so the production had to use a white woman as Miss Tyson's stand-in during the tedious lighting setups. "They light everything for her and then I'm expected to go through the same paces with the same lighting," the star complained. "Naturally, my black skin disappears on the screen. You can't see me at all." This unpleasant situation contributed to the ongoing feud between Miss Tyson and George Cukor, which finally reached such an unpleasant intensity that the great director accused her publicly of practicing Haitian voodoo against him. Not even the most potent form of witchcraft, however, could have sufficed to render the production such an utter shambles or to have provoked the bitter complaints from virtually all the principals, which soon began appearing in the American press:

ELIZABETH TAYLOR: In five months I did about a week's work.

JAMES COCO: They tell us it will finish by August, but not by August of what year. I understand Elizabeth is having Christmas cards printed.

CICELY TYSON: I came to Russia with all the juices churned up ready to work, but there was one delay after another. . . . I feel as if I've spent half my life here.

AVA GARDNER: Good parts just don't seem to come along for me anymore. At this rate I'll have to start looking for another interest. The trouble is I've forgotten how to type.

IRWIN KOSTAL, American composer: This is a ship of fools. I've got a fight with Andrei Popov, the Soviet composer, every day. He wants me off the picture . . . The problem is, he wants to write American jazz, and I want Volga boatmen music.

JANE FONDA: Things happen or don't happen on occasions that seem totally arbitrary. It doesn't matter what scene you're in the middle of . . . At 5:30 every day the plug gets pulled.

GEORGE CUKOR: A whole idiotic literature has grown

"Father Time" (Robert Morley) gives "Light" (Liz Taylor) and Tyltyl and Mytyl (Todd Lookinland and Patsy Kensit) the bad news that The Blue Bird *is hopelessly behind schedule. As James Coco (who played "Dog" before suffering a gall bladder attack) told the press: "They tell us it will finish by August, but not by August of what year."*

up about this film. I've had and continue to have a marvelous time, and the entire experience has been entirely stimulating. On the whole, however, I wish I was home.

One American who did get the chance to go home early was producer Edward Lewis, fired from the project that he himself had created and replaced by a Twentieth Century-Fox company man, Paul Maslansky. By the time the new producer came aboard, work on the picture had been suspended altogether, and it started up again only because Liz Taylor remained enthusiastic about the project. "She was terrific," Maslansky recalled, and cited her expenditure of more than $8,000 of her own money to buy additional costumes for her four roles in the film.

All in all, the finished movie turned out to be more fun that a barrel of blue birds—and the script, in fact, called for 1,000 of these feathered friends as part of the climactic scene in "The Garden of Happiness." When a call to the Commissar of Central Casting failed to turn up even a single available blue bird in the vicinity of Leningrad, producer Maslansky resolved to make other arrangements. He gave emergency orders to his Russian colleagues to locate more than 1,000 white pigeons and then to dye them blue. The makeup artists who faced the challenging task of applying nontoxic paint to the feathers of each of these aviary extras deserved the gratitude of all those concerned with the production, but instead they were questioned by the secret police assigned to the studio. Production manager Oleg Danilov recalls that the KGB officers added insult to injury by accusing the pigeon handlers of having eaten some of the choice fowl that had been purchased with government money. Though eventually cleared of these grievous charges, the birdmen of Leningrad must have wondered about the ultimate value of their efforts; when the film was released to the public, the critics treated *The Blue Bird* like an ordinary clay pigeon, despite the bright paint on its plumage.

Gruel and Syrup

The gala premiere took place in Washington on May 5, 1976, and the studio tried to suggest it was some sort of major patriotic event appropriate to the ongoing bicentennial festivities. The pretentious logo for the film showed Russian and American flags as the two wings of a creature that looked more like a dove of peace than a blue bird. The first-night audience included most of the Washington diplomatic corps, with the Iranian ambassador, Ardeshir Zahedi, winning the privilege of escorting Elizabeth Taylor. When asked their reactions to the film after the screening, these dignitaries diplomatically declined comment, except for the Mexican ambassador, who risked offending both superpowers by describing their joint effort as "poor."

The film then moved on to a festive opening in New York City, where anti-Soviet activists marred the proceedings with threats of violence. The police department offered protection to the debut crowd, but they could not defend the film against the attacks of leading reviewers, who proved far more destructive than any bomb-throwing radicals:

"If you have any naughty children you want to punish, take them to *The Blue Bird* and make them sit all the way through it."   —WILLIAM WOLF, *Cue*

"The film could just as easily have been shot in Hoboken . . . What we have is a mostly overweight movie spectacle with some awful pop songs that wouldn't have gotten beyond the front gate at the Disney Studios . . . The bore of the year to date."

—VINCENT CANBY, *New York Times*

"*The Blue Bird* turns a work for adults that children can enjoy into a charade for children that must sicken adults."   —JOHN SIMON, *New York*

"Senile and interminable."

—STEPHEN FARBER, *New West*

"A bowl of gruel and syrup."

—PENELOPE GILLIATT, *The New Yorker*

"The movie gives evidence of being heavily edited, probably in a Cuisinart. A lot of individual shots do not match. Once in a while someone breaks into song . . . Elizabeth Taylor, Ava Gardner and Jane Fonda camp it up like movie queens on an overseas press junket."

—JAY COCKS, *Time*

"A mixture of Soviet ineptitude and the American belief that the grotesque expenditure of dollars can set anything a-right."   —*London Daily Express*

The grotesque expenditure referred to above was officially (and very conservatively) estimated at $12 million, though it probably amounted to much more. The Soviet Union, which paid most of the cost, has declared all specific figures concerning *The Blue Bird* to be a state secret. It is hardly surprising that a nation that covers up news of airline disasters or unsuccessful space shots should try to pretend that this disastrous motion picture never existed. The Soviets did make a brief attempt to release *The Blue Bird* in

Russia and other Eastern bloc countries, but tepid audience response led to quick withdrawal of the film and the authoritative word that the project would henceforth become an unmentionable subject. Twentieth Century-Fox, with a security apparatus notably less efficient than that of the Russian state, allowed *Variety* to publish the dismal information that the film grossed only $887,902 in American rentals. While licking its financial wounds, the studio decided that it would not even attempt a British release of its "historic" property and jettisoned plans for the next Soviet-American co-production. This second project, *Sea Pup*, described the adventures of a baby seal who befriends Russian and American families in the area of Puget Sound; the mercy killing of this seagoing mammal before production began drew no protests from environmental activists or anyone else. To date, no one has been foolhardy enough to even attempt another joint movie project involving Russia and the U.S.

In analyzing the wretched failure of *The Blue Bird*, Soviet production manager Danilov (who has since made his way to the United States) sagely commented that when filming began "no one noticed that something important was missing: someone to take actual command. There was a Soviet production unit, and an American unit, but there was no one with the power of decision over the whole production. Committee rule seemed to be *the* rule, a situation that never really changed." The old saying has it that a horse designed by committee ends up as a camel; in this case, a blue bird designed by committee ended up as a turkey.

This creature's uncontested status as a flightless fowl—despite all the uplifting good intentions about Soviet-American co-operation—leads naturally to the next exhibit in the Hall of Shame, where we can view the earthbound wrecks of those films that attempted to rise to the loftiest and most elevated subjects of all. . . .

Cicely Tyson ("Cat"), Patsy Kensit (Mytyl), Liz Taylor ("Light"), Todd Lookinland (Tyltyl), George Cole ("Dog"), Yevgeny Scherbakov ("Fire"), Georgy Nitzin ("Sugar"), Richard Pearson ("Bread"), Margareta Terechova ("Spilt Milk") and Valentina Ganibalova ("Water"), all await guidance during a key scene in The Blue Bird. *As the Russian production manager recalled: "There was a Soviet production unit, and an American unit, but there was no one with the power of decision over the whole production."*

PROPHETS
ANDLOSSES

HOLLYWOOD'S consistent interest in religious themes has always had less to do with God than it has with Mammon. Over the years, spectacular hits such as *King of Kings* (1927), *The Sign of the Cross* (1932), *Samson and Delilah* (1949), *The Robe* (1953), *The Ten Commandments* (1956), and *Ben-Hur* (1959) left a lasting impression on the industry. Cynical producers came to believe that "inspirational" subject matter in and of itself was enough to guarantee that the faithful would flock to their local theatres. If you were going to tell The Greatest Story Ever Told, so the saying went, it didn't matter whether you produced The Greatest Picture Ever Made; Jesus was the real star of the piece, and He had a long history of proven drawing power.

In spite of this widely shared assumption, numerous sandals-and-saviors sagas have proven, time and again, that the hoary and holy formula is far from foolproof. For one thing, it costs big money to buy all those flowing robes, fake beards, and special-effects miracles; religious pictures traditionally turn out to be among the most expensive products of the major studios. The first notable bomb in the history of American movies—D. W. Griffith's *Judith of Bethulia*—told the Biblical story of Judith and Holofernes. It earned back only a small portion of its unprecedented budget of $25,000 in 1913, before its creator turned his attention to bigger and better things. Since those early years, many other uplifting epics have collapsed under their own weight, and nearly a dozen of them are listed in our compendium of disasters at the end of this book. The two most spectacular Failures of Faith in this history of Hollywood are, however, the two films on display in this wing of the museum. One of them—*The Greatest Story Ever Told*—followed a familiar and well-worn path to critical and box office Calvary. The other—*Mohammad: Messenger of God*—attempted to blaze a new trail by exploiting a major religion that previously had been all but ignored by movieland's moguls. After this film's release, the world's Muslims could take at least some perverse pride in its fate: it managed in the end to establish itself as a financial fiasco every bit as memorable as any of its Christian predecessors.

THE GREATEST STORY EVER TOLD

(1965)

United Artists
Produced and directed by George Stevens
Screenplay by James Lee Barrett and George Stevens, based on the Books of the
Old and New Testaments, Other Ancient Writings, the Writings of Fulton Oursler and
Henry Denker, and in Creative Association with Carl Sandburg

Starring Max von Sydow (Jesus Christ); Carroll Baker (Veronica);
Pat Boone ("Young Man at the Tomb"); Victor Buono (Sorak); Richard Conte (Barabbas);
Joanna Dunham (Mary Magdalene); José Ferrer (Herod Antipas); Van Heflin (Bar Amand);
Charlton Heston (John the Baptist); Martin Landau (Caiaphas);
Angela Lansbury (Claudia); David McCallum (Judas Iscariot);
Roddy McDowall (Matthew); Dorothy McGuire (Mary); Sal Mineo (Uriah);
Nehemiah Persoff (Shemiah); Donald Pleasance ("The Dark Hermit");
Sidney Poitier (Simon of Cyrene); Claude Rains (Herod the Great); Telly Savalas (Pontius Pilate);
Joseph Schildkraut (Nicodemus); John Wayne ("The Centurion");
Shelley Winters ("Woman of No Name");
Ed Wynn (Old Aram);
Robert Blake (Simon the Zealot); John Considine (John); and Jamie Farr (Thaddaeus).

Bidding on the Bible

When mounting a cinematic version of the life of Jesus, one might have thought it would be possible to rely primarily on public domain material as a source for the story line; after all, Matthew, Mark, Luke, and John have been notoriously lax in guarding their rights to their original literary property during the last few millennia. Nevertheless, in 1954, when Twentieth Century-Fox began planning a Biblical blockbuster with the modest and unassuming title *The Greatest Story Ever Told*, they first paid $100,000 for the privilege of adapting a recent novel for the big screen. The beneficiaries of this studio largesse were a senior *Reader's Digest* editor named Fulton Oursler and his associate, the immortal Henry Denker. The two gentlemen had begun cashing in on *The Greatest Story Ever Told* back in 1947 by creating a popular radio show under that name that recounted the events of the Gospels in the style of a serialized soap opera. In a triumph of creative padding, they managed to stretch their account of the Man from Galilee into more than 500 half-hour episodes, which ran without fail, once a week, between

1947 and 1957, a period substantially longer than Christ's reported ministry on earth. Having found they could make a good thing of the Good Book, Oursler and Denker proceeded to turn their radio show into a novel, which topped best-seller lists in 1949 and ultimately sold more than 3 million copies. With this sort of demonstrated popular appeal, further adaptations seemed inevitable. During the early fifties, Otto Preminger talked of producing and directing a Broadway stage version of *Greatest Story*, while irreverent wags suggested that he might approach Frederick Loewe to write the music and then call the show *My Fair Jesus*. In any event, Twentieth Century-Fox finally prevailed over the other studios bidding on the property and acquired the rights to the novel and radio show in order to churn out a logical successor to its smash hit, *The Robe* (1953). Studio chief Darryl F. Zanuck at first announced that he would "personally assume charge of the production," but perhaps sober reflection on his experience with *Noah's Ark* (q.v.) some thirty years before persuaded him to reconsider. With Zanuck more or less out of the picture, Philip Dunne seemed a logical choice to write and direct the incipient epic; he had achieved

Director George Stevens supervises the Lord's work, while supported by Jesus Christ (Max von Sydow) and John the Baptist (Charlton Heston).

considerable success in the field of religious spectaculars as the screenwriter for *David and Bathsheba* (1952), *The Robe* (1953), and *Demetrius and the Gladiators* (1954). At first, Dunne considered the challenging new assignment but later backed out with the explanation, "I simply didn't feel qualified to put words in the mouth of One whom hundreds of millions devoutly believe to be their Savior." Dunne's departure left Twentieth Century-Fox waiting for a savior of their own; the studio was stuck with a very expensive property that no one, it seemed, wanted to touch. Deliverance finally arrived in the person of veteran director George Stevens: he agreed to accept the burden of the already-troubled project in return for full and unfettered creative control of every aspect of the production (including promotion and publicity) and a personal fee of $1 million.

Visitors to the Hollywood Hall of Shame will no doubt remember Stevens as the same master filmmaker who led Liz Taylor and Warren Beatty through the wasteful motions of *The Only Game in Town*—thus making him the only director in movie history to be honored with two different films on display in the main corridors of our museum. It would be unfair to allow these twin disasters—both products of the last stages of Stevens' illustrious career—

to interfere with our appreciation of this man's overall achievement during forty-one years of making movies. Certainly, the director who created such memorable films as *Swing Time* (1936), *Gunga Din* (1939), *A Place in the Sun* (1951), *Shane* (1953), and *Giant* (1956) should not be dismissed as a lightweight. It must be noted, however, that the same basic approach that contributed mightily to Stevens' successes helped make him uniquely qualified to turn out overstuffed turkeys with wildly inflated budgets. From the beginning, this particular director would never settle for a single take. He would shoot even trivial scenes in his movies a half-dozen different ways, then combine the various versions in the editing room in order to create a complex and artful cinematic surface. As his career progressed and he began to take himself more and more seriously, this policy of "shooting everything that moves" became an essential part of the Stevens style and won the director considerable praise from his colleagues; at a dinner meeting of the Directors Guild, one of his friends and admirers proudly declared that "his initials reversed are S.G.—Screen Greatness." With these pretensions of profundity, Big George seemed a logical choice for the grand and glorious project known as *The Greatest Story*.

The Gospel According to Saint George

As he began working on preproduction details, Mr. Screen Greatness insisted that his new movie would be substantially different from any previous religious picture; he would never settle for a lackluster run-of-De-Mille presentation. "This will be a Biblical classic that has vigor in ideas," he told the press, "with no souped-up spectacles, no sword fights, no bacchanalian orgies . . . the slightest narrative with no embellishments. . . . The picture's significance will be in its words, its emotions and in the beauty and movement of its people." With this goal in mind, Stevens paid particularly close attention to the script. Before he even set to work on drafting the screenplay (along with his collaborator James Lee Barrett) he reviewed thirty-six different translations of the New Testament and compiled a giant reference book with clippings from each of them. In addition, he commissioned French artist André Girard to prepare 352 oil paintings illustrating Biblical scenes as a "facet of further study." Stevens continued this crash course by arranging "consultations" with thirty-six leading Protestant ministers and winning a personal audience with Pope John XXIII. Taking care to cover absolutely all his bases, he even discussed the script with David Ben-Gurion, though it remains unclear what, precisely, the Israeli prime minister could contribute to a project on the life of Jesus.

Despite the involvement of these various world-renowned personalities and his slow but steady progress in preparing a screenplay, Stevens still felt daunted at the prospect of penning dialogue for the Man from Nazareth Himself. Had this been a normal big studio project, the producer-director would have hired an old Hollywood hand as "script doctor" to help him over the rough spots, but writing lines for Jesus seemed even more problematic than writing them for Brando. In desperation, Stevens turned to the celebrated poet Carl Sandburg—perhaps thinking that a writer who had crafted several best-sellers out of the life of Abraham Lincoln, America's most Christlike president, would be a perfect choice to script dialogue for Jesus Christ, the Holy Land's most Lincolnesque savior. Sandburg's contributions to the finished product led to a screen credit more complex—and entertaining—than the script itself: viewers of *The Greatest Story* who bothered to read the opening titles would learn of a

Screenplay by James Lee Barrett and George Stevens, based on the Books of the Old and New Testaments, Other Ancient Writings, the Writings of Fulton Oursler and Henry Denker, and in Creative Association with Carl Sandburg.

Perhaps Stevens went to such great lengths to list all of these various sources so that blame for the final script could be widely shared. As it is, one can never be sure whether it is Mr. Sandburg, Mr. Denker, Mr. Barrett, or those intriguing "Other Ancient Writings" that should be held responsible for dialogue such as this witty repartee between The Messiah and John the Baptist:

JOHN THE BAPTIST: Who are you? I know you not, yet I know you.
JESUS CHRIST: Baptize me, John.
J.T.B.: What is your name?
J.C.: Jesus.
J.T.B.: Of what?
J.C.: Of Bethlehem.
J.T.B.: You are He! The One we've been waiting for!

Later in the film, when the Man of Men meets the teenaged James the Younger, one of his future apostles, He shows a similarly folksy approach:

JESUS CHRIST: What is your name, my friend?
JAMES THE YOUNGER: James. Little James. They call me "Little" because I'm the youngest. What is yours?
J.C.: Jesus.

JAMES: Ah, that's a good name!
J.C.: Thank you!

After reading such drivel and reviewing the general progress of their Biblical behemoth, the executives at Twentieth Century-Fox wisely decided to cut their losses and to drop the entire project. They had already spent $2.3 million, though Stevens had yet to shoot so much as a single frame of film, and the studio—deep in the throes of its *Cleopatra* debacle—simply could not afford indefinite funding of Big George's religious ecstasy. Carl Sandburg, among others, condemned their decision to the nation's press and described the big shots responsible for it as "horses' necks"—obviously deciding that "necks" sounded more poetic than the humble and familiar aspect of the equine anatomy usually used to designate studio executives. "These are fellows, who, if they don't know what's going on, go on an economy binge," Sandburg railed. "I told George I'll stick—until the last dog is hung, or until the last Roman soldier has shoved in his spear with a sponge on it."

Much to the relief of the white-thatched poet and his associates, even before the last dog was hung, fools rushed in where moguls feared to tread. Stevens began raising money on his own to keep the project alive, and the generally positive response from major investors encouraged United Artists to pick up the rights to *Greatest Story*. As part of a complicated deal involving Stevens' own production company, U.A. agreed to take over funding of the inspirational extravaganza and promised Twentieth Century-Fox that the latter studio would have its original investment returned as soon as the picture registered a total profit (ha ha!) in excess of $5 million. The various parties to this new arrangement signed contracts late in 1961 amid much cheerful speculation that the finished film would emerge as "the top grossing film in the history of United Artists."

The Second Coming

Following the timely resurrection of his brainchild, Stevens spent six weeks with three assistants scouting locations in Europe and the Middle East. Unfortunately, none of these sites seemed "lush" or "dramatic" enough to suit the director's conception of Biblical landscape, so he decided that Jesus didn't belong in Israel after all. "I wanted to get an effect of grandeur as a background to Christ," he explained to the press, "and none of the Holy Land areas shape up with the excitement of the American Southwest . . . I know the Colorado is not the Jordan, nor is Southern

Utah Palestine . . . But our intention is to romanticize the area, and it can be done better here." He admitted that shooting the film in the States would cost "a lot more," since actors, extras, and technicians would all demand greater salaries, while camels, artifacts, and elaborate sets would have to be imported. "But we feel it's all worth it," Stevens concluded, "and it's a decision we were free to make." Under the terms of his contract he was, in fact, totally free to make any sort of numbskulled decision that happened to strike his fancy: Big George enjoyed the same sort of absolute authority exercised by D. W. Griffith on *Intolerance* and Michael Cimino on *Heaven's Gate,* and as in those other celebrated instances, this unfettered license contributed in a major way to the wildly indulgent spending on the project.

By the time Stevens began building his New Jerusalem in Arizona, *The Saturday Evening Post* had anointed his picture as "the most ambitious and expensive film ever to be shot in the United States . . . Such giants as *Cleopatra* and *Lawrence of Arabia* did boast bigger budgets, but they were shot on foreign soil." In the Spring of '62, U.A. officially increased its estimate of the projected final cost of the film from $6 to $10 million, but the actual budget rose to more than $20 million before *Greatest Story* finally lumbered to its conclusion.

In order to ensure that the movie would make a decent return on this enormous investment, Stevens secured the services of literally scores of well-known stars. According to the official studio publicity, most of these celebrities were inspired by the chance to work with "the great George Stevens" and to participate in a movie of universal and lasting importance. The United Artists press office declared, with a shy understatement consistent with a project entitled *The Greatest Story Ever Told,* that "virtually every actor and actress of stature in the motion picture industry came forward and offered his services as a member of the cast." Stevens himself added, "You can't imagine the people who have called me. . . . The stars themselves have called, not their agents. There's never been a word about money, although many of these people command a million dollars a picture. They don't ask for any specific role—they just want to be in the movie, no matter how small the part." With all these stars simply "falling on him," Stevens can hardly be blamed for taking advantage of the spontaneous meteor shower, but as a result of his willingness to accommodate the likes of Shelley Winters, José Ferrer, and Pat Boone, the finished picture resembles a Biblical *Around the World in Eighty Days* or an ABC-TV Celebrity Sports Tournament. It is impossible for those watching the film to avoid the

While his costume might be more suited for **Alley-Oop** *or* **One Million Years** B.C., *Charlton Heston is actually supposed to impersonate John the Baptist in* **The Greatest Story Ever Told.** *Here, he practices his anointing techniques while director Stevens kneels with appropriate humility.*

merry game of "Spot the Star," and the road to Calvary in particular comes to resemble the Hollywood Boulevard "Walk of Fame." As Jesus sweats under the crushing weight of the cross, Carroll Baker, star of *Baby Doll, Harlow,* and *The Carpetbaggers,* suddenly emerges from the crowd and offers him a drink of water. While watching this interlude, Van Heflin, Ed Wynn, and Sal Mineo pass the time by mugging various expressions showing suffering and horror. Eventually Sidney Poitier—apparently playing a long-ago beneficiary of some affirmative action scholarship to study Hebrew in ancient Jerusalem—steps forward and helps Christ for a few moments in carrying the cross. All the while, a solemn, craggy-faced, mini-skirted Roman centurion wields a primitive sort of cattle prod to keep the procession moving along. For most viewers, it takes several moments to recognize this incongruous figure as John Wayne, looking almost as uncomfortable here as he did in playing Genghis Khan in *The Conqueror.* After the crucifixion, Wayne turns to the camera and delivers his only spoken line, the movie's single most memorable moment. "Truly," drawls the Duke, "this man *wuz* the Son of Gawd!!"

In casting the more substantial roles in his film,

The Road to Calvary is decorated with nearly as many stars as the Hollywood Boulevard "Walk of Fame": from left to right, Dorothy McGuire, Sal Mineo, Jamie Farr (in shadow), Carroll Baker, and Van Heflin.

Stevens turned to a group of little-known actors who, through some bizarre coincidence or perhaps through divine intervention, all seemed to go on to become major TV personalities. Telly Savalas took the part of Pontius Pilate, though he judged Jesus without benefit of the lollipop he later adopted as part of his *Kojak* persona. Martin (*Mission: Impossible*) Landau played the villainous Caiaphas, David (*The Man from U.N.C.L.E.*) McCallum sneered his way through the part of Judas Iscariot, while Robert (*Baretta*) Blake provided loyal service as one of Christ's apostles. It may also be possible that the flowing robe worn by Jamie Farr as the apostle Thaddaeus helped him develop the taste for feminine garb that he later indulged in to the fullest as the transvestite Klinger in *M*A*S*H.* At this rate, Stevens might have selected Jan Clayton, "Lassie's Mother" on the old TV series, to play the part of the Virgin Mary, but instead he chose Dorothy McGuire. Her maternal credentials certainly seemed in order: she had portrayed Tommy Kirk's mom in *Old Yeller* (1957) and Troy Donahue's mom in *A Summer Place* (1959), so she seemed a natural choice as The Mother of God.

This left only the very formidable problem of casting the role of The Man Himself. After his experience as Moses in *The Ten Commandments* and in the title role of *Ben-Hur*, Charlton Heston would have been the most obvious choice, but Stevens said that he wanted to avoid the obvious. He still man-

aged to satisfy Heston's many fans by throwing their boy the plum supporting role of John the Baptist, while remaining undecided on an actor for the Part of Parts. As speculation mounted, gossip naturally centered around Hollywood's biggest stars, including Burt Lancaster, Rock Hudson, Paul Newman, and Marlon Brando—though no one suggested Frank Sinatra, Jerry Lewis, or Elvis Presley for The Role, despite their presence on the list of top ten box office attractions. Stevens eventually declared his intention to cast an unknown who would remain free of secular and unseemly associations in the mind of the public. With this in mind, he turned to the Swedish actor Max von Sydow, who had won rave reviews for his performances in Ingmar Bergman's classic films, *The Seventh Seal* (1956), *The Virgin Spring* (1960), and *Through a Glass Darkly* (1961). He made his American debut in *Greatest Story*, and Stevens went to great lengths to create an air of mystery about his star. He prevented reporters from interviewing the Man Who Would Be Christ during the course of production and, as with Steven Spielberg's messianic *E.T.* some twenty years later, the director would not permit photographs of von Sydow in his shoulder-length Jesus wig until after the film's release. The actor, meanwhile, concentrated on perfecting his English: unless he managed to eliminate his Scandinavian accent, audiences would be constantly reminded of the incongruity of a big, blond Swede standing in for a Palestinian Jew tromping inexplicably through the canyon lands of Arizona and Utah. The Swedish Savior did, in fact, achieve remarkable success in developing his spoken English, while the publicity department made much of the fact that "his age, at thirty-three, is precisely the same as that of Christ at the time of his crucifixion." Such "haunting coincidences," however, did not prevent Doubting Thomases among the critics from taking a rather dim view of his characterization. *Newsweek* reported that "he skulks around as he did in Bergman's *The Seventh Seal*, this time clad in white, rather than black, garb. He hardly varies his expression, which is mild suffering, as if he had a pebble in his sandal." Had this reviewer been present on location to witness the very real suffering of von Sydow and the rest of the cast, he would have understood that there were good reasons for these expressions of discomfort.

Welcome to Wahweap

When, after more than three years of plans and preparations, Stevens finally got down to the business of shooting film, he set up shop in the village of

Wahweap, Arizona, which was about fifteen miles from the bustling metropolis of Page. To accommodate a full-time cast and crew of more than 400, United Artists paid for the construction of 115 prefabricated aluminum cottages in a tract of vacant desert just outside of town. This rustic settlement soon became known as Fort George Stevens and served as headquarters for the wide-ranging production.

From the beginning, the veteran director had an especially difficult time with his crowd scenes; in this desolate corner of the Southwest, it was a major challenge to find the appropriate extras. At one point, Stevens hired 550 Navajo Indians from a nearby reservation to act in several crucial scenes as Roman legionnaires. Despite several weeks of work, these native Americans never mastered the "centurion march," and they eventually deserted the production to go home to vote in a tribal election. They were replaced by R.O.T.C. cadets from the high school in the town of Page, many of whom can be seen in the finished film, smiling sheepishly at the camera from beneath their full battle regalia.

By far the most convincing extras in the entire picture were the lame, disfigured, and blind lepers who seem to pop up everywhere in order to give Max von Sydow the chance to demonstrate His healing powers. These unfortunates were persuasive on camera precisely because they were, in real life, the genuine article—honest-to-goodness amputees and other cripples, thoughtfully rounded up for the occasion by the Arizona Department of Welfare. When the imported charity cases arrived for work from Flagstaff, complete with their own squad of social workers and therapists (with transportation and salaries paid by United Artists), Stevens was delighted with their appearance but disappointed at their relatively small number. To create the hundreds of suffering cripples he wanted for his big miracle scenes, he offered several "normal" extras a bonus payment of five dollars a day to allow themselves to be disfigured by the makeup department so that they would blend in effectively with the hammy handicappers.

Stevens personally supervised this mixed multitude of amateur and professional actors using a handheld microphone that sent his stentorian tones, like the voice of God Himself, booming out against "the walls of Jerusalem." An elaborate replica of the ancient city had been constructed on a twenty-two-acre tract in Glen Canyon at a cost of more than $1 million. Before shooting began each day at this location, a courageous group of production assistants went to work to clear the set of rattlesnakes and Gila monsters, since these creatures might have looked

The role of Jesus is a heavy cross for any actor to bear—even one so manifestly talented as Max von Sydow. The Roman centurion to the right of the picture is John Wayne; having already humiliated himself playing Genghis Khan in The Conqueror, *he watches von Sydow's ordeal with little sympathy.*

somewhat out of place in ancient Judea. To make sure that none of the extras looked out of place, Stevens kept up a running stream of instructions and encouragement. Reporter William Trombley of *The Saturday Evening Post* witnessed the filming of the Palm Sunday scene and recorded some of Stevens' electronically amplified lines for posterity:

Good morning, folks . . . Let me tell you about this scene. You are seeing the first appearance of Jesus Christ the Lord. He mounted this little animal and rode into Jerusalem. You were the first people to see this—your faces should show wonder and awe. You can laugh and smile, but it's a strange kind of joy. Perhaps if it happened today, it is the look you would have if John Glenn landed here in his space capsule. Either expression will do—seeing Christ or John Glenn.

Later, while actually shooting the scene, Stevens bellowed forth further amplified exhortations:

Hosanna! All right, you people, this is JESUS CHRIST THE LORD! Show awe! Show awe! Hosanna, hosanna! Joy, you people in the foreground, joy! This is the Lord—wave, wave, run, folks, run! Hallelujah! Haaaaaa-lelujah! Cut!! Very good, folks. Now let's try it again.

These five little words—"now let's try it again"—were heard so often on location that they soon became the informal slogan for the entire production. Stevens had always been famous for shooting vast quantities of film and redoing even trivial scenes many times over, but on *Greatest Story,* this passion for perfectionism crossed the border into mad self-indulgence. For the Raising of Lazarus scene, for example, Stevens ordered more than thirty different camera setups and forced the actors through their paces twenty times. Veteran character actor John Considine, who played the apostle John, recalled that "the retakes were extraordinary—we progressed at an unbelievably slow pace. I only signed up for fifteen weeks on location, but I ended up staying for fifty-four. Most of the time my check for overtime would turn out to be more than my salary.

"With all the delays it got so bad that people were literally dying on the set. I remember one day in particular when our director of photography, William C. Mellor—who was Stevens' long-time collaborator and army buddy—was shooting a scene up on a huge boom. We were working away for hours and hours—as usual—when all of a sudden Mellor fell over and landed on the ground with a big thud. That was a horrible experience—the poor man just had a heart attack, fell over and died. At that point, Stevens took a break, walked over to the edge of the lake, folded his arms and looked out into the distance. It was a terrible blow to him. And then a few weeks later Joseph Schildkraut died before they were even done shooting his scenes. He was playing Nicodemus and they had to rewrite the script to work around him."

Other problems developed when, about halfway through the interminable production, the young British actress Joanna Dunham, who played the key role of Mary Magdalene, suddenly announced that she was pregnant. Despite the flowing robes provided by the costume department, her delicate condition became more and more apparent. While some of Stevens' associates urged that Miss Dunham should be replaced, Stevens decided to try to cover the embarrassing situation by using ingenious camera angles in her remaining scenes. "Well, that Mary Magdalene always was a troublemaker," he philosophically commented to *Variety.*

Joanna Dunham's example may have served as an inspiration to another member of the cast—one of the twenty-two dromedaries who had been imported from the Near East to lend color to the spectacle of Arizona. This seductive and amorous beast apparently became entangled in a liaison with one of its co-stars and eventually surprised the entire cast and crew by producing a healthy baby. As one technician observed, "This is the only picture ever made that

lasted long enough for a camel to conceive and give birth." The blessed event occurred just in time to make up for the loss of one of the older dromedaries, who had become so despondent over the endless retakes that he committed suicide by dashing his head against a desert cliff. Veterinarians speculated that the unfortunate creature may have become disoriented by the onset of cold weather—and in this he was not alone among the *Greatest Story* company.

Stevens' original plan had called for completion of his magnum opus by late fall, but as November rolled on into December the filming continued to run many months behind schedule, and no end was in sight. Like Napoleon in Russia, the great director found himself trapped by advancing winter with no avenue available for easy retreat. Temperatures dropped below freezing, and members of the cast, dressed in the sandals and tunics of ancient Judea, began suffering frostbite from the bitter cold. As one of the actors recounted his unhappy experience, "We would get there at eight in the morning, and it always took Stevens forever to set up his lights and cameras. Part of the problem was the season, because the set got no sun. It was freezing—maybe ten or fifteen degrees—but we would sit and shiver for two or three hours before they were ready to shoot. We started fires, but most of us caught colds or the flu anyway. The assistant directors were afraid Stevens might want somebody who wasn't there, and they would call everyone out." In this atmosphere, morale began to collapse and free-swinging brawls frequently erupted at the crowded mess hall back at Fort George Stevens.

The last straw, appropriately enough, fell from the heavens. Shortly after Christmas a fierce blizzard descended on Wahweap, piling huge snowdrifts against the Walls of Jerusalem. David Sheiner, who portrayed James the Elder, commented, "I thought we were shooting *Nanook of the North.*" The elaborate set faced the imminent danger of suffering irreparable damage. At the height of this crisis, an emergency meeting of the cast and the crew resolved to do whatever might be necessary to save the situation. Several hundred volunteers—including Big George himself and the good folks of Wahweap—braved the elements with shovels, wheelbarrows, bulldozers, and fifty butane flame throwers to remove the snow from the expensive replica of the Holy Land. *Variety* described this makeshift crew as "possibly the highest-salaried work gang in history"; two of the apostles suffered severe muscle strain from their exertions. It appeared for a few hours that these heroic efforts would succeed in clearing the set, but then, just when they thought it was safe to go back into the desert, it started snowing again with even greater fury than before. Reading this new misfortune as an unmistakable sign from above, Stevens ordered his production company to close up shop in Arizona, and to retreat to the relative comfort and safety of the Desilu Studios back in Hollywood.

At this point, a lesser man might have scaled down his expectations, but Stevens saw no reason why his California Holy Land should be any less grandiose than what he had abandoned to the hostile elements in Arizona. On a vast forty-acre back lot he proceeded to construct a complete replica of the ancient city of Jerusalem, including historic courtyards, the great Temple itself, and other structures. The *Los Angeles Times* enthusiastically proclaimed, "Hollywood has not known a set like this in years." With all these expensive new toys and with the U.A. executives finally running out of patience, Stevens tried to pick up the glacial pace of the production, learning to settle for eight to ten versions of every scene rather than his customary fifteen or twenty. When he finished in Hollywood, he returned to Wahweap in March to pick up some additional shots for the Palm Sunday sequence, then went on to Pyramid Lake, Nevada (standing in for the Sea of Galilee), Lake Moab, Utah (scene of the Sermon on the Mount), and Death Valley, California (where Jesus wandered forty days in the wilderness).

And lo, the Director saw that shooting had been completed, and George Stevens saw that it was good. He then disappeared into the editing room with his holy mountain of exposed film and emerged six months later with a final product with the astounding and intolerable running time of four hours and twenty minutes. As one worried studio observer commented after he emerged, blinking and yawning, from an early screening, "They should have called it *The LONGEST Story Ever Told.*"

Vengeance Is Mine, Sayeth the Critics

The gala world premiere of Stevens' cinematic sermon took place in Washington, D.C., under the official "patronage of the President of the United States and Mrs. Lyndon Johnson, the United Nations Association and the Eleanor Roosevelt Foundation." Many members of Congress, together with the ambassadors of most major nations, attended the great event, along with *Life* magazine's Shana Alexander, who commented, "Who but an audience of diplomats could sit through this thing? . . . As the picture ponderously unrolled, it was mainly irritation that

kept me awake." Ms. Alexander went on to report that "when intermission ended, everyone dutifully trudged back to his seat. Nobody, it seems, walks out on God . . . The turgid solemnity of Act Two was enlivened only by the gentle thud of heavy souvenir program books falling to the floor as the watchers drowsed."

With this sort of advance publicity, critics could hardly wait to get their hands on the film when it opened across the country. In a representative review, Brendan Gill wrote in *The New Yorker* that "if the subject matter weren't sacred in the original, we would be responding to the picture in the most charitable way possible by laughing at it from start to finish; this Christian mercy being denied us, we can only sit and sullenly marvel at the energy for which, for more than four hours, the note of serene vulgarity is triumphantly sustained." Bruce Williamson in *Playboy* succinctly described the movie as "a big windy bore."

In spite of the scathing reviews, the producers hoped that devout Christians across the country would come see the picture as a sort of sacred duty; but from the beginning, audience response was dismal. Two religious fanatics spoke for millions when they picketed *Greatest Story* outside the Los Angeles theatre at which it opened. They carried signs proclaiming, "WE AMERICANS DEMAND BETTER MOVIES!" and "PRODUCERS REPENT! THOU SHALT NOT KILL—WHY BUTCHER?"

By this time, the producers had no doubt already repented; reading box office returns, they probably wanted, like Pontius Pilate, to wash their hands of the whole bloody mess. In desperation, they ordered Stevens to begin cutting his Gargantuan Gospel down to manageable size, and the picture soon became *The Incredible Shrinking Greatest Story Ever Told.* U.A. quickly replaced the original four-hour-and-twenty-minute offering with a Revised Standard version that ran three hours fifty-eight minutes, and was in turn superseded by a United Kingdom release that lasted only three hours and seventeen minutes. Finally, the studio issued a lean, mean two-hour-and-twenty-seven-minute edition for neighborhood theatres, which remained, in the opinion of one of the editors who worked on it, "much too long. We had already taken out nearly two hours from the original, but for the most part that was easy. All we had to do was cut some of the endless scenes of people wandering back and forth, *ad nauseam*, across the desert. If you ask me, we could have cut a lot more." United Artists eventually came to agree with him, and, in the incarnation in which the movie is seen today (if at

John Wayne as "The Centurion" delivers only one line in The Greatest Story Ever Told. *Quoth the Duke: "Truly, this man wuz the Son of Gawd!!"*

all) it lasts a mere two hours, seven minutes—considerably less than half its initial length.

Despite all the frantic cutting and pasting, the studio executives, like True Believers, refused to abandon hope that their epic investment might someday pay off. In a press conference, U.A. president Arthur Krim admitted that the film would not make a profit in either '65 or '66 but predicted that over the long haul, "it would be seen by more people, over a longer period of time, than any other film in industry history." It would be, as Krim described it to skeptical reporters, "a very special—and very slow—play off."

Unfortunately, according to figures from trade publications, this special "play off" never played out. With its initial production cost of $20 million, plus additional editing and promotion charges, along with accumulated interest for delays in the picture's release, *Greatest Story* would have had to earn back at least $40 million for the studio in order to break even. As of 1983, it had grossed less than $8 million worldwide.

In the wake of this mammoth disaster, George Stevens deliberately positioned himself above all considerations of "mere" money. "The picture was not made for this year or next year," he announced to the press, "but for a long time. . . . It's hard for me to be objective with this film, but my interest in the film is for the 2000th anniversary of Christmas . . . I don't judge a film's success by money or critics, but by how long it lasts, how long it remains good. . . . I predict it will have more repetitions over the years than any picture made out here."

If "out here" meant to Stevens the specific locale

of Wahweap, Arizona, then Big George was undoubtedly correct; though *The Greatest Story Ever Told* has not exactly emerged as a popular favorite of the 1980s, it is, in fact, still seen from time to time. We happened to catch a showing during a recent one-week run at a Spanish-language theatre in the skid row district of downtown Los Angeles. For the occasion, the marquee proclaimed, *"La Historia Mas Grande Contada* con JOHN WAYNE!," ignoring the fact that the Duke delivered only one line (albeit an immortal one) in the entire picture. Perhaps the theatre owner assumed that his patrons (who paid $1.49 each for the privilege of enduring *Greatest Story* along with another inane fantasy-spectacle, *Clash of the Titans*) would be lulled into such a stupor by the narcoleptic double bill that they would blithely assume that the big fella up there on the screen playing Christ was actually John Wayne in heavy makeup.

As it turned out, most members of the ethnically mixed audience proved particularly attentive to the movie's dialogue (despite the fact that many of them read it in Spanish subtitles) and showed their appreciation of many lines with hearty and raucous laughter. During one particularly pretentious scene, Mary Magdalene (dressed, naturally, all in scarlet) is accused of adultery, and the elders decide that it's a good idea to stone her. Suddenly Max von Sydow in his long-haired wig strides scowling into the scene, bends toward the camera, and with a rock planted dramatically in his massive palm, stretches out his arm to the audience, intoning, "Let him among you who is without sin cast the first stone." At this point in the screening, a particularly enthusiastic member of the audience piped up from the darkness, "Shit, bro', give it here! *I'd* kill that bitch!" We needed no further proof that nearly twenty years after its release, *The Greatest Story Ever Told* still had a profound effect on audiences around the world.

Even more important has been its inspirational impact on other filmmakers. The movie served as an ideal target for an irreverent satire on Biblical epics, *Monty Python's Life of Brian* (1979), in which the Jesus figure, Brian, and his fellow "crucifixees" sing "Always Look on the Bright Side of Life" from Calvary. Of greater relevance for our purposes was the encouragement provided by this film (despite its disastrous fate at the box office) for a Syrian-American dreamer and visionary, who cited *Greatest Story* and other treatments of the life of Christ as a basis for feeling that his particular favorite, the Prophet Mohammad, deserved his own place on celluloid. His determination to win equal time for the Man from Mecca provided us with the next holy relic in our Museum of Mistakes. . . .

MOHAMMAD: MESSENGER OF GOD

(1977)

Tarik International Films
Produced and directed by Moustapha Akkad
Screenplay by H. A. L. Craig

Starring Anthony Quinn (Hamza); Michael Ansara (Abu-Sofyan); Irene Papas (Hind); Johnny Sekka (Bilal); Martin Benson (Abu-Jahal); and André Morell (Abu-Talib).

Impeccable Logic

On the morning of March 9, 1977, a small band of heavily armed black Muslims burst into the Washington, D.C., B'nai B'rith building with their guns blazing. When the smoke cleared, the guerrillas—members of the obscure and fanatical Hanafi sect—had taken more than 100 hostages and threatened to slaughter them all. After contacting the media by telephone, the invaders issued a series of eccentric demands, chief among them an impassioned plea for cancellation of the American premiere of the motion picture *Mohammad: Messenger of God.* Never before in the whole bizarre history of terrorism had the methods of a group of activists had so little apparent connection with their professed goals. Here was a group of devout Muslims, protesting a movie about the founder of their religion—a movie directed by a Syrian, shot in Morocco, and financed by the Libyan government—and, with impeccable logic, registering their objections by occupying the headquarters of the world's largest *Jewish* organization. In any event, the Hanafi raid in Washington made no less sense than many of the decisions behind planning and production of *Mohammad*—the very film that the terrorists went to such great lengths to protest. Leaving the innocent hostages in the hands of their crazed captors—for the time being, at least—let us consider for a moment the filmic fiasco that sparked such an energetic response and examine the checkered career of the man behind the mess.

Moustapha: Messenger of Schlock

Like most filmmakers whose work is on display in the Hollywood Hall of Shame, Moustapha Akkad is by nature a dreamer and a visionary. Born and raised in Syria, he set out for the United States as a teenager seeking fame, fortune, and immortality. Naturally, he settled in Los Angeles, where he won admittance to the film schools of U.C.L.A. and U.S.C. After graduation, he worked as a public affairs executive for CBS-TV and also claims to have served as production assistant on Sam Peckinpah's *Ride the High Country* (1962)—though no one connected with that picture seems to remember him nor did his name appear in any of the credits. Nevertheless, Akkad fancifully told the press, "my years with Sam were the most valuable experience I could ever have . . . I learned the real guts of the business from Peckinpah: Start at the top, not at the bottom, if you want to succeed."

Following this sage advice from his purported mentor, Moustapha (or Mous to his friends) formed his own company: the grandly titled Akkad International Productions. The new firm specialized in television documentary programs—with a special emphasis on the sort of informative and scintillating shows that air on local affiliate stations before eight o'clock on Sunday mornings. His principal achievement in this area was a short-lived series entitled *Cesar's World.* Early-bird viewers who rose eagerly to enjoy this show had the right to expect an historical glimpse of ancient Rome or, perhaps, a Sid Caesar comedy routine. Instead, they got a hefty dose of the "ageless and ever-popular" Cesar Romero, as host for a travelogue series featuring such exotic locales as Hunza and Addis Ababa. These presentations inspired very little appreciation from the viewing public, though Romero himself, whose only other gig at the time involved occasional appearances as "The Joker" on the *Batman* TV series, remained deeply grateful.

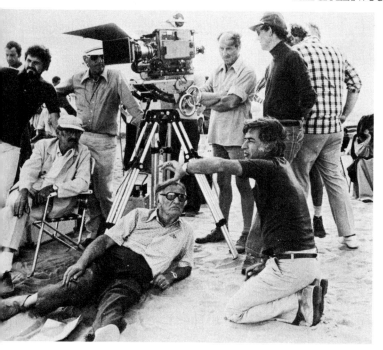

Producer-Director Moustapha Akkad (kneeling) describes his need for a broad cinematic canvas in order to contain his invisible Mohammad. Executive Production Consultant Andrew Marton (lying back in the sand) listens attentively, but is obviously exhausted from his job as director of the action scenes.

Undaunted by the lukewarm response to his "showcase" television project, Mous Akkad continued to nurse grandiose dreams for the future. In particular, he hoped to correct the abysmal ignorance of most Americans concerning the Muslim faith and its origins. "Here is a religion 700 million people believe in, yet not much is known about it in the West," he declared. For instance, historians have consistently conveyed the impression that followers of Islam have engaged from time to time in *jihad,* or holy war, involving the ruthless extermination of nonbelievers, but Akkad assured the public that these well-documented massacres never took place. "There is no case in history of *really* reckless killing in the name of Islam," he cheerfully declared. "Islam is a *very* tolerant religion." Later in the same interview, the fledgling filmmaker applied these historically tolerant principles to the current situation in the Middle East: "Israel? We should have been bloodier right from the beginning! In 1948 we should have stopped it all then."

Despite the difficulty of many Western observers in following the twists and turns of Akkad's Islamic logic, the producer felt certain that curious Americans would flock to their theatres to see a definitive and enlightening epic on the life of Mohammad. After all, the critical and commercial success of *Lawrence of Arabia* back in 1962 showed that with the right sort of sandstorm saga even the jaded audiences of the United States could fall under the spell of the Arab mystique. What's more, Akkad reasoned that a film biography of The Big M. would be a guaranteed winner even without the infidel audiences: the Muslim response alone would be enough to assure profit on The Prophet. Mous told potential backers of his project that he planned to recycle *Mohammad* year after year, timing these repeat releases to coincide with religious festivals. In this way the picture could follow the brave trail blazed by *The Ten Commandments* and *The Robe* in their annual Easter/Passover runs, or, even more appropriately, by Joseph E. Levine's *Santa Claus Conquers the Martians* in its yearly Christmas release.

Unfortunately for the success of these grand plans, Akkad blissfully ignored the facts that the Muslim world had already been saturated by nine previous Arabic-language treatments of the origins of Islam and that most Western countries neglect to celebrate the sacred month of *Ramadan.* These factors might have discouraged a lesser man, but not Moustapha Akkad. With a wealth of filmmaking experience after thirty-nine mini-travelogues and with the spirit of Sam Peckinpah to guide him (since the Arab world had always seemed like a Middle Eastern counterpart to *The Wild Bunch*), Akkad felt worthy of his monumental task. Much like his cinematic hero's original followers, who for hundreds of years crossed burning desert sands to carry their often bloody message against seemingly insurmountable odds, Mous was nobly prepared to sacrifice millions of dollars of other people's money to complete his sacred work, and once again emulating the earlier Islamic hordes, he managed to leave a legacy of wanton waste and legendary destruction in his wake.

They Said It Couldn't Be Done

Akkad's basic concept for a would-be box office bonanza faced one itsy-bitsy problem—in the same sense that the *Titanic* encountered a minor difficulty with the iceberg. According to Muslim teaching, believers are strictly forbidden from casting their eyes upon "graven images"—a prohibition that extends to all representations of the Deity or His Prophet. Therefore, the face of the leading character in the forthcoming film—Mohammad—could not be shown on screen. In the most intensely religious Islamic countries, such as Saudi Arabia, this concern with visual representation is taken so seriously that motion pictures are banned altogether, and movie theatres, or "shadow houses" as they are derisively called, are prohibited by law. One can only pity the poor teenagers of Riyadh who, denied the pleasures of *Flashdance* and *Porky's*, spend their Saturday evenings hanging around at public squares to watch heads and hands roll, or else must while away the long Arabian nights curled up in bed with their favorite hookah.

As if the touchiness about Mohammad Himself weren't enough of a challenge to a resourceful filmmaker, Islamic tradition further commands that the Prophet's seven wives, his daughters, and even his sons-in-law must be treated as sacred figures—which means that none of these relatives could be depicted by actors. That didn't leave many members of the Mohammad family for Akkad to throw up onto the screen, so through the process of elimination he had to concentrate on the Prophet's uncle, the warrior Hamza. Had he been more experienced than he was in the wonderful world of American TV, our Man Moustapha might have turned to Hans Conried to bring the lovable Uncle Hamza to life—after all, the veteran character actor had done a memorable job impersonating Danny Thomas' Lebanese "Uncle Tanoose" in the old *Make Room for Daddy* show. Instead of such imaginative (if somewhat fanciful) casting, however, Akkad made a predictable and conventional choice, selecting Hollywood's all-purpose Third Worlder, Anthony Quinn. The Mexican-born actor, who had portrayed a charismatic sheik in *Lawrence of Arabia*, seemed thrilled at the prospect of returning to the desert and described the new project as a "great event" and a "good deed."

Quinn's flamboyant acting style might help to fill the screen, but it could hardly make up for the conspicuous absence of any voice or visage associated with the title character. Even The Prophet's shadow was considered utterly taboo; the closest the filmmakers could come to The Man Himself was to offer occasional close-ups of Mohammad's "camel-riding stick"— a potent (and macho) symbol if ever there was one. The movie would also thrill the faithful with inspiring views of Mohammad's tent and of his holy camel. These images—filmed with great and solemn reverence—are intended to give a subtle sense of The Prophet's awesome but invisible presence. Meanwhile, the unfortunate actors who do appear on screen address many of their lines to no one in particular and then nod to unheard replies—as if participating in a theological remake of *Topper*. To further confuse the issue, the audience is given frequent op-portunities to watch the action of the film from Mohammad's point of view, as His followers bow and proffer offerings or His detractors wave spears directly at the camera.

In selecting a writer to concoct a script that would successfully incorporate these awkward restrictions, Akkad secured the services of one H. A. L. (Harry) Craig, son of an Irish Protestant parson and former film critic for the Manchester *Guardian*. Craig had earned his platinum-plated, diamond-studded spurs as screenwriter for lavish, overpriced, and disastrous spectacles by scripting the megaflop *Waterloo* in 1970; later in his career he managed to attach his name to such further inane fiascos as *Airport '77* and *Lion of the Desert* (1979). This extraordinary record of achievement, however, should not lead to the conclusion that Mr. Craig had an easy time turning out the scripts for such surefire turkeys; in the case of *Mohammad*, he spent two full years in research and writing before he was ready to display the fruit of his labors to the world. In particular, Muslim authorities demanded that they see the finished screenplay before allowing filming to proceed within Arab territory. These scholars and holy men considered it especially inappropriate that the job of writing the script had been assigned to an Irishman; after all,

Anthony Quinn, as Mohammad's warrior uncle, held a nasty grudge against all nonbelievers. Since Islamic law strictly forbids any rendering of the image or voice of The Prophet Himself, Quinn, as much as anyone, served as star of this confused and confusing petrodollar epic.

Islam strictly forbids indulgence in spirituous liquors. In any event, Harry Craig and Moustapha Akkad traveled in 1971 to Cairo's prestigious al-Azhar University to consult with leading representatives of The Council of Islamic Research and to seek their blessing for the project. During lengthy meetings in a Cairo hotel room, Akkad recalls "there was a great deal of discussion on religious nuances and possible areas of misunderstanding, but when we left, every page of that script had been hand-stamped as 'approved' . . . and then they were hugging Harry and praising his script to the skies." In Craig's view, "It was like writing a life of Christ and getting approval from the Pope or the Archbishop of Canterbury." Considering the betrayal by these same august scholars that took place not long after the hugs and kisses, it was actually more like *living* a life of Christ than merely writing about it, but Craig and Akkad still had several months to go before their crucifixion.

"Mohammad's Turn"

Soon after the al-Azhar meetings, *Variety* summarized the preproduction situation with one of that paper's typically urbane headlines: "JESUS, MOSES HAD EPIC PIX, NOW MOHAMMAD'S TURN AS SUPERSTAR." Unfortunately, this sort of publicity caused problems for Akkad and company before the shooting had even begun. The Saudi Arabian press soon picked up a rumor from nowhere that Peter (*Lawrence of Arabia*) O'Toole had been signed for the lead part of The Prophet and expressed "outrage and horror" that an "English infidel" would desecrate the name of their revered leader. No sooner had this rumor been squelched than the Voice of America radio station, which is theoretically in the business of winning friends for the United States, broadcast the astonishing (and totally erroneous) news that Charlton Heston, best known for his performance as that controversial Jewish boy, Moses, would now be playing the role of Mohammad. This particular propaganda coup sparked two days of spontaneous and bloody rioting by the fun-loving citizens of Karachi, Pakistan. Akkad and Heston both issued vehement denials in the hope of quelling these disturbances, but no sooner had this controversy subsided than a new one erupted. Numerous Arabic-language newspapers carried reports that "officially and definitively" (and, believe it or not, correctly) announced that Anthony Quinn would star in the film—but these same reports suggested he would be playing The Prophet Himself, rather than specifying his actual role as Mr. Big's uncle. This latest news pro-

voked additional angry protests as confusion ran rampant (so what else is new?) throughout the Middle East.

At last, Akkad reached the reluctant conclusion that Muslim believers were so sensitive about all details of this sacred project that they would not tolerate infidels in *any* of the key roles. If he hoped to cash in at the box office in the various Koran Kapitals, he knew he would have to use an all-Muslim cast; but at the same time the names of such stalwart Islamic actors as Abdulla Geith would carry little clout when they appeared on movie marquees in the U.S. and Europe. Omar Sharif was the one star who might have bridged the gap between the two worlds, but he was unacceptable to Muslim fundamentalists because he had kissed Barbra Streisand on the lips in the movie *Funny Girl*, and Miss Streisand was well-known, after all, as a "notorious Zionist" and, what's more, a native of Brooklyn.

In desperation, Akkad hit upon the idea of using two casts and, in effect, shooting two movies at once: a western version, with stars such as Quinn and Irene Papas, and a special Arabic edition, with the likes of Mona Wassif and Hamdy Said. The big battle and crowd scenes would of course be used in both versions, but the policy of "double-shooting" so many of the sequences delayed the production for months and added tremendously to its cost. Considering all the agonies he experienced over casting, it is surprising that Moustapha reacted as he did to Muhammad Ali, an international superstar and card-carrying Muslim who might have played well in both the West and the Middle East. The once and future champ, when he heard of the cinematic plans to celebrate the life of Mohammad, his Main Man, expressed interest in the role of Bilal, a black slave who becomes the first *muezzin*—a religious functionary responsible for calling the believers to prayer. Despite the obvious advantages of placing The Greatest in that role, Moustapha Akkad courageously refused to compromise his artistic principles. "Such casting would smack of commercialism," he haughtily declared, and went on to assign the role to the Senegalese actor Johnny Sekka, star of such fine, noncommercial films as *Uptown Saturday Night* (1974) and *Charlie Chan and the Curse of the Dragon Queen* (1981).

One of the reasons that Akkad could pay so little attention to mundane economic considerations was that he had been assured of up to $60 million in backing from the royal family of Saudi Arabia and other assorted petroleum potentates. But suddenly, with the script approved and the actors assigned, the Saudi monarch, King Faisal, had an unexplained

Abu-Sofyan, the evil leader of Mecca (Michael Ansara), points out his gripes against the new religion of Islam (with aid of an eloquently scowling, eyeball-rolling extra behind him) to Bilal (Johnny Sekka), a slave who has recently converted to the burgeoning faith.

change of heart. He moved swiftly to sabotage the movie's financing, at the same time that he canceled permission to film on location in Mecca and Medina. Akkad saw the fickle Faisal's unexpected opposition as only a minor problem, since there were many other sheiks to shake down; after traveling to Kuwait, Bahrain, and Iran, the persistent producer found plenty of new investors.

As for a filming location, Morocco extended a warm welcome to the Mous and his colleagues—on the condition that they would construct a $100 million film production studio before they left. The producer accepted the deal, with complete and perfect faith that Allah, somehow, would provide the money. As he boasted to the press, "I am a graduate of the U.C.L.A., U.S.C. and Sam Peckinpah film schools, and I am not without nerve." (*Chutzpah* might have been a more appropriate word, but Akkad's Yiddish pronunciation has always been somewhat deficient.) In any event, cast and crew eventually set up shop in the desert village of Ait Bouchent, fifteen miles outside beautiful downtown Marrakesh. There, using a vast pool of underpaid local laborers, the technical staff began work on an incredibly detailed replica of the city of Mecca. Moustapha proudly proclaimed that the result of these exertions would be "the biggest set since *Cleopatra*"—though he failed to predict that *Mohammad* would also turn out to be one of

the biggest *bombs* since that earlier classic set the standard for cinematic indulgence. Under Akkad's hard-driving supervision, the sweating workmen battled temperatures that sometimes reached 125 degrees. At night, the crew enjoyed the relative comfort of rooms at the local Holiday Inn, but when the air-conditioning system broke down, they were forced to sleep under wet towels. Despite these mishaps, the builders managed to complete all their work on the mirage Mecca exactly on schedule—including the construction of an exact model of the sacred *Kaaba* (Islam's holiest shrine) built at a cost of $400,000.

To populate this huge set, Akkad used as many as 7,000 extras in some big scenes and found it surprisingly easy to recruit local yokels from Marrakesh as participants in the film. The Egyptian-American actor Michael Ansara (who co-stars as The Prophet's arch-enemy, Abu-Sofyan) recalled that these Moroccans were willing to "work for next to nothing—no union scale—just give them a pig or a sheep and they were happy."

Faisal's Follies

Virtually everyone seemed to be happy, in fact, until six months into the shooting schedule when our old friend King Faisal decided to reinvolve himself in the production. After sober reflection, the megabucks monarch decided to "communicate his displeasure" to his colleague King Hassan of Morocco, suggesting that the infidel filmmakers hop the next Marrakesh Express and get out of town. Having read reports of the astonishing realism of the movie's painstaking recreation of Islam's most important shrines, the Saudi ruler became genuinely concerned that slow-witted Muslims around the world would become confused between the movie Mecca in Morocco and the real McCoy back home in Saudi Arabia. He worried in public that the perfidious filmmakers would begin luring backwoods believers away from their sacred duty to journey to the original Mecca and would lure them instead to make wrong-way pilgrimages to the abandoned movie set in the Sahara. This fear may seem somewhat far-fetched to unbiased observers, but when you happen to be absolute ruler of a country that holds about half the world's known oil reserves, the rest of humanity will most often respect your paranoia. To make sure that King Hassan respected his wishes concerning the *Mohammad* movie, Faisal threatened to ban all Moroccan pilgrims from entering Saudi Arabia, as well as planning to cut off oil shipments, unless his wishes were respected. This seemed to be an offer the Moroccans couldn't properly refuse—even if it meant giving up the fantasyland film production complex Akkad had promised to build for them. As part of the final understanding between the two kings, Faisal promised to support Morocco in its ongoing feud with Algeria over plans to annex the Spanish Sahara, and Hassan pledged to move with all due dispatch in driving the Hollywood heathens from his land. The result of all this agreement was the arrival of two Moroccan colonels and a high-ranking police official on the *Mohammad* set to supervise the dismantling of the whole operation, lock, stock, and *Kaaba,* and to escort the movie men to the border.

As a conciliatory gesture, Saudi officials informed Akkad that he would be compensated for all his time and trouble with the tidy sum of $20 million—already waiting for him in a Swiss bank—provided that he agree to shelve *Mohammad* for good. This tempting bribe would not only have covered the production's expenses to date, but would have also ensured a tidy profit for Akkad and his colleagues. Nevertheless, our foolhardy hero put all selfish considerations aside and, with cast and crew following faithfully behind, marched out of Morocco with his great work still far from completion. Like other holy men in history, Moustapha would wander the desert for years, if necessary, in order to ensure the realization of his dream. " 'Yes,' " he told the *L.A. Times,* " 'we are going to be forced to close down the film and leave Morocco because of too much controversy in the Arab world, but they can't stop us. It is the will of God that we continue! He is helping us. That man in Iraq last year who opposed our making of the film, he is dead, and now I hear King Faisal is sick.' Akkad cast his large brown eyes skyward and said gently, 'God looks after us.' "

Sure enough, Faisal met his doom at the hands of an assassin shortly thereafter (though Moustapha had an airtight alibi), and Moroccan claims on the Spanish Sahara kicked up a sandstorm of international controversy, leading to clashes with the Algerian army early in 1976. Meanwhile, and more important, the production of *Mohammad* shut down entirely for two months. Akkad continued to pay the crew in order to keep his movie alive, while he scuttled from country to country in the Middle East, searching for a new location and a new sugar daddy. Eventually, he found an unlikely patron to fund the continuation of his movie-making Allah-mode: Colonel Muammar al-Qaddafi, dictator of Libya and the world-renowned Bad Boy of Bengazi. Somehow, Qaddafi managed to take time out from his busy schedule of international terrorist activities to welcome Mousta-

pha Akkad to his capital for a private showing of an hour's worth of footage from the unfinished masterpiece. When the lights came up after the screening, the soft-hearted despot reportedly had tears in his eyes—proving himself nearly as enthusiastic a movie fan as Benito Mussolini, whose participation in *Scipio Africanus* is highlighted in another corridor of the Hall of Shame. In any event, Colonel Qaddafi immediately declared that "this was a film that had to be finished," and he assured Akkad that the oil-rich Libyan government would provide whatever funds were needed to make his epic "one of the greatest motion pictures in history." As the Hollywood trade paper *Boxoffice* reported a few weeks later: "The picture, which has been in production for more than a year and isn't finished yet, is probably the only one shooting anywhere in the world with unlimited resources."

Unfortunately, the forced exodus (pardon the expression) from Morocco had already cost a pretty petrodollar; in addition to talent overages, the producers had to pay for travel and housing expenses for some 700 people covering 2,000 miles of land and water, plus funding the expense of transporting hundreds of horses, cameras, and other equipment. When the additional expenses of constructing new sets had been included, the unexpected shift in location had cost more than $2 million. Not to worry, though; Colonel Qaddafi invited Moustapha to set up camp near the desert town of Sebha and even sent out 3,000 of his crack troops to serve in battle scenes as extras.

Under the watchful eye of the Libyan army and dictator, shooting proceeded with few additional problems—until the climactic scene re-enacting the battle of Uhud, a bitter grudge match between the faithful and the infidels. In the midst of this altercation, Mohammad's fearless Uncle Hamza (Anthony Quinn) finally cashes in his worry beads after being shish-kebabed by a particularly nasty lance. As the cameras rolled, the impaled hero staggered for several moments toward the cameras before collapsing on the sand. At this point the melodramatic script called for the villainous Hind (played by Irene Papas, Quinn's co-star in *Zorba the Greek*) to approach the hapless corpse and express her contempt by kicking it in the face. Miss Papas showed a bit too much enthusiasm for this aspect of her role; "Oh my God!" she exclaimed after filming the sequence. "I think I kicked him too hard!" By nightfall, indeed, a monstrous lump had appeared on Quinn's weatherbeaten cheek. The cast and crew could afford to laugh over the incident, since the star's role had been all but completed before the accident. Nevertheless,

Quinn's badly bruised countenance (resembling the makeup job he received in *Requiem for a Heavyweight* [1962]) served as an eloquent omen of the ultimate beating that the finished film would receive from assorted critics and crackpots around the world.

But Will It Play in Djibouti?

At one time, MGM, Columbia, and Universal Studios all bid for the distribution rights to this enticing new property, but Mous decided to shun the majors in the hope of retaining a higher percentage of the surefire profits for himself. Joining forces with Hollywood hype-master Irwin (*Roller Boogie, Laserblast*) Yablans, Akkad formed an independent distribution company called Tarik International Films. Despite production expenses that totaled more than $17 million, this dynamic duo remained confident that *Mohammad* would prove to be a worldwide smash hit.

Their chief problem in marketing the film in the West involved its focus on a religious leader who had never enjoyed a great popularity among Christians and who, moreover, failed to appear on screen. What, for instance, were the theatres supposed to use as a promotional poster—a photograph of Mohammad's camel-riding stick? Akkad and Yablans solved this problem with an impressive and lurid logo, used in virtually all the publicity materials for the film. The visual image featured a brawny forearm, whose owner remained discreetly invisible, clutching a billowing banner and waving on a horde of mounted and heavily armed Arab warriors. In the press kit for the film, this drawing appeared beneath the hysterical headline: *"IN FOUR DECADES ONLY FOUR* ... 'THE ROBE,' 'THE TEN COMMANDMENTS,' 'BEN-HUR,' AND NOW ... FOR THE FIRST TIME ... THE VAST, SPECTACULAR DRAMA THAT CHANGED THE WORLD."

The world premiere of *Mohammad: Messenger of God* was scheduled for London on July 29, 1976, but the use of the Prophet's name in the title led to bomb threats from Muslim fanatics. In response to these stern warnings, the quick-thinking British distributor three days before the opening changed the title to *The Message* "out of respect for the Muslim community in Britain"—not to mention his respect for the structural integrity of the West End movie house at which the debut was supposed to take place. This shallow ploy managed to fool the would-be terrorists, who were obviously better supplied with bluster than they were with brains, and no bombs exploded during the picture's run, except for a few lobbed hand grenades from the critics. In any event, *The Message* went on to become London's number-one movie hit for the month of August—perhaps because of the

Irene Pappas plays the villainous, idol-worshipping Hind—sort of a Middle Eastern Lady Macbeth—who, in this unforgettable scene, declaims straight to the camera, "My nails will kill you, you cutthroat, murdering beast! I will cut your heart out and taste your blood!" Much to the delight of gore fans in the audience, she proceeds to do just that in a later scene in this uplifting religious epic.

thousands of Saudis who found themselves in town for their summer shopping sprees and who, since they had no motion pictures in their own country, were willing to sit through virtually *anything* when they were abroad. What's more, Akkad's extravaganza, filled, as it was, with plenty of sand, blood, and camel dung, no doubt helped to alleviate the homesickness of these peregrinating plutocrats.

Jubilant over the encouraging reception for his film in the United Kingdom, Akkad prepared to open *Mohammad* in the United States and throughout the Arab world. The negative reviews in the American press came as no surprise: John Simon in *New York* magazine described the movie as "the last word in ponderous platitudes and stilted lifelessness," while Janet Maslin in *Newsweek* saw it as "cinematically crude and so reverential toward its subject as to seem mechanical." It was not reverential enough, however, to please Islamic religious leaders. The Supreme Council of the World Mosque Conference in Mecca officially banned the film, as did Pakistan's National Assembly, calling it "a sacrilege ... a brash

attempt to commercially exploit Islam." The unkindest cut of all came from leading scholars at al-
Azhar University in Cairo (that's right—the same
center for Muslim studies that had previously approved every page of the script) who publicly de-
nounced the movie as "an insult to Islam." Akkad
vainly protested that he himself was a loyal believer
and he had undertaken the project as a labor of love.
He further pointed out that all of those condemning
the picture had not even taken the trouble to see it,
but his voice was quickly drowned out by hysterical
jeers of protest from around the world . . .

Hanafi Hi-Jinx

. . . Which brings us back to the B'nai B'rith building
in Washington and the Hanafi Muslim terrorists who
occupied it to demand that the film's American premiere be canceled. In addition to the 100 bystanders
seized at the headquarters of the Jewish organization,
Hanafi commandos took some thirty additional hostages at the Islamic Center near Rock Creek Park
and Washington's city hall, known as the District
Building, downtown.

*Senegalese actor Johnny Sekka, as one of The Prophet's
early followers, Bilal, may have experienced a premoni-
tion of his embarrassment in front of millions of moviegoers throughout the world, as part of the devout
disaster,* **Mohammad: Messenger of God.**

The leader of this well-coordinated three-pronged
attack was Khalifa Hamaas Abdul Khaalis, who had
been seeking some form of revenge since 1973, when
five of his children were killed and one of his wives
was seriously wounded by a rival black Muslim sect.
Born in Indiana as Ernest McGee, Khaalis became a
jazz drummer in New York City after being dis-
charged from the army on grounds of mental instabil-
ity. Shortly thereafter he converted from Roman
Catholicism to the Nation of Islam, and worked
closely with Malcolm X and other Muslim leaders. In
1958 he broke with the group because of its alleged
departure from proper orthodox principles, and he
formed the intensely devout Hanafi sect. As leader of
this splinter movement, he helped to attract such celebrities as playwright Imanu Amiri Baraka (LeRoi
Jones) and basketball star Kareem Abdul-Jabbar
(Lew Alcindor).

Khaalis had carefully planned his terrorist attack
in Washington to coincide with the gala American
premiere of *Mohammad: Messenger of God.* By mid-
afternoon, he had established telephone contact with
the media from his new headquarters at the B'nai
B'rith building. Speaking to a reporter from WTOP-
TV, Khaalis delivered an unsolicited "ferocious attack" on the new motion picture. "We want that
picture out of the country," he roared. "If that picture opens in New York, heads will roll. We do not
want that picture to be shown, and I'll die for my
faith." The specific Hanafi objections to the film included alleged misquotations of the Koran, the omission of pertinent facts, and the very idea that
Mohammad should be "played by an actor"—proof
that the fanatic commandos had never bothered to
see the movie to which they so energetically objected. As the siege dragged on, some of the nervous
hostages speculated on the specific nature of the conditions for their release. "From my corner," recalled
one of the survivors, "we agreed that they wanted
some public spectacle, like the destruction by burning of the movie about Mohammad."

Though denied this ultimate satisfaction, the terrorists did succeed in interrupting the movie's premiere. At the Hollywood Paramount theatre, 300
patrons of the afternoon show groaned when the
screen suddenly went blank after thirty-five minutes
of film; the manager walked out on stage to apologize for the inconvenience, attributing the abrupt
cancellation to a "small political problem," and re-
funded their money. Three other L.A. theatres canceled their evening shows, as did four movie houses
in New York. Meanwhile, the theatres took down the
offensive title from their marquees, and threw up

signs announcing "MOHAMMAD POSTPONED." In local papers, huge blank spaces appeared in the movie sections where ads for the film had originally been slotted. Moustapha Akkad, in New York City for the American debut, had reportedly been "devastated" by the bad news. He contacted government authorities and generously offered to arrange a private screening of his movie for the gunmen and hostages in the B'nai B'rith building—perhaps relishing the notion of a captive audience. "I will destroy the film if it is offensive to them," the producer-director promised the press, but the commandos in Washington, lacking the sophistication of dedicated bad-movie buffs, turned down Akkad's friendly proposal.

As negotiations continued, Khaalis ordered one of the hostages at the Islamic Center, Dr. Mohammad (no relation) Abdul Rauf, the institute's director, to place some important phone calls. "He gave me twenty-five minutes," Rauf remembered, "to phone ambassadors of Muslim nations to tell them to take action to get the movie stopped." Finally, after much Koran quoting and direct meetings with three Islamic diplomats who promised to use their best efforts to sabotage the salacious celluloid, Khaalis and his merry band surrendered and released their hostages.

Twelve hours later, the film resumed its showings. Asked for an explanation, Akkad reasoned, "What happened in Washington is not Islamic at all. That's why I hope the film will be seen, that people may understand the true spirit of love, brotherhood and peace." One woman, at least, failed to get *The Message*. Identifying herself as "the wife of Khaalis," she called Reuters News Agency and warned that unless the movie was stopped immediately, "more trouble is coming, worse than before, all over the country." In view of the continued threats and controversy, police remained stationed outside the nine theatres in Los Angeles and New York in which the picture had opened, watching for terrorist bombs; they apparently failed to understand that the biggest bomb of all was already up on the screen.

That's Allah, Folks

Despite the patently wretched quality of the picture, the free publicity surrounding its premiere ensured tremendous first-week business. One theatre reported the surprising sale of nearly a thousand souvenir programs—a commodity that usually moves only sluggishly out the door. "It's going to be an instant hit," one local manager reported. "As far as the street re-

action goes, everyone wants to see it. Even those who didn't want to see it before, will see it now." This public response seemed to lend support to those Hollywood cynics who suggested that the entire terrorist raid had actually been set up by the producers to call attention to their film. Unfortunately, curious viewers, drawn by the air of danger and controversy, were unanimously disappointed by what they saw. They had obviously expected the sort of relevant and explosively charged epic that influences major events—such as *Taxi Driver*, which prompted the shooting of a president; *The Warriors*, which provoked several gang deaths in theatres; or *The China Syndrome*, which inspired the nuclear reactor at Three Mile Island to try to blow itself up. The producers of *Mohammad*, however, had gone to such great lengths to offend absolutely no one that the result was a bland muddle: three hours and twenty minutes of excruciating boredom in a picture that moved at the pace of a quadriplegic camel. Word of mouth soon spread that the plot of the movie was nowhere near as interesting as the plots and counter-plots surrounding its debut, and box office receipts fell off disastrously. Distributor Yablans, watching a disaster in the making, complained to *Variety* that in spite of snickers in the industry, "the Washington incident has seriously hurt the film commercially." Far more serious for its long-term prospects was its continued rejection by the Arab world: the only Muslim country to permit showings of the controversial film was, appropriately enough, Turkey. After six months, Tunisia also permitted a brief run of Akkad's cinematic spectacle, but the shadow houses of all other Islamic countries remained proudly undefiled by the offending film.

In order to break even, the producers would have had to gross at least $35 million to cover various production, promotion, and interest charges. Over the years *Mohammad*, has, in fact, won back less than $2 million in the United States, less than $5 million worldwide, proving conclusively that Allah does not in all cases reward good intentions.

Despite the fact that Akkad's inspirational epic has by now been forgotten by filmgoers everywhere, it has achieved immortality, of sorts, in the world of literature. In 1983, Richard Grenier's hilarious novel, *The Marrakesh One-Two*, offered the reading public a caustic and fictionalized view of the machinations of an Arab-American U.C.L.A. film-school graduate who produces and directs a feature film called *Mohammad, Man of Mecca*, and who, like his real-life model, manages to lose nearly $30 million.

In the face of all these humiliations and reverses,

Moustapha Akkad has maintained his faith in his own genius and in his dreams of creating memorable motion pictures. In pursuing these visions of glory, he has suffered spectacular ups and downs. His greatest triumph stemmed from his timely backing of a struggling U.S.C. alumnus named John Carpenter; the result was *Halloween* (1978), a classic horror film that grossed more than $50 million and spawned a host of sequels and imitations. This coup netted a personal bonanza of nearly $12 million (on an initial investment of $320,000) for the smiling Syrian, and he went on to additional success with a long series of low budget (and low quality) films. Akkad's biggest disaster, meanwhile, stemmed from his continued collaboration with Colonel Muammar Qaddafi and their undimmed determination to make a timeless classic celebrating Arab heroism. In 1981 they unleashed *Lion of the Desert* on an unsuspecting world, and this $35 million extravaganza, featuring Anthony Quinn (again) as Libyan folk hero Omar Mukhtar, is duly noted in the file of fiascos collected at the basement of our museum. The utter failure of their second at-

tempt at immortalizing Islamic grandeur did nothing to shake Qaddafi's commitment to Akkad; in fact they are currently planning two more epic indulgences: one of them a love story set in the romantic age of Moorish domination in Spain, the other presenting the Arab point of view of the Crusades.

Whatever the fate of these future projects, *Mohammad: Messenger of God* will always retain a very special place in the mind of Moustapha. It was, after all, his first film, and it is hard for him to abandon hope that it will someday, somehow recoup its losses. "The child is born, and there is no way you can send it back where it came from," he mused. "I think the film will impose itself . . . It is only a matter of time." As he dreams of this miraculous rebirth, perhaps Akkad speculates on what he might have done differently to ensure his film's success. Perhaps, if the main dramatic speeches in *Mohammad* had been set to music . . . the movie might not have done any better at the box office, but at least it would have qualified for the next display area in our Exhibition of Excess. . . .

MUSICAL
EXTRAVAGANZAS

IN THE 1960s, big-budget musicals provided Hollywood with some of its most glittering successes. *West Side Story* (1961), *My Fair Lady* (1964), *The Sound of Music* (1965), and *Oliver!* (1968) all walked away with Oscars as the Best Picture of the Year, while *The Sound of Music* proved by far the top money-making film of its era. The major studios could hardly be blamed for their shameless attempts to duplicate this surefire formula, but as America moved toward the seventies, box office returns provided evidence that the magic of the monster musical had begun to run out. While the studios lavished millions on films such as *Doctor Dolittle* (1967), *Camelot* (1967), *Star!* (1968), *Finian's Rainbow* (1968), *Sweet Charity* (1969), *Goodbye Mr. Chips* (1969), *Hello Dolly!* (1969), and *Darling Lili* (1970), each of these much-heralded extravaganzas proved to be a major financial disappointment. By the end of the decade this grim record of losers forced producers at long last to begin grappling with the problem of how to persuade the huge and well-heeled youth audience to divert some of the millions it lavished on rock records to purchasing theatre tickets to Hollywood musicals.

The films on display in this wing of our museum both attempted to answer this challenge by injecting self-consciously hip and contemporary elements into the familiar and time-honored formula. The resulting hybrids, *Paint Your Wagon* and *Can't Stop the Music*, resembled other ungainly examples of misguided crossbreeding by proving absolutely sterile in the long run—failing to generate even the most modest box office returns for their hopeful creators.

PAINT YOUR WAGON

(1969)

Paramount
Produced by Alan Jay Lerner
Directed by Joshua Logan
Screenplay by Alan Jay Lerner; adapted by Paddy Chayefsky
Lyrics by Alan Jay Lerner; music by Frederick Loewe; additional music by André Previn

Starring Lee Marvin (Ben Rumson); Clint Eastwood ("Pardner"); Jean Seberg (Elizabeth);
Harve Presnell ("Rotten Luck" Willie); Ray Walston ("Mad Jack" Duncan);
Tom Ligon (Horton Fenty); Alan Dexter ("The Parson");
and the Nitty Gritty Dirt Band ("The Mining Camp Band").

A Genius in Firm Command

Before *My Fair Lady*, before *Gigi*, before *Camelot*, before trying (and failing) to come up with a screenplay for the ill-fated *Doctor Dolittle*, before winning a distinguished place on lists of most-married persons with his sequence of eight wives, Mr. Alan Jay Lerner, the noted playwright and lyricist, combined with Frederick Loewe to create an eminently forgettable musical about the California Gold Rush called *Paint Your Wagon*. As Lerner himself described its initial run on Broadway in 1951, the show was "a success, but not a hit. By that I mean the reviews were mixed and the backers eventually made a small profit." Because of these marginal returns, the property attracted only mild interest from Hollywood. Industry insiders cited two key weaknesses in the original material that made it unsuitable for the big screen: a simplistic, sentimental plot and the lack of any truly memorable tunes. Despite these reservations, Warner Brothers considered using it as a vehicle for Doris Day, while Paramount talked of producing an adaptation starring Bing Crosby. In the end, Louis B. Mayer—acting as an independent producer after his departure from MGM—purchased the motion picture rights for a modest sum, but failed to get the project off the ground before his death in 1957. Unfortunately, *Paint Your Wagon* was not allowed to die with him.

In the mid-sixties, with Tinseltown thoroughly infected by the fevered craze for big musicals inspired by the epic success of *The Sound of Music*, the major studios gladly overlooked such flaws. Paramount hungrily snapped up *Paint Your Wagon*, purchasing the shopworn property from the Mayer estate, and in a wholly irrational moment, hired Alan Jay Lerner himself to serve as producer. Lerner had never before taken personal charge of a Hollywood production, but on three different occasions (*An American in Paris* [1951], *Gigi* [1958], and *My Fair Lady* [1964]) he had written screenplays for films that went on to win the Academy Award as Best Picture of the Year. These successes helped to persuade the pompous pen jockey that nothing in Hollywood was beyond his abilities; after all, as he cheerfully informed reporters, his I.Q. had once been officially measured as 175. With this self-proclaimed "genius" in firm command, the Paramount executives felt certain of success. Little did they know that they had actually hired an *idiot savant*, who should never have been permitted to stray from his typewriter.

A Wagon of a Different Color

Despite his Harvard background (Class of '38), Lerner chose Princeton man Joshua Logan (Class of '31) as the director for *Paint Your Wagon*. In addition to his record as one of Broadway's most successful and gifted directors (*Mister Roberts, Annie Get Your Gun*), Logan had compiled a formidable list of movie credits, including such memorable films as *Bus Stop* (1956), *Sayonara* (1957), and *South Pacific* (1958). Though Logan's 1967 screen adaptation of Lerner and Loewe's *Camelot* had been a critical and box of-

In the Trenches for a Long Campaign: Director Josh Logan (with dark hat, beside the camera, left) argues with his erstwhile friend, producer-writer Alan Jay Lerner, while a member of the Nitty Gritty Dirt Band seems appropriately amused by the altogether typical confusion.

fice disappointment, Alan Jay maintained enough faith in the veteran director to override all objections from the studio and to insist that his old drinking buddy be given the job. As it turned out, Logan felt more surprised than gratified at receiving this new assignment. "When Alan asked me to direct it," he recalled, "I said, *'Paint Your WAGON?'* The way you'd say, 'Sonny TUFTS?'"

Director and producer immediately agreed that the Broadway material required major revisions in order to appeal to the "with it" sensibilities of the late sixties. They simply discarded Lerner's original plot (concerning the adventures of a young girl torn between love of her father and a passion for an outcast Mexican boy) and integrated the old songs into a brand-new story line. This fresh and trendy tale (created with the help of gifted screenwriter and three-time Academy Award winner Paddy Chayefsky) took place in a Gold Rush settlement known as No-Name City, where the all-male inhabitants suffer acutely from the lack of feminine com-

panionship. When a Mormon traveler wanders into town with *two* wives, the local residents plead with him to share the wealth and leave one of the women behind. Elizabeth, the younger wife, enjoys all the male attention and agrees to be auctioned off to the highest bidder. Two hard-bitten gold-mining partners pool their resources to purchase this plum, and she is married to both men in a triple-ring ceremony, provoking no end of romantic entanglements and earthy frontier humor. This complex and provocative premise took the story far from its saccharine Broadway origins, but Lerner and Logan assumed any plot that included both polyandry and polygamy would be sure to appeal to the Youth of America.

There remained the problem of an uncomfortably thin musical score, and Lerner tried to coax his old partner, Fritz Loewe, out of retirement to provide new hit songs for the new hip show. Loewe wisely turned him down, but gave him permission for André Previn to write the music for the additional lyrics that Alan Jay Lerner planned to provide. This new creative team—Lerner and Previn—proceeded to create a series of singularly inane ballads such as "A Million Miles Away Behind the Door," "The Gospel of No-Name City," and "The Best Things in Life Are Dirty."

Despite the questionable quality of these improvements, *Paint Your Wagon* remained a hot property within the film community, and Blake Edwards— then at the peak of his power and prestige—expressed a sudden and unexpected interest in directing it. Joshua Logan, who remained less than enchanted with the entire project, eagerly volunteered to step aside, but Lerner insisted on retaining his bosom pal at the reins. This freed Edwards to work on his own megaflop, *Darling Lili* (q.v.), while Logan spent the next year in cursing his bad luck in having such loyal friends as Alan Jay Lerner.

An Unlikely Trip

The first of many nightmares encountered in the course of the production concerned the casting of the three lead roles. For the part of the rugged but tender frontier maiden who takes on the challenge of two husbands, Logan first approached Lesley *Ann* Warren, then contacted Sally *Ann* Howes (but missed a grand slam—and avoided total confusion— by ignoring Lesley-*Anne* Down). When these worthy actresses turned down the role because of other commitments, Logan settled on Jean Seberg, the farm girl

Jean Seberg shows the natural grace and agility that made her brief dancing sequences in Paint Your Wagon *stand out among the most embarrassing moments of her troubled career. Though she had shown herself a talented and sensitive actress in a number of French "New Wave" films, she was hopelessly out of place in a musical comedy.*

from Marshalltown, Iowa, who had been selected to star, at age seventeen, in Otto Preminger's celebrated flop, *Saint Joan* (1957). Subsequently, Miss Seberg had recovered from this experience and built a new career as actress in a number of French New Wave films—an experience that gave her the aura of sophisticated sexiness that Logan and Lerner wanted to bring to the Wild West of *Paint Your Wagon*.

They also wanted to bring a well-known character actor to the part of Ben Rumson—the grizzled, hard-drinking prospector who becomes Miss Seberg's senior husband. After dreaming wistfully of the musical talents of Mickey Rooney (with whom Alan Jay could compare notes on alimony payments) or James Cagney (who, after all, sang and danced in *Yankee Doodle Dandy* a mere twenty-seven years earlier), they decided in the end on the golden voice of Lee Marvin. Despite his lack of background as a crooner, he seemed perfect for the major part of the musical miner, since his long-term relationship with Michelle Triola Marvin had given him extensive experience with gold-digging. Moreover, Marvin had been prominent on the list of the top-ten box office stars for the last three years—a fact that meant far more to the studio than singing ability. The same calculation applied to the ever-popular Clint Eastwood, who won the role of Ben Rumson's soft-spoken partner (imaginatively known as "Pardner" in the script) over George Maharis and other contenders. Compared to Jean Seberg (whose songs ultimately had to be dubbed by Rita Gordon's singing voice) and Lee Marvin (whose hopelessly off-key warbling became a standing joke after release of the film), Clint Eastwood seemed a veritable Mario Lanza; at least he managed to perform his own musical numbers (in what critic Pauline Kael later described as a "light, thin little voice"), while looking steely-eyed and unsmiling out toward the horizon, suggesting that a possible ad line for the film might have been, "DIRTY HARRY SINGS!" As the great star himself commented when he first signed his contract, "I'm not exactly Howard Keel, but I think it'll work."

This attitude of "what the hey, we might as well give it a shot" typified the entire philosophy behind this sloppily planned and sorely misguided multi-million-dollar production. Equipped with dull songs that were hardly worth singing and three miscast stars who couldn't sing them anyway, the director and producer turned their attention to the energetic dance numbers from the Broadway original. At first, they approached Agnes De Mille (Cecil B.'s sister and gifted choreographer for the stage versions of *Oklahoma!* and *Brigadoon*), but she somehow managed to pass up the once-in-a-lifetime opportunity of directing hundreds of ragged miners, tramps, and pi-

Singing sensation Clint Eastwood strums another beautiful and bewitching tune as part of his role in Paint Your Wagon. *He wore the same grim, steely expression during all his songs—even when not wearing a cast on his leg and his arm in a sling.*

oneers in big production numbers from a second-rate Broadway show that already had all the earmarks of a third-rate Hollywood movie. Having failed to secure the services of Miss De Mille, Lerner and Logan decided that they didn't care about choreography after all and they might as well forget about most of the dance numbers. As a result, the miners merely wiggle without purpose while they are singing in a mineshaft, or wave their hats in the air minutes on end for the sheer joy of waving their hats in the air. As *Cue* magazine observed in its review of the film, "the vigorous choreography many remember is reduced to clomping around in the mud."

But to consider reviews at this point is to get ahead of ourselves and to miss out on all the fun and frolic involved in bringing this musical mess to its completion.

The Oregon Trail

By the time shooting finally began, the negative rumors concerning *Paint Your Wagon* had become so prevalent in Hollywood that the production team was glad to escape to a remote wilderness location in the Cascade Mountains. Lerner had personally selected an idyllic spot forty-six miles away from the nearest town—the bustling metropolis of Baker, Oregon—and there the studio builders constructed the boom town of No-Name City. The cast and crew lived in tents and rustic cabins, and suffered shortages of all sorts of equipment and amenities. The one

item, however, that no one expected to find in short supply was *trees*. Nevertheless, after the set had been completed, Logan decided that his mining town looked too barren, so he ordered some particularly scenic pine trees imported from Hollywood (honest to God) to the authentic-looking location in the midst of the Oregon woods. These nonspeaking coniferous extras were soon followed by a menagerie of trained animals who arrived from the studio to lend their talents to the production.

Shortly after their arrival, the beasts were unexpectedly upstaged by a band of 150 hippies who materialized out of the hills in which they lived to hand out flowers and kind words to the astonished filmmakers. Director Logan so admired their scraggly beards and generally "weatherbeaten" look that he immediately hired them as extras, playing the parts of prospectors, cowboys, mountain men, hobos, batik artists, and so forth. Needless to say, the hippies were delighted with their big chance to break into motion pictures, and the next day they brought more of their friends. Logan soon found himself running a bizarre circus of carpenters, trained animals, hippies, stars, camera equipment, and occasional unwelcome reporters. These newsmen reported that some of the lumberjacks who worked in the vicinity deeply resented the presence of the hippies and registered their displeasure by picking fights with the flower children or firing rifles into their encampments. Most members of the cast and crew could laugh at these mishaps, but Joshua Logan found himself ill-equipped to handle stress. He had already been diagnosed as a clinical manic-depressive, and as he later revealed, he consumed regular doses of lithium while struggling with the increasingly troubled production.

Lee Marvin sings his heart out for Paint Your Wagon; *despite his strenuous efforts, the laurels of the world's great lyric baritones remained safe. Marvin's voice (described by his co-star Jean Seberg as the sound of "rain gurgling down a rusty pipe") provided enough unintentional humor so that one of his songs ("I Was Born Under a Wand'rin' Star") became a surprise hit as a novelty item.*

Despite these problems he somehow managed to maintain a serene exterior until his long-standing friendship with Alan Jay Lerner began to disintegrate, along with his hopes for saving the picture.

Alan Jay Has His Way

Wearing the mantle of producer for the first time, Lerner felt justified in personally supervising every detail of the motion picture. He not only watched over Logan's shoulder as each scene took shape, but often countermanded the veteran director in telling the actors what to do. He particularly enjoyed setting up shots or arguing about camera angles, causing the director to feel useless and frustrated. For Logan, this awkward and unhappy situation reached a climax one evening when he returned from the set to find his wife anxiously awaiting him with a copy of the *Los Angeles Times*. The paper included a brief item by entertainment columnist Joyce Haber that gleefully reported that the filming of *Paint Your Wagon* had run into serious trouble and that the producers were ready to replace Joshua Logan with director Richard Brooks. Actually, a call to *Mel* Brooks might have made some sense, but as it was, this newspaper story only served to provide Logan with a welcome excuse for abandoning the project. Despite Lerner's assurances that the article had no factual basis and that he maintained full confidence in his director, Logan wanted to quit the picture immediately but discovered that his contract had been drawn in such a way that he could not leave without exposing himself to grave legal jeopardy. Thoroughly disgusted with the entire situation, Logan girded his loins and returned to the unpleasant business of capturing *Paint Your Wagon* on film.

As spring melted into summer in the Oregon wilderness, temperatures soared past 100 degrees, making everyone sweaty, uncomfortable, and irritable. In desperation, Logan begged the studio to save its own money by allowing him to return to Hollywood, where he could easily shoot the remaining scenes at Paramount's backlot. Showing an uncharacteristic and totally unexpected concern for "authenticity," the executives turned him down. They had already spent millions constructing grittily realistic sets in the Cascade Mountains, and they worried that a shift in location would give the film an inconsistent surface. As production costs rose to $80,000 a day, associate producer Tom Shaw told the press, "We're in one helluva fucking mess up here." A sudden rainstorm meant temporary relief from the heat, but it brought new problems in its wake. The single-lane

dirt road, which connected the movie location to the nearest town forty-six miles away, became totally impassable, and it had to be repaired—at the studio's expense—at a cost of $10,000 per mile. All of this did nothing to lift Alan Jay Lerner's spirits, and he nearly succeeded in killing himself when he tried to scramble down a 400-foot cliff in order to observe a particularly spectacular shot. Production assistants had to lower a rope to the terrified producer to pull him back to safety, but this particular adventure—so much more thrilling than the events in the script—was never recorded by the cameras.

Flower Power

Meanwhile, the several hundred itinerant flower children who had attached themselves to the production began causing so many problems that studio executives back in Hollywood jokingly suggested that a "Consultant in Charge of Hippies" should be added to the payroll. After viewing rushes on some of his crowd scenes, Logan had decided that the unkempt beards of his extras were just fine but that their hair—especially when worn in ponytails and braids—looked all wrong for the period of the Gold Rush. He demanded that the hippies shorten their locks if they expected to keep their jobs, but the young idealists were so enraged by this demand that they began handing out poison ivy along with the wild flowers they gave to everyone on the set. While this no doubt increased the budgetary allowance for calamine lotion, the hippies caused more serious problems when they organized a union and threatened to strike unless they received $25 per day (instead of the $20 that they were already earning) for their invaluable contributions to the motion picture. They also insisted that they be given daily "doggie bags" filled with commissary food in order to provide for all their hungry friends back in the hills. The filmmakers eventually gave in to these "nonnegotiable demands" and provided the young bohemians with the sense that they had made an admirable contribution to the Revolution.

When critic Rex Reed arrived on the scene to write a column about the progress of the filming, Josh Logan took advantage of the opportunity to vent his frustration. "I don't know what the hell I'm doing here," he confessed. "All these extras, all these unions to contend with. You're afraid to give anybody an extra line to say or the budget goes up another $10,000. You have to organize all these horses, all these cows, all these people, get the shot during

Magic Hour, while the sky is light enough to silhouette the nature you've come to photograph. I'm living each day to the next. I can't wait to get back to civilization." His wife, Nedda, asked the obvious rhetorical question, "Why, oh why, couldn't we have gone to Arrowhead? Or even Lake Tahoe?" Or, how about Knotts' Berry Farm amusement park? Alan Jay Lerner, as usual, had the last word. "If it's not difficult," he told Reed, "it's not worth doing."

The application of this peculiar standard would qualify *Paint Your Wagon* as one of the most worthwhile pictures ever made. Lee Marvin adjusted to the prevailing insanity by consuming huge quantities of alcohol and bringing a startling realism to his scenes as a drunk prospector. Concerning Mr. Marvin's ability to co-operate with his associates, Josh Logan commented, "Not since Attila the Hun swept across Europe leaving 500 years of total blackness has there been a man like Lee Marvin." On the opposite extreme was Jean Seberg, who developed a reputation for her accessibility and friendliness. She became a sort of mascot to the hippies and found she preferred their company on and off the set. This sort of behavior—including her service as a bridesmaid in a hippie wedding under a waterfall—went along with Miss Seberg's conception of her character. "She's sort of a nineteenth-century flower child in the middle of the Gold Rush," the actress observed. "She is deeply and genuinely in love with two men. I really dig that idea and believe it to be quite possible."

She dug the idea so much, in fact, that she proceeded to enrage her husband, French novelist Romain Gary (*The Roots of Heaven*), by falling in love with co-star Clint Eastwood. There must have been some fascinating ideological discussions between Black Panther–supporter Seberg and Eastwood, a long-time Ronald Reagan fan, but it is a well-known principle that bedfellows make strange politics. Whispers of the behind-the-scenes romance made their way from the Oregon woods to the gossip columns of the world press, and when Gary read the reports in Europe, he flew to the States immediately to take the situation in hand. The furious Frenchman confronted Eastwood at five A.M. in the kitchen of Alan Jay Lerner's cabin, loudly threatening to murder the American star unless he left Seberg alone. In his movies, Eastwood might specialize in turning his enemies every which way but loose, but this was one real-life fight that he wisely chose to avoid.

At long last, the weary company reached the climax of their lengthy and lamebrained production—a single huge scene in which all of No-Name City is supposed to collapse and fall into the earth. According to a witty premise in the script, Ben and Pardner have dug such extensive tunnels under the town in their desperate search for gold that the buildings can no longer support their own weight and are completely destroyed within a matter of moments. As one production assistant remarked while preparing the set for demolition, "$2,400,000 and seven months of construction go 'poof' for a few minutes of film." The cast and crew rejoiced as the buildings toppled, since they knew it marked the end of their long ordeal; what they failed to understand was that the symbolic scene also foretold the box office fate of the finished film.

Enlightened Consciousness

Having invested such an extraordinary amount of time and treasure on Lerner's Folly, Paramount natu-

An Aerial View of "No-Name City": It cost Paramount $2.4 million to construct this realistic replica of a Gold Rush town, deep in the Oregon wilderness, more than forty miles from civilization.

rally mounted a major media blitz on behalf of *Paint Your Wagon*. Advertising emphasized the hip and relevant aspects of this groovy musical; the studio executives reasoned that any movie in which the bearded, long-haired miners are consistently covered with mud and filth would appeal to the enlightened consciousness of the Love Generation. Peter Max, the famous designer who helped to initiate the pop psychedelic style of the late sixties, created the official logo for the film. It featured a wedding cake rendered in rainbow colors with Marvin, Seberg, and Eastwood as the figures on top. The ad line proclaimed, "BEN AND PARDNER SHARED EVERYTHING— EVEN THEIR WIFE!"

What they failed to share was popular success with their musical efforts. While critics and the public dismissed Eastwood's singing as simply inept (in particular his deadpan, earnest rendition of "I Talk to the Trees But They Don't Listen to Me"), Marvin's numbers seemed so hilariously awful that they developed a surprising popularity. Jean Seberg described her co-star's voice as the sound of "rain gurgling down a rusty pipe," while Lee Marvin himself saw it as "a combination of Tiny Tim and Wallace Beery." In any event, Marvin's adventurously atonal presentation of "I Was Born Under a Wand'rin' Star" surprised all observers by finding its way, as a novelty item, to the top of the hit record charts.

Despite this popular tune, the Peter Max designs, and the trendy advertising, *Paint Your Wagon* never came close to earning back its enormous cost. That cost, according to most estimates, amounted to $20 million, but some observers guessed that it actually ran to much more—especially in view of Paramount's conspicuous silence on this painful subject. The studio claimed that the picture grossed nearly $14 million from its worldwide release, but this announcement produced considerable skepticism for most of those close to the production. As Josh Logan tartly observed, "Whatever they tell you is not true." Even if it were, when costs of advertising and distribution had been added to the initial outlay for the production, the movie would have lost over $10 million.

Wagons Ho!

For Joshua Logan, this huge disaster marked the end of the line. He never directed another movie, but he did win revenge of sorts on his associates from *Paint Your Wagon* by providing a detailed description of their antics in his 1978 memoirs, *Movie Stars, Real People, and Me.* Jean Seberg also found it difficult to recover from her embarrassing experience in this much-heralded flop and found herself reduced to accepting parts in such worthy artistic vehicles as *Macho Callahan* (1970) and *Kill! Kill! Kill!* (1971). During the remainder of the seventies, this once promising star fought a losing battle against depression and drug addiction, with a well-publicized succession of husbands and lovers and a series of protracted stays at psychiatric hospitals. After several suicide attempts, she finally succeeded in taking her life in August 1979. Her former husband, Romain Gary, blamed himself for her tragic death, and within a year of her suicide he placed a pistol to his own mouth and pulled the trigger. Hollywood, ever eager to feast on its own carrion, apparently considers the brief life of Miss Seberg an irresistibly fascinating subject. In 1981, there was extensive talk of a film biography starring Cheryl Ladd, and a year later Oscar-winning composer Marvin Hamlisch announced plans for a musical stage play on the same subject.

Meanwhile, Clint Eastwood, who had been so closely involved with Seberg and Gary back in 1969, survived the failure of *Paint Your Wagon* with only minor damage to his reputation as a box office draw. From the pinnacle of his worldwide success in the 1970s, he could afford to look back in a philosophical frame of mind. "It was a disaster," he recalls, "but it didn't have to be such an *expensive* disaster. We had jets flying everyone in and out of Oregon, helicopters to take the wives to location for lunch, crews of seven trucks, thousands of extras getting paid for doing nothing . . . $20 million down the drain and most of it doesn't even show on the screen!" For Eastwood, the experience wasn't a total loss, since he walked out of the Oregon woods with a $500,000 acting fee and with an important lesson for his own career. He claims today that it was his education on this unfortunate film that persuaded him to form an independent production company and to direct most of his own movies in the future.

The studios also tried to learn from the grim fate of *Paint Your Wagon* and to come to terms with the fading popularity of big musicals in general. Lerner and Paramount had made a novel attempt to vary the traditional musical format by creating a racy plot and casting two nonsinging super-macho stars as the male leads. A decade later, producer Allan Carr created one of the first great musical flops of the eighties by moving in precisely the opposite direction; in *Can't Stop the Music* he mounted a highly traditional Hollywood story line and featured six flamboyant singing stars who were anything but macho. . . .

CAN'T STOP THE MUSIC

Associated Film Distribution
Produced by Allan Carr, Jacques Morali, and Henri Belolo
Directed by Nancy Walker
Screenplay by Allan Carr and Bronte Woodard
Music Composed and Produced by Jacques Morali
Choreography by Arlene Phillips

Starring The Village People (as "Themselves"); Valerie Perrine (Samantha Simpson);
Bruce Jenner (Ron White);
Steve Guttenberg (Jack Morell); Paul Sand (Steve Waits);
Tammy Grimes (Sydne Channing);
June Havoc (Helen Morell); Barbara Rush (Norma White);
Jack Weston (Benny Murray);
and The Ritchie Family.

"Everything for You Men to Enjoy"

In years to come, historians who sort through the rubble and relics of American culture in the late 1970s will search in vain for a persuasive explanation for the meteoric rise and fall of the celebrated singing group known as the Village People. For one brief shining (or at least glittery) moment, these six card-carrying eccentrics stood at the pinnacle of success—recognized as the most popular musical attraction in the country, if not the world. Their song "Y.M.C.A." sold more than 10 million copies worldwide and became the biggest hit single of the decade. The lyrics to this tender and sentimental ballad, which proclaimed the ability of lonely young men to meet one another at the "Y" and to develop meaningful relationships, all but announced to the world that in terms of their personal romantic preferences the Village People were, uh, "different."

In the past, whenever popular entertainers had projected an image of unconventional male sexuality, they went to great lengths to assure the public that they were not, in the final analysis, effeminate quiche eaters. Even the great Liberace launched several well-publicized lawsuits against those who dared to question his credentials as a red-blooded, two-fisted all-American heterosexual, while the irrepressible Tiny Tim—the 1960s singing rage with the piercing

falsetto and flowing, curly locks—answered challenges to his masculinity by marrying a pretty young lady in a ceremony broadcast live on nationwide TV.

The Village People, on the other hand, took advantage of the more tolerant spirit of the seventies to challenge the norms of straight society openly and joyously. When their songs included paeans to the charms of such well-known gay meccas as Fire Island, Hollywood, and San Francisco, or openly hailed the joys of leading a "Sleazy" life, no one could confuse these particular villagers with residents of Winesburg, Ohio.

The moving force behind the group was the French composer and record producer Jacques Morali. One fateful evening in 1976 he visited a popular Greenwich Village night spot that featured a go-go "Indian," clad only in headdress and breechclout, doing an improvised war dance on top of the bar. As the bogus brave's brown, well-oiled body twisted sinuously and suggestively to a big beat sound, Morali felt a sudden inspiration: he would assemble a group of oddball performers in similarly provocative costumes to present his original disco creations.

Using this same noble savage (one Felipe Rose) as the nucleus of the group, Morali placed an ad in several New York papers asking for "young men, with moustaches, who can sing and dance." From the hun-

Their Cup Runneth Over: One might have thought that the Village People in and of themselves would provide enough high camp for any dozen movies, but to gild the lily for Can't Stop the Music, *producer Allan Carr also secured the services of Valerie Perrine as the (very) lonely female love interest.*

dreds of respondents, he selected six and created synthetic identities for each of them that lampooned one of the classic American macho stereotypes. In addition to the Indian, the Village People included a cowboy, a hard-hat construction worker, a cop, a soldier, and a leathered biker.

The group not only won a fanatic following in New York's gay community, but surprised everyone by demonstrating an enormous appeal to prepubescent girls across the country. These teeny boppers may not have understood the suggestive lyrics of the songs, but they clearly perceived that there was an exciting air of the exotic and the forbidden surrounding these "cute," wildly gyrating young men with their outlandish costumes and tough-guy onstage identities.

Among the biggest fans of this hot new group was Allan Carr, the Hollywood producer whose ebullient personal style managed to suggest a strange meld of Alvin the Chipmunk and Truman Capote. Known for colorful caftans that snugly encased his plump body or for showing up at formal occasions clad in an ankle-length mink coat and tennis shoes, Carr made his name and his fortune as co-producer of the megahit, *Grease.* This soporific view of high school life in the "Nifty Fifties" won universal condemnation from the critics but turned out to be the largest-grossing musical in movie history, based on the magical appeal of its stars—John Travolta and Olivia Newton-John—to hordes of teenage Americans. Since the Village People had demonstrated similar popularity

with the same vast juvenile audience, Carr eagerly signed them as the stars of his next blockbuster musical.

The basic concept for this new movie seemed obvious: it would tell the story, in fictionalized and fanciful terms, of the formation of the group and its rise to stardom. An unassuming American boy named Jack Morell would stand in for real-life Frenchman Jacques Morali (get it?). To play the part of this aspiring composer, Carr hired Steve Guttenberg (who later won fame—and a measure of respectability—as the nervous bridegroom in *Diner*), a young actor described hopefully by the producer as "a Jewish John Travolta." In addition to the thrilling love affair between Jack Morell and disco music, and the progress of the Village People from obscure roots in New York City to a triumphal concert in (where else?) San Francisco, the movie needed a straight romance to broaden its appeal. Carr therefore worked with screenwriter Bronte Woodard (who was, according to the merry mogul, "a teenaged Tennessee Williams") to create a subplot concerning a high-fashion model who helps to launch the group and her love-hate relationship with an uptight lawyer from St. Louis who has a tough time adjusting to the free-spirited eighties. To play the all-important female lead, Carr wanted Olivia Newton-John but refused to give in to her demand for a $1 million fee. When negotiations collapsed, the Australian superstar moved on to act in *Xanadu*—an atrocious roller-disco musical that ultimately proved no more successful than

Can't Stop the Music (see the listing in our Basement Collection)—while Allan Carr turned to Valerie Perrine as his second choice for the role. Purists might insist that Miss Perrine boasted personal proportions far more heroic than those possessed by any high-fashion model in this galaxy, but Carr had his heart set on the girl who, in his own eloquent phrase, "saved *Superman's* life and fondled *Lenny's* private parts." To star opposite this sultry siren, the producer chose Bruce Jenner, an Olympic decathlon champion who had never acted before but who, Carr assured the press and public, would soon be recognized as "the Bob Redford of the eighties."

To direct this odd assortment of talent and to shape a unified film out of these wildly disparate elements, Carr might have called upon Ken Russell, or perhaps Mel Brooks, but instead he recruited comedienne Nancy Walker to make her debut behind the camera. Best known as "Rosie the Bounty Lady" and as Rhoda's mother from television, Miss Walker was as surprised as anyone else that Carr, her former agent, wanted her as his director. When he called and asked her, "Nancy, are you ready for a change of life?" her immediate response was "What do you mean, professionally or menopausally?" Her only apparent qualifications for the job were her sense of humor and her record of outspoken and courageous participation in several gay-rights political battles.

"A Gorgeous Love Affair"

Despite the presence of "a Jewish John Travolta," "a teenaged Tennessee Williams," "the Bob Redford of the eighties," a producer who modestly described himself as "another Mike Todd," and a lavish budget of some $20 million, Carr seemed nervous about the future of his big project. "A lot of people in Hollywood, the ones who trade in mediocrity, think I'm crazy," he told reporters. "Nancy never directed a movie. Bruce never acted in one. Valerie has no name at the box office.... Well, I don't give a damn what people think. At some point in your life you've got to realize you're good and trust your instincts. You have to go with the things you believe in." Now, wait just one moment: is this Sir Richard Attenborough discussing the making of *Gandhi* or Allan Carr describing the making of a tacky, exploitative musical extravaganza designed to cash in on the big disco craze? "I have a lot of perseverance with those things I believe in, whether they're in vogue at the moment or not," Mr. Carr solemnly intoned. "I do what I think has real value."

Unfortunately, the Village People themselves failed to see the timeless value in the movie vehicle that the crusading, high-minded producer had so nobly designed for them. Said group member David Hodo ("The Construction Worker"): "When I first read the script, I threw it across the room. I thought it was a piece of crap. It read like one of those stupid old Judy Garland and Mickey Rooney pictures ... We didn't believe in the movie, but no one would listen to us! You can only go on for so long being a joke." Another Village Person, "Cowboy" Randy Jones, met the authors of this book during a joint TV appearance in Australia and told us that *Can't Stop the Music* should have been included in *The Fifty Worst Films of All Time*. During the preproduction planning sessions, screenwriter Bronte Woodard showed little concern over the Village People's obvious lack of enthusiasm for his script. "It's the musical numbers that they do that they're famous for," he assured the press. "All they have to be is charming and kind of funny in the other scenes." Carr and company also wanted a title that would be "charming and kind of funny," so they came up with *Discoland: Where the Music Never Ends!*, hoping that all fans of

The Merry Mogul: That well-known visionary and idealist, Allan Carr, explained the genesis of Can't Stop the Music *by telling the press, "You have to go with the things you believe in ... I do what I think has real value."*

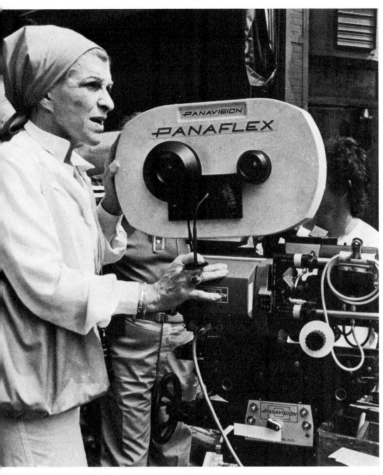

First-time director Nancy Walker, best known as "Rosie the Bounty Lady" from television commercials, explains the similarities between a motion picture camera and a roll of paper towels.

America's hot new sound would get down and boogie-oogie-oogie over to their local theatre to join in the fun. Unfortunately, in the midst of production, some of the producer's assistants forced him to face the grim news that the worldwide disco craze had obviously peaked, while buttons and bumper stickers declaring that "Disco Sucks" proliferated among hard-core rock 'n' roll fans. Carr therefore agreed to drop the controversial word "disco" from the name of his costly new film and instead delivered an order in stern, imperative terms to the fickle public. *You Can't Stop the Music!* shrieked the new title of the movie, and it was later shortened to the more catchy designation, *Can't Stop the Music.* In either case, this declaration represented a striking example of wishful thinking.

Meanwhile, old hands at the MGM lot, where the company spent eight weeks of its eleven-week shooting schedule, came up with their own name for the production. As one veteran studio employee recalled, "Usually, studio people are a hardened bunch. I mean, we have seen everything. But the group who worked on that movie was just too much. The costumes! We were used to seeing Nazi soldiers or spacemen on the lot, but not this! Every day it was like Mardi Gras at New Orleans. It was a stomach-turning experience. It wasn't just Carr and the Village People, but all the pals and hangers-on they brought along. We were just inundated. After a while, we started calling the film, *Can't Stop the Faggots.*"

One of the highlights of the film involved a huge production number, à la Busby Berkeley, in which literally hundreds of muscular young men clad only in bikini bathing suits and glistening body oil dance through a series of well-choreographed calisthenics to celebrate the glories of the Y.M.C.A. and to provide background for an on-screen performance of their hit song. Director Nancy Walker considered this stirring scene her greatest achievement. "What I'm working for is a sense of rhythms," she explained, "and our cinematographer Bill Butler is unbelievable. How he handled all those nude dancers in the Y.M.C.A. number is a study for psychologists in people management . . . This whole film is just a gorgeous love affair."

That love affair reached its climax with the filming of the movie's finale: a gala concert at San Francisco's Galleria. With the production already running well above budget, Carr proved reluctant to pay extras to act the part of the enthusiastic audience. Instead, he staged a live performance by the Village People and asked the public to pay $15 a seat for the privilege of attending and appearing in the film. To the press, Carr described the event as "just a little party for three thousand of my closest friends." From a cinematic point of view, the filmmakers faced a major problem when a disturbingly high percentage of those close friends turned out to be drag queens in feathers and finery. This was not exactly the image that either Carr or the Village People wished to convey to the American public, so the concert footage required extensive splicing and cutting and the utilization of various cunning camera angles to emphasize the presence of a few "ordinary" teenagers while calling attention away from the large contingent of wildly enthusiastic transvestite San Franciscans.

When Carr completed work on the film and invited industry insiders to advance screenings, their opinion was unanimous: *Can't Stop the Music* was an inept and pointless piece of work, but its peripatetic producer, fresh from his triumph with *Grease,* had another commercial blockbuster on his hands. "Start counting the bucks," *Film Journal* predicted. *Playboy* commented that "Milos Forman's *Hair* and Bob Fosse's *All That Jazz* were ten times more skillfully made. *Music* will probably make ten times more than either of them." While *Variety* worried about the new film's bloated budget, it eventually reached the same optimistic conclusions: "Cost aside, the box office prospects seem promising . . . Carr has got a hot property that will doubtless appeal widely; maybe he's already considering a sequel to be called *Can't Stop the Money.*"

In order to make sure that his picture fulfilled these expectations, the party-mad producer launched a lavish worldwide publicity blitz with a budget in excess of $10 million. "Glamour, I want Hollywood glamour all over the world!" he told the press. "This picture lends itself to partying. It's fun and upbeat and I want people to feel like having a good time *afterwards.*" Perhaps these good times "afterwards" would help audiences forget the lousy time they had inside the theatres. Carr certainly did his best to hide his movie's meagre entertainment value behind a multi-colored smokescreen of inventive hoopla. In Los Angeles, the unveiling of a *billboard* advertising the film inspired more hype and received more attention than the actual premiere of most other pictures. To facilitate the billboard's debut, modestly billed by Carr as "The First Major Event of the Eighties," the police closed off traffic for three blocks on busy Sunset Boulevard. To join in the spirit of this joyous afternoon, the city council declared April 10 as "Can't Stop the Music Day" and Mayor Tom Bradley, who attended the unveiling in person, presented Carr with an official City of L.A. resolution honoring him as "The Master Showman of the Eighties." When the fateful moment arrived, and the Master Showman himself gave the signal, Valerie Perrine lifted her skirt, extended a shapely leg, and stepped on a "magic lever" that caused the curtains to suddenly drop and exposed the Great Billboard to the world. Because of Carr's commitment to the advertising firm that owned the space, this 300-foot-long white elephant remained in place for five months—long after *Can't Stop the Music* had disappeared from the screens of even fifth-run skid row movie houses—and served as a vivid reminder of the film's laughable failure.

Can't Stop the Rotten Eggs

The first hint of that failure was provided by the gleefully savage reviews:

"It's true . . . you really can't stop the music, no matter how much you want to, and at times you'll want to very, very much . . . This Allan Carr–produced extravaganza is less a movie than some kind of bizarre artifact, a forced marriage between the worst of sitcom plotting and the highest of high camp production numbers."—*New West*

"Some scenes could pulp and solve the paper shortage, they're so wooden." —*Variety*

"Watching it was akin to witnessing a disco interpretation of the dance of the seven veils in which Salome turned out to be a male chorine who Couldn't Resist the Chiffon." —*Film Comment*

"One doesn't watch *Can't Stop the Music.* One is attacked by it." —*New England Entertainment Digest*

"Producer Allan Carr's guiding principle seems to be: shoot everything that moves, throw it on the cutting room floor, give the editor a vacuum cleaner and hope that it will all work out. It doesn't." —*Time*

The fabulous chorus line featured in the epic "Y.M.C.A." sequence of Can't Stop the Music. *Busby Berkeley, eat your heart out!*

Valerie Perrine can't seem to attract the attention of an excited Bruce Jenner after he has been exposed to the more subtle charms of the Village People in Can't Stop the Music.

"Considering the low level of wit in this film, perhaps the Village People should consider renaming themselves the Village Idiots." —*Los Angeles Magazine*

"This shamefully tacky musical extravaganza fails on every aesthetic level." —*Los Angeles Herald-Examiner*

To the surprise of virtually everyone, the film also began to fail on a commercial level. Carr and his apologists blamed these disappointing returns on "bad timing"; at the historical moment the movie was released, record sales and other indicators pointed clearly to the fact that America (at last!) had been cured of disco fever. Nevertheless, the picture suffered a rejection so massive and so universal that it obviously had as much to do with its own wretched quality as with the ever-shifting currents of musical taste. Even the gay community—the core audience for the Village People—felt betrayed by the coy and sanitized approach of the film. In one key scene, construction worker David Hodo indulges his "favorite fantasy" (to the accompaniment of a musical number called "I Love You to Death"); the audience discovers, much to its surprise, that his most secret thoughts are exclusively—and safely—heterosexual. In movie houses in gay neighborhoods in New York, Hollywood, and San Francisco, the angry patrons greeted this sequence—and the entire film—with derisive booing and, in several instances, with rotten eggs heaved at the screen.

Despite mounting evidence of box office disaster, Carr continued down the promotional primrose path, taking the Village People, Bruce Jenner, Miss Perrine, and other members of his traveling circus and road show throughout the Midwest and up and down the East Coast for one well-publicized party after another. The merry mogul himself had no difficulty whatever in ignoring the hostility of critics and the public, but less stout-hearted members of the grand tour began dropping out one by one. As *People* magazine reported, "By Boston, most of the cast had remembered urgent business elsewhere and fled the scene." At the end, only June Havoc and Steve Guttenberg remained with Captain Carr aboard his sinking ship.

When all the pixie dust had finally settled, they did, in fact, stop the music: according to annual reports in *Variety*, Allan Carr's $20 million indulgence managed to gross *less* than $2 million domestically. Foreign returns proved little better, as *Can't Stop the Music* turned out to be a resounding flop in every country in which it opened—with the singular exception of Australia, where it did spectacular business and managed to set box office records. (Perhaps the Aussies merely wanted to express their gratitude at the fact that their own Olivia Newton-John had, despite Carr's best attempts, been spared the title role in this fatuous Yank fiasco.) The producer, in any event, rewarded the good folks down under for their loyal support by establishing the annual "Allan Carr Awards" at the Australian Film and Television School. The lucky winners—selected by the faculty for their creative promise—earned the right to work for three glorious weeks as "trainees" on a future Allan Carr production. No one could predict the number of weeks it would take these poor unwitting students to *un-learn* the boneheaded filmmaking principles they were bound to pick up at the feet of

the master.

Needless to say, the Village People never recovered from the poisonous aftereffects of the embarrassment surrounding their film debut. Later in 1980 they tried an uneventful guest spot on ABC's *The Love Boat* and played for a week at Las Vegas' Riviera Hotel—with notoriously disastrous results. By this time, country singer Kinky Friedman had begun referring to the has-been group as "The Shalom Retirement Village People." In 1981, they made a desperate attempt at a comeback, abandoning their familiar macho man costumes in favor of the space age Elizabethan outfits first popularized by David Bowie. Abandoning their outdated disco sound, signing with a new record company, giving themselves a stylish new designation as "The V.P.'s," they cut a new album hopefully entitled "Renaissance." It quickly bombed, as the group faded even further into obscurity.

Nancy Walker, meanwhile, confounded the critics who said that in light of the utter ineptitude of *Can't Stop the Music*, she would never again get a job as a director. In 1981, she did, in fact, direct a new production of *The Odd Couple*, in which she co-starred with Eve Arden, at the Burt Reynolds Dinner Theatre in Jupiter, Florida. The play drew mixed reviews, and Miss Walker continues to be best known as Rosie, Paper Towel Queen of Television.

As for Allan Carr himself, the failure of his magnum opus proved only a temporary setback in his career. In 1982, he unleashed *Grease II*—another major bomb—but set to work shortly thereafter on a remake of the George Hamilton–Connie Francis classic, *Where the Boys Are*. Despite disappointments, he maintains to this day an admirable zest for living and for his career. "It's fabulous," he confided to reporters, "I love it. I think secretly everyone else wants to do what I do, too, but few people do it. It's my life . . . It's like a talk show!"

Mr. Carr deserves our admiration for his effervescent enthusiasm in the face of adversity, and his light-hearted abandon will be sorely missed as we move along toward the solemn, portentous, self-consciously artistic cinematic spectaculars that are displayed in the final corridor of our main exhibition area. . . .

DELUSIONS
OF GRANDEUR

REVEREND Sun Myung Moon believes he is the Messiah.

It is not our place to assail that conviction, but rather to examine what happens when this exalted self-image and sense of divinely appointed mission are applied to the business of making movies. *Inchon*, Reverend Moon's unforgettable adventure in the world of motion pictures, offered a $48 million answer to that question.

Heaven's Gate represented a similarly expensive indulgence by a highly touted director with messianic delusions all his own. Though Michael Cimino, to the best of our knowledge, has never attempted to heal the sick with a touch of his hand, claimed a direct hot line to heaven, or ordered his followers to peddle flowers at street corners, he supervised the production of his wild, wild Western with such unshakable faith in his own infallibility that the crew began referring to him as "The Ayatollah." In the cases of both of these movies, spiritual, mystical, and "artistic" considerations took precedence over the common-sense calculations of ordinary earth-bound filmmakers.

These flights of fancy resulted in fiascos of breathtaking and monumental scope. Though inflation adjustments would give *Cleopatra* the inside track for the all-time title, the films displayed in this last gallery in our tour are, in terms of raw dollars-and-cents figures, the two most expensive movies made to date and the most costly failures in the history of entertainment. In this sense, at least, the grandeur they achieved is no delusion.

HEAVEN'S GATE
(1980/81)

United Artists
Produced by Joann Carelli
Directed by Michael Cimino
Screenplay by Michael Cimino

Starring Kris Kristofferson (Marshal James Averill);
Christopher Walken (Nathan D. Champion); John Hurt (Billy Irvine);
Isabelle Huppert (Ella Watson); Sam Waterston (Frank Canton);
Jeff Bridges (John H. Bridges); and Joseph Cotten ("The Reverend Doctor").

The Emperor Unclothed

The title *Heaven's Gate* has become a byword for disaster in the English language—like "Watergate," "Waterloo," or perhaps most appropriately, "Armageddon." The merest mention of this film conjures up images of folly and failure on an epic scale; though few people have actually seen it, nearly everyone makes jokes about its laughably low quality. No other motion picture in history has received such universal and such enthusiastic scorn.

Several factors help to explain this movie's unique notoriety. First and foremost is the sheer size of the debacle—the production costs of *Heaven's Gate* rose to the record-breaking level of $44 million and the studio's total losses on the project, with various interest and promotion charges included, easily exceeded $55 million. Moreover, it is safe to say that no film within memory has delivered less "bang for its buck"; for all the squandered money and production delays, *Heaven's Gate* remains nothing more than a dreary little Western, bereft of superstars, massive orgy sequences, special-effects miracles, or spectacular battle scenes. The picture's bungled release—with the much-heralded opening canceled at the last minute to allow for re-editing—further contributed to the negative reputation of the project. And finally, there was the colorful personality of the film's creator, Michael Cimino, which generated a particularly strong reaction from the world's critics, commentators, and comedians.

In the public eye, Cimino represented the well-

publicized group of Hollywood *wunderkinder* who had taken the industry by storm in the 1970s. Brash young directors such as Steven Spielberg, George Lucas, and Francis Ford Coppola might spark a certain amount of resentment from the Hollywood establishment, but no one could deny that the people "out there" loved their movies. When Spielberg dropped his gigantic bomb *1941*, or Coppola perpetrated the wildly expensive failure *One From the Heart*, they escaped full-scale public contempt because of lingering affection for *Close Encounters* and *The Godfather*. Michael Cimino, on the other hand, had never enjoyed that sort of massive acceptance. His one cinematic triumph—*The Deer Hunter*—had inspired grudging respect rather than widespread enthusiasm. No one—perhaps not even Cimino himself—understood what this controversial movie was about, but the critics agreed it was "original" and "important," and the Academy presented it the Oscar for Best Picture of 1978, so "serious" filmgoers dutifully trooped to their local theatres. Two years later these same movie fans, along with insiders from the Hollywood community, reacted with ill-disguised glee when *Heaven's Gate* began collapsing around its creator. It was true, they agreed, that the overpraised Emperor wore no clothes, and years of pent-up resentment against "artsy-fartsy" directors and their grand pretensions found a juicy target in Michael Cimino.

The object of this obloquy was born in New York City in 1943, the son of a prosperous music publisher. From his earliest years, young Michael knew he was a genius, but it took him a while to discover the right field for his unique talents. At first he dreamed of glory as a great architect and won an architecture degree from Yale in 1963. After serving a brief stint as a medic at an army training camp (he never made it to 'Nam), Cimino studied painting in Paris with Jackson Pollock's brother, took ballet lessons, and after catching the show biz bug, enrolled in the Actors Studio back in New York. This led to a job with a documentary film company, which led in turn to steady work as a director of TV commercials. In this capacity, he created a series of memorable thirty-second spots for worthy products such as Lustre Creme and Nescafé. Unfortunately, the chief lesson of successful advertising—"economy in story-telling"—was apparently forgotten by Our Man Mike when he graduated to feature films.

The Script That Wouldn't Die

This big transition came in the early seventies, while Hollywood was still trying to come to terms with the enormous success of *Easy Rider* (1969), and the major studios courted anyone under thirty who had a beard and a script. Though Cimino remained clean-shaven throughout his career, he did qualify on the other two counts and managed to break into the motion picture business on the strength of his screenplay *Silent Running*—an environmentalist sci-fi adventure that he had co-written with two friends. It became a Universal picture in 1972.

The year before this first creation made its way to the big screen, Cimino had already completed his second script: *The Johnson County War*, a romanticized treatment of an obscure incident in the history of Wyoming. The new screenplay told the story of wealthy and greedy cattlemen who try to protect their range land by driving impoverished homesteaders from their farms. Its combination of melodrama and social conscience appealed to producer David Foster, who optioned the property and tried to win backing from major studios. "It was wonderful. I was freaked over it," Foster recalls. "But even back then there was already this knock against anything that smelled of a Western, and nobody was willing to take that shot."

While *Johnson County War* bounced from one executive office to another, the boy wonder got lucky on another front: he did a rewrite for Clint Eastwood on his *Dirty Harry* sequel, *Magnum Force*. Cimino's slick, efficient contribution to this enormously successful project so impressed Eastwood that the magnanimous star offered the young screenwriter his first

Director Michael Cimino emphasizes the exacting eye for detail that helped to bloat the budget for Heaven's Gate *beyond $40 million. "If you don't get it right," he told the press, "what's the point?"*

chance to direct. The result was the Eastwood–Jeff Bridges vehicle *Thunderbolt and Lightfoot* (1974), based on Cimino's original screenplay. As the pressbook for that buddy-buddy road picture aptly pointed out, "For Cimino, it's a male Cinderella story come true—with Eastwood being his Prince Charming." Bridges won an Academy Award nomination as Best Supporting Actor, and the $4 million picture went on to gross more that $25 million worldwide. *Time* magazine praised the thirty-one-year-old director for his "scrupulously controlled eye," but the budget had been scrupulously controlled by Eastwood—who knew how to keep an eye on his directors.

Over the next four years Cimino worked on various scripts, including *The Dogs of War* and *The Rose*, but labored most energetically on *The Johnson County War*. After every studio in Hollywood had turned away this ungainly pet, he sat down to write a major revision under the fresh new title *Paydirt*. Twentieth Century-Fox took an option on the refurbished property in 1975 but had no idea what to do with it. Cimino made himself something of a pest with his tenacious refusal to abandon the project; like the dull pain of a canker sore, it continued to fester in his consciousness.

In 1977 the British company EMI Productions asked Cimino to pitch them some script ideas, and he came up with the basic concept for *The Deer Hunter*. When the English producers expressed strong interest in the project, Cimino demanded the chance to direct the picture as well as writing the screenplay; somewhat to his surprise, EMI agreed. In view of the young filmmaker's limited directorial experience, Her Majesty's moguls were in fact imitating the characters in the story who put partially loaded guns to their heads and spin the cylinders. While Cimino repeatedly reassured the press that "there are no problems with the budget of *Deer Hunter*," the final cost of the film wound up at $15 million—nearly twice what the producers had planned. Nevertheless, commercial and critical prospects looked promising, so what's a few million dollars among friends? Despite the ominous demonstration of his deep-seated propensity for budget busting and perfectionism, Cimino had suddenly become a recognized rising star as a filmmaker.

Even with his newfound prestige, the studios still found it easy to say no to Michael Cimino when he tried, once again, to peddle his warmed-over *Johnson County* script. While he waited for the release of *The Deer Hunter* in the summer of '78, he prepared a third version of the screenplay and submitted it to Twentieth Century-Fox. A story analyst's report judged the result as "not a wholly satisfying piece of work, lacking in pace and humor, and being obscure and oblique." By this time, a lesser man would have abandoned the fight and moved on to more promising material, but Cimino had developed a ferocious obsession with his subject matter. The long, frustrating struggle to get the film made no doubt contributed to his total lack of perspective when he finally had the chance to realize his dreams.

That chance came following a much-publicized management shake-up at United Artists. In a move that became known as "The Great Walkout," many of the top executives and production supervisors abandoned U.A. after a pay dispute and went on to form the Orion Company. To fill the empty positions, United Artists bumped its middle-management people up to the top decision-making slots, where they struggled to prove themselves "for real" before their Fairy Godmother turned their new Mercedes limousines into pumpkins. These various Peter Principle appointees naturally looked for cinematic saviors: hot young directors who would make them look good in a hurry. According to Steven Bach, the new vice president in charge of production: "There was absolutely no question that we wanted to be a part of,

however distant, a Michael Cimino movie." With that kind of blind faith, Cimino could have been pushing a $12 million story about the development of peat moss and the U.A. brass would have exploded in orgasms. They proceeded to snap up the rights to *The Johnson County War* (Big Mike having returned to the original title), while ignoring the obvious flaws in the script that Twentieth Century-Fox had pinpointed so accurately. Said Steven Bach: "Reading a Michael Cimino screenplay is a very deceptive thing, because what *you* see when you read is not necessarily what *Cimino* sees." This difference in vision certainly applied to the numbers in the budget, for which U.A. initially committed the relatively modest sum of $7.8 million.

To make sure that Cimino stayed within his assigned parameters, United Artists sensibly assigned his girlfriend and former secretary, Joann Carelli, as "line producer" for the project. Though the top executives must surely have recognized that her relationship with the director might color her judgment, they apparently felt confident that her vast cinematic experience would allow her to overcome this bias: after all, Carelli had served as a "production consultant"—or glorified researcher—on *The Deer Hunter*, her first (and only) prior film credit. Cimino, quite naturally, welcomed the participation of his longtime *amore* as overall supervisor of the project. So long as somebody had to be around to sign checks and monitor cost overruns, it might as will be someone with whom him he could—shall we say—stay on top of the situation.

In retrospect, the inexplicable decision to give Carelli the chance for on-the-job training as producer of *Heaven's Gate* may have been the single most fateful factor in the unfolding fiasco. At the time, however, it seemed a small price to pay for the privilege of signing up an "enormous talent" such as Michael Cimino. The young director had precisely the sort of reputation that U.A. needed to change its "sinking ship" image within the industry; in fact, they trumpeted their new association with full-page ads in the Hollywood trade press. These announcements, under the heading "The Company We Keep," showcased various "creative" people who had agreed to work with the studio, but most prominently featured Cimino and Carelli (Carelli?). Beneath a photograph of the fledgling producer, the text congratulated "United Artists, where creative newcomers like Joann Carelli traditionally find a welcome." For Cimino, the copy began, "You might guess from Michael Cimino's expressive hands and face that he's a masterful storyteller. You'd be right."

Merrily They Roll Along: Federal Marshal James Averill (Kris Kristofferson) and independent businesswoman Ella Watson (Isabelle Huppert) strut their stuff at the Heaven's Gate roller skating arena in Johnson County, Wyoming, while to their left, Jeff Bridges prepares for the spectacular tumble he will take, along with the rest of the cast, once the film is released.

(And he certainly told them an expressive and masterful story about the millions of dollars they would make from his *Johnson County* extravaganza!) In an ironic concluding statement at the bottom of each of the ads, a slogan proclaimed, "UA—THE INTERESTING PLACE TO BE . . . THE PLACE TO BE INTERESTING." Had the unsuspecting executives realized in advance just *how* interesting the next two years would be, they no doubt would have preferred to find a less intriguing place for themselves.

Great Expectations

Cimino finally began shooting on his long-delayed Western on the morning of April 10, 1979. Just one week earlier he had walked away with five Academy Awards for *The Deer Hunter* (including Best Picture and Best Director), and the top officials at United Artists had already begun congratulating one another on their genius in signing up Cimino's new project. By the time filming began in Montana, that project had undergone a name change. The old title, *The Johnson County War*, conjured up prosaic images of Hatfields, McCoys, and hillbilly feuds, while the new designation, *Heaven's Gate*, seemed more poetic, portentous, and appropriate in light of the vastly increased prestige—and pretensions—of the Academy Award–winning director.

Those pretensions became painfully obvious when Cimino described *Heaven's Gate* to a reporter who visited the set as "an American *Great Expectations*." It is hard to imagine any points of similarity whatever between his Western adventure and Dickens' masterpiece, except for a possible resemblance between the director's increasingly grand delusions and the sad fantasy world of Miss Havisham. Cimino's story centers around Harvard graduate James Averill (Kris Kristofferson), who, motivated by burning idealism, serves as a U.S. marshal in the raw, unsettled Wyoming Territory. Averill naturally sympathizes with the starving homesteaders, most of them immigrants from Eastern Europe, who are forced to steal and butcher stray cattle in order to feed their families. This bit of frontier self-reliance arouses the ire of a group of wealthy cattlemen, who seem to combine all the worst personality traits of Simon Legree and J. R. Ewing. The leader of this pack of scoundrels is Frank Canton (Sam Waterston, complete with a little moustache that gives him an unmistakable resemblance to Adolf Hitler), who hires a gang of fifty hitmen to knock off 125 settlers who are suspected of rustling. In this ambitious project, the imported thugs will have the assistance of an uncouth but lovable local gunslinger, Nathan D. Champion (Christopher Walken). In the leisure time left over from these murderous pursuits, Walken competes with Kristofferson for the favors of the young tart (Isabelle Huppert) who runs the local brothel, known as "The

Christopher Walken plays Nate Champion, a sensitive gunfighter, in Heaven's Gate. *We know he is sensitive because of the heavy layers of mascara around his eyes.*

Hog Ranch." In a climactic scene, all of the downtrodden Johnson Countyites assemble at their local roller-skating rink (which is called Heaven's Gate, hence the title), where they are inspired by the example of their Ivy League marshal to organize for the purpose of defending their lives and their homes against the capitalist bully boys.

Cimino's final shooting script emphasized some commercially viable elements to add spice to this otherwise unsavory stew, including the romantic triangle between two cowboys and a whorehouse madam, a bloody cockfight (not between two men, but with real chickens), lots of nudity, loads of violence, a graphic rape scene, and a fun-filled, musical roller-skating sequence as a sort of *hommage* to *Xanadu* or *Roller Boogie*. Unfortunately, the story lacked the conventional happy ending expected by fans of Hollywood horse operas; when the U.S. cavalry rides over the hill at the conclusion of the film's interminable battle sequence between the ragged homesteaders and the cold-blooded mercenaries, they arrive just in the nick of time to save the *bad* guys! Before this uplifting conclusion, the villains have succeeded in slaughtering literally hundreds of innocent people by trampling them with horses, shooting them in the head, or crushing them under the wheels of a moving barricade.

In actual, historical fact, only two individuals died in the real Johnson County "war"—a minor discrepancy that Cimino cheerfully ignored. "It was not my intention to write a history book," he snapped at reporters who questioned his version of events. "The specific facts of that incident recounted in a literal way would be of no interest . . . One uses history in a very free way." Unfortunately for the budget of his film, the director felt no such freedom when it came to minor details of his production. "Every article of clothing, every structure, every sign," he boasted to the press, "is based on a photograph of the period . . . Even when detail is there but not seen, I still feel it contributes something. It's a necessity for me to feel the presence of that detail in order to work properly on a set, or a location." To make sure that this temperamental *artiste* could "work properly" on a scene that showed the "huddled masses" arriving in Wyoming, he "had people scouring the country for a standard-gauge steam locomotive. And when we found it, we had to have it and the rest of the train brought in on flatbed cars from Denver across five states! And before shipping, the cars were rebuilt inside and out." For the fabled roller-skating sequence, "we had to find 250 people, men, women, and children, properly cast, who could skate. Or they had to be taught to skate. Each of them was given a cassette

"The Huddled Masses, Yearning to Breathe Free": Brad Dourif addresses a meeting of immigrant settlers while Jeff Bridges looks on, obviously impressed by his eloquence.

of the music they would be skating to, and they were sent off for six months. Then they were brought back and individually wardrobed for the period, according to old photographs."

In addition to developing their expertise as roller skaters, Cimino initiated required classes for his actors and extras in the other most important "frontier skills," including horseback riding, bullwhipping, wagon driving, and waltzing. (It is unknown whether the director based this curriculum on an antique photograph showing an Arthur Murray studio in nineteenth-century Johnson County.) At Cimino's command, Isabelle Huppert prepared for her role as an immigrant prostitute by spending three days in a Wallace, Idaho, bordello—though the French actress declined to specify just how deeply she pursued her research. Meanwhile, a former Green Beret specialist gave instructions to the entire cast in firing handguns, an exercise that, in the eloquent words of the director, "sensitized the actors in how to use weapons not as props, but as lethal aids."

Constantly Busy

Despite this carefree summer-camp atmosphere, with plenty of arts, crafts, and recreational activities to keep all his campers constantly busy, Cimino ran into serious trouble stemming from his choice of location. Before shooting began, the director and his associates had traveled some 20,000 miles throughout the western United States, searching for scenery grand enough to serve as a backdrop for the forthcoming cinematic masterpiece. They finally settled on the magnificent mountain vistas of Glacier National Park and the appropriately rustic streets of the nearby town of Kalispell, Montana. Before granting permission for the movie makers to move in, officials of the National Park Service extracted a solemn promise from Cimino that he would scrupulously respect the delicate ecology of all protected public lands and would restore the wilds to their virgin state before the company returned to Hollywood. In light of these assurances, the nervous park rangers naturally became concerned when the *Heaven's Gate* crew began dumping several tons of dirt onto the huge parking lot near Two Medicine Lake. It was Cimino's intention to construct the set of the frontier town of Sweetwater on top of this layer of imported soil, but his workmen, in their enthusiasm, had not only covered the asphalt parking lot but had also crushed nearby sensitive plants. Even worse, the trucked-in tonnage was found to contain some foreign weeds that might have had a devastating effect on the park's fragile ecosystem.

After stern warnings from the appropriate officials, Cimino promised to behave himself, but shortly thereafter the rangers noticed that beautiful Two Medicine Lake had a shiny new look to it. Since no oil drilling rigs had been spotted in the immediate vicinity, they decided to check the *Heaven's Gate* set—where they discovered that Cimino's little elves had been at it again. Apparently, the crew members had been trying to make their newly constructed buildings look appropriately weatherbeaten by tinting them with an oil-based stain, and as an inadvertent by-product of the antiquing process, the lake had acquired a slimy brown sheen of its own.

Additional complaints arose when the movie men covered acres of unspoiled grasslands with brown and yellow paint (antiqued grass?), hauled in hundreds of unauthorized trees from outside the park, and damaged several miles of roads by running heavy trucks over them during spring thaw. The final confrontation, however, concerned Cimino's announced intention to film the gruesome slaughter of several cows on the open range. In past years, several campers at Glacier Park had been killed by rampaging grizzly bears, and the rangers worried that the gory scenes Cimino planned would provide the pesky critters with just the excuse they needed to run wild once again. Despite the director's cross-my-heart-and-hope-to-die assurance that he would avoid honest-to-goodness blood and guts, a park official who visited the set found three cow carcasses in various stages of butchery. Shortly after this bum steer incident, the *Heaven's Gate* company found itself banished from the park for "alleged damages and unkept promises."

In addition to the rude treatment extended to the unfortunate cows, the A.S.P.C.A. later protested "documented suffering inflicted on horses, steers, chickens, and fighting cocks." Although Cimino and company denied these charges, everyone admitted that at least one unlucky horse was sent to pony heaven after being blown to bits by an accidental explosion of gunpowder. As deservingly disgruntled as

the various animals (including the local grizzly bears) may have been, their plight was no worse than that of the underpaid extras.

For the privilege of appearing in a Michael Cimino film, the 1,200 local residents who participated in the fun received $30 a day for ten hours of work, less $3 a day for food. Cimino, apparently, was willing to spare every expense to make sure that the folks got into the right frame of mind to portray members of the oppressed masses. In addition to their embarrassingly low wages, the extras found themselves subjected to various gratuitous indignities: they received a printed notice, for instance, telling them, "Please do not approach the actors or crew members," as if the locals were highly contagious lepers. While cast members and technicians were free to use the portable toilets that had been provided for their personal needs, the lowly extras were expected to "make do" with primitive outhouses or in the great outdoors.

Cimino, great humanitarian that he was, looked upon these people as so many pieces of inanimate scenery, to be manipulated along with his sets and camera angles. He made sure that all of his extras were correctly dressed, down to the last coat button, boasting to the press that he had personally approved each one of the more than 1,000 costumes, but he showed an utter disregard for their physical well-being. Accidents occurred almost daily, and after one particularly hectic ten-hour shoot, some sixteen extras were injured seriously enough to require medical attention. Filming of the climactic scene in which 250 immigrants rush out of the Heaven's Gate roller rink to do battle with the baddies reflected Cimino's real-life attitude toward the "common man" far more accurately than the preachy script. After the sequence had been filmed time and again over several days, an order came down from on high to speed up the action. "If people don't move out of your way," one of Cimino's loyal assistants instructed a wagon driver, "then you'll just have to run them over." Not surprisingly, the Montana extras began defecting in droves, which, of course, only served to further slow down the shooting schedule.

While the abused extras suffered on the set, their capitalist colleagues back in Kalispell won revenge of sorts by taking advantage of the Hollywood honchos at every opportunity. In addition to selling innumerable pairs of overpriced cowboy boots to the visitors from California, local entrepreneurs managed to unload a matched set of two shiny new black jeeps for those amorous *auteurs*, Cimino and Carelli. City slicker Cimino eventually found himself so enchanted by the mountain scenery that he invested in

156 acres of Montana soil—at several times the going price. After several months of enduring outrageous ripoffs on even the most trivial purchases, producer Joann Carelli began to sense a pattern. "The longer you stay in a place like this," she indignantly observed, "the more people seem to think you have a lot of money." This conclusion seemed particularly unwarranted since, at the time she made her observations, Carelli and company had spent only $15 million. Meanwhile, the astute businessperson went on to complain about the price of shoes. "They really start to rip you off," she declared, "when one would have a pair of boots resoled, and that would normally cost three to seven dollars. Well, after a while they'd start charging seventeen to twenty ... The same thing happened with the land we used for filming. After we made the deals, before production started, every landowner changed his mind. 'You can't use my land,' he'd say, 'unless you give me another $50,000.' What choice did we have? In some cases we did try to find new locations, and that would take more money, too. It was like holdup time without a gun." Considering that the script they were filming emphasized the perfidy of greedy landowners, why the sudden shock? Furthermore, even though this was Joann's first job as a producer, hadn't someone told her about signing contracts with people once a deal was cut?

The local men of property were not, in any event, the only ones getting rich as the production dragged on months and months behind schedule. Literally hundreds of technicians—all protected by Hollywood unions—raked in a fortune as part of what became known in the industry as "The Montana Gold Rush." The good luck of these crew members stemmed from Cimino's idiosyncratic insistence that his technical people remain on call for twelve to eighteen hours a day, seven days a week. As one of these employees fondly recalled, "It was absolutely incredible. He wanted all of us there all the time, just in case he woke up in the middle of the night with a brilliant idea. He did this for six months." According to union rules, this little indulgence meant paying his crew for twenty-four-hour shifts—even if they worked less than half that time—and most of those hours were billed at triple time. When various other union-sanctioned penalties had been added in, the average weekly paycheck, which should have been $1,000, took a breathtaking leap to $5,000. Despite this largesse, crew members could not resist making fun of the peripatetic New Yorker who captained their obviously sinking—or at least badly listing—ship. In honor of his imperious and inscrutable ways,

they dubbed him "The Ayatollah." By the time he had held cast and crew hostages for nearly a year, it proved to be a particularly appropriate nickname.

Cimino, of course, managed to justify (at least to himself) the incredible outflow of cash and, in a TV interview, even offered his own version of the celebrated "trickle down" theory of economics. "I've been asked by many people," he explained, " 'Don't you think it's immoral to spend so much money on a film?' Well, where do people think that money goes?! That money goes to pay people's salaries. In the little town we worked in, Kalispell, in Flathead County, they were going through a recession the year we made the picture. Had that film not been located there at that time, three-fourths of the town would have been on relief. So it's not a question of immorality. A lot of people survived that year because of the work we did." Had United Artists known of Cimino's unselfish and charitable intentions, they no doubt would have filed for tax-exempt status as a nonprofit corporation before he went off on his mission of mercy. According to rumors, the city of Detroit has begun lobbying hard to persuade Cimino to base his next picture there.

Meanwhile, Back at the Studio ...

Despite their infatuation with their distinguished director's plans and pretensions, the U.A. executives realized they were in deep trouble within one week after shooting began. The preproduction problems had already caused the estimated budget for the picture to skyrocket from its initial level of $7.8 million up to the vicinity of $12 to $15 million. Then came the first six days of shooting, during which Cimino managed to impress nearly everyone by falling five full days behind schedule. This startling achievement so amazed the powers that be at U.A. that Dean Stolber, Vice President for Business Affairs, convened "serious discussions about closing down." As production chief Steven Bach recalls, "The handwriting was already on the wall," though the penmanship apparently remained illegible to the top decision-makers, who refused to put *Heaven's Gate* out of its misery.

Joann Carelli, who eventually took much of the blame for the unprecedented extent of the cost overruns, presented her side of the story in an interview with *Rolling Stone.* "After the first week," she recalled, "U.A. kept calling and asking, 'How can we stop this?' I told them I would show them exactly how, but they would have to back me up ... We should have said, 'No, Michael, no. You cannot build the town larger than you said you would. No, Michael, no. You cannot have 1,000 extras when you said 100.' Everyone was afraid to say no to Michael. It was an impossible situation." Therefore, even though little Mikey was a bad boy who wouldn't listen to the adults when they told him no, these executives dared not discipline him because, in their own words, "it would have created a crisis of confidence that would have been psychologically intolerable for Michael." In other words, the big-hearted big shots resolved that rather than risking permanent emotional scars on their boy wonder, they would simply have to eat $44 million. They may have lost their jobs as a result of this decision, but at least they had clear consciences.

Despite all the noble intentions, the atmosphere at the studio, as Steven Bach recalls, became "tense, and it was tense on a daily basis. For many months there were a lot of plane trips to Montana, friendly trips, but concerned trips. Michael was always very shrewd with us. He would always offer an assemblage of footage, and he knew we would recognize that this was no ordinary movie." This description of *Heaven's Gate* may rank as one of the great understatements in motion picture history.

Heaven Must Wait

"It's hard to finish a film," confessed the beleaguered director. "One loves the fact that things are getting larger, richer, deeper." An impartial observer might have noticed that things had already gotten so deep that Cimino was in way over his head. Nevertheless, he managed to retain the admiration of his chief compatriots in catastrophe. Kris Kristofferson publicly compared him to Fellini and Bergman, but Steven Bach went even further. "Cimino has been like Michelangelo," he enthused, "feverishly painting the Sistine Chapel, carried away with an artistic vision. But I am confident we'll make our money back on it. It's going to be another classic." This comment prompted a response from veteran producer Samuel Z. Arkoff, acknowledged master of low budget/high profit movie making, who observed, "You can bet when the Pope hired Michelangelo he told him exactly how much he could spend to paint the ceiling."

Meanwhile, the intrigues and excesses on location in Montana made even Michelangelo's Medici patrons look like pikers. Rumors reached Hollywood that the crazed director had decreed the destruction of an entire street, built to the precise specifications of his blueprints, simply because the spacing "didn't look right" to his artistic eyes. Cimino wanted both sides of the set torn down and moved back three feet each, but the construction boss suggested that it would be easier and cheaper to leave half of the street as it was and to simply shift the other one the entire six feet. Cimino, however, using the carefully trained vision of a former architecture student, refused to compromise when, in his mind, immortality was at stake with every frame of film. Reportedly, at his command, both sides of the completed street were razed and reconstructed at an estimated cost of more than half a million dollars.

However whimsical the director's decisions concerning set construction, the endless shooting and reshooting of even the most trivial scenes made scarcely more sense. For one sequence in which Kris Kristofferson is required to bullwhip a crowd of extras (as if they didn't have enough problems), Mr. Mike ordered fifty-three—count 'em, fifty-three—separate takes. Another memorable scene featured a fat, vulgar capitalist removing his pants and baring his keester as a sign of contempt for the immigrant masses during the climactic battle scene. At Cimino's insistence, this inspiring sight was filmed no less than thirty times until the entire cast and crew were hopelessly moonstruck. As one disgusted cameraman impatiently inquired, "I mean, how many different ways can a guy drop his pants? I thought we were going to stop after the fifteenth take, but Michael—jerk that he was—wanted to try it again and again until he was satisfied."

When descriptions of this unorthodox search for satisfaction reached Cimino's *amore cum producer* Joann Carelli, she may well have found grounds for concern, but for United Artists, after all of the alarming reports from their filmic funny farm in Montana, the last straw apparently was the one stuck up somebody's nose. Various illegal substances, or "chemical production aids," are not at all uncommon as a source of inspiration for today's actors and technicians, but according to the breathless gossip back home in Hollywood, the snow had never before fallen as heavily as it did on location for *Heaven's Gate*. An assistant cameraman who camped in Montana for the duration of the shoot recalled the experience with a wistful smile. "A lot of people don't understand how Cimino could possibly spend so much money on a picture like *Heaven's Gate*," he sighed, "but I can tell you how he did it. It's simple! There was about $20 million for overall production costs, and another $20 million, you can bet, to buy all that cocaine for the cast and crew."

Through it all, having a blast, there was Michael Cimino at the helm—happily oblivious to such mundane concepts as "budget" and "schedule." This merry megalomaniac confided to his colleagues that one of his secret goals on the project was to break the previous record—set by Francis Ford Coppola on *Apocalypse Now*—for the amount of film exposed on a single motion picture. To no one's surprise, Cimino realized this dream: on September 6, 1979, he hosted a gala champagne party on location to celebrate the exposure of his one millionth foot of celluloid. To put this grand achievement in proper perspective, it should be noted that the average film consumes considerably less than 100,000 feet. As the happy director told a reporter on the scene, "The absolute best time for me is on location . . . There's not much adventure left in the world today, but making a movie is still so much an adventure on so many levels." U.A. investors, of course, might have preferred that Cimino seek his kicks from hang-gliding—or perhaps, still better, Russian roulette—rather than movie making, but when he came to them with a unique concept for additional cinematic thrills and spills, they didn't have the heart to say no.

Postgraduate Education

By mid-October, with the core of his film finally in the can (or, to be more precise, dozens and dozens of cans), mad Mike refused to concede that his fun was over. No sooner had he returned to Hollywood from the wilds of Montana than he began dreaming of shooting two "bookends" for his tale: a freshly conceived prologue and epilogue that had never appeared in the original screenplay or any of the subsequent drafts submitted to the studio. By this time, *Heaven's Gate* had already run more than $20 million over budget and some six months behind schedule, so the executives at U.A. might have been forgiven had they reacted to the suggestion for further filming with the same sort of open-minded enthusiasm usually reserved for greeting earthquakes, floods, nuclear war, and other surprises. Cimino, however, could be a persuasive salesman when he had to be. As Steven Bach explained, "He called me up one day and said, 'I have an idea that I think might take the onus of being a Western away from the picture and which might also illuminate the characters' backgrounds' . . . the question at U.A., quite honestly, was: will those qualities of tone, texture and memory be worth the money? It was very hard to defend the expenditure of the money, but I felt strongly that it was worthwhile. The prologue, in a sense, haunts the rest of the movie." It also haunted United Artists—to the tune of some $5 million.

This extra artistic touch depicted the Harvard graduation ceremonies for the Class of 1870 in an elaborate (but utterly inept) attempt to reveal the comfortable, upper-crust eastern world that the Kris Kristofferson and John Hurt characters escaped some twenty years before the events depicted in the main body of the film. Cimino saw a strong contemporary relevance in the idea that these rich, liberal idealists had to go west and befriend the "toiling masses" in order to find meaning in their pampered, empty lives. "What causes the chemistry between Bobby Kennedy and Cesar Chavez?" the director asked rhetorically. "I think some of these comparisons are inescapable with the character of Averill."

What *was* inescapable to viewers of the finished film was the tedious irrelevance of the lavish Harvard sequence. It ran for more than twenty-five minutes on screen and featured marching bands; hundreds of impressively costumed, highly excited young men running nowhere with great enthusiasm; a throng of students listening to uplifting speeches by Joseph Cotten (as "The Reverend Doctor") and John Hurt; a beardless Kris Kristofferson, wandering through the crowds looking lost and, frankly, embarrassed at the idea that he is supposed to portray a fresh-faced twenty-one-year-old; plus 200 collegiate couples waltzing endlessly around a tree in a college courtyard to the nostalgic strains of "The Beautiful Blue Danube."

With his passion for meticulous and realistic detail, Cimino naturally wanted to film this elegant opening on location at Harvard, but after initially approving his plans, the university suddenly changed its mind and refused to co-operate. Perhaps the administrators, hearing of the director's controversial exploits at Glacier National Park, worried that his presence on campus might upset the delicate ecosystem of Cambridge, Massachusetts. In any event, recent experience with another U.A. production called *A Small Circle of Friends*—where the filmmakers left a horrible mess after their departure—convinced Harvard's decision makers that the university could survive without the incomparable honor of serving as a backdrop for the prologue to *Heaven's Gate*. After Harvard said no, Cimino applied to Yale as his second choice but found himself no more welcome at his own alma mater than he had been at its ancient rival. At this point, the logical step would have been to move the production to one of several dozen other New England colleges, or even prep schools, that easily could have doubled for nineteenth-century Harvard. The visionary director, however, felt certain that such minor institutions could never exude that

intangible "feel" of a great educational center that
he wanted for his film, so he decided to schlepp his
entire cast and crew across the Atlantic to shoot the
precious Harvard graduation at . . . Oxford. Yes,
that's in England. And to purists who might object
that the British university's venerable Gothic architecture bore not the slightest resemblance to the
Georgian red brick of the *real* Harvard, Cimino insisted that his new location was "a place which just
seemed *spiritually* right." Besides, why turn down a
chance for a jolly jaunt with literally hundreds of
your friends and co-workers to merry olde England?
Incredible as it may seem, United Artists approved
the plan, deciding that the prior Herculean efforts of
Bach's Bad Boy in the Montana wilderness entitled
him to an all-expense-paid vacation at a more civi-
lized locale. When the traveling circus arrived in Old
Blighty, Cimino set to work with his usual thorough-
ness. While looking for an appropriately impressive
tree to serve as a "central focus" for the outdoor
waltzing sequence, he happened to spot a lovely oak
three miles outside the city. No problem—he ordered his production assistants to chop it up and ship
it to Oxford, where it was neatly reassembled. Of
course, the U.A. bosses were delighted that he didn't
need a tree specially delivered from Montana, so
they kept quiet. The Oxford students who served as
extras, however, did not. They soon became as disgruntled as their Kalispell counterparts, but in the
finest tradition of British trade unionism, the Oxon-
ians struck for higher pay twice in ten days—with
U.A. giving in to their demands both times. They
certainly should have demanded hazardous duty pay,
since one day's shooting, with more than 200 people
involved, suddenly erupted into a skull-bashing free-
for-all, with numerous extras carted off to the hospital. Despite these minor setbacks, Cimino managed
to delight (and amaze) his studio bosses by finishing
the filming at Harvard-on-the-Thames precisely on
schedule.

There still remained the job of shooting the epilogue—two and a half minutes of film showing Kris
Kristofferson as an old man on board his yacht at the
luxurious resort of Newport, Rhode Island. As he
strolls about the deck, his handsome visage covered
in latex face putty to indicate the passage of time, he
watches the sun go down and thinks of those long-
ago, wonderful days of the Johnson County War. For
the conclusion of the film, he goes to his cabin below
deck where a mysterious woman (Is it his wife? mistress? backup singer?) awaits him. She finally speaks
the last line of the whole epic drama: "I'd like a ciga-
rette," she drawls, while the weary audience at this

point would no doubt prefer something considerably
stronger. To capture these subtle, poetic concluding
touches for posterity required a full week's rental of
an antique yacht, plane transportation for the entire
crew to the new location in Rhode Island, and last
but hardly least, a special trip to San Diego to shoot
the unique, glorious sunset Cimino "needed" as an
establishing shot for the beginning of the sequence.
All in all, the cost for the epilogue ran close to $1
million, making it one of the most expensive two-and-
a-half-minute afterthoughts in the history of motion
pictures.

"Let's Take a Look at That Again . . ."

With no new worlds to conquer, and no new trouble
to make, U.A.'s prodigal son settled in for the enormous job of cutting his film down to size (something
the critics would accomplish with no trouble at all
after the movie's release). He certainly had enough to
work with: an unprecedented total of more than 500
hours of *developed* film. Editor William Reynolds,
assigned to assist Cimino in shaping the finished
product, sifted through the confused and confusing
mass of celuloid with a sense of mounting dread. "I
had never seen so much footage in my entire life," he
recalls. "This was a guy who printed everything he
shot. I mean everything!'

The editor and the director soon set to work at the
MGM sound studio, known for the most sophisticated
mixing equipment in town (though the U.A. investors
would probably have preferred Cimino in a cement
mixer). Problems arose from the beginning. "The
sound effects overwhelmed the dialogue," Reynolds
remembered. "Characters would be speaking but
you wouldn't be able to hear them because of all Michael's authentic noises—rumbling, galloping, whis-
tling, whatever—he wanted to throw it all in. I told
him that no one in the audience would understand
what his people were saying. Then he played it back
again and said, 'I don't know what you're talking
about. I can understand every word!' Well, of course,
he understood—he was the one who wrote it in the
first place! But he wasn't really looking for advice
from anyone else. Any time I tried to cut down some
extra footage he'd just go back and undo it all."

This indulgent approach to the task at hand ensured that the editing dragged on for more than four
months. To keep nervous producers and curious reporters from "interfering" with his creative process,
Cimino hired an armed security guard to stand as a
sentry in front of the mixing room around the clock,

We-Know-the-Cost-of-Higher-Education-Is-Going-Up-But-This-Is-Ridiculous Department: The "Prologue" to Heaven's Gate *depicted commencement ceremonies for the Harvard Class of 1870 and featured (in front of the group) John Hurt (left) and Kris Kristofferson (right) as eager and idealistic graduates. To capture this subtle moment, Michael Cimino dragged his cast and crew to England's Oxford University, which the director had chosen to stand in for Harvard. The total cost of this excursion amounted to nearly $4 million, but after the ruthless re-editing of the original film, the resulting footage occupied less than ten minutes on screen.*

blocking entry even to U.A. executives. A filmmaker who worked in a nearby office recalled that, "Michael didn't just want respect. He wanted awe. The idea was that the miracle man is in his workshop now, and he's doing his magic, so we just have to stand back and leave him alone. The level of pretension in that editing room was matched only by the level of disaster later on."

After ruthlessly paring away all the inessential material, Cimino came up with a first cut that he was prepared to show to the studio brass. This "bare bones" version of his story ran five and a half hours. The top executives, most of whom had seen only snippets of film so far, reacted with amazement and horror. "It was deadly at that length," Steve Bach confessed. "You really needed a transfusion afterwards." Cimino returned to the editing room for another two months, then emerged with a new, slim-and-trim three-hour-forty-five-minute version.

The studio officially judged this second cut to be "more reasonable" but continued to worry over its plodding pace and soporific effect on audiences. "We definitely knew we had something," said one insider. "Even if it wasn't a movie, it was at least a good cure for insomnia." Despite these misgivings, the bosses at United Artists decided to rush the movie into release. Normally, they would have tested public reaction in sneak previews and specially arranged evaluation screenings, but Cimino's foot-dragging in the editing process left no time for these safeguards without postponing the already scheduled premiere engagements. Hollywood gossips had already adopted U.A.'s "problem picture" as a major topic of conversation, and further delays would only intensify the negative speculation. As they tiptoed nervously toward the end of the plank, the harried executives at last decided that the only alternative was to cover their eyes and jump.

Now You See It . . .

In the three weeks immediately preceding the gala
opening day, U.A. lavished some $1.5 million on
print ads to increase public awareness of the film.
These newspaper layouts—personally supervised by
former ad agency whiz Michael Cimino—featured a
dim, out-of-focus image of Marshal Kristofferson,
along with the hauntingly prophetic line: *"What One
Loves About Life Are the Things That Fade."* Meanwhile, the Eastman Kodak Corporation sank hundreds of thousands of dollars of its own in a related
advertising program that attempted to sell film and
cameras by emphasizing the precision and perfection
of *Heaven's Gate.* This memorable pitch featured Cimino's personal motto in the headline: "If You Don't
Get It Right, What's the Point?" It is hard to believe
that even suffering, as he did, from a terminal case of
elephantiasis of the ego, the demented director could
remain totally unaware of the self-parodistic potential of this quote.

On Tuesday morning, November 18, 1980, an
eager crowd of invited guests—primarily critics and
reporters—assembled in New York for the first-ever
public screening of Michael Cimino's long-awaited
masterpiece. The director sat quietly in his first-row
balcony seat, trying to gauge the audience response
in the darkened theatre. After ninety minutes—less
than half the total running time—there had been
more than enough moans, groans, and derisive laughter to affront the delicate equilibrium of the sensitive
cinematic artist. Cimino got up in the middle of the
screening, walked to the lobby, and placed a long-
distance call to the U.A. executive offices back in
L.A. When he returned to his seat he asked editor
Bill Reynolds, who happened to be sitting beside
him, "What would you think if we cancelled the
opening in L.A. and Toronto?" As Reynolds recalled,
"I nearly fell out of my chair!"

The ever-astute Steven Bach observed, "The first
time I saw the entire film with an audience, I said to
myself, 'We have made a mistake . . .' " The next day,
the critics who had seen the film unanimously echoed
his sentiments. Vincent Canby led the attack on the
pages of the *New York Times.* "*Heaven's Gate* fails so
completely," he wrote, "that you might suspect Mr.
Cimino sold his soul to the Devil to obtain the success
of *The Deer Hunter*, and the Devil has just come
around to collect. . . . Mr. Cimino has written his
own screenplay, whose awfulness has been considerably inflated by the director's wholly unwarranted respect for it . . . *Heaven's Gate* is something quite rare
in movies these days—an unqualified disaster."

. . . Now You Don't

Within hours after the appearance of Canby's review, Cimino had written to United Artists president
Andy Albeck, begging him to yank the film from release. "I believe we have learned an invaluable lesson
from our very first public showing," he pleaded.
"Once again, I call on your remarkable faith, understanding and cooperation." The picture had been
scheduled for reserved seat "exclusive engagements"
in New York, Toronto, and Los Angeles. It was too
late to stop the first week of screenings in the Big
Apple, but Cimino suggested canceling the much-
ballyhooed openings in the other cities. Reaching
deep into their seemingly endless supply of "faith,
understanding and cooperation," the studio bosses
agreed. They sent personal cancellation telegrams to
1,200 California ticket holders, while running special
newspaper ads to announce their unprecedented
step.

The sudden postponement of the premiere became a major news story across the country, as
Americans in all walks of life watched the embarrassment of the movie moguls with obvious relish. In Hollywood, T-shirts suddenly appeared bearing the legend: "RELAX . . . You could be selling
HEAVEN'S GATE!" Meanwhile, New York film buffs
and curiosity seekers rushed over to Cinema One in
Manhattan like gleeful onlookers at the scene of a
bloody accident to catch the film in its original version before it concluded its one-week run. Vilmos
Zsigmond, director of photography on the project,
attended one showing with some thirty friends, all of
whom wore black armbands for the occasion. Various
commentators began wondering aloud why the studio had chosen to cancel the opening altogether,
rather than simply re-editing the film as it continued
in release. In response to these questions, one U.A.
exec explained candidly (and anonymously), "It's not
the sort of movie you can salvage in a weekend. It's a
wholesale disaster." *Time* magazine reported, however, that the studio would do all in its power to save
the picture: "U.A. is expected to invest another $10
million for the reclamation project. The South Bronx
should be so lucky . . ."

Once More, With Feeling

While dodging the brickbats that had begun flying at
him from every direction, Cimino retreated to his
editing room for another try at transforming his miles
and miles of disconnected footage into some form of
coherent entertainment. He promised the studio he

would present them with a new, improved *Heaven's Gate* within ten weeks, but naturally, the recutting process lasted for an additional twelve weeks past his deadline. Cimino remained, if nothing else, admirably consistent. While he snipped and fretted at his delicate work, Steve Bach sheepishly announced to the press that at this point, the revised version of his prize project would have to gross at least $140 million (!) simply to *break even*. As they reputedly say in Japanese: "Rotsa Ruck!" The board of directors of Transamerica, U.A.'s parent corporation, reviewed the terrifying numbers and then graciously accepted the resignation of studio president Andy Albeck—a thirty-two-year veteran of the company. His was the first of many heads due for the chopping block in order to satisfy the vengeful wrath of *Heaven*.

The remaining executives commissioned a marketing survey to devise an effective strategy for selling the re-edited film to a skeptical nation. In conversations with the press, they naturally went to great lengths to put an optimistic face on the results of their research, and to point out the "hidden benefits" of the film's notorious history. "Short of calling it *Gone With the Wind*," one studio source told *The Wall Street Journal*, "you couldn't get more noticed than we have been. . . . We know some people will go to see the picture simply to say, 'I told you it was a bomb!'"

This unusual marketing strategy might have led to some intriguing ads for the film, but U.A. decided instead to use their lavish new $6.5 million promotional budget to counter one of the major problems cited by numerous preview audiences: the movie's unmistakable anti-American message. While Cimino whined over the advertising decisions being taken out of his hands, the studio devised a ludicrous layout showing a billowing image of Old Glory behind the heroic faces of Kris Kristofferson and Isabelle Huppert, with the patently misleading headline: "THE ONLY THING GREATER THAN THEIR PASSION FOR AMERICA . . . WAS THEIR PASSION FOR EACH OTHER." One can only imagine the surprise of some patriotic bumpkin, lured by the promise of a flag-waving, John Wayne–style horse opera, who is exposed instead to Cimino's muddled, atmospheric neo-Marxist polemic.

With the new sales approach locked in place, and Cimino's substantive changes—including a de-emphasis on the shocking violence, a drastic reduction in the length of the prologue, a new voice-over narration to help viewers avoid confusion, and the overall excision of ninety minutes' running time from the first edition—the studio felt ready to make another run at the public. In March 1981, Jerry Esbin, newly appointed marketing director for U.A., told the press that "the picture has been locked up and put to bed," though while they were at it they should have also put it to sleep. Infected by the newfound optimism of studio officials, the *L.A. Herald-Examiner* predicted that the new *Heaven's Gate* would "come out in the spring and make a mint." Half an accurate prediction is better than none; the movie did, indeed, come out in the spring.

Unqualified Disaster: Take Two

The world premiere of the deflated *Heaven's Gate* took place on April 23, 1981, as the closing-night attraction of Filmex (the Los Angeles International Film Exposition) at Grauman's Chinese Theatre. The demand for tickets easily made the event the most popular of the festival, and it won additional publicity from pickets repesenting the American Humane Association. They carried signs decrying the suffering of numerous animals in the film, though at least one viewer yelled to them at the conclusion of the premiere, "The worst cruelty is for the audience who sits through this thing!"

The first indication of the public reaction to the new edition came midway through the screening at Grauman's Chinese when a woman, sobbing hysterically, stormed out of the theatre and confronted a man pacing restlessly in the lobby. "This is the most disgusting, degrading and horrible film I've ever seen!" she cried, apparently unaware that the hapless fellow listening to her verdict was none other than Michael Cimino. Inside the crowded theatre, the bulk of the audience booed lustily when the credits came up at the end of the film, easily drowning out the sound of scattered applause.

This opening-night response wounded Cimino's pride, but it in no way prepared him for the magnitude of the bad news that arrived from across the continent in the next few days. During its first weekend, his picture played in 810 theatres in the U.S. and Canada but managed to gross only the paltry sum of $1.3 million. The *L.A. Times* reported that these figures averaged out "to just over $500 a night for each of the 810 theatres, which will barely pay for the film cans used to transport prints of *Heaven's Gate*." New York's Astor Plaza cinema faced a typical situation with the film in which the gross after the first three days totaled only $10,105—less than *half* the theatre's operating expenses. Many other cities reported that filmgoers were totally ignoring *Heaven's Gate* and staying home in record numbers.

In the face of mounting evidence of a box office disaster of historic proportions, United Artists tried to keep a stiff upper lip. One studio executive expressed his confidence that the film would eventually perform well enough so that corporate losses on the project, when advertising and interest charges had been included, could be held to a mere $50 million. Newly appointed U.A. president Norbert Auerbach finally admitted, "We have repeatedly said that we were guardedly optimistic, but let's face it—the picture has been rejected by the public, and most of the press, even in its new version. . . . We don't have to pull it; they're doing it for us. We don't have to take any action at all . . ." Marketing chief Jerry Esbin, who had earlier assured everyone that "the masses will love it," now mourned, "It's as if somebody called every household in the country and said, 'There will be a curse on your family if you go see this picture.' I've been in this business a long time, and I've never seen anything like this in my life." Though U.A., for understandable reasons, never issued a press release with information on the final dimensions of the debacle, informed estimates suggest that with the additional editing, advertising, distribution, interest, and all other charges involved with their born-again fiasco, the studio lost *at least* $100 million on Cimino's Folly.

Despite his embarrassing involvement with every stage of the deepening disaster, Steven Bach expressed great confidence that he would retain his position as head of production. He told the press that both studio president Auerbach and Transamerica chairman James Harvey had "gone out of their way to be supportive and understanding." Auerbach himself issued a statement on May 5, 1981, that declared that "Steve not only has my confidence, but the confidence of Transamerica. I am not going to make any changes in my production team . . . We have repeatedly said we're not blaming Steven for *Heaven's Gate*."

Six days later, Bach was unceremoniously fired, joining former president Albeck and four other top officials who had already—you should pardon the expression—been given The Gate. Later in the same month, Transamerica, not satisfied with sacrificing some overpaid and under-talented executives, decided to dump the entire U.A. operation. On May 21—less than thirty days after the nationwide failure of *Heaven's Gate*—the parent corporation sold off its ailing United Artists subsidiary to MGM. Though various corporate spokespeople tried to deny a direct connection, all of Hollywood knew that Transamerica's resolve to unload its troubled studio stemmed from the massive losses associated with the recent detonation of the industry's biggest bomb.

Passing the Megabuck

With a failure as gigantic as *Heaven's Gate*, there is always plenty of blame to go around. No sooner had the dust settled from the picture's final, pathetic box office collapse than the key players in the costly game began pointing fingers at one another.

Former production head Steven Bach, after a calm, totally objective review of the motion picture's melancholy history, generously absolved himself and his executive colleagues of all responsibility and lay exclusive blame for the massacre at the doorstep of the director. "In a sense, Cimino had us by the throat," he sighed. "We knew what was going on. It was not a case of a bunch of uncaring executives sitting around just letting it go wild. . . . Believe me, if controls had not taken place, he'd still be shooting."

A leading member of the crew, meanwhile, singled out producer Joann Carelli as the main culprit. "She didn't even begin to do her job," he charged. "Instead of trying to control Michael's obvious insanity, she actually encouraged him to run amuck. She backed him all the time, in everything. She always fended for him when the executives would complain. She happened to be a very obnoxious young woman, extremely aggressive at the same time she was totally unknowledgeable about the film business. She made enemies left and right, not only for herself, but for Michael as well."

Carelli, for her part, threw the onus of responsibility right back at the studio executives. As she told *Variety*, "For a long time U.A. has been trying to pin this thing on Michael and myself. In fact, things probably never would have gotten to the point they did if there had been proper support for the film's producer from the studio." An objective observer might have classified $44 million as "proper support," but Carelli apparently wanted spiritual as well as financial backing. "U.A. may have seemed supportive in one sense," she explained, "but they actually did an injustice to the creative people involved by allowing them to go wild." In other words, the studio sinned against those two crazy but lovable kids, Mike and Joann, by turning them loose in the Montana wilderness without any sort of proper supervision. By this same logic, a teenaged girl who gets into trouble would attack her parents for having failed to institute a rigorous curfew.

To no one's surprise, the most imaginative explanation for what went wrong with *Heaven's Gate* came from Michael Cimino himself. Sure, he may have made a few itsy-bitsy, teeny-weeny mistakes, but in an interview after the fact, he stepped forward and courageously placed the blame right where it belonged—squarely on the shoulders of the American moviegoing public. "A friend of mine said that he thinks we made the picture for the wrong generation," Cimino lamented. "I think we were once a country that valued craftsmanship and valued individuality. I think we are gradually in the process of losing the value we placed on those qualities. A good example that many people may now be familiar with is the case of John DeLorean, and his extremely tough and difficult fight to build his own automobile." Cimino failed to comment on DeLorean's extremely tough and difficult fight to avoid going to jail, because at the time of these remarks the automotive *auteur* had not yet been indicted for his dubious dealings in cocaine. In any event, considering the reports of high times on location in Montana, it is doubtful whether DeLorean's troubles with the law would have prevented Cimino from saluting a kindred spirit. "Many people tried to stop him," the director continued. "Many people stood in his way. But DeLorean never gave up. But what it's taken for him to do it has been a tremendous cost."

And so, with this paean to a fellow high-roller, Michael Cimino closed *Heaven's Gate* behind him. Unlike his hero, the former boy wonder need not worry about a term in prison as the consequence of his excesses, but he has had a difficult time in finding a job. The brief chronology below will serve to bring his inspiring story up to date:

March 7, 1979—Cimino is announced as director for *The King of Comedy*, a project that will reteam him with his star from *The Deer Hunter*, Robert DeNiro.

November 10, 1979—Because of various missed deadlines and his continued preoccupation with the editing and re-editing of *Heaven's Gate*, Cimino is yanked from *King of Comedy*; the job goes to Martin Scorsese.

November 14, 1979—Anticipating a huge hit with *Heaven's Gate*, Cimino announces to the press that he is already planning his next project, another Western, called *Conquering Horse*. Conservatively budgeted at $20 million, this generational saga would trace the history of the Sioux Indians in America—with the entire film to be told in authentic Sioux dialogue with English subtitles. (Cimino obviously recognized the vast Sioux-speaking film audience out there that had been neglected for too long.) Needless to say, the project never got off the ground.

December 11, 1981—Cimino is announced as director of *Live on Tape*, a movie about camera crews for CBS Theatrical Films. In May of '82, after

disastrous release of the revised *Heaven's Gate*, these plans are abruptly canceled. The desperate director then pitches CBS a gangster story based on the life of crime chief (no, not John DeLorean) Frank Costello, entitled (appropriately enough) *Proud Dreamer*. His proposed lavish budget wins a hasty "no thanks" response.

December 12, 1981—Cimino is signed by producer Daniel (*All That Jazz*) Melnick to direct *Footloose*, a youth-oriented musical comedy. A clause is added to his contract providing that if the film goes over its strict $7.5 million budget, then every penny will come out of Cimino's own pocket.

January 18, 1982—Just as *Footloose* is about to start shooting, Cimino calls on Dan Melnick and asks for an additional $250,000 to rewrite the screenplay and for an indefinite delay in the start date. Melnick fails to see the humor in the situation and asks our boy to take a walk; he is replaced by Herbert Ross.

April 1, 1983—In what many insiders initially believed to be an April Fool's joke, Cimino is signed to direct the next movie of fellow perfectionist Dustin Hoffman. One longtime film pro, who has worked with both artists in the past, remarks; "Now there's a team for ya! If that picture *ever* gets done it will be a miracle!" The project, tentatively titled *The Yellow Jersey*, is written and produced by Carl (*High Noon*) Foreman. The inspired pairing of Cimino and Hoffman—two of the most temperamental and demanding talents in the history of Hollywood—promises behind-the-scenes battles reminiscent of *King Kong versus Godzilla*. We breathlessly await further news on the forthcoming clash of the ego titans.

The roller-coaster ups and downs in Michael Cimino's brief career should not obscure the fact that the man is still in his early forties; as the *Heaven's Gate* adventure gradually fades from memory, he is all but certain to make a comeback. When he does, however, it is safe to assume that whichever studio employs his services will watch closely every move he makes and every dollar he spends. In fact, Cimino's sobering example led to a major change in the attitudes of the entire industry. Never again, the mainstream moguls vowed, would a creative artist be given such free rein to indulge his artistic whims and to waste tens of millions of studio dollars.

But then, One Way Productions is no mainstream studio; its Guiding Light is no normal (or mortal?) Hollywood executive; and *Inchon*—the final picture in our Rogue's Gallery—is in no way an ordinary motion picture. . . .

INCHON

(1982)

One Way Productions
Distributed by MGM/UA
Special Advisor: Sun Myung Moon
Produced by Mitsuharu Ishii
Directed by Terence Young
Screenplay by Robin Moore and Laird Koenig

Starring Laurence Olivier (General Douglas MacArthur); Jacqueline Bisset (Barbara Hallsworth); Ben Gazzara (Major Frank Hallsworth); Richard Roundtree (Sergeant Gus Henderson); Toshiro Mifune (Saito-san); John Pochna (Lieutenant Alexander Haig); Noom Goon Won (Park); David Janssen (David Field); Rex Reed (Longfellow); Sabine Sun (Marguerite); and "The Little Angels."

The Moon Also Rises

While making your way through the exhibits in our museum of mistakes, you have already encountered a fair number of eccentric and colorful individuals; characters such as Howard Hughes, Joseph Goebbels, Moustapha Akkad, and Allan Carr could hardly be classified as the boys next door. Of all the dreamers who have created Hall of Shame motion pictures over the years, however, none have been more bizarre—or ambitious—than the visionary responsible for the most recent film in our main collection. Sun Myung Moon was no mere movie maker reaching for fame, greatness, or immortality; as the Son of God he already had all that. To him, the film business was only another means of fulfilling his heavenly mission and teaching "The Divine Principle"—his personally formulated interpretation of Biblical prophecy, which, among other "Great Truths," reveals that a Communist-free Korea will ultimately emerge as the spiritual center of the universe and that a suspiciously familiar Korean evangelist will expose himself—or at least announce himself—as the new Savior of the World.

Born in 1920, Moon grew up in a Presbyterian home in the northern part of Korea and studied in Japan during World War II. At the impressionable age of sixteen, the young man had his first face-to-face meetings with Jesus, when Christ appeared to him for the apparent purpose of giving some key pointers about the Messiah business. In the years that followed, Moon enjoyed similar late-night conversations with a number of other distinguished guests, including Moses and Buddha, though much like the viewers of *Mohammad: Messenger of God*, he never did get to see the Muslim representative. When the Communists took control of North Korea after World War II, they remained unimpressed by his nocturnal visitations and arrested him twice for his activities as a Christian evangelist. He had served half of his five-year sentence when U.N. forces reached Hungnam prison during the Korean War and released him. As Moon recounts his experiences in jail, he emphasizes the admiration the other prisoners felt for him because he could do twice as much work on half the rice quota they received. He disciplined himself to do the most distasteful work: carrying 1,300 bags of fertilizer to the scale every day. Clearly, this prepared him for bringing 250,000 feet of celluloid manure to his film company's editing room. Moon also recalled that while toiling away in prison, he had a vision of himself as the star of a motion picture being shown simultaneously to his ancestors and his descendants.

After getting out of jail and traveling south to Pusan, Moon decided on a career as a religious, rather than a screen, idol. His stint in a North Korean prison had not only developed his expertise at piling manure but had also taught him some fine points of the subtle arts of persuasion and brainwashing—all of which stood him in good stead as he pursued his lofty messianic vision. In 1954, spouting a confusing message of anti-Communist militancy and apocalyptic Christianity, he founded the Unification Church with a handful of followers. Soon after that, disquieting reports reached the American embassy that when teenage girls joined the movement, Moon would personally purge them of "satanic forces" by putting them through sexual initiation rites. He was jailed for three months, this time by *South* Korean authorities, on charges of draft evasion (let somebody else have the honor of stopping the Commies, he reasoned), forgery, "pseudo religion," and false imprisonment of a university coed (who apparently didn't swallow his Divine Principle without a struggle). But nobody said that saving mankind was going to be easy.

Moon's second prison experience convinced him that in order to rule the world he had to start with South Korea. With this altruistic goal in mind, he recruited several army officers into his thriving cult and developed strong ties with the Korean Central Intelligence Agency (K.C.I.A.). The most important among his new establishment contacts was Bo Hi Pak, the assistant military attaché at the Korean embassy in Washington, and as Moon's man in the U.S., Pak became one of the leading practitioners of the church's officially sanctioned "Doctrine of Heavenly Deception," which teaches that lying is frequently necessary when doing God's work; in fact, according to the enlightened words of "Father" (as Moon is addressed within his movement), the Lord Himself often will deliberately mislead humanity. How else could one explain His decision to place so grand and beautiful a soul in so unprepossessing a package as Reverend Sun Myung Moon?

Pak Man Conquers the Free World

With a flair for public relations and high-level maneuvering, Bo Hi Pak quickly established a Moonie power base in North America. In 1962, inspired by a concert of the Vienna Boys Choir, he organized the first of literally hundreds of front groups for the Unification Church: a choral ensemble composed exclusively of Korean orphan girls and known to the world as "The Little Angels." Who could resist these beatifically smiling tykes, warbling Korean folk tunes and religious hymns to soothe the hurt of their lonely orphaned state? In point of fact, the parents of nearly all the girls were alive, well, and contributing gen-

"That Old Devil Moon": Reverend Sun Myung Moon wears full battle regalia in order to perform one of the solemn and inspiring rites of his Unification Church. Neither his prayers nor a record-busting production budget of $48 million could induce American filmgoers to accept his battlefield epic, Inchon, *which* Newsweek *described as "a turkey the size of Godzilla."*

erously to the Unification Church—which urged them to go along with the Heavenly Deception that helped to ensure the popularity of their daughters' singing group. In promoting the Angels in the United States and Western Europe, Pak never mentioned the choir's connection with the controversial Reverend Moon and so succeeded in signing up former Presidents Truman and Eisenhower, former Vice President Richard Nixon, labor chief George Meany, and many other dignitaries as official "sponsors" of the group. The Angels appeared on stage with that ageless matinee idol, our own Liberace—though Mr. Glitter surely would have preferred the Vienna Choir Boys.

While these "Tuneful Ambassadors of Good Will" toured the world with their message of universal love, Father instructed his followers back home in Korea to concentrate on building weapons. His Tong Il ("Unification") Industries developed an exclusive contract with Colt Industries to produce and sell M-16 rifles, as well as manufacturing parts for the Vulcan antiaircraft gun, the M-79 grenade launcher, and the M-60 machine gun. But even the profitable production of these convincing, anti-Communist, Christian motivators was kid's stuff compared to the fertile economic ground discovered by the church in America. Protected by the First Amendment right to freedom of religion, Moon set up a wide variety of businesses and scams that generated literally tens of millions of tax-free dollars. He started major newspapers in several cities, purchased a leading bank in Washington, bought the better part of a fishing village in New England, established restaurants and tea houses, while becoming increasingly involved in food processing, shipbuilding, furs, candle making, and jewelry. With most of his enterprises staffed by obedient, glassy-eyed Moonies who spent their spare time wandering the streets and peddling candles or flowers to raise even more money for their ever more prosperous movement, Father had the opportunity to handle huge quantities of cash. One former high-ranking church member estimated that Moon's tax-free income from the enthusiastic efforts of his "children" amounted to no less than $28 million annually. Among cult members, the leader's multi-millionaire status caused not the slightest hint of embarrassment or discomfort. An official training manual used the sophisticated language typical of the movement to explain the seemingly magnetic mutual attraction between money and Moon: "Do you like to make green bills happy? When green bills are in the hands of a fallen man, can they be happy? So many green bills are crying. . . . But they are all destined to go to Father . . . We must offer it to Heavenly Father through Father to use for a heavenly purpose." Those "heavenly purposes" obviously included the purchase of country estates, the acquisition of Rolls-Royce limousines, providing expensive "gifts" to various public officials, and a bold, lavishly financed attempt to break into the motion picture business.

In 1974, Sun Myung Moon informed his key lieutenants that he intended to form a film production company. Not content with producing mere rifles and machine guns, he obviously wanted a chance to produce big bombs as well. To head this glamorous new enterprise, the good Reverend turned to his long-time disciple and business associate, a wealthy Japanese newspaper publisher named Mitsuharu Ishii. This seemed an ideal choice because of Ishii's invaluable background in the entertainment business: he had once booked a successful Little Angels concert tour of Japan. As far as the portly press baron's experience in producing movies, Moon apparently had faith in the Doctrine of Heavenly On-The-Job Training.

Ishii Kitschie Koo

With Ishii comfortably established as president of the newly organized One Way Productions and shuttling back and forth between corporate offices in Los Angeles and Tokyo, the Moon men next faced the all-important question of what sort of movies they wanted to produce. The obvious choice—a film biography of Jesus—was briefly considered, but Father worried about finding a script that would meet the well-known "high standards" of the Man from Nazareth. After all, if they went ahead and produced a mediocre, critically assailed film such as *The Greatest Story Ever Told*, it would create a highly awkward social situation the next time Moon and Christ got together.

After setting aside Jesus (for the time being) as the subject for a film, Mitsuharu Ishii turned next to the logical second choice: Elvis Presley. Ishii traveled to the States for several meetings with Presley's managers, hoping to lure the King of Rock 'n' Roll to the Far East for a triumphant concert tour and the starring role in a Moonie movie to be shot at Japan's Toho Studios. This plan might have resulted in a memorable cultural confrontation under the heading *Elvis Meets Godzilla*, but alas, the singer's untimely 1977 demise abruptly terminated the negotiations.

With tens of millions (in cash) to spend on a movie but no suitable subject ready at hand, Ishii turned (where else?) to divine revelation. According to the official pressbook released with the movie *Inchon*, the fledgling producer at this point suddenly recalled a mystical episode from 1971. At that time, during a visit to Seoul, South Korea, Ishii found himself suddenly overcome with emotion and "for no apparent reason" burst into uncontrollable tears. (No, his spiritual vision had nothing whatever to do with the ultimate financial fate of *Inchon.*) After six days of nonstop crying, "he sought refuge in a movie theatre in order to escape from the strange looks he was receiving in the street." As it happened, the film before his brimming eyes turned out to be a grade B local feature about the Korean War. The pressbook continues, "As he sat in contemplation, he noticed the tears had stopped [causing him to miss the world's record by twenty-four days], and he became convinced that God wanted him to undertake the mission of bringing a fresh awareness of the War to a worldwide audience through a major film." Ishii apparently forgot this assignment for the next five years until, as president of One Way Productions, searching for a way to spend Father's money, frustrated by the unavailability of Elvis and Jesus, it all came back to him. He immediately commissioned a study of the Korean War and thereafter decided to focus his movie on one of its most heroic episodes: General Douglas MacArthur's surprise landing at Inchon harbor in 1950, which turned the tide of the initial North Korean assault. As a later Moonie press release explained, "So audacious was MacArthur's plan and so vigorous was his insistance [*sic*] on it that Ishii felt that the General may have received divine guidance."

To support this point of view, the One Way publicists trotted out an old photograph that had been published in a 1950 issue of *Paris-Match.* According to their imaginative propaganda, an American jet pilot at the Korean front had seen "a dazzling white light in the sky and, although he could see no details, took a photograph. When developed, the face of Jesus Christ could be discerned as if indicating Jesus' protection of Korea." If this hard evidence of the sacred nature of Ishii's movie mission failed to convince confirmed skeptics, he could refer them to another unimpeachable source, a "renowned psychic," who was reputedly Jeane Dixon. According to Ishii, the art director for his production company had snapped a blurry picture of MacArthur's Tokyo headquarters from the Korean War years, then submitted the photo to Ms. Dixon for analysis. At first, she mistakenly identified a shadowy face as George Washington, but then, as she prayed over the snapshot in her hands, MacArthur's voice boomed out from the spirit world, "If you lower the forehead and turn the head more to the left, you will recognize it is *me.*" According to the official *Inchon* pressbook the old soldier who never died went on to say, "I am very happy to see this picture being made because it will express my heart during the Korean War . . . I will make more than a 100% effort to support this movie."

Of course, this promise turned out to be nothing more than showbiz bluff, since ol' Doug wouldn't even make himself available for some simple talk show promotion—but go argue with a spirit! In any event, this mysterious blast from the past persuaded Ishii and Moon to ignore the abject failure of a recent film biography of MacArthur starring Gregory Peck and to press ahead with plans for their ultimate war epic—featuring blood, guts, God, love, and plenty of Commie atrocities, and the most pointless waste of time and treasure this side of *Heaven's Gate.*

Moore Is Less

After the exhaustive research period, Ishii settled on a curious title, *Oh, Inchon!* (allegedly inspired by the heroic sound of "Oh, say can you see . . ."), and began searching for an established screenwriter to translate his divine vision for the big screen. Acting upon the recommendation of his "personal friend" Jeane Dixon, Ishii secured the services of Robin Moore, author of the books *The Green Berets* and *The French Connection* and the scriptwriter for *The Happy Hooker.* Moore once told a reporter that the secret of his astonishing productivity was that he always worked while standing nude in front of a typewriter. "While I'm writing I don't even have a wristwatch on," he confessed. "I find that clothing is a barrier to creativity." This unique approach may have signaled confusion on the part of the writer between *Oh, Inchon!* and *Oh! Calcutta!*, but at least offered the advantage of greater speed, since Moore had access to additional digits with which to strike the keys. Lest anyone assume that the screenwriter's new association with officials of the Unification Church reflected a religious reawakening for the chronicler of *The Happy Hooker,* one of his close friends reassured the public that "they offered him a fortune to do the script. What you have to understand about Robin, above all, is that he will do absolutely anything for money."

The Moonie movie makers soon discovered that many other Hollywood luminaries operated on the same basis. By the end of 1977, they had signed studio veteran Andrew McLaglen (*Shenandoah, The Wild Geese*) to direct *Oh, Inchon!* and planned to begin production at Tokyo's Toho Studios. The Japanese production company, best known for giving the world such classics as *Matango: The Fungus of Terror, Ghidrah: The Three Headed Monster,* and the seemingly endless installments of the *Godzilla* series, agreed that Ishii's opus looked stupid and shoddy enough so they could proudly affix the Toho name as co-producers. With a budget set at $18 million, it looked as if the minor matter of shooting the film would be a piece of rice cake, but then, without warning, Ishii's Japanese plans were Nipped in the bud by Satanic forces.

No Go at Toho

Spurred by reports in the press that *Oh, Inchon!* would be an anti-Communist political diatribe designed to bring wealth and respectability to the controversial Reverend Moon, hundreds of left-wing Toho studio workers threw down their equipment in protest and went out on strike. They threatened to close down the entire movie company and to keep it closed until One Way Productions had been given a one-way ticket out of town. Faced with this grim ultimatum and literally surrounded by thousands of angry, chanting demonstrators, the Toho executives had little choice but to offer a sincere "so solly" to the visitors from Korea and to wish them ruck elsewhere. Since there had already been rotsa ruckus surrounding the project—and this only at the pre-production stage—the normally lion-hearted director, McLaglen, chickened out. He abandoned his binding contract with One Way (starting a dispute that was later settled out of court) and left Ishii and company in a quandary. With no experience whatever in filmmaking (not even thirty-second commercial spots) they knew they needed to find some sort of "successful director," so they turned once again to that mystical movie maven, Jeane Dixon.

This time, the psychic reached into her black hat and pulled out the name of Terence Young, director of three highly successful James Bond films: *Dr. No* (1962), *From Russia With Love* (1963), and *Thunderball* (1965). After screening a sample of Young's work, Ishii decided he liked the style (Forget the characters! Plenty of action!) and signed the British filmmaker for the astounding fee of $1.8 million. As part of the deal, Young brought several well-paid cohorts on board with him, including screenwriter Laird Koenig, who made a half-hearted attempt to redeem Robin Moore's dreadful script. Even at this relatively early stage, participants in *Oh, Inchon!* could scarcely believe the huge sums the Moonies proved willing to pay for even the most trivial tasks, but in the months ahead they gleefully watched all sanity depart in a senseless shower of "happy green bills."

The Moon and the Stars

When Ishii began announcing a series of all-star casting coups for his forthcoming feature, longtime industry observers seemed hard pressed to explain the willingness of some of the biggest names in the movie business to go to work for the Moonies. These puzzled pundits had apparently forgotten the eternal wisdom in the profound philosophical principle, "Money Talks, Nobody Walks." As one production insider candidly described the hiring process: "Never before has so much gone to so many for so little." One prime beneficiary of the producer's largesse was Jacqueline Bisset, fresh (and still dripping) from her starring role in *The Deep*. Critics agreed that her acting talents may not have been evident in this adventure yarn, but she filled a wet T-shirt like nobody since Jane Russell in *Underwater!* (q.v.). For a relatively minor part as a bored American army wife caught unexpectedly in the crossfire of war, Bisset received $1.65 million—which comes to $825,000 per breast.

When Nick Nolte (Jackie's co-star in *The Deep*) turned down $1.5 million for the role of her warrior husband in *Oh, Inchon!* the part went to Ben Gazzara, whose cleavage must have been considerably less appealing than Bisset's (or Nolte's) since he signed on for the bargain-basement price of only $750,000. To prove he was an Equal Opportunity Santa Claus, Ishii also hired Richard Roundtree, the original *Shaft* (who himself got shafted with a comparatively measly paycheck of $200,000); ex-*Fugitive* David Janssen, in the last role before his death, as a cynical war correspondent ($300,000); and Rex Reed, as an art critic turned front-line reporter ($6,000 per week—his first major role since an unforgettable 1970 debut as Raquel Welch's transsexual twin in *Myra Breckinridge*); and Toshiro Mifune, whose part had been specially written by his friend, director Terence Young, in the hope of attracting a large Japanese audience. For the all-important starring role of General Douglas MacArthur, one crew member recalled, "They wanted the very best that money could buy, so they went out and they got the world's greatest actor."

Et Tu, Larry?

Lord Laurence Olivier in a Moonie movie?

One might as well baste horsemeat with Dom Pérignon.

Fortunately, the aging thespian made it clear to his many admirers that he had not sold his soul to Moon, only to Mammon. After climbing aboard the *Oh, Inchon!* gravy train to the tune of $1.25 million, Lord Larry explained to co-star Rex Reed, in perhaps one of the most tragic soliloquies: "People ask me why I'm playing in this picture. The answer is simple. Money, dear boy . . . I'm like vintage wine. You have to drink me quickly before I turn sour . . . I'm almost used up now and I can feel the end coming. That's why I'm taking money now . . . I've got nothing to leave my family but the money I can make from films . . . Nothing is beneath me if it pays well. I've earned the right to damn well grab whatever I can in the time I've got left."

As if to prove that, indeed, *nothing* was beneath him, this once proud giant of stage and screen has accepted roles in such notorious turkeys as *Khartoum* (1966, in blackface and flowing Arab robes, as a murderous Sudanese chieftain); *The Shoes of the Fisherman* (1968, portraying a sabre-rattling premier of Russia); *The Betsy* (1978, where he gleefully rapes his own daughter-in-law, played by Katharine Ross); *Dracula* (1979, as a fearless vampire killer with an outrageously bogus Dutch accent); *The Jazz Singer* (1981, with a *Yiddish* accent yet, as Neil Diamond's father and a neighborhood cantor on the Lower East Side); and *Clash of the Titans* (1982, in a Zeus suit, no less!). After this string of public humiliations, he may even have welcomed his new role in *Oh, Inchon!*; as Douglas MacArthur, at least, he would have the chance to hide much of the time behind a corncob pipe and sunglasses.

The Invasion of Korea

With all his celebrated headliners firmly in place, Mitsuharu Ishii recruited an experienced technical crew of 225 Italians, Japanese, Germans, Englishmen, Frenchmen, and Greeks and descended on Korea in January 1979. By this time, it had become clear that it was the intention of the Moonies to re-stage the Korean War in all its anti-Communist glory, so government officials—who were just then attempting to negotiate a long-delayed peace treaty with their northern brothers and hoping to reduce tensions—did everything they could to discourage their presence. These powerful political crosscurrents interfered with the otherwise strong connection between the Unification Church and the Chung Hee Park regime, so that key bureaucrats took their sweet

Jacqueline Bisset tries to comfort Ben Gazzara over the humiliation of appearing in a Moonie movie. His acting fee of $750,000 provided more substantial reassurance, while Miss Bisset received $1.65 million for her role in Inchon.

time in responding to permit applications and requests for military equipment. As one member of the crew complained, "Korea's not like Hollywood. You can't just go out there and shoot whatever you want to. You can't do *anything* without the government's permission." The only progress during this frustrating period involved a change in the title, when Ishii and Moon decided that the simple, unadorned designation *Inchon!* would be quite enough, thank you, and let the *Oh* go. Finally, in April, after nearly ninety days of frustration, the Moonie minions received the official green light to begin shooting in early May.

But May came and went, with the entire cast and crew drawing full pay (at a cost of $200,000 a day) for hanging around their Seoul hotel rooms as they waited two months for their electrical, sound, and lighting equipment to clear customs. Since no major Hollywood film had ever been shot in Korea (with the strong likelihood that none will be attempted again in the near future), the country had no studios, production expediters, or extra equipment available—everything had to be done from scratch. In the face of these difficulties, the fast-aging Young confessed he might be tempted to make *Inchon!* in Hollywood, with only background shots in Korea, but decided against it because "that would be cheating."

This exemplary display of conscience soon found its divine reward. One of Father's faithful disciples, who assisted in the production, recalled a sudden and seemingly miraculous deliverance. "One day, something changed," he said. "God was there to intervene for us, and the permits somehow came through. There were many obstacles in our way—but we always felt that it was God's will that this movie should happen." If this, indeed, was the Lord's opinion, He found a strange way of expressing Himself in the weeks that followed.

The Last Typhoon

As *Inchon!* inched forward, the production team soon realized that they could not possibly stick to their twelve-week shooting schedule due to the unpredictable weather. One day the pouring rain would wash out the day's plans; the next morning the scorching sun would make work unbearable. Under these circumstances, trying to match shots became a source of constant frustration to Terence Young, and even more an irritation to Jackie Bisset's devoted costume designer, Donfeld. This sensitive couturier (whose original name was the less artistic "Don Feld") draped the star under big, floppy hats throughout most of the movie, explaining with exasperation, "I was *terrified* because of that bright sun in Korea! When Jackie squints, she looks like an onion."

No sooner had old Sol been shielded by welcome clouds, than two local typhoons named Irving and Judy decided to pay a call to the film set. During their visits, they managed to demolish an elaborate replica of the Inchon lighthouse. After the storms came another calamity: an inconsiderate earthquake that caused a fourteen-ton camera crane to be washed out to sea in the resulting twenty-four-foot-high tides. The disastrous weather also produced mudholes in which heavy tanks sank to their turrets, and once again, cast and crew had to sit and wait—this time for the earth to dry. Oddly enough, through all these natural disasters, the loyal Moonies never paused to consider that the unceasing string of catastrophes just might have been a message from above that they should give up their foolish thoughts of filmmaking and go back to selling flowers.

While the waters settled and the winds calmed, the cast members had a chance to express to the press some of their pent-up feelings about the entire project. In a classic understatement, Ben Gazzara told reporters, "this is not an actor's picture." "That's

right," David Janssen quickly agreed. "It's a movie about guns going off. All you can really do is say your lines as fast as you can and get out of the way before you get your ass blown off . . . Hell, in a week's time I forget who I'm playing."

One Way Productions chose to believe that Lord Larry, on the other hand, took his role more seriously. As a Moonie spokesman solemnly intoned, "Olivier had a very compelling, strong feeling after he did the part. I think he enjoyed learning the role of MacArthur, who was a very religious man. It was not just another movie; he could really get wrapped up in it." The famed actor certainly did get wrapped up in layers and layers of makeup; it took four hours every day to prepare him for the cameras. After learning that the real-life MacArthur had been so vain about his personal grooming that he used to wear corsets and lipstick for his public appearances, the makeup artists decided to go all the way. They began with a putty schnozzola that weighed nearly a pound, followed by a latex-thickened chin. After Olivier's noble head had been covered with a shiny black toupee (which stuck to his noggin like a piece of fresh seaweed), they applied thick layers of lipstick, rouge, and mascara. As a film critic for *The Village Voice* correctly observed: "Olivier subverts the entire project by appearing in the appropriate guise of a broken-down tart."

While suffering the gross indignities of this superficial transformation, Lord Larry approached the finer points of his role with thoroughgoing professionalism. He researched MacArthur's speech, mannerisms, and personal habits in tapes, films, Pentagon files, photographs, and William Manchester's best-selling biography, *American Caesar*. He also talked with five generals who had been active in the Korean campaign, including Alexander Haig. As a young lieutenant, Haig had served on MacArthur's personal staff, and in the course of a three-hour meeting, he startled Olivier with the revelation that the great general "sounded just like W. C. Fields." The diligent actor took this description to heart and, never giving a sucker an even break, fashioned his American accent in the movie after Fields' classic intonations—with strong hints of Slim Pickens and Jimmy Durante thrown in for good measure.

Unfortunately, during the course of the filming it was Jacqueline Bisset, and not Olivier, who came down with laryngitis. She languished in bed for a week, perfecting her impersonation of Liz Taylor on location, while the prearranged shooting schedule ground to a halt. Left once again with nothing to do, the other members of the cast and crew made the most of their free time by pursuing the delights of that gay and elegant capital city that had become like a second home to each of them.

Seoul Food

Night life in Korea differed markedly from the situation back home, in that there wasn't any. The police and the military strictly enforced the eleven P.M. curfew, and anyone found on the streets after that hour faced the virtual certainty of arrest. The local food also proved something of a disappointment to those pampered Hollywood types who had grown accustomed to the fare at Ma Maison and Chasen's. One of Korea's most popular (and omnipresent) delicacies is called *kimchi*, which consists of raw garlic and rotten cabbage. The authentic method for preparing this exotic treat is simple: bury it until it putrefies. Serves eight.

Another popular dish enjoyed throughout the country is barbecued dog—a snack which produced a mixed reaction among the representatives of an industry that had given the world Lassie, Rin Tin Tin, Benji, Phyllis Diller, and Muki the Wonder Hound. The widespread enjoyment of shish ke-puppy inspired the oft-heard line among the cast, "The dogs have stopped barking—it must be time to eat!" The corner grocery store, meanwhile, offered little relief, since inflation had driven the price of a small jar of instant coffee to $38, while a bottle of brandy could set you back $250.

In spite of these discomforts and inconveniences, producer Ishii tried hard to show his employees the best sort of down-home Far Eastern hospitality, making frequent trips to Tokyo and returning each time with suitcases filled with happy green bills. One crew member recalled, "They wasted tremendous amounts of money in every way imaginable. Always in cash. I got the feeling they were trying to make it cost as much as possible." Costume designer Donfeld felt particularly grateful for this approach. "They treated us like royalty," he said. "I've never seen a movie company treated so splendidly." Another high-ranking crew member recounted, "Moon had this obsession about spending money—he thought he was the Oriental David O. Selznick. They had so much cash coming in, I guess they had to do something with it. Whenever I asked for money, Ishii would simply go into a room, open up one of those suitcases, count out the cash, and hand it to me. In all my days in the business, I had never seen such a thing."

For the climactic re-enactment of the decisive

Et Tu, Larry?: Lord Laurence Olivier, less than delighted with his hilariously inappropriate casting as General Douglas MacArthur, contemplates a bust of Julius Caesar and considers the fleeting and temporary nature of all earthly glory.

landing at Inchon, Ishii must have brought along a footlocker of cash: the call sheet for that one day's shooting included a half-dozen destroyers, a fleet of transport convoys, six F-86 fighter-bombers, eight tugboats, eight twenty-ton tanks, twelve trucks, ten jeeps, three Red Cross ambulances, 1,500 foot soldiers, and one bagpipe marching band. At least some of the manpower came cheap, however, as a production auditor confirmed that "the Japanese and Korean Unification Churches supplied lots of free labor and extras for background scenes." This might explain why the thousands of dead soldiers strewn throughout the film look so utterly convincing; perhaps Reverend Moon convinced some of his followers to make the ultimate sacrifice for the sake of the film.

In any event, the single most impressive moment in the movie involved a grand total of 300 ships, steaming into Inchon harbor in perfect formation. Moon insisted that this stirring sequence must be staged at the precise location of the original events, despite the fact that the same tricky tides that had made MacArthur's landing so risky an enterprise in the first place now caused enormous problems for the movie makers. Director Terence Young struggled to overcome these difficulties and spent many days planning the logistics of the show-stopping production number. His final instructions called for the armada to make an abrupt turn to the left that would bring all the ships suddenly into the camera's view for maximum dramatic impact. After waiting for hours for the perfect light to coincide with appropriately manageable waves, the fateful moment arrived: Young cried out "ACTION!," expecting his seacraft to make their big turn to the left, but watched helplessly as they all turned right (and out of camera range) instead. When the ensuing curses died down, the nightmarish mistake could be traced to a Korean assistant director. "It turned out that the idiot's walkie-talkie was broken," Young recalled, "but the damned fool didn't tell anybody because he was afraid of losing face!" The spectacular snafu cost the production company close to a half-million dollars, but it seemed a small price to pay to preserve the self-respect of the embarrassed aide—especially for an operation that could waste even greater sums on some considerably less challenging scenes.

"A Spiritual Sensation"

The film's final sequence features a victory parade in Seoul after MacArthur's successful campaign. The General waves from his limousine, then steps inside Government House, where he is greeted by a cheering throng. As the vast room falls into a hush, a radio announcer makes sure he has our attention by whispering into his microphone, "America's greatest sol-

Major Frank Hallsworth (Ben Gazzara) and Sergeant Gus Henderson (Richard Roundtree) worry that they may have made a disastrous wrong turn at the 38th Parallel in one of the stirring battle scenes from Inchon.

dier is about to make a statement that may change world history!" At this point, Olivier, with pursed and painted lips, responds by reciting the entire Lord's Prayer to the assembled multitude. As the cameras zoom back, the music swells and the crowd rises to offer a standing ovation, followed by a montage of the South Korean and United Nations flag, and the credits come up.

This triumphal conclusion—lasting only three minutes on screen—seems simple and straightforward in both the script and the finished film, but due to the breathtaking incompetence of the producers it had to be shot over the course of four months in three different countries, and then pieced together at great expense. Moon himself created most of the difficulties: when he saw the original version of the crowd of flag-waving citizens, he felt there weren't enough people in the mob and asked Ishii to try again. This meant bringing the entire crew back to Korea at a total cost of nearly $1 million. The resulting footage pleased Father Moon (who at this point was acting a bit like Daddy Warbucks), but with the larger number of people on the street, the new sequence failed to match the previously filmed view of MacArthur in his limousine. Since Olivier had already returned to England, he declined the opportunity for another thrilling trip to Korea for the sake of redoing this one trivial shot. The Moonies had to satisfy themselves with transporting their star to Dublin, where they rented a studio, placed Olivier in a stationary car, and filmed him in front of a tacky-looking rear projection of the happy hordes. Fortunately, the interior shots of Government House had already been shot in Rome, of all places, where One Way Productions had worked out a "special deal" with one of the Italian film companies. Mitsuharu Ishii also worked out a very special deal for *himself* in this last scene, where he appears in the uniform of a South Korean general. The pudgy producer is on screen for several seconds, standing just behind MacArthur and unable to prevent himself from smiling straight into the camera. With this cameo appearance, Ishii apparently intended to emulate Alfred Hitchcock, though his only real connection with that great director was the fact that he may well be a *Psycho*, and his finished product is definitely for *The Birds*.

Ishii's presence in the scene only added to the awesome intensity of the moment, so that when Olivier recited the Lord's Prayer to the group of 300 extras and 175 crew members, the entire crowd experienced "a spiritual sensation" and felt moved to tears over the veteran actor's convincing impersonation of W. C. Fields. As the pressbook solemnly proclaims: "It was as if the greatest Old Soldier of the century had indeed never died nor even faded away but was living again through the century's greatest actor." Ishii, never prone to underestimate the significance of his work, told the *L.A. Times*, "I knew MacArthur's spirit was there. It was the first time in Hollywood history that the subject of a film helped from the spirit world." After reviewing his costs on *Inchon!*, Ishii must have realized that he would need all the help he could get.

Pennies From Heaven

According to figures released at the time, the price for principal photography came to $26 million—which in itself represented a lot of flowers, but amounted to little more than half the cost of the finished film. The additional expenses, including massive reshooting in Korea, England, Ireland, the United States, and Italy, and a prolonged editing process (which rivaled Michael Cimino's postproduction adventures on *Heaven's Gate*), added an astounding $22 million to the overall budget. Producer Sidney Beckerman, who accepted a $350,000 "consulting fee" to advise Ishii on re-editing the film, saw little connection between the final price tag of $48 million and the shoddy quality of what ultimately appeared on the screen. "In their position," he said, "I'd be embarrassed to tell anyone how much I spent."

Ishii, on the other hand, felt no such embarrassment. He boasted of *Inchon!*'s bloated budget and repeatedly told the world that his creation deserved recognition as "The Most Expensive Film Ever Made." It was only when reporters pressed him concerning the source of his money that the proud producer turned suddenly coy and inscrutable. While admitting his personal membership in the Unification Church, he vigorously denied rumors that church funds had been used to finance the production. He insisted that he himself had provided thirty percent of the budget, with the remaining seventy percent split among three Japanese banks and the First National Bank of Boston. According to an official press release from One Way Productions, Reverend Moon's only contribution to the project came in the form of Fatherly advice. "Since producer Mitsuharu Ishii didn't experience the war himself," this propaganda patiently explained, "he turned to Sun Myung Moon as Special Advisor for this historical Inchon project. . . . Moon saw the film in various stages of production and also gave artistic suggestions." Apparently, these "artistic suggestions"

proved so uniquely valuable that the genius who provided them received more generous acknowledgment on the screen than the director, producer, or any of the stars.

The Heavenly Deception concerning the money behind the film eventually proved too much even for Reverend Moon, and in January 1980, Father abruptly acknowledged paternity of his deformed celluloid child. Cheerfully contradicting all of Ishii's denials, Moon told a group of church leaders in New York that he had contributed some $35 million toward the making of *Inchon!* and that he planned to "work with veterans' groups and former generals to promote the film and, ultimately, the Unification Church point of view."

As members of President Nixon's White House staff might have put it, this unexpected announcement made all previous stories suddenly "inoperable." Faced, at last, with incontrovertible evidence of the Moon-made nature of the production, dozens of cast and crew members issued public statements claiming they *never* suspected the involvement of the controversial religious leader. Even Jeane Dixon, the producer's paranormal pal, insisted that on this one issue, her psychic powers inexplicably failed her. "Ishii *swore* to me that there was not one dollar of Moon money in that film," she told the press, and then rushed to a startling conclusion: "I guess he lied to me, didn't he?" The United States Department of Defense (which had supplied 1,500 American troops stationed in Korea to serve as fighting extras) and associate producer Red Hershon eventually reached the same conclusion and requested that their credits be removed. Officials of One Way Productions found it vaguely amusing that so many of those associated with the film should feel the need for disingenuous disclaimers. As one production assistant observed, "Of course, they all knew where the money was coming from! How many productions, do you think, pay their employees out of big suitcases filled with millions of dollars in cash? The fact was that all of the stars and all of the technical people were getting enormous sums, so they decided not to ask questions."

Can't Stop the Moonies

The increasingly controversial Korean war epic received its world premiere in a special showing at Washington's Kennedy Center, staged as a benefit for retired Navy personnel and sponsored by U.S. Senator Alfonse D'Amato (Republican, N.Y.). When the newly elected senator, however, heard the news that

Moon himself planned to attend the gala affair, D'Amato responded by staying home and boycotting his own event. The chief excitement at the debut screening came from the Marine Corps Drum and Bugle Corps, whose martial music helped to drown out the shouts of angry demonstrators, protesting the "brainwashing" of their children by the Unification Church. Despite the fuss and fanfare concerning his planned appearance, that old sly boots, Moon, went into eclipse and failed to show up.

Considering the hostile reaction of the audience to what they saw on the screen, he undoubtedly made the right decision. The public response at all preview screenings proved so negative, in fact, that the major U.S. distributors wanted nothing to do with the multi-million-dollar mess. In desperation, Ishii hired a brand-new staff to try to shape a silk purse out of his cinematic sow's ear, and they spent more than a year re-editing the film and cutting its original running time of two hours and forty minutes by nearly a third.

In this new slim-and-trim incarnation, *Inchon!* played the Cannes Festival in the spring of '82, where, together with Pia Zadora's grand entrance in a tushy-baring black G-string, it proved to be one of the most eagerly awaited offerings. One critic suggested that the only possible explanation for the excitement surrounding *Inchon!*'s reappearance was the open invitation to all festival-goers to attend a lavish banquet following the film's premiere. One Way Productions provided literally dozens of tables heaped high with every conceivable gourmet delicacy (except for barbecued dog), but the ungrateful critics persisted in finding the gratis grunts considerably more appetizing than the warmed-over movie.

The One Way wonders fared no better in their attempts to lure Lord Olivier into co-operating with their efforts to hype the finished film. They invited him to make an appearance at Cannes, and to show their gratitude in advance, they bought him a 1982 Rolls-Royce Corniche, which they would present to him in a well-publicized ceremony as soon as he arrived. Though the great actor had previously declared that *nothing* was beneath him, the Moonies may have finally proved him wrong; the idea of flying to the carnival at Cannes to pick up the keys to a new car as part of an outright bribe from Reverend Sun Myung Moon proved a bit too tacky for even Olivier's notoriously strong stomach. Lord Larry stayed home, happily counting the money he had already received, and left Ishii and company with the problem of finding some other use for their elegant new car.

The distributors, meanwhile, still could find no use whatever for their elegant new *Inchon!*, so the Moonies began talking of handling the public presentation of the film on their own. As one distribution expert recalled, "They came to me for advice, because they were planning to rent the theatres outright, and have their people sell tickets, run the projection booth, and pop the popcorn all by themselves. I told them it was a very crazy idea, but some of these people were not always rational." In the end, the church leadership decided it would be more profitable to keep the Moonie minions pounding the pavement, so Mitsuharu Ishii approached MGM/UA with an offer they couldn't refuse. Though precise details never appeared in the press, it was understood in the industry that the studio received a fat up-front fee—in cash, naturally—for releasing the film domestically. Even so, the executives at MGM/UA wanted a number of changes before they agreed to handle the film. First, they suggested that the exclamation point be dropped from the title *INCHON!* because they feared that the public might look at print ads and billboards with the mistaken notion that they were reading about a new pasta dish called *Inchoni*. Second, the Hollywood bosses prevailed upon One Way to modify Sun Myung Moon's gigantic above-the-titles credit from "*Spiritual* Advisor" to "*Special* Advisor" in order to play down the controversial religious associations of the film. The Moonies eventually complied with these requests, leading the ailing, recently merged studio to a sense of guarded optimism concerning their new product. As one MGM/UA veteran described their state of mind at the time: "We felt that if we could survive Michael Cimino, then we could survive anything." Little did they know that the critical and box office response to *Inchon* would make *Heaven's Gate* look like a triumphant blockbuster in comparison.

Inchon Unchained

A saturation campaign of television, radio, and newspaper ads prepared the country for the movie's nationwide release on September 17, 1982—the thirty-second anniversary of MacArthur's fateful landing. While making much of this historical coincidence, neither the film itself nor any of the hundreds of pages of promotional material released along with it made any mention of the fact that a mere seven months after his great triumph at Inchon, Big Mac was relieved of command by President Truman. It seems that "America's greatest soldier" had pulled a monumental boner by pursuing the Korean Commies up to the Chinese border, giving the Red Chinese an excuse to enter the war and nearly blowing the entire ball game for the United States—but then, everybody's entitled to a few mistakes. The ads for the film promised "LOVE. DESTINY. HEROES. WAR CHANGES EVERYTHING." but might more appropriately have read, "STARS. EXTRAS. MONEY. INCHON WASTES EVERYTHING." The mess on screen managed to combine comically pompous speeches by Olivier/MacArthur; touching domestic scenes between the general and his wife ("I shall return—but not too late for dinner!"); cliché-ridden marital conflicts between embattled Major Ben Gazzara and Jackie Bisset, his interior-designer wife; kiddie interludes about Korean war orphans, as portrayed by (who else?) members of the Moonie singing group, The Little Angels; and plodding, interminable battle scenes, through many of which Ms. Bisset dodges exploding shells in a revealing polka-dot bikini top. While such a titillating spectacle might appear strikingly out of place and uncharacteristically incendiary in a film sponsored by the Unification Church, true disciples need not have worried. Father Moon's indoctrination program prepared cult members to conquer their natural sex drives by taking cold showers ("Satan hates cold showers"), so that his pubescent proselytes could be kept well in hand—unlike the rambling and confusing film.

According to one of the film editors, one major problem with the final cut of Inchon was Reverend Moon's personal insistence on numerous scenes showing North Korean atrocities: "He couldn't get enough of the blood and guts. He just wanted more and more and more." As a result, we see vivid and horrifying sequences showing South Koreans ruthlessly murdered, maimed, tortured, pillaged, raped, and forced to eat kimchi by the Godless Commies. Throughout the film, these unspeakable baddies pronounce not one word of dialogue, which helps to render them into subhuman scum, worthy of nothing but mass extermination. But, after all, Moon-style anti-Communism means never having to say you're sorry.

While Ishii and the Reverend pushed Inchon past its already exorbitant budget to new, hitherto unexplored financial frontiers in the name of achieving an unequaled standard of authenticity, somehow their eye for detail proved notably less exacting than fellow fanatic Michael Cimino's. In one of MacArthur's long speeches, his pants are so moved by the general's eloquence that they change color twice: he is first clad in beige trousers, then, in a long shot, they are dark green; only to revert to beige at the end of

his exhortation. Later, we watch with horror as Sergeant Richard Roundtree is caught in the explosion of the Han River Bridge; he plummets in his jeep into the water far below. But take heart, Shaft fans! . . . less than two minutes later, Roundtree reappears in precisely the same jeep, without a scratch and perfectly dry, to help Jackie Bisset fix her car.

This sort of idiotic inconsistency helped to win for The Most Expensive Movie Ever Made some of The Most Vicious Reviews Ever Penned. Included in the chorus of condemnation were judgments such as:

"The worst movie ever made . . . A turkey the size of Godzilla . . ." —JACK KROLL, Newsweek

"Quite possibly the worst movie ever made . . . Stupefyingly incompetent." —PETER RAINER, L.A. Herald-Examiner

"A near total loss as well as a laugh . . ." —BRUCE WILLIAMSON, Playboy

"As military spectacles go, one of the sorriest in movie history." —RICHARD SCHICKEL, Time

"Hysterical . . . The most expensive B movie ever made." —VINCENT CANBY, New York Times

"The movie attributes the 'winning' of the Korean War to an act of God. It may take more than that to foist this dreck off on the American public." —J. HOBERMAN, Village Voice

That Old Devil Moon

In the face of such withering and overwhelming scorn, the Moonies tried a suitably silly promotional gimmick to lure crowds to the theatres. One might think that "THE INCHON MILLION DOLLAR SWEEPSTAKES!!!" was just a typical piece of Hollywood hype, but One Way Productions insisted that their raffle had a higher, deeper purpose: "The Inchon Sweepstakes is being held to call attention to the motion picture and the need for America to see MacArthur's spirit in a new light—the love of God, country, man, and resistance of [sic] Communism."

And what, dear reader, do you think was offered as the grand prize in this uplifting exercise? A gigantic American flag that had been flown over Arlington National Cemetery? A tactical nuclear weapon for your very own garage? A free hour of consultation with Jeane Dixon? No! The Moonies generously offered a brand-new, 1982 Rolls-Royce Corniche . . . a glamorous vehicle fit for Lord Olivier himself. (No one ever accused these clever cultists of being unresourceful.) Other gifts from Moon the Munificent included ten paid vacations to South Korea, televisions, cameras, "MacArthur style" aviator glasses, and last, but certainly least, "50,000 beautifully illustrated *Inchon* souvenir books."

Unfortunately, the *Inchon* Sweepstakes backfired almost immediately; as a *Variety* headline reported: "SOME SEE *INCHON* CONTEST AS MOONIE RECRUITMENT DRIVE." According to this report, many potential moviegoers feared that the Unification Church would "use the mailing lists drawn from the contest to seek new cult members" or that "Moonies would be present at theatres and will attempt to recruit others there." If the Reverend's loyal disciples were, in fact, on hand at the theatres where *Inchon* had opened, they would have become painfully lonely before the end of the first week; by that time, the motion picture had already shaped up as a box office disaster of historic proportions.

This grim situation called for extraordinary action. Full-page ads in newspapers across the country featured an "open letter" from the Divine Mr. M. that began "DEAR AMERICAN PEOPLE: I note with sorrow how motion picture critics have reacted to the new film, *Inchon* . . . What saddens me most is that this should happen in the United States which is, and always has been, the champion of freedom of religion." In other words, Moon reasoned that those critics who hated his film had actually violated his First Amendment rights; we are only surprised that the A.C.L.U. failed to rush forward to take up his case.

After the ads appeared, one embarrassed publicity man tried to explain to the press what had happened. "I told them I thought it was a bad idea. It was Ishii's idea. He's deeply sorry the film isn't doing any business. [We'll bet he is.] He feels the public is being essentially misled that the movie is a church message rather than what it is—a war movie." It all makes perfect sense—a message directly from their church leader will convince the American movie-going public that the film has nothing to do with religion. Slick move, but then Father knows best. In any event, according to figures in the Hollywood trade press, *Inchon* grossed only $1.9 million in its U.S. and Canadian run—only slightly more than *Heaven's Gate*'s preposterously paltry $1.5 million, but then Ishii's "most expensive movie" had reportedly cost $4 million more to make. By its second week of release, *Inchon* had already been double-featured with such notable classics as *The Last American Virgin* or *The Incubus,* and *Variety* had reported that it was "fast becoming a larger bomb than any dropped during the Korean police action."

In a last-ditch effort to salvage something from the debacle, the Unification Church dispatched some of its best flower children to local airports and street corners across the country. Armed with their usual flowers and "Please Contribute" literature the Kiddie Korps also carried a new weapon in its arsenal, neatly tucked inside the familiar leaflets. This special message bore the sad plea, "GO SEE *INCHON*." These noble efforts, however, much like their leader's lamentable letter, only served to enhance the film's already potent negative associations. The *Los Angeles Herald-Examiner* summarized the situation just three weeks after the picture's initial release: "It all adds up to one of the worst disasters in either entertainment or military annals."

To add insult to injury, Laurence Olivier and Terence Young, not satisfied with collecting their agreed-upon fees of $1.25 million and $1.8 million respectively, turned around after the film's release and sued One Way for an additional $1 million *each* as compensation for overtime charges. Moon also suffered well-publicized personal problems, with a crippling conviction on tax evasion charges.

But then, just as the darkness seemed most oppressive and most intense, came a thin ray of hope in the distance . . .

Waiting for Divine Guidance

In mid-1983, Mitsuharu Ishii tried to emphasize the up side of *Inchon*. Sure, he was *at least* $50 million in the hole, but the film had not yet played any overseas markets at all, and no ancillary rights (television, video cassette, and cable) had yet been negotiated.

This raises an obvious question: what are the Moonies waiting for? For Lord Olivier to die—with a flurry of favorable publicity? For MacArthur to make his much-promised promotional tour ("I shall return—but not too late for a good foreign sale")? For Reverend Moon to send cast and crew back to Korea for a fifth time? No, producer Ishii is humbly awaiting "Divine Guidance." Sooner or later, according to his way of thinking, God is going to tell him, "Quick—offer the film to CBS for $6 million," or "Do not sell Tasmanian rights until 1994." Apparently, Ishii is also expecting word from Above that will help to determine the right moment for his planned American rerelease of the film—this time in its unexpurgated two-hour-and-forty-minute version, with an even more generous selection of Communist atrocities. He also nurses the fond hope that his film will clean up with the unspoiled audiences of Asia—

Why Is This Man Smiling?: The gentleman to the left, toasting completion of Inchon *with Laurence Olivier, is none other than Mitsuharu Ishii, the movie's irrepressible producer. After his triumphant cameo appearance for several seconds on screen as a general in the South Korean army listening to MacArthur's dramatic victory speech, Ishii is ready to move upward and onward with his motion picture career. Currently in the "planning stages" are a series of Moonstruck adaptations of the Bible, with the initial budget estimated at $1 billion.*

particularly the Philippines, where MacArthur is revered as a secular saint.

In the aftermath of *Inchon*, one might reasonably expect that One Way Productions would have learned its lesson—that Moonies and movies don't mix—but Mr. Ishii's continued and indefatigable efforts to make cinema history show just how hard, if not impossible, it is to keep a good man down. Ishii's new project involves a series of ten to fifteen full-length feature films, all based on different books of the Bible. This series has been modestly budgeted at $1 *billion*—enough to make twenty-four *Heaven's Gates* or 200 *Chariots of Fires*. The first film in this ambitious sequence will deal either with the life of John the Baptist or with "new research" on the life of Jesus—including, no doubt, the surprising revelation that he made many visits to South Korea. Ishii's office also indicates that Robin Moore is once more stripped down and ready for action—hard at work preparing the screenplay for the new picture, which is planned for release some time in 1987. When asked if they are worried about tying up so much time and

money in a project that won't come to fruition for another four years, a One Way spokesperson told us, "Well, it took Richard Attenborough twenty years to make *Gandhi*, didn't it?" In response to the all-important question of who will be funding these new productions, producer Ishii replied with a straight face, "I expect, sooner or later, to make a lot of money from *Inchon*."

If these Bible stories are ever completed, bad-movie buffs in the years ahead will have more fun than a barrel of Moonies, and the Hollywood Hall of Shame might have to open a new wing. Mr. Ishii and Reverend Moon—if you are listening now—a donation, please, to cover the cost of construction would be most sincerely appreciated. We'll even throw in a small bronze plaque—and a prayer rug—at no extra charge.

If you fail to respond in a timely fashion, we may be forced to relegate your worthy new films to our already overcrowded Basement Collection, where so many memorable movie mistakes must compete for attention. . . .

THE BASEMENT COLLECTION: A COMPENDIUM OF NOTABLE FILM FLOPS

AS WE WARNED at the very beginning of our tour, the movies displayed in the main gallery of the Hall of Shame have been chosen on a purely subjective basis. We selected those financial disasters that we *wanted* to research and describe in depth, while hoping that in the process we could provide a representative sampling of the wondrous ways in which Hollywood has contrived to lose money over the years. We recognize that different curators would no doubt have decided differently.

For our Basement Collection, on the other hand, we have tried to be inclusive, displaying all of the most important big-budget busts that came to our attention. Despite our energetic efforts, we understand that we have most certainly missed many worthy contenders, and we can only suggest that you correct some of these omissions by writing to us at the address provided at the back of the book.

In addition to those deserving motion pictures from the past that we have unintentionally excluded, there are countless contemporary bombs that could not be listed here because they have exploded altogether too recently. In the high-stakes, reckless gambler's atmosphere of today's Hollywood, new financial disasters turn up every month—if not every week—and monitoring all these fast-fading flops would be in itself a full-time job. In the last analysis, the history of human failure and fatuity is a subject timeless in dimension and infinite in scope.

Gary Cooper, as that suave Italian globetrotter, Marco Polo, teaches Sigrid Gurie (the Khan's daughter) how to kiss in the best European style. Producer Samuel Goldwyn had high hopes for Miss Gurie as "The Norwegian Garbo," but she never made it; neither did The Adventures of Marco Polo.

John Wayne as Davy Crockett (with sidekick Chill Wills, right and young disciple Frankie Avalon) looks longingly toward the horizon for some sign of deliverance from his personal financial dilemma as producer, director, star, and chief backer of The Alamo.

THE ADVENTURES OF MARCO POLO (1938)

What do Gary Cooper, Rory Calhoun, Horst Buchholz, and Desi Arnaz, Jr., have in common? They all played the lead in bad movies about Marco Polo, and in all four cases the projects flopped. This trailblazing turkey—with Coop, Basil Rathbone, Ward Bond, and a bit part for young Lana Turner—boasted high production values, a lavish $2 million budget, and more dismal box office returns than any of its successors. The film is best remembered today as the debut vehicle for Sigrid Gurie, producer Sam Goldwyn's much-touted "Norwegian Garbo." Shortly after the movie's release, private detectives discovered that this exotic beauty actually hailed from Flatbush, Brooklyn, a revelation that assured that both Miss Gurie and her first film faded into well-deserved obscurity.

THE AGONY AND THE ECSTASY (1965)

Ponderous, slow-moving spectacle about history's most celebrated paint job. Michelangelo (Charlton Heston) bickers interminably with Pope Julius II (Rex Harrison) over the interior-decorating scheme for the Sistine Chapel, which had been specially recreated for this movie as the world's largest indoor set. The picture cost a staggering $12 million, earned back only $4 million (domestic gross), and caused executives at Twentieth Century-Fox to hit the ceiling with a good deal more agony than ecstasy.

THE ALAMO (1960)

"This picture is America," said John Wayne. "I hope that seeing the Battle of the Alamo will remind Americans that liberty and freedom don't come cheap." Neither, apparently, do overblown epics. The Duke produced, directed, and starred (as Davy Crockett), sinking most of his personal fortune into financing the film. A ludicrous list of co-stars, including Richard Widmark, Laurence Harvey, Chill Wills, Linda Cristal ("The Pepper Pot of the Pampas"), and Frankie Avalon (Frankie Avalon?) helped to doom Wayne's sincere and noble intentions. The picture earned back only half its initial $15 million cost, despite eleven Academy Award nominations. The elaborate replica of the Alamo, built for the film at a cost of $1.5 million, still stands on the Texas plains and has become an appropriately tacky tourist attraction known as "Alamo Village."

ALICE IN WONDERLAND (1933)

Paramount stuck closely to the episodic story line of the Lewis Carroll classic, designing costumes and abstract sets from the famous illustrations by John Tenniel. Inside the elaborate, surreal outfits the studio placed some of its biggest stars, including Gary Cooper as the White Knight, Cary Grant as the Mock Turtle, and W. C. Fields as Humpty Dumpty. All of this only served to confuse or frighten the children for whom the film had been intended, while adults found it mannered and dull. As a result, the picture emerged as one of the biggest bombs of the 1930s, leading the studio to cancel its plans for other adaptations of children's literature. Strangely, the far inferior Disney animated version paid off quite handsomely in rereleases during the 1960s when audiences finally began to understand what the Caterpillar had been smoking. Paramount, however, never did rerelease their curious treatment of the story, and it remains known only to devotees of the late, late show.

The $42 million cost of Annie *(with perky newcomer Aileen Quinn in the title role) would have made a dent in even the vast fortune of Daddy Warbucks (Albert Finney).*

ALL NIGHT LONG (1981)

No, the title does not refer to the sexual prowess of its two high-powered stars (Gene Hackman and Barbra Streisand) but rather to Hackman's depressing job as manager of an all-night drugstore. Both he and his son (Dennis Quaid) have affairs with the hotsy-totsy married neighbor lady, as rendered by La Barbra, in what would have been a low-budget comedy except for the record-breaking $4 million fee paid to Streisand for her part.

ANNIE (1982)

Columbia set a record by paying $9.5 million for the rights to film the successful Broadway show, and the budget for *Annie* went on from there. Producer Ray Stark selected John Huston to direct, despite the fact that the seventy-four-year-old filmmaker had never before attempted a musical. Before the dust had cleared, the picture cost $42 million, placing it in the magic circle with *Inchon* and *Heaven's Gate* among the prize porkers of recent years. Ray Stark told the world, "This is the film I want on my tombstone," to which *Time* magazine responded, "Funeral services may be held starting this week at a theatre near you." Studio sources estimated that the film would have to earn more than $150 million in order to break even, and to date the picture has grossed about half that. Stark blamed vicious and unfair reviews for its dismal performance and is currently working on a movie about film critics.

The celebrated romantic chemistry between Charles Boyer and Ingrid Bergman could not save Lewis Milestone's Arch of Triumph *from utter failure at the box office.*

ARCH OF TRIUMPH (1948)

A soggy and soporific adaptation of a best-selling novel by Erich Maria Remarque, which single-handedly sank a short-lived but promising operation known as Enterprise Studios. Charles Boyer, as an anti-Nazi Austrian surgeon, and Ingrid Bergman, as a self-pitying lady of the night, are thrown together in prewar Paris. Charles Laughton, in one of his worst-ever performances, plays a monocled, sadistic Gestapo agent with an accent that is pure Katzenjammer Kids. A $5 million budget and a $1.4 million gross made this over-publicized offering an Arch of Disaster for its struggling studio.

ASH WEDNESDAY (1973)

Liz Taylor's on-screen husband (Henry Fonda) runs off with a younger woman, so our heroine decides to transform herself through the magic of cosmetic surgery into a radiant beauty. "Look at these breasts! Aren't they beautiful?" she asks her wayward hubby, who eventually sees her point. This trashy soap opera spent millions on surgical scenes so detailed and realistic that they revolted most viewers.

AT LONG LAST LOVE (1975)

"If this film were any more of a dog, it would shed," commented critic John Barbour, and the movie merited inclusion in that invaluable 1978 reference book, *The Fifty Worst Films of All Time*. Director Peter Bogdanovich earned these distinctions by presenting sixteen Cole Porter songs through the golden voices of his good friend, the former (and future) model, Cybill Shepherd; that dancin' fool, Burt Reynolds; and the ever-enchanting Madeline Kahn. The choreography set new standards for flat-footed incompetence, while Bogdanovich's perfectionist refusal to lip-synch the musical numbers drove the budget through the roof. To date, the movie has earned back less than one-fourth its cost of $6 million.

AUSTERLITZ (1960)

Silent era director Abel Gance tried for a comeback with this ambitious multi-national co-production shot in France, Germany, Italy, and Yugoslavia. Gance made his reputation with an audacious screen biography of Napoleon in 1929, but here the Little Corporal seems lifeless and stilted. The picture cost one billion French francs (or about $4 million) and nearly bankrupt producer Alexander Salkind, who later recovered to team with his son, Ilya, as producers of the *Superman* series.

THE BATTLE OF BRITAIN (1969)

Celebrated actors such as Laurence Olivier, Michael Caine, Michael Redgrave, and Ralph Richardson are all utterly wasted in this melodramatic, confusing view of "their finest hour." The British producers somehow managed to keep a stiff upper lip while losing $10 million.

BEAR ISLAND (1980)

The most expensive Canadian film ever made features Vanessa Redgrave and Richard Widmark, with hilarious Norwegian and German accents, respectively. Donald Sutherland, the only card-carrying Canadian among the stars, plays an American biologist in this "action adventure" about a U.N. scientific expedition—and phantom Nazi submarines—in the icy waters around Norway. Audiences found it un*bear*able, and it lost virtually every penny of its $12 million cost.

BEAU BRUMMEL (1954)

The fop flops, and Liz Taylor does it again! This handsomely mounted historical romance tells the story of a famous eighteenth-century dandy (Stewart Granger) who is forced to leave England and dies in poverty, thereby foretelling the fate of the producers. Young Elizabeth is the love interest, though she is not the quarry in an overlong fox hunt that is central to the plot. The *New York Times* reported that "the dialogue is atrocious and the picture moves like a tired elephant."

BEYOND THE FOREST (1949)

Bette Davis *always* hated this turgid melodrama about a small-town bad girl itching to run away to the big city, and the star felt a similar itch to run away from this project. She walked out on it several times, driving the budget skyward, but Jack Warner refused to release her from her contract. The box office failure of this lavish howler marked a sad end to Miss Davis' long association with Warner Brothers; she remembers *Beyond the Forest* as "a terrible movie," in which she played "the longest death scene ever seen on the screen."

THE BIBLE (1966)

The inspiration for this sprawling adaptation of the perennial best-seller reportedly came to producer Dino De Laurentiis one night in a hotel room: "I wake up inna middle ofa night, I say to myself, 'Whatsa greatest book ever wrote?' The Bible! So I makea movie of the Bible!" The ambitious movie maker failed in his attempts to persuade Igor Stravinsky to write the score, Laurence Olivier to provide the voice of God, or Maria Callas to play the role of Sarah, but he did succeed in signing "the greatest director inna world!," John Huston, to supervise the film. Huston also spoke God's lines from behind the camera and played Noah as if he were a long-lost cousin of the Beverly Hillbillies. Other stars included George C. Scott as Abraham, Ava Gardner as Sarah, Richard Harris as Cain, and Peter O'Toole as an angel. A pretentious pageant budgeted at $18 million, it went into release at the same time as *The Greatest Story Ever Told* (See the *Prophets and Losses* exhibit) and surprised nearly everyone by outperforming its New Testament competitor, but still fell far short of earning back its hefty cost.

THE BIG FISHERMAN (1959)

This story of Saint Peter, starring Howard (*Carousel*) Keel in the nonsinging title role, used seventy-three sets in the San Fernando Valley to recreate Galilee. A favorite of bad-film fanatics, it features klieg lights and microphones dangling into many scenes, while temptress Martha Hyer clearly displays the vaccination mark on her bare arm. A generous $4 million budget couldn't stop the *Hollywood Reporter* from commenting: "The picture is three hours long and, except for those who can be dazzled by big gatherings of props, horses and camels, it is hard to find three minutes of entertainment in it."

BIG WEDNESDAY (1978)

The only $11 million surfing picture in Hollywood history, it describes the adventures of three tightly bonded buddies who conduct a tedious search for the perfect wave. The boys finally find enlightenment, along with heavy philosophical lines, such as "You can't surf forever!" The picture, however, feels as if *it* can go on forever, under the ham-handed direction of John Milius, who later gave the world *Conan the Barbarian*. *Big Wednesday* never succeeded in shooting the glassies and suffered a spectacular wipe out after just one week in most theatres.

THE BLUE BIRD (1976)

See the *Child Abuse* exhibit.

BOBBY DEERFIELD (1977)

A slick tearjerker with Al Pacino as a sensitive Grand Prix driver who falls in love with Marthe Keller, an Italian lady of leisure (with an inexplicable German accent) who is, naturally, dying of a mysterious disease. The audience suffers far more painfully than she does. Sydney (*The Way We Were, Tootsie*) Pollack

not only lost his touch for directing this unintentionally hilarious stinker, but managed to lose nearly substantial amounts of the investors' money in the process.

BOOM! (1968)

See *The Elizabeth Taylor Wing*.

BRIDE OF VENGEANCE (1949)

This big-budget costume drama tries to rehabilitate the reputation of that Renaissance good time girl, Lucrezia Borgia, who is best remembered for her poisonous proclivities. With Paulette Goddard in the lead role, Lucrezia is portrayed as a sweet kid who is unfortunately misled by her bearded baddie of a brother, Cesare, as played by Broadway star John Lund. Paramount, painfully aware of the shoddy quality of their product, held back its release date for more than a year while trying to devise some strategy for selling this lemon to an unsuspecting public. They obviously failed, since after it opened, the critics all slammed *Bride* with a vengeance. Said the *Los Angeles Times*: "A dud. . . . It just couldn't be that bad by accident." In New York, the picture opened and closed within a week, and the few people who actually saw the picture laughed uproariously at its excesses. David Chierichetti, biographer of the film's hapless director, Mitchell Leisen, reported: "It was a complete failure at the box office . . . *Bride of Vengeance* was such a catastrophe, Paulette Goddard never worked on the Paramount lot again."

BRIGHAM YOUNG (1940)

When Darryl Zanuck suddenly discovered that several million Mormons in the United States believed that Joseph Smith and Brigham Young were Latter-Day Saints, he decided that these good people deserved their own answer to *King of Kings*. He cast Vincent Price as Smith, founder of the religion, and Dean Jagger as Young, the charismatic polygamist who led the Mormons west. Tyrone Power and Linda Darnell are also on hand as devoted disciples who join the trek to the Great Salt Lake. Twentieth Century-Fox tried to emphasize its star power and to downplay the religious elements (eventually retitling it *Brigham Young, Frontiersman*), but the picture still failed, even in Utah.

CABOBLANCO (1980)

A lamebrained remake of *Casablanca*, but this time, apparently, they spelled the title wrong and decided to set the action in Peru. Charles Bronson takes the

Humphrey Bogart part, Dominique Sanda stands in for Ingrid Bergman, with Jason Robards, Fernando Rey, and Gilbert Roland along for the ride. When studio executives viewed the finished product, they decided to cut their losses and gave it only a limited release; the picture still lost well in excess of $8 million.

CAESAR AND CLEOPATRA (1945)

This ambitious film version of George Bernard Shaw's witty play lost the equivalent of more than three million American dollars, establishing itself as the greatest fiasco in the history of British film up to that time. Vivien Leigh is persuasive as a young, kittenish Cleopatra, trying to attract an aging Caesar (played by Claude Rains), but for movie makers the Queen of the Nile has always been a bust. Spectacular sets and battle scenes irritated the eighty-nine-year-old Shaw by taking attention away from his finely honed lines, and director Gabriel Pascal shocked colleagues and associates with his unparalleled extravagance. At one point he organized a trip to Egypt with cast and crew for which he brought along his own, gigantic papier-mâché Sphinx. Feuds on the set, a miscarriage and serious illness for Miss Leigh, bad weather, and a few Nazi bombing attacks in the last years of the war all contributed to long delays in the production. The resulting disaster nearly forced the Rank Organization into bankruptcy and virtually ended the career of the film's profligate director.

CAIN AND MABEL (1936)

See *The Titans and Their Toys* exhibit.

CAMELOT (1967)

A $17 million adaptation of the hit Lerner and Loewe musical, which featured the authentic, wafer-thin voices of Richard Harris and Vanessa Redgrave. Filmed in Spain, France, England, and on a gorgeous $2.5 million set in beautiful downtown Burbank, the film presented an unarguably beautiful surface that led critic John Simon to describe it as "three hours of unrelieved glossiness, meticulous inanity, desperate and charmless striving for charm." Director Joshua Logan managed to avoid the sort of crushing disaster he later achieved with *Paint Your Wagon* (see the *Musical Extravaganzas* exhibit), but considering the quality of the original material and the high hopes for another *Sound of Music*, it still proved a major box office disappointment for Warner Brothers.

CAN'T STOP THE MUSIC (1980)

See the *Musical Extravaganzas* exhibit.

CAPTAIN FROM CASTILE (1947)

A swashbuckling treatment of the conquest of Mexico by Cortez, as portrayed by Cesar Romero, with Tyrone Power and Jean Peters. Under Darryl Zanuck's watchful eye, the budget ballooned from an original figure of $2 million all the way up to $4.5 million, setting new records for Twentieth Century-Fox. The stirring Alfred Newman score is remembered as a Hollywood classic and helped the picture do respectable business at the box office, but the grossly inflated expense of the production ensured an overall loss of $1.5 million.

THE CAPTAIN HATES THE SEA (1934)

This zany comedy about a luxury liner gave John Gilbert, the faded Adonis from the silent era, his last role. With celebrated alcoholics such as Gilbert, Victor McLaglen, Walter Connolly, Walter Catlett, and Leon Errol working together and having a ball, the picture naturally ran way over budget. Harry Cohn, head of Columbia Studios, dispatched an angry cable to director Lewis Milestone in the midst of production: "Hurry up! The cost is staggering!" to which Milestone responded, "So is the cast!" When released, the picture sank almost immediately beneath the waves and achieved some of the lowest grosses of the year in theatres across the country.

CARAVANS (1978)

Such enlightened despots as Benito Mussolini (see the *Fascist Follies* exhibit) and Muammar Qaddafi (see the *Prophets and Losses* exhibit) made big-budget movie flops, so why not the Shah of Iran? On the eve of revolution, His Serene Highness, the Light of the Aryans, managed to come up with $14 million to finance this sprawling adaptation of James Michener's best-seller, described by some critics as a Persian version of *The Searchers*. Jennifer O'Neill joins a nomadic tribe led by that barbaric old standby, Anthony Quinn, and diplomat Michael Sarrazin is ordered to bring her back. The first (and undoubtedly the last) Hollywood film ever made in Iran, it earned less than $1 million, though by the time of its release the Shah and his pals were already preoccupied with even more costly disasters.

Jennifer O'Neill, as the rebellious daughter of a U.S. Senator, "blossoms like a desert flower" under the approving eye of that macho, nomadic rascal, Anthony Quinn, in the Made-in-Iran adaptation of James Michener's Caravans.

CASINO ROYALE (1967)

A disorganized spoof guided by five different directors, it turned out to be the only James Bond adventure ever to lose money. David Niven plays 007, hoping to bring his nerdy nephew Woody Allen into the family secret-agent business. Deborah Kerr, Orson Welles, Peter Sellers, Ursula Andress, William Holden, Charles Boyer, John Huston, Peter O'Toole, Jean-Paul Belmondo, and Jacqueline Bisset are all utterly wasted in this $12 million extravaganza, which provoked contempt from both James Bond fanatics and civilian audiences.

THE CHARGE OF THE LIGHT BRIGADE (1968)

Director Tony Richardson, whose *Tom Jones* had won the Oscar for Best Picture just five years before, brought this dramatization of Alfred Lord Tennyson's poem to cinematic life. It was United Artists' major release for '68, and the studio assumed that the cast of Trevor Howard, John Gielgud, David Hemmings, and Vanessa Redgrave would spur moviegoers half-a-league onward to the box office. Those who expected Errol Flynn heroics, however, discovered that *Charge* was no typical blood-and-thunder war epic; its scenes of battle were secondary to social satire and political examination of Victorian England. Despite good reviews, the producers of this $5 million adventure found cannon to the right of them, cannon to the left of them, and the measly $1 million gross made the slaughter of the noble six hundred seem mild by comparison.

CHITTY CHITTY BANG BANG (1968)

This musical adaptation of a children's classic by James Bond–creator Ian Fleming features a flying car in the title role and such memorable songs as "You're My Little Chu-Chi Face!" Dick Van Dyke, who had succeeded so notably in *Mary Poppins*, plays an inventor who creates the airborne auto in order to entertain lonely children, but the saccharine film crashes on takeoff and earned back only half of its $10 million budget.

CIRCUS WORLD (1964)

Time magazine declared, "To sit through this film is something like holding an elephant on your lap for two hours and fifteen minutes." John Wayne plays the owner of a globe-trotting circus, whose 4,000-ton ship capsizes in Barcelona harbor sending screaming humans and roaring animals into the drink in a fitting climax to this dull, confusing mess. After the picture's release, it managed to lose virtually every penny of its absurdly reckless $9 million budget.

CLEOPATRA (1963)

See *The Elizabeth Taylor Wing.*

THE CONQUEROR (1956)

See *The Titans and Their Toys* exhibit.

CONQUEST (1937)

Charles Boyer plays Napoleon and Greta Garbo impersonates his Polish mistress, Marie Walewska, in this laughable romance. MGM intended the project as a natural follow-up to Garbo's great triumph the year before with *Camille,* but the studio experienced severe problems from the beginning. Seventeen writers worked on the script, but despite all the rewrites, the final version still included lines such as "Are you real, or born of a snow drift?" and "My son is not only an Emperor—he is also a *man!*" The original title for the project was *Marie Walewska,* but the studio worried (quite sensibly, it seems to us) that Americans would have a tough time pronouncing it; just imagine if Meryl Streep had turned in her 1982 Oscar-winning performance in a picture called *Sophie Zawistowska.* No matter what the title, everyone agreed that the troubled production dragged on far too long. After five months, an organization sprung into being on the MGM lot known as the *Walewska-Must-End Association,* composed of all members of the cast and crew. At $2.8 million, *Conquest* became the second-most expensive film in the studio's history to that time (after the 1926 *Ben-Hur*) and fell far short of justifying its expense.

CROMWELL (1970)

A thick slice of underdone English history from the director of *Chitty Chitty Bang Bang* (Ken Hughes), featuring Richard Harris as Oliver Cromwell and Alec Guinness as Charles I. It was intended to capitalize on the success of *A Man for All Seasons,* but earned back only $3 million of its $9 million cost. The producers had hoped to save money by avoiding the unpredictable British weather and using Spain to stand in for the English countryside, but they were rewarded for their efforts by one of the dampest and stormiest seasons in Spanish history. The rain in Spain caused almost as much pain as Richard Harris' overreaching performance, and through the course of the film the star reportedly remained as well-watered as the landscape.

THE CRUSADES (1935)

Cecil B. De Mille's greatest failure, which helped to weaken his reputation as a director with the surefire golden touch. When Paramount's boss, Adolph Zukor, heard the news from his accountants that his fair-haired boy's latest venture had lost at least $700,000, he reportedly clasped his hands to his head and cried, "The King is dead!" The movie itself is certainly lifeless, except for such magic moments as Queen Berengaria (Loretta Young) telling King Richard the Lion-Hearted (Henry Wilcoxon): "You've just *gotta* save Christianity, Richard! You gotta!"

DARLING LILI (1970)

See the *Star-Crossed Lovers* exhibit.

THE DAY OF THE DOLPHIN (1973)

George C. Scott talks to the fishies and helps them to avoid participation in a nefarious plot to assassinate the President. Dolphin voices are provided by screenwriter Buck Henry, who seems to be imitating Tweety Pie from the old Warner Brothers cartoons. Mike Nichols directs a film that might otherwise have offered a tempting subject for a devastating Mike Nichols–Elaine May routine. Described by Judith Crist as "the most expensive Rin Tin Tin movie ever made," it cost $8.5 million, with a domestic gross of $2.3 million, leaving a lingering stench of dead fish.

DEEP WATERS (1948)

Another fish story! Lobster fisherman Dana Andrews

C. Aubrey Smith (as "The Old Hermit") and Henry Wilcoxon (as Richard the Lion-Hearted) persuade a crowd of strong-armed extras to offer their swords to Cecil B. De Mille's lost cause, **The Crusades.**

befriends juvenile delinquent Dean Stockwell, and is rewarded for his kindness by falling in love with the young punk's beautiful social worker, Jean Peters. The supporting cast features the irrepressible Cesar Romero as another kindly fisherman. By the end of the picture, the audience wants to feed all these goodie-goodies to the lobsters. *Variety* reported that *Deep Waters* ran into deep trouble: "Its grosses are so low that Twentieth Century-Fox won't even talk about it."

DOCTOR DOLITTLE (1967)

See the *Child Abuse* exhibit.

DOWN TO THEIR LAST YACHT (1934)

Fish, fish, and more fish! This time Mary Boland is a blond queen on a South Seas island who amuses herself by throwing grade-B actors into the shark-infested drink. The socialites who are marooned on this troubled paradise perform elaborate, unforgettable musical numbers to tuneful treats such as "Tiny Little Finger on Your Hand," "Funny Little World," and "South Sea Bolero." Producer Lou Brock (no, not the ballplayer!) received his pink slip as soon as this wretched wreck exploded at the box office. One critic described it as "the worst film ever produced by RKO . . . so bad that it's almost good."

DRAGONSLAYER (1981)

It took two studios (Paramount and Disney) to absorb the $12 million loss generated by this $18 million sword-and-sorcery debacle about a plucky apprentice (Peter MacNicol) who uses special-effects magic to take on a mechanical monster.

THE EGYPTIAN (1954)

Royal on-screen intrigue at the court of the ancient pharaoh, paralleled royal off-screen intrigue at Twentieth Century-Fox concerning this starring vehicle for Darryl Zanuck's mistress, Bella Darvi. Victor Mature as a captain of the guard adds to the fun by delivering the immortal line: "More wine, you waddling toad!" A quintessential sandals-and-sandstorms schlockbuster from the same producer (Zanuck) and director (Michael Curtiz) who gave the world *Noah's Ark* (see the *Silent But Deadly* exhibit) some twenty-five years earlier. As it was, the picture returned only a small fraction of its $5 million budget, but just think how much they could have lost had they stuck with their original casting idea of placing Marlon Brando (instead of Edmund Purdom) in the romantic lead.

ESKIMO (1933)

This wildly extravagant documentary left MGM out in the cold to the tune of $935,000. Director W. S. Van Dyke traveled to the Arctic to try to duplicate the success of *Nanook of the North*, carrying all his equipment (including an electric refrigerator) by dog sled to remote locations. The result was artistically impressive but failed to arouse any interest from Depression-era moviegoers.

EXORCIST II: THE HERETIC (1977)

Linda Blair apparently failed to pay her exorcist bills and is repossessed. Richard Burton as a befuddled priest is a laugh a minute in the soporific sequel to William Friedkin's huge hit of four years before. Warner Brothers blew $11 million on a thoroughly repulsive piece of work, chosen in a poll of our readers (as published in *The Golden Turkey Awards*) as the second-worst film of all time. It did most of its business in the first two weeks, before word of mouth set in to warn patrons away from the theatres. *The Wall Street Journal* reported: "Rarely, if ever, have box office receipts declined so drastically."

THE FALL OF THE ROMAN EMPIRE (1964)

Producer Samuel Bronston's personal losses on this one three-hour megaturkey amounted to $18,436,625, making it, when figures are adjusted for inflation, one of the biggest disasters of all time. Only the release of *Cleopatra* the year before prevented this similar stinker from receiving the recognition it so richly deserved. *The Fall* featured Sophia Loren, Alec Guinness, James Mason, Stephen Boyd, the Spanish Army as the Visigoths, the Barbarians, and the Romans, and last, but not least, Christopher Plummer as Commodus—an appropriate part for a picture that went right into the toilet.

A FAREWELL TO ARMS (1957)

Farewell to $5 million! Director John Huston described this second screen version of Hemingway's novel as "a debacle . . . an unhappy experience for everyone connected with it." Producer David O. Selznick, in his neurotic Last Hurrah, fired Huston in the middle of the production. His constant interference with even the most trivial details produced unnecessary feuds with actors, technicians, and

Barbarian John Ireland (you can tell he's a barbarian because he hasn't shaved in weeks) threatens to blind the Roman philosopher Timonides (James Mason), unless he divulges the secret plans to avert The Fall of the Roman Empire. *In an effort to persuade the baddie to spare his eyes, Mason eagerly (and with a straight face) responds, "Let's look upon this logically . . ."*

reporters. Above all, Selznick wanted to make his wife, Jennifer Jones, look good in an ingenue role for which the thirty-eight-year-old actress was totally unsuited. At the end of the film, Jones dies in childbirth, leading her co-star, Rock Hudson, to intone straight to the camera: "Poor kid! Maybe this is the price you pay for sleeping together." Selznick, as it turned out, paid an even more inflated price for the same privilege, since the dismal failure of this World War I romance terminated his distinguished career.

FINIAN'S RAINBOW (1968)

Fred Astaire's last Hollywood musical turned out to be a multi-million-dollar loser as directed by a young

Francis Ford Coppola in a warm-up for his later money-eating achievements on *One From the Heart.* A leprechaun (Tommy Steele) magically appears in the American South to combat racism (and heightism, presumably) by turning Keenan Wynn into a black man. One of those inane late-sixties imitations of *Sound of Music* in which characters spend their lives running down grassy hillsides singing to cameras overhead.

THE GREAT GATSBY (1974)

Paramount spent a total of $13 million on this third-time-around film treatment of F. Scott Fitzgerald's classic novel, with nearly half the money paying for the most intense promotional campaign in memory. Expenses for the magnificent recreation of the 1920s turned out to be particularly irresponsible, but then what could be expected for a movie portrayal of the most romantic big spender in American literature? Robert Redford seemed to many an ideal choice as Gatsby, but casting of Mia Farrow as Daisy provoked pointed criticism from the project's script writer, Francis Ford Coppola, and most other movie mavens throughout the country. The slow-moving pace of the finished film doomed *Gatsby* to a slow-moving response at the box office, but Paramount's presold booking arrangements limited the studio's losses. In retrospect, most critics agreed that the original 1926 silent movie treatment of the material remained in every way superior. Sorry about that, Old Sport! And so we beat on, boats against the current, borne back ceaselessly into the past . . .

THE GREATEST STORY EVER TOLD (1965)

See the *Prophets and Losses* exhibit.

HAVING WONDERFUL TIME (1938)

Based on an endearing Broadway hit about Jewish immigrants on summer vacation in the Catskills, it received the Hollywood treatment with such well-known and authentic ethnic types as Ginger Rogers, Douglas Fairbanks, Jr., Eve Arden, Red Skelton, and Lucille Ball. The bland result—like a hot pastrami sandwich on Wonder Bread smeared with butter—proved singularly unappealing and lost $300,000 for RKO.

HEAVEN'S GATE (1980/81)

See the *Delusions of Grandeur* exhibit.

HELEN OF TROY (1955)

The immortal Rossana Podesta heads a no-star cast as "The Face That Launched a Thousand Ships." Helen runs off with a Trojan but becomes pregnant anyway, leading her husband and his Greek colleagues to horse around shamelessly with their newfound adversaries. Ads for the picture promised: "ALL THE TUMULTUOUS WONDERS AND TREMENDOUS DRAMA IN THE STORY OF HISTORY'S MOST FAMOUS RUNAWAY LOVERS! SOON THE WHOLE WORLD WILL KNOW OF ITS GREATNESS!" Soon the whole world knew about Warner Brothers' big loss on the project, totaling nearly $4 million.

HELLO DOLLY! (1969)

Good-bye budget! Costs rose to the ridiculous level of $24 million, while Fox paid five years' worth of interest charges before the troubled production finally reached the screen. The recreation of Little Old New York was so expensive that it remains standing to this day, with Twentieth Century-Fox trying to reduce their losses by renting it out to other productions. The miscasting of a much-too-young Barbra Streisand in the role of a lovable matchmaker initially intended for Ethel Merman or Carol Channing, helped to transform the second-*most* successful musical in Broadway history (to that time) into the second-*least* successful musical in Hollywood history (topped only by *Darling Lili*—see *Star-Crossed Lovers*.) When the dust and glitter cleared after a massive publicity campaign, Fox found itself some $15 million in the hole.

HELLO EVERYBODY! (1933)

See the *Disastrous Debuts* exhibit.

HITTING A NEW HIGH (1937)

Lily Pons, the legendary French opera diva, is utterly humiliated as "Ooga-Hunga the Bird Girl," a primitive jungle creature with a great voice. She is forced to dress in feathers and to twitter as she talks, but worst of all, she must endure the companionship of Jack Oakie as a Hollywood publicist who shapes her career. Neither Miss Pons' admirable high Cs nor her sweet smiles could prevent the picture from hitting a new low at the box office. The bitter response from both critics and the public made sure that this, her third starring role, would also be her last.

HONKY TONK FREEWAY (1981)

British director John (*Midnight Cowboy*) Schlesinger blew a bundle on this cynical view of the American Dream, which, in view of its obvious stylistic debt to Robert Altman, might appropriately be described as *Nashville* on wheels. The fragmented, episodic plot features Beverly D'Angelo driving nowhere with her mother's ashes in an urn on the dashboard; William Devane as the energetic mayor of Ticklaw, Florida; Beau Bridges as the frustrated author of that adorable children's book, *Randy the Carnivorous Pony*; plus car crashes, bank robberies, a frustrated nun abandoning old habits, a charging rhinoceros, and Bubbles the Waterskiing Elephant. Bubbles unquestionably steals the show because she is the only vaguely likable character in the whole dreary mess. Schlesinger's bloody *Freeway* pileup somehow cost $25 million to make, while racking up an absolutely pathetic domestic gross of $500,000.

HOTEL IMPERIAL (1936–1979)

See the *Star-Crossed Lovers* exhibit.

HURRICANE (1979)

A remake of the South Seas classic with Dorothy Lamour, this time starring Mia Farrow, who has neither of her predecessor's obvious assets. Much of the hype concerning this blow-hard spectacle centered on the "discovery" of Dayton Ka'ne, a sizzling Polynesian delicacy who was supposed to be Bora Bora's answer to John Travolta. His big moment in the film comes as he lifts the willowy Farrow off the ground and breathes: "If the gods had meant me for another . . . then why . . . why . . . did they send you? Marry me at once . . . or leave my island!" By this time, we'd all like to leave the island, thank you very much, and the film actually left most theatres within a week. It cost Dino De Laurentiis $22 million, of which *at least* $17 million was gone with the wind.

I TAKE THIS WOMAN (1940)

MGM studio head Louis B. Mayer interfered personally with every aspect of this production due to a desperate desire to make his Viennese discovery, Hedy Lamarr, into "a star of stars." Three directors (Josef von Sternberg, Frank Borzage, and W. S. Van Dyke) came and went, finding Mayer's expensive obsession

In I Take This Woman, *Spencer Tracy played a noble physician with a doomed passion for* femme fatale Hedy Lamarr, *while stoically enduring so much interference in the production from studio head Louis B. Mayer that the project became known at MGM as* I Re-Take This Woman.

to be totally intolerable. At the studio, the picture became known as *I Re-take This Woman* because of the producer's insistence on shooting every scene time and again. The madness continued for eighteen months, and "Mayer's Folly" lost $1.5 million at the box office. Looking back, Louis B. placed the entire unfortunate incident in philosophical perspective. "I told them they were making a lousy picture," he said, "but they wouldn't listen to me!"

INCHON (1982)

See the *Delusions of Grandeur* exhibit.

INTOLERANCE (1916)

See the *Silent But Deadly* exhibit.

THE ISLAND (1980)

Universal paid novelist Peter (*Jaws*) Benchley $2.5 million for the rights to his new best-selling potboiler about pirates in the Bahamas who attack fat and unsuspecting tourists. On screen, the family fun includes scenes of a boy taught to kill his father, a cat skinned alive, several throats slit, stabbings, shootings, bloody leech attacks, and Michael Caine raped by a pirate hag all to the accompaniment of a rousing, upbeat score by Ennio Morricone, who apparently never saw the movie. The studio lost more than half its investment of $22 million in this sordid shipwreck; audiences would have a far better time visiting the "Pirates of the Caribbean" ride at Disneyland.

IT CAME FROM HOLLYWOOD (1982)

In 1980, Paramount acquired the rights to that blazingly brilliant best-seller, *The Golden Turkey Awards*, with the idea of making a compilation film about "the worst achievements in Hollywood history." In the process of bringing this concept to the screen, the studio managed numerous worst achievements of its own, particularly by ignoring the advice of the book's authors, who are nonetheless credited as "Special Consultants." After two years of editing and re-editing, plus the inclusion of inane, largely irrelevant skits by Dan Aykroyd, Cheech and Chong, Gilda Radner, and John Candy, the producers totally abandoned the original concept, included some fine films along with the celebrated stinkers, and managed to waste more than $5 million on a picture that should have been done for one-fifth that amount. Naturally, the putrid pastiche bombed at the box office. As Variety reported, "*It Came . . . and Went.*"

JET PILOT (1951-1957)

Howard Hughes spent $9 million on this Cold War action-adventure about jet jockey John Wayne chasing curvy Commie Janet Leigh from Palm Springs to Alaska. Nearly half the budget went into the absurdly extended post-production process, which lasted *six years* as Hughes fretted endlessly over every scene in his favorite film. By the time of the picture's ultimate release, some eight years after shooting began, the up-to-date aerial hardware, which the producer had gone to such great lengths to secure, had already become obviously obsolete.

JUDITH OF BETHULIA (1913)

D. W. Griffith horrified his contemporaries by spending $25,000 to bring this Biblical story to the screen in an era when most movies cost no more than $1,000 per reel. His colleagues scoffed at D. W.'s attention to detail with sets, costumes, lighting, and camera work, predicting that he could never earn back enough from a mere movie to justify the heavy expense. *Judith's* weak performance at the box office proved them right—just two years before Griffith had his ultimate vindication through the tremendous success of *Birth of a Nation*.

JUMBO (1962)

Based on a 1935 Rodgers and Hart musical about a traveling circus and a "pusillanimous pachyderm"

MGM's biggest star takes a break during filming of the elephantine flop that bears his name.

who plays cupid to a pair of singing star-crossed lovers. The property was hopelessly dated by the time it finally reached the screen, and the casting—Doris Day, Stephen Boyd, Jimmy Durante (as "Pop Wonder"), and Martha Raye (as Lulu)—didn't help. Producer Joe Pasternak fell from the high wire without a safety net on this one, losing $5 million for MGM.

THE KING OF JAZZ (1930)

The title refers to portly Paul Whiteman, a popular bandleader of the twenties and thirties who has been described by jazz critic Leonard Feather as "the Lawrence Welk of his generation." Here, he shares center stage with hundreds of dancing girls, a man playing "The Stars and Stripes Forever" on a bicycle pump, Bing Crosby and the Rhythm Boys performing "Happy Feet," the Russell Market Girls, a grand piano the size of the *Titanic*, and various other oddities and attractions. Essentially a 1930s version of *The Gong Show*, this wildly disjointed revue cost Universal $2 million to produce, and its total failure at the box office came close to driving the studio into bankruptcy.

KOLBERG (1945)

See the *Fascist Follies* exhibit.

LAND OF THE PHARAOHS (1955)

Newspaper ads boasted that the film contained "1,600 CAMELS! 104 SPECIALLY BUILT BARGES! 9,753 PLAYERS IN ONE SCENE ALONE! 21,000 WORKERS AND TECHNICIANS! FILMED IN EGYPT BY THE LARGEST LOCATION CREW EVER SENT ABROAD FROM HOLLYWOOD!" Instead of emphasizing camels and barges, Warner Brothers might have done better to point to the formidable talent associated with the production: Nobel prizewinner William Faulkner wrote the script; Howard Hawks directed; and Dmitri Tiomkin composed the atmospheric score. What went wrong? Faulkner later admitted he tried to make the Pharaoh sound "like a Kentucky Colonel"; pyramid building is boring to watch; and the studio was so busy rounding up camels that it forgot to provide big-name stars. Joan Collins, at age twenty-two, is already playing an ambitious, amoral, and bitchy temptress in the era of ancient Egypt's Fourth *Dynasty*. As the promotional material proudly proclaimed: "Her treachery stained every stone of the pyramids!" After its release, the picture stained every page of the studio's ledgers—with red ink—as it made back less than a third of its $6 million budget.

Actors and extras writhe in agony at the lava pouring down from Mount Vesuvius, and at the utter failure of the 1926 version of The Last Days of Pompeii. *This lavish loser helped to seal the doom (temporarily, at least) of the once flourishing Italian film industry.*

THE LAST DAYS OF POMPEII (1926)

Also known as "The Last Days of the Italian Film Industry," this idiotic spectacle, along with the 1925 *Quo Vadis?* (see the *Silent But Deadly* exhibit in the main gallery) lost so much money that it forced the closure of several Roman studios. Despite the fact that the producers economized by shooting on location in the actual ruins of Pompeii, it still cost 7 million lire, making it one of the most expensive productions in history to that time.

THE LAST VALLEY (1971)

Written, produced, and directed by James Clavell, who also contributed vast sums from his own pocket to pay the $8.5 million production costs. The story describes the adventures of a band of weary soldiers in 1641, at the height of the Thirty Years War, who suddenly discover a remote, unspoiled valley in the Swiss Alps. Michael Caine is their commander, Omar Sharif is a runaway philosophy professor, and the dynamic Florinda Bolkan provides love interest, such as it is, as the quintessential Valley Girl. It had all the elements of a successful action-adventure film, including pillage, rape, torture, death at the stake, and grand scenery, but still managed to lose more than $7 million. Following this fiasco, Clavell concentrated on writing fiction, with far happier results, including best-sellers such as *Shogun* and *Noble House.*

THE LEGEND OF THE LONE RANGER (1981)

Noting the success of the *Star Wars* and *Superman*

series, producers Lew Grade and Jack Wrather reached the conclusion that any recreation of B movie serials could make millions. Wrong again, Kimo-sabe! Here, the boyhood and youth of the Lone Ranger are treated with Wagnerian solemnity, and key plot points are underscored with hilarious voice-over narration from balladeer Merle Haggard. This picture also served to unleash on the world the acting abilities of one Klinton Spilsbury, who added to the already excessive budget by delivering his lines so badly that the producer had to hire another actor (James Keach) to redub all his dialogue. This sad, cynical exercise ultimately bit the silver bullet, losing at least $10 million of its $18 million cost, and at last report, the Spilsbury doughboy is now wearing a paper bag in place of his black mask.

LION OF THE DESERT (1981)

After snookering Libyan strongman Muammar Qaddafi and other Arab adventurers into losing tens of millions on *Mohammad: Messenger of God* (see the *Prophets and Losses* exhibit in our main gallery), flamboyant Syrian-American producer Moustapha Akkad faced a difficult challenge in trying to top his previous achievements. A magazine article on the famed Bedouin warrior Omar Mukhtar, who fought Italian fascist colonialists in the 1920s, gave him the idea he had been waiting for. Akkad went back to Colonel Qaddafi and asked for more movie money, apparently inspired by W. C. Fields' *Never Give a Sucker an Even Break.* Qaddafi, in a generous mood, came up with $35 million for the purpose of illuminating this stirring chapter from Libya's glorious past. Anthony Quinn, fresh from his triumph as the Prophet's uncle in *Mohammad,* took the title role and roared at worthy enemies such as Oliver Reed as a sadistic Italian general and Rod Steiger as Mussolini. Akkad's hopes for box office success suffered a major setback with the taking of American hostages in Iran, since Quinn's cunning Arab chieftain bore a striking physical resemblance to the Ayatollah Khomeini. When the Iranian leader makes his long-awaited comeback in American popularity polls, this film may stand a chance; but having so far grossed all of $1 million against its initial cost of $35 million, it still has a long way to go.

THE LITTLE PRINCE (1974)

Another lavish Lerner-Loewe loser, adapted from the popular fable by Antoine de Saint-Exupery about an aviator who befriends a young boy from outer space, but the entire project should have been left on Mars. Gene Wilder portrays a talking fox, Bob Fosse plays a snake, and British child star Steven Warner plays the Little Putz.

THE LONG SHIPS (1964)

Sidney Poitier starring in a Viking movie shot entirely on location in Yugoslavia? No jive? The press-book explained the otherwise confusing situation by touting "SIDNEY POITIER IN HIS FIRST NON-NEGRO ROLE!" Here, he plays a Moorish chieftain who battles Richard Widmark as leader of the tenth-century seagoing Swedes. At the end of the game, the final score showed Vikings–zero; Moors–zero; Movie–biggest zero of them all. It cost $6 million to make and managed to lose nearly all of it. Sidney Poitier said after the fact: "To say it was disastrous is a compliment."

LOOKIN' TO GET OUT (1982)

Jon Voight and Burt Young are a pair of New York banana brains who go out to Las Vegas to make a killing, where they team up with former call girl Ann-Margret. Director Hal Ashby tried to create a tale of lovable losers who manage to break the bank at a big casino, but he succeeded only in breaking the bank at a big studio (Lorimar). The picture cost $17 million and returned only $300,000 in its first six months.

LOST HORIZON (1973)

Known in the industry as *Lost Investments,* this hopelessly incompetent remake of the 1937 Ronald Colman classic features such memorable Burt Bacharach–Hal David songs as "The World Is a Circle," "Share the Joy," and "Different People Look at Life from Different Points of View." Peter Finch, Liv Ullmann, Sally Kellerman, George Kennedy, and Michael York all find their way to Shangri-La, where they dance on rocks, waltz through libraries, and wave their arms at gaggles of giggling children. The production took $7 million, the huge promotional campaign cost nearly as much, but the picture returned only $3 million to Columbia studios.

THE MAGIC OF LASSIE (1978)

A musical tearjerker in which Jimmy Stewart sings even more tunefully than the title character, though the finished product is still a dog. Despite the presence of Pat and Debby Boone, the project never had a prayer and lost several million for its independent producers.

THE MAGICIAN OF LUBLIN (1979)

What could one expect from an Israeli-German co-

Lucille Ball mounts a banana (or is it a moon? . . . well, never mind . . .) as part of the family fun in Mame.

production? Menahem Golan, the Irwin Allen of the Middle East, produced and directed this incomprehensible adaptation of I. B. Singer's short story. Alan Arkin, Shelley Winters, Lou Jacobi, and Valerie Perrine (as the token shiksa) appear and disappear through the course of the picture, but the investors' $8 million—the biggest budget ever for an Israeli film—vanished without a trace.

MAME (1974)

A $12 million adaptation of a successful Broadway show, which was in turn an adaptation of the successful 1958 Rosalind Russell movie, which was in turn a screen treatment of a successful Broadway play, which was in turn a stage version of a successful Patrick Dennis novel. By 1974, we would have thought we had quite enough of Mr. Dennis' lovably iconoclastic relative, and Lucille Ball's ludicrous, frog-voiced performance as the durable Auntie

Mame in the new musical film soon had the world yelling "Uncle!"

MAN OF LA MANCHA (1972)

United Artists' desire to make a fortune on this big-screen treatment of the long-running Broadway musical proved to be an impossible dream. Despite the $12 million budget, Peter O'Toole, Sophia Loren, and James Coco spent most of their time on two dingy studio sound stages, which O'Toole lovingly described as "the most depressing sets that ever existed." Producer-director Arthur Hiller ingeniously coped with the shortage of hit songs from the original show by giving each of the major characters the chance to sing "The Impossible Dream" at least twice. *Newsweek*'s review of the picture suggested that its creators had "pitched this screen version of the celebrated Broadway musical as low as possible

The dreary big-screen version of the hit musical Man of La Mancha *featured the golden-voiced trio of James Coco (Sancho Panza), Peter O'Toole (Quixote), and Sophia Loren (Dulcinea), looking appropriately depressed in some of the most tacky and unconvincing sets ever used in a major motion picture.*

without sinking beneath the screen altogether." Box office receipts promptly sank to the same Death Valley level shortly after the film's release.

MARCH OR DIE (1977)

A Foreign Legion movie in 1977? Give us a break! Catherine Deneuve, Gene Hackman, Max von Sydow, and 3,000 Arabs co-star with assorted camels and sandstorms. Cost: $9 million. Domestic gross: $1 million.

THE MASTER GUNFIGHTER (1975)

Billy Jack's off his normal winning form in Tom Laughlin's absurdly indulgent paean to himself. Ron (*Superfly*) O'Neal turns up during our hero's Mexican wanderings to provide spiritual enlightenment on the nature of violence and the meaning of life. Laughlin spent $3.5 million of his own money to produce this horrible home movie, then blew another $3.75 million on a series of angry ads attacking critics (who unanimously hated his film) as "frustrated writers who failed to make it in show business."

MEGAFORCE (1982)

Megaflop. This $20 million turkey didn't even make

back the cost of Hollywood hunk Barry Bostwick's sequined jumpsuit. A technological fantasy about a new breed of tanks, motorcycles, and machine guns as used by a squad of sexy international supercops. The machines turn out to be as dull and predictable as the actors.

METEOR (1979)

A killer meteor aims straight for the heart of Manhattan and engulfs the New York subway system—and the viewer—in a tidal wave of sewage. *Boxoffice* magazine called it "one of the worst big budget films in recent memory . . . There are moments that make *Godzilla* look like a masterpiece." Henry Fonda, Sean Connery, Karl Malden, Natalie Wood, and Trevor Howard all make brief appearances before the end of the world at the hands of a menace from the great beyond, which, according to the *New York Times,* "looks like a big hunk of week-old bread." The $20 million used to produce the klutzy klinker and the $6 million wasted on promotion are, at last sighting, lost in space.

THE MISSOURI BREAKS (1976)

United Artists paid big money for Jack Nicholson and Marlon Brando to conduct an on-screen competition in overacting for this heavy-handed Western. Brando wins, thanks to his habit of slipping into and out of a blatantly bogus Irish brogue, in an Arthur Penn picture that is so much blarney. Much of the key action takes place in frontier bathrooms, which is only fitting for an obnoxious stinker that quickly disappeared down the drain.

MOHAMMAD: MESSENGER OF GOD (1977)

See the *Prophets and Losses* exhibit.

MUTINY ON THE BOUNTY (1962)

Marlon Brando again—whatta guy! As Fletcher Christian in this waterlogged remake of the 1935 Clark Gable classic, he proved so tediously temperamental that he personally cost MGM no less than $6 million in unnecessary delays. Director Lewis Milestone said, "This picture should have been called *The Mutiny of Marlon Brando.*" Co-star Richard Harris fondly recalled: "The whole picture was just a large, dreadful nightmare for me." In addition to Brando's intolerable antics, the exotic Tahiti location, disastrously poor weather, and a huge replica of H.M.S. *Bounty* sent total costs well over $24 million. But by the end of the shooting schedule, Marlon Brando had

Sean Connery didn't seem to know what hit him after he decided to appear in Meteor. *American International Pictures, which had traditionally specialized in dreadful (but generally profitable) cheapies such as* Viking Women and the Sea Serpent *or* The Thing With Two Heads, *proved with this film that they could achieve the same low quality while spending $20 million.*

inflated even more dramatically than the budget—his *Bounty*-ful belly reflected the fact that his weight had ballooned from 170 to 210 pounds. By the time he shot his last scenes in the film, the great star resembled Elvis Presley at the end of his life, while his lispingly ludicrous British accent made him sound more like a swishbuckler than a swashbuckler. "It was the worst experience of my acting career," Brando moaned, but MGM deserved pity far more than he did. The studio spent the astounding equivalent of $65 million in 1984 dollars, and lost more than half its investment.

MYSTERIOUS ISLAND (1929)

Intrepid undersea explorers discover bizarre bubble-blowing creatures who resemble E.T. in this pioneering, expressionistic sci-fi adventure. Director Maurice Tourneur walked out in the middle because

Appropriately enough, Marlon Brando played a bounty hunter in The Missouri Breaks; *both he and co-star Jack Nicholson received $1.25 million for their roles.*

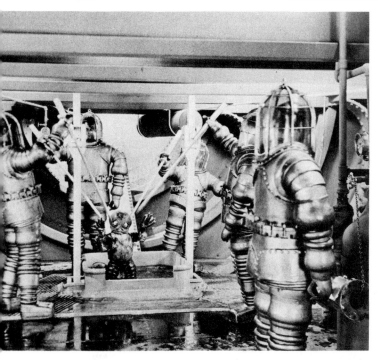

A lovable undersea creature receives a royal hazing from insensitive divers in search of the Mysterious Island.

of artistic differences with MGM production chief Irving Thalberg. These problems, and the ambitious special effects, resulted in a total cost of $1,130,000, while the incoherent and laughable product resulted in a net loss officially reported at $878,000.

NICKELODEON (1976)

Peter Bogdanovich's $9 million unfunny valentine to the good old days of the silent screen, starring Burt Reynolds as a cowboy star, Ryan O'Neal as a bumbling director (no, not Peter Bogdanovich), and Tatum O'Neal as a kid genius screenwriter, who should have been hired to doctor this particular script. As a promotional gimmick on opening day, Columbia Studios invited curious crowds to come see the movie for the "old time" price of one nickel. In New York City, many of those admitted on this basis felt they were overcharged and demanded their money back.

1941 (1979)

Nobody's perfect—not even Hollywood's most magnificent money maker, Steven Spielberg. Along with all his celebrated triumphs, he turned out this one resounding dud at a cost of $31 million—three times the cost of *E.T.*! The premise—mass hysteria in Southern California over a suspected Japanese invasion just a few weeks after Pearl Harbor—might not strike impartial observers as a promising basis for an overblown slapstick comedy, but Spielberg had his own subjective response. "When I first read the script I gagged on it," he recalled. "Moments were so funny that I vomited from laughter." Meanwhile, executives at the two studios (Universal and Columbia) that co-produced this multi-megabuck bomb were vomiting with horror as the budget soared. "The whole film is a noisy drunken brawl," Spielberg chortled. "For me, it was like making huge toys." John Belushi's personal problems added to the insanity, as did Spielberg's perfectionist approach to this awestruck homage to the Three Stooges. After an $11 million advertising campaign, it still managed a domestic gross of only $23 million, indicating that despite the picture's popularity in Japan (*Banzai!*), the worldwide returns fell *at least* $20 million short of earning back the movie's various costs.

NOAH'S ARK (1929)

See the *Silent But Deadly* exhibit.

John Belushi tries to walk away from the wreckage of Steven Spielberg's $31 million comedy flop, 1941. *Several key scenes took place on a painstaking recreation of Hollywood Boulevard that constituted one of the largest interior sets ever built for a motion picture.*

THE OLD MAN AND THE SEA (1958)

Hollywood-agent-turned-movie-producer Leland Hayward came up with the odd idea of adapting Ernest Hemingway's terse, symbolic novella for the big screen, then gave in to Warner Brothers' daffy demand that Spencer Tracy play the title role (the old man, not the sea) of a starving Cuban fisherman. To ensure maximum authenticity for the climactic moment in which Tracy managed to hook a gigantic marlin (the fish, not the Brando), Hayward dispatched four fish-and-film expeditions to different corners of the world in the hope of capturing on celluloid a genuine struggle with a huge "miracle fish." By the time all four fishing parties (including one led by Hemingway himself) returned from their voyages empty-handed, Hayward had already exceeded his projected $2 million budget and had less than four minutes of film to show for it. At this point, director Fred Zinnemann decided that this particular project had best be looked upon as "the one that got away" and abruptly resigned. His replacement, John Sturges, still dripping from his experience directing *Underwater!* (see our exhibit on *The Titans and Their Toys*), decided to forget about authenticity and to shoot the entire film in a little studio tank with a mechanical foam-rubber fish. Sturges himself described the result as "technically the sloppiest film I have ever made," but that didn't prevent Tracy's Academy Award nomination as Best Actor (for keeping a straight face through lines such as, "Fish, I love you and I respect you very much"). The *Motion Picture Herald* understated the situation in reporting, "This is not a picture audiences are going to tear down the doors to see." Hemingway himself summarized the situation, proving once again that Papa knows best, when he growled to reporters that, "No picture with a fucking rubber fish ever made a dime!"

ONE FROM THE HEART (1982)

After investing his considerable proceeds from the *Godfather* films in making Zoetrope Studios the finest facility in Hollywood, Francis Ford Coppola felt such a burning desire to try out all his shiny new toys that he settled for this utterly unsuitable property as the basis for a major film. The puerile plot concerns two restless blue-collar lovers (Teri Garr and Frederic Forrest) who must experiment with infidelity in order to learn how much they actually need each other. Under these circumstances, it is hard to blame Coppola for finding the sets and equipment infinitely more intriguing than his two-dimensional characters, and the movie unspools as an ultimate and sterile triumph of technology-in-the-service-of-technology. As

critic Pauline Kael aptly observed: "It isn't one from the heart, or from the head either; it's one from the lab." Among Coppola's many stunning achievements was a duplication of George Stevens' feat in *The Only Game in Town* (see *The Elizabeth Taylor Wing* of our main gallery) of recreating the entire city of Las Vegas on a studio sound stage. For a mere $6 million, the Czar of Zoetrope managed to erect casinos, hotels, auto junkyards, and vast streetscapes far more attractive and colorful than their real-life counterparts back in Nevada. While Coppola reveled in his film-school fun and games, the total budget blimped up to $26 million, with $14 million provided from the director's personal funds. When *One From the Heart* opened, it became obvious that, in commercial terms, it was One for the Toilet: it grossed less than $1 million in its first year, causing various banks to close down Zoetrope Studios while making determined attempts to go after Coppola's home and other personal possessions.

THE ONLY GAME IN TOWN (1970)

See *The Elizabeth Taylor Wing.*

PAINT YOUR WAGON (1969)

See the *Musical Extravaganzas* exhibit.

PARADISE ALLEY (1978)

The Italian Stallion goes down for the count! Sylvester Stallone did *everything* on this picture other than brew coffee on the set—he scripted, directed, starred (as a two-bit hustler named Cosmo Carboni), sang the theme song in a toneless bellow (the immortal "Too Close to Paradise"), and even wrote the novelization that appeared in bookstores prior to the film's release. None of the fuss and bother could redeem the

Sly Stallone, director, screenwriter, and star of Paradise Alley, *tries out his singing voice on one of his co-stars. He was obviously pleased with the reaction, since he included his all-but-unintelligible rendition of the song "Too Close to Paradise" on the soundtrack.*

pointless story about three tenement-born brothers who struggle to make it big (even though all three are rather large to begin with) in the chic, glamorous world of professional wrestling. The picture's commercial failure drove home the point that Stallone's *Rocky*less Horrid Pictures Show-ed little promise at the box office.

PARNELL (1937)

For "The King of Hollywood" (Clark Gable), this dreary film could only be described as an act of regicide. MGM equipped its biggest star with hilarious muttonchop whiskers and a lilting Irish brogue for his role as the tragically doomed Parliamentary leader who fought for home rule for the Emerald Isle in the nineteenth century. The presence of Myrna Loy as Parnell's beautiful mistress, Kitty O'Shea, diverted audience attention from Gable's embarrassment only occasionally. Prerelease promotion for the picture in the trade press showed two boxing gloves with the caption, "SOCK COMING!" Little did MGM know that the studio itself would absorb the punch, along with a loss of $600,000.

PENNIES FROM HEAVEN (1981)

In this challenging film, Steve Martin jerks his way through half-dozen Depression-era production numbers, but off camera the comedian and director Herbert Ross must have given the executives at MGM/UA an even more persuasive song and dance to convince them to fund this project to the tune of $22 million. Martin's fans already knew that comedy wasn't pretty, but they were not prepared to accept their hero in a grim, gripping surrealistic fantasy of ill-fated illicit love. *Pennies* deserved better than its miserable $3.6 million gross, which left Hollywood with the conviction that Steve Martin in serious roles made no cents.

THE PRODIGAL (1955)

Hailed by the *New York Times* as "a big, expensive, gaudily arrayed and absolutely atrocious whang dang of a movie which represents Hollywood at its costly worst," this Biblical behemoth offered a feeble excuse for Sweater Girl Lana Turner to appear sans sweater (and most of her other clothes). Her love interest here is the charismatic Edmund (*The Egyptian*) Purdom, playing a good-hearted Hebrew kid from the Old Neighborhood who gets into trouble for running around with a shiksa. Needless to say, the hussy (Turner) who ensnares him is no ordinary temptress: she is a blond, fair-skinned Syrian, and a high priest-

ess of Baal, but he persists in chasing after her until he finally gets Baaled himself. Much of the $5 million budget behind this nonsense went to pay for costumes. There are 4,000 changes of clothing—including 292 for the leads—in the 114-minute movie. Turner herself later described it as "a costume stinker . . . It shoulda played Disneyland!" Old Walt, however, never would have accepted the off-camera machinations of the stars. During filming of *The Prodigal*, Edmund Purdom enjoyed a sizzling affair with starlet Linda Christian, who happened to be married to Tyrone Power, who happened, in turn, to be an ex-lover of Lana Turner's, who, as the world turns. . . .

QUO VADIS? (1925)

See the *Silent But Deadly* exhibit.

RAGTIME (1981)

A serious, well-meaning realization of E. L. Doctorow's best-selling novel depicting a broad slice of American life in 1906. Milos Forman replaced Robert Altman as director of the much-publicized project, which featured Mary Steenburgen, Brad Dourif, Howard Rollins, Jr., Elizabeth McGovern, Pat O'Brien, Donald O'Connor, Norman Mailer (yes, *that* Norman Mailer), and James Cagney, returning to the screen after a twenty-year hiatus. Extensive shooting on location in Manhattan plus handsome sets and period costumes drove the budget up to $32 million. Despite critical praise and Oscar nominations for newcomers Rollins and McGovern, the picture left audiences cold and grossed only $11 million for the hapless Dino De Laurentiis organization.

RAISE THE TITANIC! (1980)

The U.S. Navy learns of a killer chemical more powerful than H-bombs but which lies inconveniently at the bottom of the sea. The container that holds this potent treasure is that lovable old hulk, the S. S. *Titanic*. How did this secret weapon end up inside the sunken luxury liner? Don't ask! And don't, by all means, waste time with this seagoing stupidity in which, yes, the *Titanic* is finally raised, but it takes them nearly an hour to get it up. Everything went wrong with this Lew Grade presentation, which won particularly low grades for preproduction planning. The filmmakers spent $350,000 for a devastatingly detailed fifty-five-foot model of the old ship, only to find it was too large for the studio tank in which they planned to shoot much of the film. The solution? Build a brand-new tank with a few extra feet on all

Lord Lew Grade insisted on using a considerably larger and more elaborate model of the featured craft in Raise the Titanic! *than the one displayed here by the movie's star, Jason Robards. This decision enlarged the already inflated budget by several million, but added little to the realism of the finished product.*

sides, at a cost of an additional $6 million. With this sort of quick thinking, no wonder the picture's overall budget rose to $40 million (making it Britain's all-time biggest bomb), before it sank without a trace—bringing in less than $7 million at the box office.

THE RED TENT (1971)

An Italian-Russian co-production about Arctic explorers whose 1928 dirigible expedition runs out of gas. Claudia Cardinale is the love interest but fails to thaw the frozen pacing; Peter Finch is sorely miscast as an Italian general who is the sole survivor of the group's misfortunes. The movie suffered misfortunes enough of its own to earn a place in history, and in

the end it managed to lose at least $13.1 million of its $14 million production cost.

REDS (1981)

Try to imagine that you are a top executive at Paramount responding to the latest scheme by superstar Warren Beatty. This time around, Beatty proposes to make one of the most expensive movies in Hollywood history, on the love life of John Reed—America's most famous Communist agitator—a man so revered by the Soviets that he is actually buried in the Kremlin wall. What do you say to Mr. Beatty's bright idea? Do you ask him if it will play in Peoria? Do you suggest that he take a long, leisurely vacation until he feels less agitated? Do you propose that he change the title to *Commie Dearest*? In the end, the real-life bosses at Paramount happily handed their bright-eyed boy the keys to the studio treasury and told him to go out and have a good time. In light of his track record for making unlikely projects pay off (*Bonnie and Clyde, Shampoo, Heaven Can Wait*), their confidence in Beatty's gifts as a producer-star overcame their fears about the obviously limited appeal of his controversial subject matter. Nevertheless, after Wonder Warren disappeared with cast and crew into the icy wastes of Finland and costs and delays mounted alarmingly, Paramount came close on several occasions to killing the project. Despite all obstacles, Beatty managed to finish *Reds*, and the resulting motion picture represented a personal artistic triumph for the determined individual who produced it, directed it, co-wrote the script, and co-starred in the finished product with his off-screen flame, Diane Keaton. Cinematic achievement, however, does not guarantee commercial success; the positive reviews and a flurry of Oscar nominations could only temporarily mask the true dimensions of the box office debacle. During its first two years, the film grossed less than $21 million, after a production budget estimated at close to $45 million. Had the movie fulfilled the widely held expectation that it would win the Academy Award as Best Picture of the Year (instead of losing to British underdog *Chariots of Fire*) it might someday have come close to breaking even. As it was, Paramount's overall loss, after promotional and interest expenses are included, may approach $50 million. In his grave in Red Square, John Reed must feel intense satisfaction at his success in delivering a posthumous hammer blow against an evil capitalist studio.

THE ROAD TO RENO (1937)

Another Hope road picture . . . but this time it's not

Bob, it's *Hope* Hampton, the mistress (and later wife) of Kodak tycoon Jules Brulator. This indulgent sugar daddy first financed his sweetie's attempts at a career in grand opera, but when that failed he managed to push her into movies. Brulator bribed Universal to use his tone-deaf tootsie as star of a major musical by offering the studio low-cost, extended credit for the purchase of film stock: the company took the bait but lived to regret it. Universal dropped a bundle along *The Road,* largely because they gave Miss Hampton the chance to sing eight songs in the course of the picture, including a show-stopping production number set in divorce court called "I Gave My Heart Away."

ROAR! (1981)

The most expensive home movie ever made. Noel Marshall wrote the script, directed, and starred, along with his wife, Tippi Hedren, three of their children, some 150 lions, leopards, tigers, cheetahs, and other big cats, whose witty ad-libs gave the film its title. In a sense, this is a reprise of Miss Hedren's famous role in Alfred Hitchcock's *The Birds,* but this time it is ravening jungle beasts who assemble in flocks to invade an otherwise quiet home where they chase the humans up and down stairways and from one room to another. The film took eleven years to complete and suffered every conceivable cat-astrophe, including maiming of actors and technicians by temperamental tigers, flood, fire, foreclosure, and a deadly disease that decimated the feline cast. At the end of the picture, the human stars lion up on the side of the beasts and reach the conclusion that the cuddly critters have turned mean only because they are misunderstood by the people around them. This plea for sympathy for the big cats, and for preservation of endangered African wildlife in general, seemed so important to Marshall and Hedren that they mortgaged virtually all their personal property to prevent the production from shutting down. Their triumph in bringing the $17 million message to completion proved short-lived, however; *Roar!* has to date played for a total of one week in only a handful of American theatres, and its *worldwide* gross is reported at well under $2 million.

SAINT JOAN (1957)

Otto Preminger's costly assault on G. B. Shaw's celebrated play cast seventeen-year-old Jean Seberg in the title role after a much-ballyhooed nationwide "talent search." Seberg's career barely survived the burning at the stake she received from critics, but

fortunately she managed to regain her momentum and went on to triumphs such as *Kill! Kill! Kill!* and *Paint Your Wagon.* (See the *Musical Extravaganzas* exhibit in our main gallery.) Preminger maintained his personal affection for *Joan,* calling it "my most distinguished flop," and thereby slighting his many other noteworthy failures including *Porgy and Bess* (1959), *Bunny Lake Is Missing* (1965), *Hurry Sundown* (1967), *Skidoo* (1968), *Tell Me That You Love Me Junie Moon* (1970), *Such Good Friends* (1971), and *Rosebud* (1975). They all lost money—though Preminger maintained the seemingly ottomatic ability to keep budgets within reason, so that few of his films lost heavily enough to merit inclusion as individual entries in even the Basement Collection of our museum of major mistakes.

THE SCARLET EMPRESS (1934)

This bizarre, atmospheric evocation of Old Russia and the rise to power of Catherine the Great featured Marlene Dietrich, as directed by her alter ego, Josef von Sternberg, in the most expensive—and indulgent—of their seven collaborations. The multi-million budget horrified Paramount executives, who suspected that the title might refer not only to the reputation of the *Empress* but to all the red ink into which she had plunged the studio. Though considered a cult classic today, the film caused bewilderment among moviegoers in 1934. "What a headache at the box office!" a representative theatre manager told the *Motion Picture Herald.* "Poorest business this year."

SCIPIO AFRICANUS (1937)

See the *Fascist Follies* exhibit.

THE SHOES OF THE FISHERMAN (1968)

No, it's not another fish story. Nor is it fetishist fun about smelly feet. What we have here is the story of a Russian Roman Catholic bishop who tries to step into the spacious size-fourteen slippers of Saint Peter himself (see *The Big Fisherman* elsewhere in the Basement Collection) as Pope of the Holy Mother Church. The result is one holy mother of a snoozer, enlivened only by the curious miscasting of Anthony Quinn in the lead role. For the most part, *Shoes* resembles an $8.5 million "Let's Visit the Vatican" travelogue and became known to industry insiders as *Zorba the Pope.* When he is not wandering the back streets of Rome, looking for unfortunate orphans to assist, Pope Anthony finds time to avert nuclear war between Russia and China and pray for the poor of all nations. Someone should have prayed for the poor executives at MGM, who lost so heavily with this one and with other big-ticket blunders of the period (*Goodbye Mr. Chips* and *Zabriskie Point*, q.v.) that the studio showed an impressive overall loss of $37 million for the year 1969.

THE SILVER CHALICE (1955)

Paul Newman called this bundle of Biblical bunkum "*The* worst film of the 1950s," and he certainly ought to know: Newman played the lead role of Basil the Defender in a Hollywood debut so howlingly horrid that it is a tribute to his talent and persistence that he did manage to work again. In what the film presents as the pre-eminent sporting event of First Century Judea, all the major characters compete for the coveted "Christ Cup"—seeking possession of the holy relic that Jesus used at the Last Supper. Jack Palance provides additional excitement as Simon the Magician, who believes he has learned how to fly through the air, but the picture itself never gets off the ground. Given the two-dimensional operatic quality of the sets, the sloppy handling of all technical details, and the absence of established big-name stars, the fact that this tendentious twaddle actually cost (and lost) $4.5 million is nothing short of a miracle.

SINCERELY YOURS (1955)

See the *Disastrous Debuts* exhibit.

SORCERER (1977)

When director William Friedkin followed up his triumph with *The Exorcist* by creating a new film called *Sorcerer*, fans of the occult quite reasonably expected another chilling journey into the world of spirits and demons. When they showed up at the theatres, however, they received the shock of their lives to find a macho action picture that might more appropriately have been titled *Trucker*. Roy Scheider, who starred in the film, lyrically described it as "a story of the relationship between men, their trucks and the terrain." *Sorcerer* was, in fact, the name of one of the big rigs that played a prominent part in the action, transporting Scheider and his pals through the remote back country of the Dominican Republic with a load of highly unstable nitroglycerine. This gritty remake of *The Wages of Fear*, a memorable French film of 1953, suffered from bad weather, poor planning, and unsuitability of the jungle location, senseless subplots filmed in Jerusalem, Paris, and Elizabeth, New Jersey, and Friedkin's obsessive drive for absolute real-

ism—all of which caused the budget to jump from its original level of $9 million all the way to $22 million. Box office receipts failed to make a similar leap, and stalled (permanently) at $5.9 million.

SPHINX (1981)

An ill-conceived Egyptology thriller designed to capitalize on the trendy popularity of the traveling exhibition of artifacts from the tomb of King Tut. Lesley-Anne Down is a glamorous archaeologist who has obviously mastered the ancient Egyptian secret of searching through ancient tombs and tunnels without stirring a single hair of her elaborate coiffure. The enduring riddle of this particular *Sphinx* was why so pathetically few moviegoers went to see it. The mummy's curse seemed to be on the project from the day it opened, and its overall gross of $800,000 on a production budget of more than $14 million made it a candidate (along with similarly themed projects such as *Land of the Pharaohs* and *The Egyptian*, q.v.) for inclusion in the *Egyptian Book of the Dead*.

STAR! (1968)

From its inception, this project seemed a surefire smash, reteaming that singing sweetie pie, Julie Andrews, with Robert Wise, her director on the monster hit, *The Sound of Music*. This time the gold-dust twins collaborated on a glitzy film biography of 1920s Broadway star Gertrude Lawrence. Shooting lasted for eight months in Hollywood, New York, and the French Riviera. Miss Andrews' gowns alone cost $347,000, while the overall production budget reached $14 million. When reporters began criticizing some of the on-location excesses, director Wise responded, "Gertrude Lawrence was a glamorous, exciting personality who lived a flamboyant and extravagant life. We feel she would have heartily endorsed our budget." But would she have subsidized it? When the top-heavy turkey opened to disastrous business, Twentieth Century-Fox pulled it from release with the intention of re-editing for greater impact and providing the zippy new title, *Gertie Was a Lady*. When the film finally did reappear, trimmed down a full forty minutes to a svelte new two-hour form, the *Gertie* designation had been somehow lost in the shuffle; it bore instead the wishful-thinking monicker *Those Were the Happy Times*. Maybe so, but not for the producers, who lost more than $10 million, while driving yet another solid-gold nail into the already crowded coffin of 1960s big-budget musical flop-busters.

During the late sixties, Julie Andrews' career was suddenly bedeviled by participation in some of Hollywood's biggest flops; here she pleads for deliverance from the Robert Wise production of Star!

SUTTER'S GOLD (1936)

The *Heaven's Gate* of the 1930s, the budget for this idiotically expensive Western ran over $2 million at a time when the average film from its studio (Universal) cost $100,000. Like Cimino's famous folly, the plot concerns idealistic immigrants who are disillusioned by the realities of the Old West, with, in this case, a focus on Johann Sutter, who owned the land on which the California Gold Rush began. Again like *Heaven's Gate*, *Sutter's Gold* fared so badly with the critics and the public that it was withdrawn, then rereleased, with even less success than it had enjoyed the first time around. Edward Arnold looked out of place and uncomfortable in the lead role, perhaps because neither he nor anyone else could understand the heavy spending for spectacular scenery and "au-

thentic" sets that led Universal stockholders to believe that studio head "Uncle Carl" Laemmle had contracted a bad case of gold fever. The movie lost virtually every penny of its hefty investment; not for forty years (until *The Wiz*, q.v.) did Universal Studios experience a more costly cinematic disaster.

THE SWARM (1978)

"I never would have dreamed it would turn out to be the bees!" says a beleaguered Michael Caine in this unintentionally hilarious disaster movie. "They've always been our friends!" Schlockmeister Irwin (*The Towering Inferno*) Allen certainly hoped that the popular insects would be *his* friends; he planned to use them in this sloppy end-of-the-world fantasy to make box office honey but found himself badly stung instead. Neither the presence of Caine, Henry Fonda, Katharine Ross, Richard Chamberlain, José Ferrer, Slim Pickens, and Fred MacMurray nor the fact that the inept action begins at a small town flower festival could remove the pervasive stink from this project. Warner Brothers planned the broadest release pattern in the studio's history, with the bumbling bees invading a record number of theatres across the country. After a production budget of $13 million and an additional $8 million spent on advertising, the movie's $10 million gross proved a major disappointment.

SYLVIA SCARLETT (1935)

This was, in many ways, a film ahead of its time; forty-five years before *Tootsie* and *Victor/Victoria* parlayed the old formula of transvestite transformation and bisexual innuendo into highly profitable worldwide success, this George Cukor romp featured Katharine Hepburn dressed as a boy falling in love with Brian Aherne, but unable to reveal her feelings because of her masquerade. The handsome and expensively mounted production attempted to duplicate rural Britain on the RKO lot, costing the studio more than $1 million. Ads for the picture at the time of its release proclaimed to the world, "SHE'S A BOY! . . . IT'S MR. HEPBURN TO YOU!" but they might more appropriately have announced, "SHE'S A DUD! . . . IT'S MR. TURKEY TO YOU!" The public response to the *Scarlett* lady proved so hostile, in fact, that producer Pandro S. Berman told Cukor and Hepburn that he never wanted to see either of them again; at the time, the net loss of $363,000 represented a major setback for RKO. As Miss Hepburn herself wistfully recalls, "It was a disaster—and a very expensive disaster for those days!"

Cossack leader Yul Brynner leads a troop of Argentine gauchos into battle during a climactic scene in the steppes-meet-the-pampas spectacle, **Taras Bulba.**

TARAS BULBA (1962)

The pampas of Argentina might not seem the most logical place to recreate the world of sixteenth-century Ukrainian Cossacks, but producer Harold Hecht hoped that he could hold down costs by choosing a South American location. Nice try, Harold, but for several reasons it didn't work. For one thing, the 7,000 gauchos who stood in for the Cossack hordes turned out to be a headstrong and temperamental bunch, who fought one another with much greater ferocity off camera than they did during the filming. Then Tony Curtis, playing a Cossack horseman with his thick Brooklyn accent firmly in place, fell in love with his co-star, the seventeen-year-old German actress Christine Kaufmann. This caused Mrs. Curtis, Janet Leigh, to pack up their children and fly back to Hollywood, while the resulting personal (and press) turmoil caused several weeks of costly delays. By the time director J. Lee (*The Guns of Navarone*) Thompson managed to wrap the picture, its cost had risen to $7 million. Despite a massive publicity campaign and a decent performance by Yul Brynner in the title role the public refused to buy the muddled result. The movie suffered in particular from its faithful adaptation of the tragic ending of the famous Nikolai Gogol novel on which it was based: after slogging and slicing his way through tedious battles too numerous to count, Taras Bulba (Brynner) kills his own son (Curtis) for betraying the Cossack cause. Most audience members would have been ready to kill Curtis themselves by the end of the picture—and would doubtless have been encouraged by the actor's soon-to-be ex-wife—but this downbeat conclusion ensured tepid returns at the box office and a loss of more than $3 million for United Artists.

TORA! TORA! TORA! (1970)

Boring! Boring! Boring! A documentary-style presentation of the Japanese attack on Pearl Harbor that ignores character, plot, and dramatic tension (after all, most people know who won the battle) to concentrate on a painstaking recreation of the actual bombing. Director Richard (*Doctor Dolittle*) Fleischer commented, "bombing Pearl Harbor must have been a lot easier than making a movie about it," and as if to prove his point, he lost two civilian pilots in a fiery crash, then sent six U.S. Marine Corps extras to the hospital for ten weeks in the aftermath of a shipboard explosion. In addition to these flesh-and-blood casualties, Twentieth Century-Fox burned $25 million to bring this epic to the screen—making it, next to the studio's own *Cleopatra*, the most expensive movie in history at that time. Much to the chagrin of Fox president Darryl Zanuck, U.S. audiences resisted the charms of a picture that emphasized the enemy point of view in re-enacting the most disastrous episode in the history of the American military. *Tora!* grosssed only $14.5 million domestically, so despite the fact that it proved to be a major hit in (surprise!) Japan, Fox fell *at least* $8 million short of breaking even. Along with other battlefield fiascos such as *The Alamo* and *Waterloo*, the failure of *Tora!* served to underscore the seemingly obvious point that moviegoers will not spend their hard-earned money to relive celebrated military defeats, no matter how heroically they may be presented.

THE TRAIL OF '98 (1928)

A $2 million MGM misadventure about the Alaskan gold rush that left audiences out in the cold. Director Clarence Brown took Dolores Del Rio, Ralph Forbes, and 2,000 extras to a snowy location in the Rockies to ensure realism, but stormy weather (and temperatures that dropped to −60°) caused endless delays and cost six lives. These difficulties helped seal the fate of the struggling production—by the time of its release, nearly a year behind schedule, talkies had already invaded theatres across the country, and the public had little interest in a soundless spectacular that is remembered today as one of the most expensive—and least successful—silent movies ever made.

UNDER THE RAINBOW (1981)

Forty-five years after Hollywood thrilled the world with *The Terror of Tiny Town*—a musical Western with an all-midget cast—Orion Pictures felt ready for a costly variation on the same theme that managed to dwarf Tinseltown's previous achievement. This tasteless comedy centered on the adventures of several hundred plucky midgets who find themselves at MGM in 1938 for the filming of *The Wizard of Oz* and who manage to defeat a nefarious plot hatched by Nazi munchkin Billy Barty. Those sizzling international sex symbols Carrie Fisher and Chevy Chase provide love interest for normal-sized viewers, but the lasting impression one takes away from the theatre is one of idiotic, interminable slapstick that remains decidedly short on positive production values. To date, the producers have hardly found a pot of gold *Under the Rainbow*, earning only $8.3 million on an investment of more than $20 million.

UNDERWATER! (1955)

See *The Titans and Their Toys* exhibit.

VENDETTA (1950)

Howard Hughes spent $4 million on this stodgy, black-and-white costume melodrama intended to advance the career of his star-of-the-month—the lovely but untalented Faith Domergue. The hackneyed plot concerns a hot-blooded honey in old Corsica who is determined to avenge the murder of her father. As Hughes-ual, the billionaire producer demanded endless reshooting and re-editing that, in this case, dragged on for more than two years. By the time of the film's release, however, he had apparently lost interest in Miss Domergue, since RKO deposited this expensive valentine at theatres across the country with scarcely a whisper of advertising or promotion. *Vendetta* lost virtually every penny invested in its production.

VIRUS (1980)

With a budget of more than $17 million, this doomsday extravaganza about a naughty killer germ that escapes its isolation canister and proceeds to destroy humanity holds the record as the most expensive Japanese film ever made. Most of the money went for location shooting: in order to give his daring venture the broadest possible international appeal, producer Haruki Kadokawa dragged his long-suffering cast and crew to scenic natural settings in Russia, East Germany, Great Britain, Japan, the United States, Canada, China, and Antarctica. He also hired stars such as Glenn Ford, Robert Vaughn, Chuck Connors, Olivia Hussey, and George Kennedy, but language problems between the English-speaking actors and the Japanese crew caused frequent delays. A fitting climax to the entire ill-fated production occurred when the Swedish steamer carrying the company to its Antarctic location struck a submerged reef and nearly sank, leaving the movie (and the movie makers) dead in the water for four tense and icy days. When released in Europe, bad luck continued to plague the project, and it played in most countries for less than a week before closing. In light of this miserable performance, the picture has not yet opened for so much as a single night's engagement in the United States, leaving the producers—despite their film's great popularity on Japanese television— more than $15 million in the hole.

WATERLOO (1970)

Soviet director Sergei Bondarchuk made his international reputation by creating a six-and-a-half-hour version of Tolstoy's *War and Peace*, which some ex-

Napoleon gets the bad news on **Waterloo.** *Rod Steiger's shameless overacting as the former French Emperor helped to ensure that this $25 million battlefield massacre earned back less than $1.5 million at the box office.* **Waterloo's** *director, Sergei Bondarchuk, aptly observed: "One cannot direct an explosion—and Steiger is an explosion."*

perts believe to be *the* most expensive movie ever made. When taking into account the value of several years of free co-operation from the Russian army and government, estimates of the equivalent cost in American dollars of Bondarchuk's magnum opus range up to $100 million. Soviet officials insist that they broke even on this massive project, because millions of Russians flocked to see the film four and five times in yet another triumphant demonstration of the cultural advantages of enlightened state socialism. No such fanciful claims, however, could be advanced concerning Bondarchuk's next undertaking, *Waterloo*, which he and the Russians made in conjunction with four western production companies in the full glare of uncensored international publicity. The presence of Christopher Plummer (playing the Duke of Wellington) and Orson Welles (as Louis XVIII) helped give the project that "big picture" aura, though critics agree that it was Rod Steiger's hysterical and ham-boned impersonation of Napoleon that determined, more than any other factor, the ludicrous tone of the finished product. Steiger's off-camera feuds with Bondarchuk made the real-life grudge match between Napoleon and Wellington look like a love feast by comparison; at one point, the self-centered star demanded that the title of the film be changed to *Napoleon* in order to give his grotesquely exaggerated performance even greater prominence. These problems contributed to an overall budget conservatively estimated at $25 million, which led co-producer Dino De Laurentiis to announce, with his usual reserve (and his usual disregard of the facts), that he had just helped to make "the most expensive spectacle in history." This tedious battlefield pageant certainly did offer a spectacle of sorts when it finally marched before the public. Critics savaged the picture, audiences ignored it, and theatre owners reported a pitiful domestic gross of $1.4 million. The results, in other words, were not so much a Waterloo as they were an Hiroshima.

THE WEDDING MARCH (1928)

In his acting career, Erich von Stroheim gloried in the title "The Man You Love to Hate," but as a director, the hatred he inspired from studio bosses proved real and destructive. Von Stroheim's exquisitely crafted silent extravaganzas *always* ran over budget and very seldom packed the sort of punch at the box office that his producers demanded. *The Wedding March* represented a particularly extreme case. Set in the director's native Vienna, this decadent, bittersweet love story cost Paramount more than $1 million but won no response from the public in either its original form or in a clumsily re-edited version that appeared a few months later. The film is best remembered today as the debut vehicle for Fay Wray and as the occasion for a now legendary demonstration of von Stroheim's fanaticism concerning even the most trivial production details. In dressing a squadron of hussars for the all-important wedding scene, von Stroheim not only polished every gold button and inspected every visible stitch; he also ordered specially made silk underwear, complete with the monogrammed insignia of the Austrian army, so that his extras could feel—in the most intimate and fundamental sense—the grandeur of the era they were supposed to recreate on film.

THE WEDDING NIGHT (1935)

Four years before he failed miserably in his efforts to make a star of "The Norwegian Garbo," Sigrid Gurie (featured in *The Adventures of Marco Polo*, q.v.), producer Samuel Goldwyn spent a fortune in similarly futile efforts to launch the career of another "sensational" discovery, Anna Sten. In her three starring roles, this Russian actress received such an intense and exaggerated buildup and performed so feebly on screen, that she won the retrospective title "The Edsel of the Movie Industry." *The Wedding Night* was her most expensive and heavily promoted vehicle, and would-be star-maker Goldwyn labored breathlessly to consummate her bid for the big time. During the filming of a dramatic love scene with Gary Cooper, the proud producer became so excited that he pushed aside director King Vidor and gave the two stars personal instructions on how to caress one another. "If this scene isn't the greatest love scene ever put on film," Goldwyn declared, "then the whole goddamned picture will go right up out of the sewer!" Viewers found the finished film as complex and muddled as Goldwyn's characteristic and inimitable syntax, and the utter failure of the project helped end the career of an actress who had already become known to her many detractors as "Anna Stench."

WHEN TIME RAN OUT (1980)

Having already exploited the dramatic potential of burning office buildings, submerged luxury liners, and man-eating bees, producer Irwin Allen eagerly turned his attention to the explosive subject of killer volcanoes. The result featured a malevolent mountain in Hawaii pouring tons of lava over Paul Newman, Jacqueline Bisset, William Holden, Ernest Borgnine, Red Buttons, Barbara Carrera, Burgess Meredith, James Franciscus, and Veronica Hamel. Apparently, Allen spent so much on his cast he had nothing left for special effects, which are unbelievably shoddy for a movie that cost $22 million. Much to the producer's delight, Mount St. Helens thoughtfully contrived to blow its top just in time to publicize the movie's release, but not even this unsolicited assist from Mother Nature could coax patrons into their local theatres. When the new picture grossed only $1.7 million—following the prior failure of *The Swarm* (q.v.), *Viva Knievel*, and *Beyond the Poseidon Adventure*—time finally seemed to have run out for Hollywood's "Master of Disaster." Most recently Allen has applied his formidable talents to producing TV specials and designing a theme park ("Winter Wonderland") for Marineland, in Palos Verdes, California.

WILSON (1944)

This sincere but heavy-handed attempt to pay tribute to the memory of the twenty-eighth President astonished the industry by running up a budget far higher than that for *Gone With the Wind*. Instead of battles and burning cities, *Wilson* offered a minutely detailed replica of the White House and loving recreations of several dozen of the late President's most

Paul Newman (left) attempts to lead some of his co-stars (including the producer's wife, Sheila Allen, second from right)
in escaping from the wreckage of **When Time Ran Out.**

famous speeches, as rendered by Broadway star Alexander Knox. The emphasis on oratory gave the picture a stuffy, textbook quality that caused great concern among the top executives at Twentieth Century-Fox—as did the downbeat ending, with Wilson suffering a near total physical breakdown as he lost his battle with the Senate over the League of Nations. In response to these marketing problems, the studio devised perhaps the most misleading and mendacious promotional campaign in the history of entertainment—creating tuneful, upbeat trailers that

seemed to promise audiences a toe-tapping, light-hearted musical romp down memory lane. Before the picture's release, studio chief Darryl F. Zanuck nervously declared, "If *Wilson* fails, I will never make another picture without Betty Grable." Though his gigantic experiment in presidential biography lost more than $2 million of its $5.5 million budget, Zanuck failed to keep his promise—as evidenced by *Tora! Tora! Tora!, Captain from Castile, Cleopatra,* and the many other films associated with his name on display in our museum.

Diana Ross as Dorothy in The Wiz *helped ease Universal Studios on down the road toward one of the most costly disasters in its history. The yellow-brick Congoleum that paved this colorful pathway to perdition in itself cost the producers some $250,000.*

THE WIZ (1978)

In 1975, a musical reworking of *The Wizard of Oz* with an all black cast became a smash hit on Broadway. In response to its critical and commercial success, Universal Studios bought the film rights as a fateful first step in easing on down the road to an $11 million loss. The most important mistake in the events that followed concerned the casting of the central role: superstar Diana Ross seemed at least twenty years too old to play Dorothy. The producers responded to this obvious dilemma by adjusting the material to fit Miss Ross and turning Dorothy into a lonely schoolteacher who is supposed to be somewhere in her mid-twenties. In this context, Dorothy's friendship with Scarecrow, Tin Woodman, and Cowardly Lion seemed entirely out of place, as did the stage play's fundamental premise that the heroine had never left Harlem to explore "The Emerald City" below 125th Street. Director Sidney Lumet

contributed to the ensuing fiasco by frequently bringing his camera to within a few inches of his aging star's straining tonsils—as if looking into her mouth would convince the audience that despite her mature exterior, Miss Ross, inside, remained pure as a child. Inventive and brilliantly executed sets, costumes, and dance numbers—along with diverting performances by Michael Jackson (as the Scarecrow) and Richard Pryor (as the Wiz) made the film barely endurable—but not for Universal executives. The dismal $13 million gross after the $24 million cost on production sent shock waves through the industry that helped to destroy interest in black-oriented projects at all the major studios.

XANADU (1980)

After the inexplicable success of *Grease*, Hollywood assumed that Olivia Newton-John's star power would prove potent enough to redeem any and all material, no matter how awful. To test this hypothesis, Universal placed her in this dreadful pastiche, in which Miss Newton-John plays the ancient Greek muse, Terpsichore, reincarnated as a white-gowned Australian roller skater living near the beach in Southern California. Gene Kelly appears as an aging big-band clarinetist who had once been inspired by the muse, and so, for old times' sake, now learns roller skating and constructs the world's gaudiest roller-disco palace as a monument to his former love (and current bad taste). Along the way we encounter animated cartoon sequences, prepubescent rock 'n' roll fantasies, and nostalgic, thoroughly embarrassing tributes to

dancer Kelly's own past triumphs—including an excruciating rendition of "Singin' in the Rain" on skates. All the overblown musical numbers seem to go on forever and succeed in making the comparable moments in *Can't Stop the Music* (see the *Musical Extravaganzas* exhibit) look like models of mature and well-balanced restraint. This $20 million modern-day Xanadu, in short, is no stately pleasure dome, and in view of its relentless stupidity, it deserved an even more hostile response from the public than the one it actually received. In the final tally, it grossed $11 million, while grossing out nearly every moviegoer who ventured anywhere near it.

Olivia sings! Olivia dances! Olivia bombs! Concerning this climactic scene from Xanadu, the press book exulted: "Olivia Newton-John, in her role as a goddess, is totally hot! Dressed in black leather boots and a tiger skin vest, she sizzles, steams, and sets the screen ablaze!" The producers, meanwhile, set nearly $10 million ablaze—turned to ash by the well-deserved failure of this insufferable movie.

Eddie Albert as a worried artist's manager, Luciano Pavarotti as the world's greatest tenor (and a champion pasta chef), and Kathryn Harrold as a fashionable physician, all join in the uproarious fun of director Franklin (Patton) Schaffner's $19 million aborted opera buffa, Yes, Giorgio.

YES, GIORGIO (1982)

No way, Luciano. Despite the fact that this $19 million romantic comedy featured the world's greatest tenor voice, a lovely and charismatic co-star, a lively score by John Williams (with help from Puccini, Verdi, and other friends), and handsome location photography in Italy, New York, Boston, and San Francisco, it still grossed a pathetic $1 million at the box office. What, then, went wrong? First, there were obvious problems with the plot. Luciano Pavarotti plays a happily married Italian opera star who seduces Kathryn Harrold, a Boston throat specialist

(that's a doctor, not a call girl), without the slightest thought of leaving his wife. As a profound expression of his burning love, Luciano nobly promises his new mistress, "When I am in America, I am all yours." This seems a viable offer, precisely because there is so much of him to go around. Despite valiant attempts at a major diet before shooting began, Pavarotti remained the most generously proportioned singing sensation since Kate Smith (see the *Disastrous Debuts* exhibit), and audiences of the world were not prepared to accept a male sex symbol with such heroic dimensions. The script, meanwhile, served to accent rather than obscure the inherent weaknesses in the plot premise and the casting. "You are a thirsty plant, Pamela," Pavarotti purrs at one point to his *amore.* "Giorgio can water you!" In the end, MGM investors were the ones who were watered on, as their expensive trial balloon for making unlucky Luciano the Mario Lanza of the eighties ran out of hot air and crashed.

ZABRISKIE POINT (1970)

This pretentious piece of pap took its title from the name of a promontory in California's Death Valley—the lowest spot in the United States and an appropriate setting for a movie that fell so far below sea level in both artistic and commercial terms. In an effort to show how hip they could be, MGM executives handed carte blanche to the much-praised Italian director Michelangelo Antonioni, and like a rebellious teenager with Daddy's credit card, he pro-

ceeded to run wild. In order to guarantee the box office success of his controversial film about idealistic youth confronting a heartless power structure, the Italian *auteur* secured the services of such bankable international stars as Mark Frechette, Daria Halprin, and The Magic Theatre of Joe Chaikin. After negotiating these costly contracts, Antonioni still had to find a way of spending what must have been nearly $6,995,000 remaining in his generous budget of $7 million, so he set to work using five different cameras to film the explosion of refrigerators, washing machines, television sets, and other "worthless" material possessions. These apocalyptic Blow Ups forecast the future detonation of this overbudgeted bomb, which immortalized all the most idiotic clichés about 1960s flower children, and "blew it" at the box office with a gross below $1 million. This grade Z disaster ultimately won a well-deserved place in the Medved brothers' *Fifty Worst Films of All Time* . . . but then, egotists that we are, how could we help but give ourselves the last word?

A NOTE TO OUR READERS . . .

In both of our previous books on movies, we invited the public to send in suggestions for our future work in this field, and the literally thousands of responses that we received have proven extremely valuable to us over the years. Though we do not at the moment plan another project on Hollywood's greatest embarrassments we still welcome the opportunity of hearing from you. We'd be pleased to learn of your reactions or recommendations concerning the contents of this volume or on any other subjects that come to mind. You can write us at the following address:

THE MEDVED BROTHERS
610 S. Venice Blvd. #4094
Venice, California 90291

Meanwhile, we have enjoyed the opportunity of guiding you through the Hollywood Hall of Shame, and we hope that your personal plans and projects will always meet with greater success than the movies presented in our museum.